Charles Messe ger served for nine   officer and
thirteen years as a Territorial in   Regiment. He has
written over forty books on historical and defence matters, including a number on the two world wars. He has carried out several historical analysis studies for the Ministry of Defence and has written and helped direct a number of TV documentary series. He lectures widely and is an occasional battlefield guide. He is a member of the Army Records Society, the British Commission for Military History and the Society for Army Historical Research.

CHARLES MESSENGER

COMMANDOS

The Definitive History of Commando Operations in the Second World War

WILLIAM
COLLINS

William Collins
An imprint of HarperCollins*Publishers*
1 London Bridge Street
London SE1 9GF
www.WilliamCollinsBooks.com

First published in Great Britain by William Kimber & Co. Ltd in 1985
Published by Grafton Books in 1985
This paperback edition published by William Collins in 2016

1

Typeset in Baskerville

Printed and bound in Great Britain

FSC
www.fsc.org

FSC™ is a non-profit international organisation established to promote the responsible management of the world's forests. Products carrying the FSC label are independently certified to assure consumers that they come from forests that are managed to meet the social, economic and ecological needs of present and future generations, and other controlled sources.

Find out more about HarperCollins and the environment at
www.harpercollins.co.uk/green

Contents

List of Illustrations

Amphibious training, 1940 (*RM Museum*)

Toggle bridge demonstration (*W Boersma*)

The *Maid Honor* before the war (*Charles Howe via 'Red' Wright*)

The *Duchessa d'Aosta*, seen as the *Empire Yukon* (*Canadian Pacific via 'Red' Wright*)

Castelorizzo – the harbour (*Lt Col Stephen Rose*)

Charles Vaughan, the Commandant at Achnacarry (*W Boersma*)

Abseiling at Achnacarry (*RM Museum*)

Achnacarry (*Commando Association*)

Practising an assault landing (*RM Museum*)

Assault Landing Craft returning from Hardelot (*Imperial War Museum*)

Lord Lovat talking to Admiral Sir Bertram Ramsay (*Imperial War Museum*)

MTB 344 (*Mrs Margaret Prout*)

Members of the Small Scale Raiding Force (*Tom Winter via Mrs Margaret Prout*)

1 SS Brigade going ashore on D-Day (*Imperial War Museum*)

RM Commandos of 1 SS Brigade land on 6 June 1944 (*RM Museum*)

Commandos digging in at Merville (*RM Museum*)

Army Commandos with men of 6th Airborne Division (*RM Museum*)

Charley Head, John Durnford-Slater and Peter Young (*Commando Association*)

The run-in to Walcheren (*RM Museum*)

Weasels and Buffaloes in the Westkapelle Gap (*RM Museum*)

Walcheren—RM Commandos round up prisoners (*RM Museum*)

Commando Vickers machine gunners give covering fire at Wesel (*RM Museum*)

Bringing in a wounded man near the River Maas (*RM Museum*)

4 Commando Brigade 3in mortar crew (*RM Museum*)

LIST OF MAPS

FOREWORD TO THE FIRST EDITION
by
Brigadier Peter Young DSO MC MA FSA

The Commando Soldiers of the Second World War are, in the nature of things, a dwindling band, fading away as old soldiers are supposed to; their exploits already History. It is a peculiar feeling to be a historical character in one's lifetime – not unlike being a character from fiction I suggest, for much of what passes for Military History is little more. The temptation to write provocatively about the Campaign of Normandy or the career of Field Marshal Montgomery is too much for many an aspiring historian. The eyewitnesses are often astonished to read what the next generation has to say of their exploits, but I believe the survivors of the Commandos will find that Charles Messenger has researched thoroughly and described accurately our battles of forty years ago. I believe, too, that they will find in these pages much that will be fresh to them, as well as recalling experiences shared with great men.

PETER YOUNG
March 1985

Introduction to the First Edition

There have been many accounts written on the Commandos of the Second World War, both general and personal. Yet, there has never been what might be termed a definitive 'regimental' or official history published. The closest to this was *The Green Beret* by Hilary St George Saunders, who had been the official Recorder at Combined Operations Headquarters. In his preface he made it clear that the book was not the official history, and, indeed, at the time he wrote it (it was published in 1949) he was forced to leave much unsaid for security reasons. Yet, even so, while he undoubtedly captured the Commando spirit, the book contains a numbers of errors of fact, which have unfortunately been perpetuated in some more recent works on the subject.

It was my publisher's original intention that *Commandos* should be just an anthology. In order to gather the necessary material, I made contact with the Commando Association and was invited to attend one of the monthly meetings of the London Branch. The members quickly made it clear to me that they feared that I was embarking on something which would merely regurgitate all the old fallacies. It was this that prompted me to adopt a different approach and to concentrate on primary source material, which meant many hours of research in the Public Record Office, Royal Marines Museum, Imperial War Museum and other institutes. I then began to realise what they meant when I compared my findings to secondary works on the subject. Throughout all this time I maintained my contact with the Association, especially the London Branch, and the encouragement given to me spurred me on, even though at times I was daunted by the task I had set myself.

A major problem which I struck was how to draw up clear parameters, especially over the often blurred dividing line between Commandos *per se* and other Special Forces. In the end, I decided to concentrate on the Army and Royal Marine Commandos, and to merely give something of the origins and method of operating of other specialist units spawned by them and Combined Operations. I do hope, therefore, that former members of the Special Boat Section,

Royal Navy Beachhead Commandos, Combined Operations Pilotage Parties and others will forgive me. If I had treated their exploits in the same detail, the result would have been a totally unwieldy book. A further problem I found was over the availability of records. In many cases they are fragmented and for a number of reasons. The pressures of war often gave little time for precise records to be made. Some also fell victim to post-war 'weeding', while others, especially if connected with the Special Operations Executive and No 30 Commando, remain classified to this day. In cases where I have not been able to substantiate a particular occurrence, I have so indicated with footnotes.

I make no apologies for the fact that I have retained something of the anthological approach. Not having been a Commando myself, let alone being old enough to have taken part in any of the momentous events described in this book, I have relied much on contemporary accounts and the often very clear memories of the ex-Commandos themselves. These have an authenticity which I could never hope to reproduce in my own words. Indeed, without the help of so many members of the Commando Association and other affiliated organisations, this book could not have been written, and it is to them and their comrades who have gone on before that I dedicate *Commandos*.

While to list the names of all who have helped me would take up almost a book in itself, there are a number who have given me particular assistance. In particular I would like to single out two individuals. Henry Brown MBE is, as the Secretary of the Commando Association since 1946, a household name among all ex-wartime Commandos. His constant advice and encouragement, as well as allowing me to quote from his wartime diary, have been invaluable to me. Likewise Lt Colonel Stephen Rose OBE, Hon Secretary of the Middle East Commandos Historical Research Group, opened up his complete archive on the early Middle East Commandos for me, and I spent a number of fascinating days at his house at Eastbourne with him. Without the benefit of this archive, the story of the Middle East Commandos could not have been told.

As for the others, there are a number of individuals at the Royal Marines Eastney to whom I am most grateful – Major A.J. Donald RM (Corps Historical Officer), Major A.G. Brown MBE RM (Curator, RM Museum), Captain D.A. Oakley MBE RM, (Editor, *Globe and Laurel*), Bridget Spiers (Archivist) and Harry Playford (Photographic Librarian). Many thanks go too to Lt Colonel Sam Pope OBE

RM for giving me the necessary introductions. The Editor *Navy News* kindly published a letter asking for former Commandos to get in touch with me, and James Ladd, himself the author of a number of books on the Commandos and Royal Marines, gave me some valuable leads. A number of Honorary Secretaries of subsidiary Commando Old Comrades groups were most helpful in putting me in touch with their members – Norris Peak (43rd Royal Marines Commando Re-union), G. 'Jungle George' Fagence (RN Commando Association) and Peter Jemmett (30 Commando Association). Clive Hughes of the Department of Documents, Imperial War Museum, produced a number of collections of papers held by the Museum, and the Staff of the Photographic Department were as helpful as they always are. I was also given further contacts by David Smurthwaite, Keeper of Books and Archives, National Army Museum, and John Harding of the Ministry of Defence (Army Historical Branch). Andrzej Suchcitz of the Polish Institute and Sikorski Museum, London, gave me much information on Polish Commandos, as did W. Boersma of the Airborne Museum at Arnhem on the Dutch Commandos. Likewise, I am most grateful to Christopher Woods CMG MC, SOE Adviser to the Foreign and Commonwealth Office, for throwing much light on the activities of the Small Scale Raiding Force (SSRF). In this connection, M.R.D. Foot, who served at Combined Operations HQ 1942–44, also helped by answering a number of my questions, as did Patrick Howarth and Mrs Margaret Prout. I am, too, especially grateful to Henrietta March-Phillipps, daughter of Gus, who commanded the SSRF, who gave me the benefit of the researches which she carried out on her father for a BBC Radio programme transmitted in 1972, and for allowing me to quote from the transcript. F.H. Lake of the Whitehall Library, Ministry of Defence, helped with his extensive knowledge of service wartime periodicals, and John Cloake CMG, biographer of Field Marshal Templer (to be published by Harrap in 1985), gave me some useful background to his subject's involvement with the V Corps School of Raiding. Vice Admiral Sir Peter Gretton KCB DSO OBE DSC very kindly lent me an account which he had written on 3 Commando Brigade's operations in Burma, and Bryan Perrett also loaned me material on the 19th Lancers' involvement in the Arakan. Terry Norman gave me biographical detail on the Congreve family. Rosemary Baker carried out much of the basic research at the Public Record Office. Lt Colonels George Forty and the late Ken Hill of the Tank Museum, Bovington, provided information on the SS Squadrons RAC. Cecilia Weston-

Baker grappled with the typing of the manuscript with her usual cheerfulness and enthusiasm, and my thanks go too to Image Photographic of Shepherd's Bush, London for their skill in reproducing many of the unique photographs included in the book.

As for those who served with or alongside the Commandos during 1940–45, I would like to mention the following in gratitude for the time and trouble which they took on my behalf – L.G. Heirons (RN Commandos), Peter Smithson (40 & 41 RM Cdos), Stan Buckmaster (2 Cdo), Carlo G. Segers (4 (Belgian) Tp, IO(IA) Cdo), Major General R.B. Loudon CB OBE (43 RM Cdo), the late General Sir Campbell Hardy KCB CBE DSO (46 RM Cdo, 3 Cdo Bde), Major Jeff Beadle MBE MC (40 RM Cdo), Sir Alfred Blake KCVO MC (2 Cdo Bde), Ken Phillott (4 Cdo, I Cdo Bde), A.J. Kemp (RN Commandos), John Hill (RN Commandos), the late Colonel J. Neilson Lapraik DSO OBE MC TD (51 ME Cdo, SBS), Joe Edmans (I Cdo), Fred Walker (4 Cdo), Colonel B.G.P. Pugh (2 Indep Coy, I Cdo), Trevor Glanville DSC (30 Cdo), Paul McGrath DSM (30 Cdo), Ltd Commander Patrick Dalzel-Job DL (30 Cdo), Desmond Rochford (2 Cdo), Lt Colonel R.S.M. Laird OBE (5 Cdo), Pat Barber TD (V Corps School of Raiding), Colonel George Young DSO (50 & 52 ME Cdos, D Bn Layforce), who very kindly read and commented on my draft chapters on the Middle East Commandos, Brigadier A.E. Holt MC (5 Cdo), Peter Kemp DSO (SSRF), Tom Winter MM (SSRF), Jan Nasmyth *(Maid Honor* Force) and Bill Westcott (V Corps School of Raiding).

In addition, I wish to thank the following for allowing me to quote from their papers: Major General F.C.C. Graham CB DSO, Colonel B.W. de Courcy-Ireland DSC RM Retd, Major F.C. Townsend OBE RM Retd, Stan Weather all and The Reverend Joe Nicholl MC. Colonel David Smiley very kindly permitted me to reproduce some of his photographs and Major Christopher Congreve gave me permission to quote from the diaries of his brother, Commander Sir Geoffrey Congreve Bt DSO RN.

Finally, I am deeply indebted to Brigadier Peter Young. Apart from reading through the manuscript and providing much valuable comment, as well as writing the Foreword, it was he who set me off on the path towards becoming a military historian when I was an Officer Cadet at RMA Sandhurst 25 years ago.

CHARLES MESSENGER
London
March 1985

Introduction to the 1991 Paperback Edition

SINCE THE ORIGINAL edition of this book was published a number of those whose names and exploits are mentioned in the text have passed on. In particular, I would like to single out Brigadier Peter Young, who kindly wrote the original Foreword, and to dedicate this new edition to his memory. He epitomised the Commando spirit and I also owe him a personal debt for the help and encouragement in the field of military history which he gave me over the years.

I would also like to thank the many former Commandos and others who have written to me. Unfortunately, economics have prevented me from incorporating all their suggestions and new information. Indeed, the only significant amendments to the original edition have been made as a result of investigations by the Commando Association which established that one of my primary sources was of doubtful validity.

CHARLES MESSENGER
London
August 1990

Introduction to the 2016 Paperback Edition

IT IS DIFFICULT to believe that twenty-five years have gone by since the last edition, and very few of those I have written about are still with us. Yet their spirit undoubtedly lives on in today's Royal Marine Commandos.

I have made no major revisions in this new edition, but have tightened the text and, in one or two places, updated it. I am very grateful to Essie Cousins and Steve Guise of HarperCollins for enabling *Commandos* to see the light of day once more.

CHARLES MESSENGER
London
November 2015

CHAPTER ONE

In the Beginning

The term 'Commando' originates from the South African War of 1899–1902. The Boers had no regular forces, apart from the Staat Artillery, which was officered by Dutch and Germans, and their police. Consequently, they raised bands of men based on electoral districts. These were called Commandos, and each man was responsible for providing his own horse and received no pay or uniform. Commando tactics were marked by lightning strikes on the British forces, with the Boers fading away into the veldt before the British could react. Although by October 1900, the British had virtually defeated the Boers in the field, it was the activities of the Commandos, who would not surrender, which caused the war to drag on for another eighteen months. Apart from the reforms brought about by the war to bring the British Army into the twentieth century, little note was taken of the Boer method of fighting. It was merely considered to be guerrilla warfare in which regular armies did not indulge.

The only element of the British Army to undertake anything approaching Special Forces operations, as they are known today, during the First World War was T.E. Lawrence and his Arabs in the Middle East. However, another characteristic which was to dominate Commando operations during the Second World War did surface. Although the idea of making amphibious landings on opposed shores had become quite commonplace during the Eighteenth and early Nineteenth Centuries, the conduct of the landings in the Dardanelles in the spring of 1915 demonstrated that what lessons had been learnt in the past had been long forgotten. Indeed, the general view was that amphibious operations were too difficult, and the concept was only saved by a dramatic operation which took place on the night of 22/23 April 1918. This was the blocking of the port of Zeebrugge by the Royal Navy and Royal Marines under Admiral Roger Keyes in order to deny its use to the German U-boats. This was a classic Commando operation, but its significance was not to be realised for some years.

Between the two world wars, lip service only was paid to amphibious operations. It was studied in staff colleges, but that was all, and the general concept was that the assaulting forces would go ashore from destroyers and cruisers, using ships' whalers and covered by naval bombardment. Admittedly, in 1922 a water-jet-propelled Motor Landing Craft (MLC) made an appearance, and two more were built by the end of the decade, with another six being authorised in the mid Thirties, but there was little effort made to develop concepts for their use. Much of the reason for this lay in the prevalent belief that air power would dominate wars of the future, making an amphibious operation even more hazardous than hitherto. As for the troops involved, it was accepted that this should be a Royal Marine responsibility. The Madden Committee of 1924 recommended that a 3,000 strong Royal Marine brigade be set up to undertake amphibious operations, which were seen as raids on the enemy coastline and bases in the Zeebrugge mode, and the seizure and defence of temporary bases for naval use. Financial restrictions, however, prevented this from becoming any more than a paper concept.

In 1937, General Sir Ronald Adam, then Deputy Chief of the General Staff, assisted by Admiral Sir Andrew Cunningham, Deputy Chief of the Naval Staff, managed to get started a small inter-service committee. Known as the Inter-Service Training and Development Centre (ISTDC), its charter was to examine the whole question of inter-service operations, and it consisted of one sailor, Captain L.E.H. Maund RN, one soldier and one airman. It was based at Eastney. By early July of that year their influence was such that an amphibious exercise was actually laid on, with three battalions of Brigadier (later Field Marshal) Montgomery's 9 Infantry Brigade coming ashore at Slapton Sands in whalers from the troopships *Lancashire* and *Clan MacAlister*. The Centre also wrote a number of farsighted papers covering various aspects of amphibious landings, which were considered by the Deputy Chiefs of Staff Committee, but nothing could be done because of shortage of money. There was also the continued feeling that combined operations as such were not relevant to the practicalities of modern warfare and, for a short time, during the Munich crisis, the Centre was even temporarily disbanded.

With the outbreak of war, the future of the ISTDC became somewhat uncertain. Both the sailor and the airman were posted to other jobs, leaving merely the soldier, Lt Colonel M.W.-M. MacLeod DSO MC RA, who now headed it, although Captain Maund was shortly to appear in another Combined Operations post.

As far as irregular operations were concerned, a branch of the War

Office, General Staff (Research) (GS(R)) had been set up in the mid Thirties to study this, and in 1938 this was headed by Major J.C.F. Holland DFC RE, who had supported T.E. Lawrence as a pilot during the First World War, and then had been badly wounded in Ireland. He studied reports on Boer tactics, T.E. Lawrence and the various civil wars which had been and were still raging throughout the world. In the spring of 1939, his office was moved from being under the Director of Military Operations to that of Military Intelligence and became MI(R). Here Holland was joined by Lt Colonel C. McV. Gubbins MC RA, who had served with him in Ireland, as well as in North Russia in 1919. MI(R) now produced a number of pamphlets on guerrilla warfare. Gubbins also went on two intelligence gathering trips, one to the Danube valley and the other to Poland and the Baltic states. Then, a week before war broke out, he returned to Poland as a member of General Carton de Wiart VC's Military Mission, escaping to Bucharest when Poland was overrun.

With the outbreak of the Russo-Finnish War in November 1939 came the opportunity to put some of MI(R)'s ideas into practice. Thought was given to sending a force to help the embattled Finns, and, in view of the nature of the terrain, MI(R) proposed the raising of a ski battalion capable of operating behind enemy lines. This was formed as 5th Battalion Scots Guards, but was never sent because of Norwegian and Swedish refusal to allow Allied troops to traverse their territory and the eventual defeat of the Finns. The battalion was disbanded, but MI(R) continued to work on schemes for producing battalions specifically organised for irregular warfare.

The Independent Companies

On 9 April 1940, the Germans invaded Norway. A British force under Major General P.J. Mackesy was landed north of Narvik on the 14th, and a further force was put ashore at Namsos on the 16th. Norway's long coastline was very vulnerable and there were not sufficient troops to defend it all. It was therefore decided to form a separate force with the object of covering the coast between Namsos and Narvik and preventing the Germans setting up submarine and air bases. Although the Royal Marines were in the process of raising a striking force of four battalions, which would have been ideal for this task, they were still under training and not available.

Consequently, MI(R) now stepped in with a proposal that 'Guerrilla Companies' be formed.[1] Within a few days the name had been changed to 'Special Infantry Companies'[2] and then finally 'Independent Companies'. It was decided, with time being very pressing, to raise these from volunteers among the second line Territorial Army divisions still in the United Kingdom. Tom Trevor, who was to command No 2 Independent Company, describes how they were organised:

> The companies were recruited from volunteers. Each brigade found a Platoon and each Battalion a Section. The Sections were led by officers. The Headquarters of the Independent Companies had a section of the Royal Engineers under an officer and an ammunition section, provided by the Royal Army Service Corps, in which every trade of the Corps was represented. There was also a medical section, composed of personnel of the Royal Army Medical Corps and an Intelligence Section. There was no 'Q' side proper, but between 50 and 60 tons of stores of all description were allotted to the Independent Companies and administered by Headquarters.
>
> The idea was that each Independent Company should be organised as a ship-borne unit. The ship was to be their floating base and to take them to and from operations. For this reason they were not provided with any transport.[3]

Each company had an establishment of 21 officers and 268 other ranks, and they were raised as follows:

No 1 Company Formed 20 April 1940 at Martock, Somerset from 52nd Lowland Division. OC was Captain J. Ballantyne, Cameronians, and later Major A.C.W. May HLI.

No 2 Company Formed at Ballykinler, N Ireland on 25 April 1940 from 53rd Welsh Division. OC was Major H.C. Stockwell RWF, and later Major T.H. Trevor, Welch Regiment.

No 3 Company Formed at Ponteland on 25 April 1940 from 54th East Anglian Division. OC was Major A.C. Newman, Essex Regiment.

No 4 Company Formed at Sizewell from 55th West Lancashire Division on 21 April 1940 with Major J.R. Paterson, Liverpool Scottish, in command.

No 5 Company Formed at Lydd from 56th (1st London) Division on 21 April 1940 with Major J. Peddie, London Scottish, commanding.

No 6 Company Formed at Buddon Camp, Carnoustie, Fife from 9th Scottish Division on 25 April 1940 with Major R.J.F. Tod, Argylls, in command.

No 7 Company Formed at Hawick on 25 April 1940 from 15th Scottish Division under Major J.D.S. Young DSO MC HLI.

No 8 Company Formed at Mundford, Norfolk from 18th Eastern Division under Major W.A. Rice, Suffolk Regiment.

No 9 Company Formed at Ross-on-Wye in late April 1940 from 38th Welsh Division under Major W. Siddons DCM R WF and later Major W. Glendinning, Welch Regiment.

No 10 Company Formed from 66th East Lancashire Division under Major I. de C. Robertson, TA General List.

Of these early commanders, a few would go on to be famous and their names will crop up again. Tom Trevor would command No 1 Commando; Charles Newman would likewise command No 2 Commando and win the Victoria Cross at Saint Nazaire, while Ronnie Tod commanded No 9 Commando and then 2 Commando Brigade.

Within ten days of its formation, No 1 Company was embarked in SS *Orion* and was on its way to Norway. It was ordered to the port of Mo and an Admiralty signal told the Officer Commanding:

> Your mobility depends on your requisitioning or commandeering local craft to move your detachments watching possible landing places.
> Keep attack from the air always in mind.
> Disperse and conceal but retain power to concentrate rapidly against enemy landing parties.
> Keep a reserve.
> Get to know the country intimately.
> Make use of locals but do not trust too far.
> Use wits and low cunning. Be always on guard.[4]

On 4 May, the company arrived at Mo, to be followed a few days later by No 3 Independent Company, then Nos 4 and 5, and finally No 2. Appointed in overall command was Lt Colonel Colin Gubbins, who set up his headquarters at Bodo, where No 3 Independent Company was deployed. His force was nicknamed Scissors Force, and his orders, which had been given to him before he set sail for Norway, were:

> Your first task is to prevent the Germans occupying BODO, MO and MOSJOEN. This they may try to do by small parties landed from the sea or dropped by parachute. Later, the Germans may be expected to advance Northwards on MOSJOEN from the TRONDHEIM area via GRONG. You will ensure that all possible steps are taken by demolition

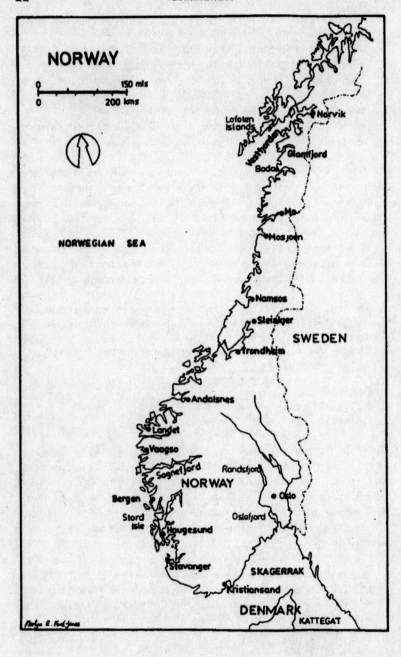

NORWAY

0 ——————— 150 mls
0 ——————— 200 kms

NORWEGIAN SEA

Lofoten
Islands

Narvik

Vestfjorden

Glomfjord

Bodø

Mo

Mosjoen

Namsos

Steinkjer

SWEDEN

Trondheim

Andalsnes

Langet

Vaagso

Sognefjord

Randsfjord

NORWAY

Bergen

Oslo

Stord
Isle

Oslofjord

Haugesund

Stavanger

SKAGERRAK

Kristiansand

DENMARK

KATTEGAT

and harrying tactics to impede any German advance along this route. Your Companies operating in this area should not attempt to offer any prolonged resistance but should endeavour to maintain themselves on the flanks of the German forces and continue harrying tactics against their lines of communications.[5]

Some idea of the confusion and lack of intelligence about Norway can be gained from the experience of Major Paterson, OC No 4 Independent Company, who visited the War Office for a briefing on 2 May and returned with 'a batch of our "maps" which consist of an illustrated guide to the beauty of Norway as a holiday country and enclosing map'.[6] Indeed, this confusion would persist throughout.

The experiences of No 4 Independent Company are typical of them all. They left Sizewell for the north on 4 May, with no idea as to what their port of departure was. Arriving at Gourock, near Glasgow, early on the 5th, they were told that they were to be put aboard the *Ulster Prince*, where breakfast awaited them. 'About 3 hours later, we did get aboard to find nothing had been arranged, the ship having arrived early that morning, and in addition there was no fresh food, bread or meat aboard.'[7] Eventually, they sailed and Paterson finally received some orders, which informed him that he was to be taken to Mosjoen, there to transship into local boats and make his way to Sandnessjoen, west of Moesjoen and at the mouth of the fjord. Little was known of the situation in the area. Then, the orders were changed, with both Nos 4 and 5 Companies disembarking at Moesjoen. They finally arrived just after midnight on the night 8/9 May. Having offloaded as much of their stores as they could before the ship sailed again, they moved two or three miles north of Moesjoen and dispersed into platoon positions.
Next day. . . .

> . . . I heard that a Norse ship with Germans aboard had been reported and I was told to keep a watch westward. I went to 1 Platoon who were about a mile and a half along the coast road on a bicycle and took one officer along to a look-out spot. I came back to my head-quarters ready for lunch, when Colonel Gubbins turned up in a 'flap'. I was ordered to take up a defensive position some 2 miles south of Moesjoen to cover the withdrawal of No 5 Coy who had been engaged by the enemy. The Norse troops were in retreat and the situation very uncertain; lorries were being sent for my men. I was to move at once!!!!

The move went smoothly, helped by the low cloud which prevented any interference by the Luftwaffe. Once in position, No 5 Company had a satisfactory brush with the enemy, killing a number of cyclist troops, and some Norwegian riflemen came back through them. The main German body was some five miles away, but did not follow up. Late that night the companies pulled back to Moesjoen. They were then taken by ship to Sandnessjoen. On the night 11/12 May they moved again by sea, this time to the Bodo area. On the 16th there was a scare that enemy parachutists and seaplanes had landed on the coast north of Bodo, which kept the company busy throughout the day. Otherwise, apart from the occasional air raid and various local redeployments, life was comparatively quiet. Then, on the 22nd, they were ordered to a new area, Valnes, where they spent three days before the German advance began to threaten once more. By now Lt Colonel (later General Sir Hugh) Stockwell had taken over command of Scissors Force from Colin Gubbins,* and on the 27th he gave Paterson orders to take up an outpost line in the area east of Finneid, which included responsibility for a bridge prepared for demolition. Next day, Stockwell told Paterson that, when the time for withdrawal came, No 2 Company, which was on the left of No 4, was to be placed under his command. The problem was that his only means of communication with them was by runner.

I had no sooner started talking about this than, BANG! Up went the bridge, the enemy were at our gates ... I gave orders ... telling No 2 Coy to withdraw on their own but not to become involved, but before withdrawing to inform No 2 Platoon of my Company what they were doing. In order to be sure this message was carried out I sent my Intelligence Officer with it. Actually by the time he got there, they had started their withdrawal. . : . We then sat and waited. After a short time the Boshe [sic] got a mortar going and a machine-gun which covered the road between Fauske and Finneid with long range fire. Copland† came up in a car and got chased, also a lorry which turned up to get some explosives out of Finneid. The road into Finneid was also under fire about 200 yds from my Headquarters. As soon as Copland and the lorry stopped the mortar started to try and find them, fortunately, we were behind the hill. No 1 Platoon whose weapon-pits were on the forward slope were getting quite a lot of mortar attention.

---

* He was reputedly removed for having sacked a Guards battalion commander who had been temporarily under his command.
† Captain W.O. Copland, South Lancs, 2IC No 4 Independent Company. He would later command this company and then distinguish himself at St Nazaire as 2IC No 2 Commando, winning a DSO.

That evening, Paterson decided to withdraw to the main position, but was sent back to the outpost line by Stockwell.

By this stage, the German advance had reached so far north that there was little left for Scissors Force to do, and it was decided that they should be evacuated. Paterson was made aware of this at about midday on the 29th, but it took him some hours to establish when, where and how it would be carried out. Eventually, 'I was handed typewritten orders to the effect that a destroyer would be at Bodo at midnight, that is, between 28 and 30 miles away. The time by now was 6.30 pm.'

Gathering his scattered platoons together, they eventually got to Bodo on time, where the destroyer took them off. 'Thus ended our Norway trip! Did we do our job? I don't know!' By 10 June all five companies were back in Scotland.

The remaining five Independent Companies had suffered an even more frustrating time. They were all eventually moved to Gourock on and around 21 May and actually went on board ship ready to go to Norway, but, in view of the worsening situation, never sailed. For the time being they remained training in the Glasgow area.

The Commandos are Born

On 10 May 1940, while Nos 1-5 Independent Companies were in Norway, the long awaited German invasion of France and the Low Countries began. By the end of that month, the British Expeditionary Force was being evacuated back to England from Dunkirk. Two weeks later, the French capitulated and the British braced themselves for a German invasion.

Although priority had now turned to the defence of Britain, Churchill himself was concerned that an offensive spirit must be fostered. He made this plain in a minute written to the Chiefs of Staff on 3 June:

> The completely defensive habit of mind, which has ruined the French, must not be allowed to ruin all our initiative. It is of the highest consequence to keep the largest numbers of German forces all along the coasts of the countries that have been conquered, and we should immediately set to work to organise raiding forces on these coasts where the populations are friendly. Such forces might be composed by self-contained, thoroughly equipped units of say 1,000 up to not less than 10,000 when combined.[8]

Two days later he wrote:

Enterprises must be prepared with specially trained troops of the hunter class, who can develop a reign of terror first of all on the 'butcher and bolt' policy.

I look to the Chiefs of Staff to propose me measures for a vigorous enterprising and ceaseless offensive against the whole German occupied coastline.[9]

His ideas were considered by the Chiefs of Staff at a meeting on 6 June. In particular, they were directed to draw up plans for organising 'striking' companies, transporting and landing tanks on the beach, setting up a comprehensive system of espionage and intelligence along enemy held coastlines, and the creation of a 5,000 man 'barrage' force. Their first thoughts were to base a striking force on a regular formation, and Major General B.L. Montgomery's 3rd Division, which had done well in France, was selected. They quickly realised, however, that this division would be better employed preparing for the German invasion, and instead decided to call for volunteers to form the striking companies.

On 10 June 1940, General Sir John Dill succeeded General Ironside as Chief of the Imperial General Staff (CIGS), and one of his first tasks was to consider how the striking companies should operate. Indeed, the wheels had turned fast, for on 9 June the War Office had sent out a letter to Northern and Southern Commands calling for the names of forty officers and one thousand other ranks to join a special force for 'mobile operations'. This was followed a couple of days later by a similar letter to the other commands. The ultimate aim was to have a force of 5,000 men. General Dill's Military Assistant at the time was Lt Colonel Dudley Clarke:

> At that time I was GSOI to the CIGS and General Dill spoke to me one day on this subject. I told him I had some ideas to put forward, based upon experiences gained as his GSOII in Palestine at the time of the Arab Rebellion, and was told to put up a paper for him to consider. I wrote it in my flat late that night and, I think, suggested the name 'Commando' from the very start.
>
> At least it was arrived at without much effort and I don't remember any rival titles having been seriously considered – although it was a long time before War Office circles would unbend sufficiently to use the word in official papers without visible pain. I think it was Denis [Denys] Reitz's books,* read against the background of a South Afri-

---

* *Commando* (Faber, 1932) and *Trekking On* (Faber, 1933)

can childhood, which had brought it so easily to mind, but it did seem at once to suggest exactly what was wanted, and the historical parallel was not very far-fetched. After the victories of Roberts and Kitchener had scattered the Boer Army, guerrilla tactics by the Commandos snatched victory for many months to come from an enemy vastly superior in numbers and arms. I had myself seen the Arab armed bands in Palestine do much the same against a whole Army Corps from Aldershot aided by thousands of auxiliaries. Guerrilla warfare was always in fact the answer of the ill-equipped patriot in the face of a vaster though ponderous military machine; and that seemed to me to be precisely the position in which the British Army found itself in June 1940. And, since the Commando seemed the best exponent of guerrilla warfare which history could produce, it was presumably the best model we could adopt.

A little further thought seemed to show one conditions far more favourable than most guerrillas had had to contend with. First, we had in England a safe and well-stocked base from which to operate within close range of many tempting targets: second, we had plenty of intelligent and trained soldiers who could individually be just as well armed as their opponents: and third, we had in the sea lines of approach and retreat where we could expect to be more mobile and more secure than our opponents. So the idea crystallised into the raising from the still formidable resources of the British Army picked bands of guerrilla fighters who would harry the long enemy coastline in order to make him dissipate his superior resources. Two conditions were imposed from the start, which too often have been over-looked by critics of the Commandos at later stages. It was axiomatic from the very start that no existing units of the Army could be made available for raiding operations for many months to come – not one single one could be diverted from the overwhelming needs of Home Defence. It is this which must give the answer to so many officers who have thought since that raiding might have been more efficiently carried out by selected battalions with special training.

The second condition was one of stringent economy. So urgent was the need of every sort of arm and equipment to refit the B.E.F. that raiding had to be carried out on a Woolworth basis. For this reason the Commandos were armed, equipped, organised and administered for one task and one task only – tip-and-run raids of not more than 48 hours from bases in England against the Continent of Europe. It is only fair to keep this in mind before confronting the Commandos with those administrative difficulties which arose when the same system was expected to suffice on arrival in the Middle East after an eight weeks' voyage. So short, in fact, had been the supplies of arms that the Commandos at first had only a small training scale of weapons and each in turn drew up its full complement off Tommy-guns etc., from a communal store on the eve of a raid!'[10]

Two types of operation were initially envisaged. The 'regular' type was defined as being 'of the Zeebrugge type downwards', while 'irregular' were the 'cloak and dagger' operations coordinated by MI(R). Both would be combined under one commander, and Major General J.F. Evetts, then on the North-West Frontier of India, was initially recommended for this post as having the right qualities of offensive spirit, a good knowledge of all three services, good organisational ability, drive and youth, energy and powers of imagination. His formal title would be Commander, Offensive Operations. He would come directly under the Chiefs of Staff and his area of operations would cover Norway, Holland, Belgium and France. He would be allowed a free hand to prepare and execute any plans, subject to clearance by the Chiefs of Staff, and would have the Commandos and the Royal Marine Brigade, which had now completed its training, at his disposal. Evetts, however, could not be released in time, and General Sir Alan Bourne, the Adjutant-General Royal Marines, was appointed in his place.

As for the original Commando concept, this is best described by a memorandum sent out by the Director of Military Operations and Plans, Major General R.H. Dewing:

It is intended to form these irregular volunteers into a number of 'Commandos', and I have prepared this memorandum to explain the purpose of the new force and the way in which it is proposed to organise and employ it.

The object of forming a commando is to collect together a number of individuals trained to fight independently as an irregular and not as a formed military unit. For this reason a commando will have no unit equipment and need not necessarily have a fixed establishment. Any establishment that may be produced will be for the purposes of allotting appropriate ranks in the right proportions to each other.

Irregular operations will be initiated by the War Office. Each one must necessarily require different arms, equipment and methods, and the purpose of the commandos will be to produce whatever number of irregulars are required to carry out the operations. An officer will be appointed by the War Office to command each separate operation, and the troops detailed to carry it out will be armed and equipped for that operation only from central sources controlled by the War Office.

The procedure proposed for raising and maintaining commandos is as follows. One or two officers in each Command will be selected as Commando Leaders. They will each be instructed to select from their own Commands a number of Troop Leaders to serve under them. The Troop Leaders will in turn select the officers and men to form their own

Troop. While no strengths have yet been decided upon I have in mind commandos of a strength of something like 10 troops of roughly 50 men each. Each troop will have a commander and one or possibly two other officers.

Once the men have been selected the commando leader will be given an area (usually a seaside town) where his commando will live and train while not engaged on operations. The officers and men will receive no Government quarters or rations but will be given a consolidated money allowance to cover their cost of living. They will live in lodgings, etc., of their own selection in the area allotted to them and parade for training as ordered by their Leaders. They will usually be allowed to make use of a barracks, camp, or other suitable place as a training ground. They will also have an opportunity of practising with boats on beaches nearby.

When a commando is detailed by the War Office for some specific operation arms and equipment will be issued on the scale required, and the commando will be moved (usually by separate Troops) to the jumping-off place for the operation. As a rule the operation will not take more than a few days, after which the commando would be returned to its original 'Home Town' where it will train and wait, probably for several weeks, before taking part in another operation. It will be seen from the above that there should be practically no administrative requirements on the Q. side in the formation or operation of these commandos. The A.* side must of course be looked after, and for this purpose I am proposing to appoint an administrative officer to each Commando who will relieve the commando leader of paperwork. This administrative officer will have permanent headquarters in the 'home town' of his commando.

The commando organisation is really intended to provide no more than a pool of specialised soldiers from which irregular units of any size and type can be very quickly created to undertake any particular task.

The main characteristics of a commando in action are:
a) Capable only of operating independently for 24 hours;
b) Capable of very wide dispersion and individual action;
c) Not capable of resisting an attack or overcoming a defence of formed bodies of troops, i.e., specialising in tip and run tactics dependent for their success upon speed, ingenuity and dispersion.[11]

For ease of administration, it was decided that the various Commands within the United Kingdom should be responsible for forming Commandos from the troops under their command. The allocation was made as follows:

No 1 Commando From disbanded Independent Companies,

---

* 'Q' represented stores and equipment, and 'A' personnel matters.

but never formed at this time as the Independent Companies remained in existence for the time being.

No 2 Commando To be raised as a parachute unit with volunteers from all commands.

No 3 and No 4 Commandos Southern Command.

No 5 and No 6 Commandos Western Command.

No 7 Commando Eastern Command.

No 8 Commando Eastern Command, but actually raised from London District and the Household Division.

No 9 and No 11 Commandos Scottish Command.

No 10 Commando Northern Command.[12]

In the event, Northern Command were unable to find sufficient volunteers for No 10 Commando to be formed, but a No 10 would eventually be raised with a unique organisation in summer 1942. A little later, at the beginning of August 1940, No 12 Commando was also raised from the forces stationed in Northern Ireland, but this had a strength of only 250 men, half that of the other Commandos.

The main point of difference between the Commandos and the Independent Companies was that the former were trained to fight as individuals while the latter fought as self-contained units. The Commands selected the Commando leaders, who were then made responsible for selecting suitable volunteers, travelling around the units to interview them. Geoffrey Appleyard, an RASC subaltern serving at HQ II Corps at Aldershot, who had been in France and had a pre-war international reputation as a skier, and later to become the famous 'Apple' of the Small Scale Raiding Force, has left an account of how he came to join No 7 Commando:

March-Phillipps* (he has just got the MBE in France) was selected by Col Lister (the OC) as 'B' Troop leader. He was told that he could have a free hand in picking two volunteer subalterns from the whole of Southern Command (about 30 volunteered) for his two section leaders. Colbeck (Royal Tank Corps) had volunteered and was immediately picked and after interviews by the War Office was selected. Until then I had not heard anything about this at all, and then I heard March-Phillipps discussing it and knew it was the thing for me. I know him very well and after he knew I wanted to volunteer he accepted me as the other subaltern immediately. The proposal went up to Col Lister together with

---

* Later Major 'Gus' March-Phillipps DSO MBE RA OC Small Scale Raiding Force.

my 'on paper' qualifications and March-Phillipps's strong recommendation. Col Lister accepted it and approached the War Office and communicated with Brig Gale of this HQ who apparently 'did his stuff by me', and yesterday evening the War Office wired that I was appointed![13]

Another, who was selected for No 4 Commando, was Ken Phillott, who had also been in France and was now serving with the Glosters at Bristol, enduring the German blitz on the city:

At this time I read in Battalion orders that volunteers were wanted for Special Duties. This seemed to offer something different, although I had no idea what these Special Duties would be. I informed my Company Commander that I wished to volunteer.

In due course, with some 20 or more of the Regiment, I was called before this officer and asked a number of questions as to my previous military experience. I was told to wait outside. Here I saw an officer wearing a uniform I had never seen before – green with yellow piping. I then noticed that he was a Lt Col!*

Shortly afterwards I was again called into the room; this time the unknown Colonel was sitting behind the desk. He then started to ask me questions such as: 'I see you have already seen active service. Tell me, can you swim at least 500 yards in full kit?' I replied that I was a good swimmer and I thought I could do so. 'Can you drive a car and ride a motor-cycle?' I replied that I could. He then asked what my pre-war hobbies had been to which I replied swimming, boxing and motor-cycling. I was asked if I had done any climbing and satisfied him when I said that I had been born and lived on the edge of Exmoor where there was nothing but hills and moorland. He then asked: 'Can you stand plenty of bloodshed?' I laughed and replied: 'Well, if anyone else can, I am sure I can!' 'Good' he replied, 'Wait outside.'

In due course I was again recalled, together with five of six others. This time we were asked: 'Do you know what you are volunteering for?' We replied that we did not. He then said: 'A lot of bloody fools aren't you not knowing what you are volunteering for! Well, I will tell you. We are forming units which will hit back at the enemy. You may be dropped by parachute, landed on enemy territory by boat or submarine and given certain tasks to perform. There may only be two or three of you, there may be more, but you must realise that you may have to find your own way back again. We cannot always promise to rescue you. If anyone feels he wants to pull out, now is the time to say so.' I think one man decided to do so; the remainder of us stood firm. Having heard us, our Company

*Lt Colonel C.P.D. Legard, 5th Inniskilling Dragoon Guards, original Commander No 4 Commando.

Commander was so impressed that he asked whether he could join us. He was a very big South African and a great rugby player. The Colonel agreed.[14]

A point that must be stressed is that all volunteers were merely seconded to the Commandos. They retained their own cap badges and remained on the books of their own regimental pay and record offices for pay. The greatest punishment which could befall them was to be 'Returned to Unit'. For the Army Commandos this policy would remain in force throughout the war.

The First Raids

MO9 Branch was set up under the Director Military Operations and Plans to undertake planning for Commando operations, and Dudley Clarke was to head it. Because Commando activities would involve both ships and aircraft, it was clear that there would need to be close cooperation with the Royal Navy and the Royal Air Force, General Sir Alan Bourne, who was Adjutant-General Royal Marines at the time:

> I was told on Wednesday, 12th June 1940, that the Chiefs of Staff had decided that I should be in command of Offensive Operations as it was called at that stage. I had been asked by the First Sea Lord, I think the day before, whether I would welcome such an appointment if selected and naturally replied that I would. Instructions from the Prime Minister gave birth to this new department. I got, as being the quickest method of starting, an allotment of 4 rooms in the Admiralty that afternoon and saw the Naval Assistant to the First Sea Lord in connection with my staff and had Capt Maund RN and Capt Garnon-Williams RN appointed. . . . Next morning I arranged with the War Office for Major (Acting Lt Col) A.H. Hornby MC RA, who was GSOI at the War Office, to be put on my staff. I used his advice and experience to collect the remainder of the Army Staff. I also approached the Air Ministry for an Air Officer; one was detailed but did not put in an appearance for a long time. . . .
>
> The original proposal was to call the Director of Combined Operations 'Cochrane', but I felt that it was going to be difficult to get anyone to realise that this new development was in existence, that to call it 'Cochrane' would kill it at birth, so I proposed to be called 'Director of Combined Operations' and that was accepted.[15]

In the meantime, Churchill was impatient for action, but, as yet the resources to begin carrying out raiding operations were very slender.

The Commandos were still being formed, and all that was available were the Independent Companies. While Nos 1-5 and 10 Independent Companies were based in Scotland, it was decided to send Nos 6-9 Independent Companies to Cornwall, to help guard against invasion both there and on the Scilly Isles. Before they left Scotland, however, volunteers were called for to form a fresh Independent Company, No 11, for special operations. It was to consist of 25 officers and 350 other ranks and was to be commanded by Major Ronnie Tod. It was to be this unit which was to carry out the first of the Commando operations.

No 11 Independent Company was officially formed on 14 June 1940, and moved to Southampton. A week later, Ronnie Tod received a warning order to be prepared to carry out operations on the French coast. He was told that there were a number of RAF Crash Boats available at Dover, Ramsgate and Newhaven and that he was to split his company among these three ports. On the afternoon of 23 June, he received detailed instructions from the War Office ordering him to make landings at various points on the coast with the object of carrying out reconnaissance of the defences and capturing Germans. After a conference with the Royal Navy, at which he was told that only nine out of the promised twenty boats were available, he decided to split his force into five. Two parties would set out from Ramsgate, each with two boats, to operate in the Hardelot area, a third, with one boat, from Dover would also land at a different spot in the same area, while the two parties from Newhaven would land at Stella Plage and north of Berck. The landings would take place at midnight, and the parties were to be allowed eighty minutes ashore.

Operation *Collar* took place on the night of 24/25 June. Of the Ramsgate groups, the first landed some four miles south of Boulogne and noted the enemy using searchlights and firing Very lights, but met no opposition, spotting what they thought might be oil or ammunition dumps. The boats of the second became separated and landed in two different places. The first boat landed just south of Hardelot and met an enemy patrol which fired at them and made off. Fire was not returned. The other was not afterwards able to pinpoint where it had landed, but saw nothing, apart from coming under machine-gun fire during re-embarkation. The Dover party arrived too late to land, although they did come under some machine-gun fire. The party landing at Berck found nothing, and only the Stella Plage group, which actually landed at Merlimont Plage, had a proper brush with the enemy.

An enemy patrol of 2 men was encountered and both killed by sub-machine gun fire at a range of 15 yards. Nothing was removed from the bodies. A large hotel was found to the North of the landing which was wired in but no enemy sentries were observed. Cars were seen in the compound. A coastguard hut was found to be unoccupied. As the boat was leaving, fire was opened from the hotel, estimated at 1 MG (slow rate of fire) and about six rifles. This fire ceased when our troops in the boat opened accurate fire in reply.[16]

The only casualty of the raid came in this last action when Dudley Clarke, who had gone as an observer, was hit behind the ear, but not seriously. There had been little tangible result, but it provided a good tonic for the general public when it was written up in the press. In connection with this, General Bourne recalled:

Having been told that in the last war most of the leakages were from high places, it was decided that the details for this raid should not be given to those in high places. Consequently the first the Cabinet knew about the raid was when it appeared in the public press. I was told, by one of those present, that the Cabinet were furious at its publication (possibly because they did not know beforehand) and decided that the officer responsible should be Court-Martialled. Mr Anthony Eden then Minister for War, I was told, took a more lenient view and I got away with it.[17]

The origins of the second raid lay in a memorandum by the Prime Minister to General Ismay on 2 July, two days after the Germans had occupied the Channel Islands:

If it be true that a few hundred German troops have landed on Jersey or Guernsey by troop-carriers, plans should be studied to land secretly by night on the Islands and kill or capture the invaders. This is exactly one of the exploits for which the Commandos would be suited.[18]

A War Cabinet meeting that same day approved a plan for 140 men to be put ashore on Guernsey with the object of killing Germans and destroying German aircraft and facilities on the airfield there. Major John Durnford-Slater's No 3 Commando, the first to be formed, was to join No 11 Independent Company for the raid. Codenamed *Ambassador*, it was launched on the night of 14/15 July. The plan was to land at three separate points on the southern coast of the island. Forty men of No 3 Commando under Durnford-Slater himself were to land in Moulin Huet Bay, supported by the destroyer HMS *Scimi-*

tar. The other two landings were to be made by No 11 Independent Company at Le Jaonnet Bay and Pointe de la Moye. The idea was that the raiders would embark in the two destroyers and then trans-ship to the crash boats which would make the trip under their own steam once off the Guernsey coast. The convoy set off from Dart-mouth at 1845 hours. It hove to off the coast in poor visibility with mist and drizzle, and in a slight swell.

Durnford-Slater's party arrived at the correct beach on time, but could not land dry-shod because of the rocky nature of the beach. Nevertheless, they all got ashore. Patrols were sent out, a roadblock established and the Jerbourg peninsula searched, but no enemy were found. Durnford-Slater now ordered re-embarkation. While this was going on, an enemy machine-gun opened up to the south, but then ceased fire. Re-embarkation proved difficult, however, because of the heavy rollers and one man was presumed drowned. Eventually some had to swim out to the crash boats and three, hav-ing made one attempt to wade out, decided to give it up. They were given additional supplies of French currency – every man had been issued with 300 francs – and told to make for a certain RV in two nights' time, where the Navy would pick them up. The three were, however, captured and, in any event, C-in-C Plymouth vetoed the attempt to rescue them. Neither of the two No 11 Independent Company parties managed to get ashore, having failed to find suit-able beaches, and all then returned to Dartmouth. The main lessons to come out of it were the need to land the raiders at the right place and the right time and the unsuitability of the crash boats for this type of operation.

Rationalisation of Raiding Forces

In those early days after his appointment as DCO, Bourne had a constant struggle to obtain clearcut policy from the Cabinet. He received conflicting demands from the various ministries, and won-dered whether some of these, like an idea to land rifles on the coast of Brittany to start a revolt against the Germans, had really been properly thought through. At the beginning of July he therefore drafted a paper on raiding policy, to which Churchill gave general agreement, and also sought a member of the War Cabinet to repre-sent Combined Operations interests, Hugh Dalton, then Minister for Economic Welfare, being appointed. His other problem was suit-able ships:

On the 29th June the actual landing craft we had received were 6 ALC, 3 MLC and I SLC*. I went to the Third Sea Lord (Controller) Rear Admiral Fraser† and asked him for certain vessels and boats which, with the assistance of Capt Maund, I had decided was the minimum to make a start with. He was splendid in his co-operation. He gave everything that was humanly possible. He gave me two Dutch and 6 Belgian steamers without a word as troop carrying vessels. He also ordered, through the United States, all the Anti-Rum Running US Customs Cutters which were available – 38 in number. We realised that these would probably not be fully suitable but were better than the 7 RAF Crash Boats. At the same time he ordered 50 Eurekas and a provisional order for 50 more. We also looked around the country and managed to raise 30 salmon cobbles. These, with the three Glens [naval supply ships], were well designed ships already being completed under instructions from the Combined Operations Training Development Centre, the 2 LNER Train Ferries and an MLC carrier composed the fleet at the time. The last three were being converted (this is speaking from memory).[19]

The two relevant establishments when Bourne took over were the Combined Operations Development Centre mentioned above and the Irregular Warfare School which had been started by MI(R) at Inverailot in May 1940. Bourne now established a number of small boat bases at such ports as Warsash, Brightlingsea and Falmouth. The running of these was a Royal Navy responsibility, and a headquarters had been set up on 15 June in His Majesty's Yacht *Melisande*, headquarters of the Solent Patrol. Then, after *Collar*, this was moved to the Household Brigade Yacht Club at Warsash and in August 1940 was designated HMS *Tormentor*. Later, in October 1940 a Combined Training Centre for amphibious warfare was started at Inveraray.

Considering that Bourne was 'double-hatted', continuing as Adjutant-General Royal Marines throughout, it is remarkable what he did manage to achieve. Nevertheless, by mid-July he was feeling the pressure and asked to relinquish the post of Adjutant-General. On 17 July, Winston Churchill decided to appoint his old friend Admiral of the Fleet Sir Roger Keyes, as DCO, and Bourne was asked whether he would like to serve on as Keyes' deputy, which he agreed to do, temporarily relinquishing the post of Adjutant-General. Keyes installed himself in Richmond Terrace, Whitehall,

---

*ALC = Assault Landing Craft. MLC = Motorised Landing Craft. SLC = Ship Landing carrier.
†Later Admiral of the Fleet Lord Fraser of North Cape.

and this was to be the headquaters of Combined Operations for the remainder of the war.

Although General Bourne had, in early July, proposed two more raids – against a wireless station at Ushant and the Cherbourg Peninsula – it was clear that a long term plan was needed to develop Combined Operations. This was considered by Anthony Eden, the Secretary of State for War, and the Chiefs of Staff, and they presented a memorandum to Churchill on 22 July. They envisaged four stages. Firstly, there was the reconnaissance and experimental phase of small coastal raids, as represented by *Collar*, and then the 'guerrilla warfare' stage, 'when constant smash-and-grab raids by numbers of irregular troops are carried out up and down the enemy's long coast-line'. Next all three services would combine in 'deliberate attacks upon important and well-defended objectives'. Finally would come the 'knockout' phase when 'advances inland are intended'. They accepted that the phases would overlap, but the 'guerrilla' stage, which would have involved parties of upwards 200 men making two raids a week and remaining ashore for periods of up to 24 hours, could not be started until there were sufficient landing craft available. The two later phases would employ conventional army formations, and the RAF would have to build a troop-carrying fleet for the parachutists then under training.[20]*

Churchill, with the failures of *Collar* and *Ambassador* uppermost in his mind, replied that, while the gaining of intelligence in the occupied countries was essential, this was the responsibility of the Ministry of Economic Warfare, which had also been placed in charge of the newly created Special Operations Executive,† which would organise contacts with the local people and the planting of agents.

> It would be most unwise to disturb the coasts of any of these countries by the kind of silly fiascos which were perpetrated at Boulogne and Guernsey. The idea of working all these coasts up against us by pin-prick raids and fulsome communiqués is one to be strictly avoided.

Instead, he tasked Keyes to begin planning for three raids by

---

*The paper also recommended the development of gliders and helicopters to transport men and equipment.
†This was formed in July 1940 and was a merger between MI(R) and Section D of the Secret Intelligence Service, which was responsible for sabotage and subversion in enemy territory.

between five and ten thousand men, which would be mounted during the winter and once the invasion threat had receded. Once these had taken place, 'there will be no objection to stirring up the French coast by minor forays'. He was also keen that 'during the spring and summer of 1941, large armoured irruptions should be contemplated'.[21] The Joint Planning Sub-Committee did warn that unless the Independent Companies and Commandos were given the opportunity to prove themselves in some minor operations, they would become disheartened.[22] Keyes, however, strongly supported Churchill, and the latter's proposals carried the day.

Meanwhile the raising of the Commandos continued, with training remaining the responsibility of each Commando unit.* It continued, for the time being, to be directed towards small-scale operations, with much emphasis on building up individual endurance. Geoffrey Appleyard describes in a letter home how B Troop of No 7 Commando was tackling this at the beginning of August:

We are all [the whole Troop] in a large house in Newmarket, and the Provost Company (to whom we are temporarily attached for pay, rations, etc.) has lent us two cooks. John [Colbeck] and I share one room, M-P [March-Phillipps] has a room to himself, the sergeants have a room, the men are about eight to a room. The house is entirely unfurnished except for tables and benches that we have got together. There is a bathroom and a lavatory with running water. We three officers eat exactly the same food as the men, but in a different room. And it is very good.

Our transport consists of M-P's car (a terrific 30-98 Velox!!), two motor cycles and a 30-cwt lorry. But we don't use it much. When we want to go anywhere, we walk, as our preliminary objective is to get as tough as possible. When we finally move from here to a new location on the coast, we shall walk – 60 or 70 miles – in two or three days, bivouacking at nights in barns and haylofts and living on our ration allowance of 6/8d a day.†

Today's programme has been typical. Reveille 6.30, training run 7 (about a mile) followed by PT, breakfast 8, parade 9, inspection, route march 8-10 miles (with arms, in battle dress, belts etc.) at fast pace, including cross-country work, map reading, compass work, moving through cover, etc. Lunch 1, swimming parade 2.30 for 1½ hours' swim-

---

*It was suggested in early July that Inverailot, under the new title of the School of Special Warfare, should be responsible for training both the Independent Companies and Commando cadres and that an Inspector of Irregular Forces be appointed. This was not followed through.[23]

†Officers received 13/4d per day and other ranks 6/8d.

ming, running, exercising etc. Tea at 4.30. Lecture by M-P for three-quarters of an hour at 5. Free for the evening at 6. A fairly full day and hard work, but makes one feel grand, even though a little stiff! Later on, of course, there will be weapon training, range practice, cross-country runs, hare and hounds, treasure hunts, mock operations, night operations etc. The training programme can and will be made very fascinating.[24]

On 25 August Churchill sent a minute to Anthony Eden:

If we are to have any campaign in 1941 it must be amphibious in its character and there certainly will be many opportunities of [sic] minor operations all of which will depend on surprise landings of lightly equipped mobile forces accustomed to work like packs of hounds instead of being moved about in the ponderous manner which is appropriate. These have become so elaborate, so complicated in their equipment, so vast in their transport that it is very difficult to use them in any operation in which time is vital.

For every reason therefore we must develop the storm troop or Commando idea. I have asked for 5,000 parachutists and we must also have at least 10,000 of these small 'bands of brothers' who will be capable of lightning action. In this way alone will those positions be secured which afterwards will give the opportunity for highly trained regular troops to operate on a larger scale.[25]

The problem was that, with the Battle of Britain now at its height and invasion threatening, it was clearly impossible to cream off this number of elite troops from the formations and units then defending the British coasts. Nevertheless, Eden realised that some form of rationalisation of the existing Special Forces needed to take place. He replied to the Prime Minister on 5 September stating that the Commandos and Independent Companies would be merged into twenty Special Service Companies under the direct control of the Director of Combined Operations.[26] Indeed, the Chiefs of Staff had already agreed on 9 August that the two should be amalgamated.[27] It would, however, be a little while yet before the merger could be brought about. The Independent Companies were committed to the defence of Britain, apart from No 10 Independent Company, now under command of Major A.C.W. May, who had won an MC with No 1 Company in Norway, which had been sent on the abortive expedition to Dakar (Operation *Menace*) with the Royal Marine Striking Force. The Commandos were still under training, and between mid-September and mid-

October they were removed from the operational control of Keyes to that of Home Forces because of the threat of invasion.

Eventually, in early October, a plan for the reorganisation began to take shape. The Independent Companies, together with Nos 5, 6 and 11 Commandos would be formed into three Special Service* Battalions. The battalion would have two 500-man companies, each formed from an existing Commando. Two more battalions would then be raised from Nos 3, 4, 7 and 8 Commandos.[28] They would make up a 'Special Brigade' and reorganisation was to be completed by 10 November. In addition, No 12 Commando, then based at Strangford Lough, N Ireland, under Lt Colonel S.S. Harrison MC RA, was also available. In the end, the reorganisation took place as follows:

1 Special Service Battalion Formed from Nos 1, 2, 3, 4, 5, 8 and 9 Independent Companies, and based at Dartmouth and Paignton in Devon. CO: Lt Col W. Glendinning, Welch Regiment.

2 Special Service Battalion Formed from Nos 6 and 7 Independent Companies and Nos 9 and 11 Commandos and based at Whiting Bay in Scotland. CO: Lt Colonel J.M. Saegert RE.

3 Special Service Battalion Formed from Nos 4 and 7 Commandos and based at Girvan in Scotland. CO: Lt Colonel D.S. Lister MC, The Buffs.

4 Special Service Battalion Formed from Nos 3 and 8 Commandos and based at Largs. CO: Lt Colonel R.E. Laycock RHG.

5 Special Service Battalion Formed from Nos 5 and 6 Commandos and based at Helensburgh. CO: Lt Col T. Featherstonhaugh KRRC.

No 2 Commando became 11 Special Air Service Battalion and was based at Ringway, near Manchester, the first parachute training centre. It would eventually become the 1st Parachute Battalion and then the Parachute Regiment. No 12 Commando remained outside the Special Service Brigade and, indeed, was not at this stage under the control of DCO, being earmarked for possible operations in the

---

*According to Dudley Clarke, the term 'Commando' was considered as 'scarcely an appropriate title to appear in the formal nomenclature of the Ministry, and so seriously was this taken that for a time all documents (with the blissful disregard to the sinister parallel of Hitler's SS) referred to them exclusively as 'Special Service Troops'.[29] Indeed, as we shall see, the 'SS' title remained in being until the end of 1944, but was never used at unit level except during the SS battalion experiment.

Republic of Ireland in the event of a German invasion or occupation of that country. Appointed on 9 October 1940 to command the Special Service Brigade was Brigadier J.C. Haydon DSO OBE, who had commanded the Irish Guards in France with much distinction and had earlier been Hore-Belisha's Military Assistant when he was Minister for War. His headquarters was eventually established at Theale in Berkshire, with the Signals Section at Brightlingsea.

It was at this time that the first of many specialist Commando sections was formed. On its formation in July 1940, No 6 Commando raised a special troop for sea-raiding, obtaining some civilian Folboat canoes. No 8 Commando also had in its ranks a canoe enthusiast, Lieutenant Roger Courtney, who, in between gold prospecting and big game hunting in Africa, had before the war undertaken many long distance canoeing trips. He persuaded Bob Laycock, commanding No 8, to allow him to experiment with canoes as a means of sabotaging ships, and, as a result of an exercise against the *Glengyle* and a submarine depot ship, Keyes agreed that a Folboat Section of twelve men under Courtney should be formed, and this would accompany Laycock to the Middle East at the end of January 1941. They did their training on the Isle of Arran, and the original intention was to form a Folboat Section in each Commando, but, apart from that in No 6, which was called 101 Troop, this never materialised.

No 10 Independent Company eventually arrived back from West Africa at the end of October and was disbanded at Fort William. Some of its members went to Special Service Battalions, while others, like in all the Independent Companies,* voluntarily returned to their units, as did a certain number of those in the Commandos. Much of their dissatisfaction is summed up by the comments of Major Bill Copland, about to relinquish command of No 4 Independent Company and join No 1 Special Service Battalion:

And so, into another new organisation goes the cream of the Independent Companies which were born in muddle, suffered in the chaos of Norway, wasted months of valuable time at home when tasks which

---

*One Independent Company did, however, continue to survive. This was the Independent Company, Gibraltar, formed in October 1940 from units in the garrison. Its role was as small assault parties should the enemy gain a lodgement on the Rock and short raiding operations. Members did undergo Commando training at Achnacarry from July 1942. It carried out no operations and was eventually disbanded in August 1944 after the Allied landings in the South of France.

other troops botched could have been done well by them. The diary closes with the hope that the new formation will 'give them a break' and that the new staff will be more worthy of them than ever was the staff which controlled their Norwegian destinies.[30]

CHAPTER TWO

A Year of Frustration
1941

Sir Roger Keyes was keen to use the Special Service Brigade on the lines of Churchill's concept of large-scale amphibious operations. Appreciating that these were not feasible against the coastline of France and the Low Countries, he looked at the Mediterranean, and proposed to the Chiefs of Staff on 30 October 1940 that Pantellaria, a small island off Sicily, should be captured and used as an alternative to Malta, as well as an aircraft staging post and a useful means of disrupting the Italian lines of communication to Libya. He considered that four Commandos would be sufficient to capture it. Admiral Sir Andrew Cunningham, C-in-C Mediterranean Fleet, was opposed to this on the grounds that it would be an intolerable burden on his already overstretched resources, since once captured it would have to be held. The Chiefs of Staff, after some hesitation, approved the plan, provided that it did not interfere with another scheme, Operation *Brisk*, the seizure of the Azores should Spain enter the war on the Axis side. Codenamed *Workshop*, Keyes was given responsibility for its conduct, and began to organise the Special Service Brigade for it.

While Churchill quickly became enthusiastic about *Workshop*, Cunningham continued to voice his doubts, as he did over Keyes' other proposal, which was to seize islands in the Dodecanese. The Commandos began to train for it, but on 5 December the Defence Committee, which acted as a link between the Chiefs of Staff and the War Cabinet, expressed their doubts as to the probability of success of the operation, believing that lack of surprise and a shortage of destroyers would be serious disadvantages. Then, during the next few days came news of success by Wavell in the Western Desert, and the Defence Committee reconsidered *Workshop*. Although still doubtful over its success, they agreed that it should go ahead, provided that Cunningham was able to keep the garrison maintained after its capture. Keyes' Commandos should sail to take the island, although the Defence Committee reserved the right to cancel the operation at any time. The force was scheduled to sail on 14 December, but on that very day, it was decided, in view of fears of a German invasion of

Spain, that it should be postponed by at least a month, although it would still remain a top priority as far as plans were concerned. For the Commandos themselves, Bob Laycock later recalled:

> Time went on and no other raids took place, though everyone was keyed up. Several projects were planned, but none took place and these cancellations had a disheartening effect on the men. Patience is a virtue for everyone, and the Commandos certainly learnt it.[1]

Cunningham, however, had now become interested in the Dodecanese, and believed that their denial to the Italians would give encouragement to the Greeks, who were at the time successfully holding the Italian offensive through Albania, which had been launched in early November. This grew in attraction as an alternative to *Workshop*, especially after the Luftwaffe had been deployed to Sicily in early January, and was seen as the means of maintaining the British hold on the Eastern Mediterranean as well as preventing the Italians from striking the Mediterranean Fleet base at Alexandria from the air.

Churchill fought a rearguard action over *Workshop*, considering that the Chiefs of Staff view was too defensive minded, and even advocated the attack of either Sardinia or Sicily. Eden and the Chiefs of Staff, however, now played a trump card, pointing out that if the Italians remained in the Dodecanese they would effectively cut maritime communications with Turkey, which it was hoped might enter the war on the British side. Churchill relented, and it was agreed that the operation against the islands was to go ahead, but not before a sufficient sized force, spearheaded by Special Service troops sent from England, had been built up. Consequently, at the end of January, part of the SS Brigade, Force Z, set sail for the Middle East, and their experiences will be related in Chapter Four.

At this time each Special Service battalion was organised into two companies, each of ten platoons or troops of fifty men. The platoons were further broken down into two sections, which in turn were split into two sub-sections of six NCOs and five private soldiers each. Although the departure of Force Z had reduced three of the battalions to one company, Brigadier Charles Haydon still felt that it was too cumbersome an organisation. On 1 February 1941 he recommended to Sir Roger Keyes that the Special Service Brigade revert to the original Commando establishment on the grounds that the Special Service battalion concept had never been popular in the bri-

NORTH SEA

NETHERLANDS

GREAT BRITAIN

BELGIUM

London

Ostend
Dunkirk
Gravelines
Dover
Les Hemmes
Calais
Ambleteuse
Newhaven
Boulogne
Hardelot

Merlimont

Poole
Portsmouth
Onival

ENGLISH CHANNEL

Berneval
St Valery en Caux
Dieppe
Teignmouth
Fecamp
Etretat
Harfleur
Plymouth
Hanfluer
Paris
Cherbourg
Deauville
Omonville
Houlgate
Channel
Islands
Courselles
La Riviere
Arromanches
Port en Bessin
St Laurent

St Malo

Ushant
Brest

FRANCE

Lorient

Nantes

St Nazaire

Isle de Yeu

BAY OF BISCAY

Bordeaux

**CROSS-CHANNEL
RAIDS**

R. Adour

0   50   100   150   200   250 Kms

Bayonne

SPAIN

Morton R. Dowlingen

gade, it was difficult to control and did not satisfactorily match the capacities of existing shipping. This was agreed[2] but before it could be put into effect, the brigade was given a warning order for another operation.

Operation Claymore

The target for this operation was the Lofoten Islands, Norwegian-owned and lying just inside the Arctic Circle. Here there were a number of factories which converted cod and herring oil into glycerine for munitions, and it was felt that these should be destroyed. Haydon selected Nos 3 and 4 SS Battalions, now each reduced to one company as a result of the departure of Force Z, for the task. They set sail, accompanied by Brigadier Haydon and his headquarters and a party of fifty Norwegian sailors in HMS *Queen Emma* and *Princess Beatrix* and a naval escort, on 21 February from Scapa Flow. They stopped at the Faroe Islands for final training and here the No 3 SS Battalion Company became No 4 Commando once more, under command of Lt Colonel Lister, while the No 4 Company was designated No 3 Commando again under Lt Colonel Durnford-Slater. Then, on 1 March, they set off for the final lap. Ken Phillott remembers the voyage well:

> Here we were in mid Winter, crowded into a small ship, some 500 of us. It was a ship [*Queen Emma*] with a shallow draught and made top heavy with landing craft. Anyone who knows the North Sea even in Summertime is aware of its roughness, but this was Winter. That ship did everything but turn upside down and I am sure that everyone was seasick, even the Captain.[3]

They arrived off the Lofoten Islands in the early hours of 4 March:

> We climbed into our landing craft, in which we were packed like sardines. Even so, we were freezing. A warship escorted us towards the shore, where already we could see the twinkling of lights. Obviously little attention was being given to a black-out in such a remote northerly place. After all, this was the first real Commando landing and no one expected such a thing.
>
> The cold was so intense that as the spray swept over us the sea water froze on our gas capes which we were wearing both as camouflage and protection against the elements. Suddenly we heard the craft hitting something solid. The ramp was lowered and we tried to rush ashore as we had done so many times in training. This time there was a difference; everywhere was solid ice and on the quay were piles of frozen cod fish.

Our surprise had been perfect. Even the Norwegians on their way to work thought we were German troops in training and gave a half-hearted Nazi salute. With my partner Frank Moore, a real Cockney, I raced, or at least tried to hurry over the slippery ice towards the back door of a large hotel. We had been told to shoot anyone seen leaving by that particular door. I say 'shoot', but we were so cold that we could hardly hold our rifles let alone pull the trigger. We could see the staff being kept in the kitchen on instructions from an officer. Then we heard a shot, then another. Lt Webb, together with his batman, and some Norwegian officers had gone upstairs to arrest two of Goebbels' Propaganda Ministry officials who were sleeping there. The door was locked. One shot blew it open and, upon entering, a chamber pot was seen below the bed. No one could resist such a target and so another shot was put into the target. I understand that the two half conscious bodies performed a feat of levitation unmatched by any conjuror! By now everyone one was fulfilling their allotted tasks. Fish oil factories and military installations were being blown up as well as ships. The Norwegians by now had realised that we were British and were giving us hot ersatz coffee and some of their meagre rations. They pointed out the Quislings and others who had assisted the Germans, particularly the girls.

One of the funniest sights I saw that day was a very small officer's batman bringing down the street a very big German prisoner. This Commando must have been a cartoonist's dream; he had his rifle and bayonet across his shoulders, there were knives in his belt, a revolver in his holster and, in his hand pointing towards the back of the running German, a Very pistol. Suddenly our Commando friend slipped on the ice and fell. His huge prisoner, sensing what had happened, stopped, looked round, walked back, picked up the unfortunate Commando and then collected the pistol and replaced it in his hand. He then turned again, placed his hands above his head and, with our intrepid Commando friend now fully recovered, continued running down the street to the compound![4]

There were, too, other humorous incidents which became part of Commando folklore. Lieutenant R.L. Wills sent off a telegram from the telegraph station at Stamsund. Addressed to A. Hitler, Berlin, it read: 'You said in your last speech German troops would meet the British wherever they landed. Where are your troops?' Lord Lovat, who had recently joined No 4 Commando, took a bus to a seaplane base and captured the staff. The commander afterwards complained of his unwarlike behaviour and said that he would report it to the Führer.

By midday, their tasks completed, the Commandos began to re-embark. Commander Sir Geoffrey Congreve Bt DSO RN, the Commandos' Senior Landing Officer since July 1940, noted in his diary: 'Confess to great disappointment in not having any fighting, but it would be unpleasant in this cold I suppose. . . . Got some stamps at PO [Post Office]. A nice morning ashore.'[5] This summed up the feelings of most of those who took part. Nevertheless, it was a significant fillip to morale after the months of frustration. Furthermore, apart from the destruction of the glycerine factories and military installations, there was something concrete to show for what they had done when they arrived home in the shape of 315 volunteers for the Norwegian forces, sixty Quislings and 225 German prisoners. All this had been achieved at the cost of one casualty, an officer who accidently shot himself in the thigh. One success, which could not be made public at the time, was the boarding of the trawler *Krebs*. She was equipped with an Enigma cypher machine and, although the crew managed to throw this overboard, the boarding party did seize a set of spare rotors which was of great help to the cryptanalysts at Bletchley Park.

New Commando Organisation
Immediately on return from the Lofoten Islands, the reorganisation of the Commandos was completed and by mid March 1941, the structure was as follows:

No 1 Commando Formed from No 1 SS Battalion. Commanded by Lt Colonel W. Glendinning, Welch Regiment, and based at Dartmouth.

No 2 Commando Formed from No 1 SS Battalion. Commanded by Lt Colonel A.C. Newman, Essex Regiment and based at Paignton, but shortly to move to Weymouth.

No 3 Commando Formed from No 4 SS Battalion. Commanded by Lt Colonel J.F. Durnford-Slater RA and based at Largs less A Troop in the Middle East

No 4 Commando Formed from No 3 SS Battalion. Commanded by Lt Colonel D.S. Lister MC, The Buffs and based at Troon.

No 5 Commando Formed from No 5 SS Battalion. Commanded by Lt Colonel W.S.S. Sanguinetti, The Hampshire Regiment and based at Barrhead, but shortly to move to Falmouth.

No 6 Commando Formed from No 5 SS Battalion. Commanded by Lt Colonel T. Featherstonhaugh KRRC and based at Inveraray.

No 7 Commando Formed from No 3 SS Battalion. Commanded by Lt Colonel F.B. Colvin, Dorset Regiment and in the Middle East.

No 8 Commando Formed from No 4 SS Battalion. Commanded by

Lt Colonel D.R. Daly, Scots Guards and in the Middle East.

No 9 Commando Formed from No 2 SS Battalion. Commanded by Lt Colonel J.M. Saegert RE and based at Criccieth.

No 11 Commando Formed from No 2 SS Battalion. Commanded by Lt Colonel R.R. Pedder HLI and in the Middle East.

No 12 Commando Had retained its separate identity throughout and was still under command of Lt Colonel S.S. Harrison MC RA and now based at Warsash, where it had been since early January.

Brigade Headquarters remained at Theale.

*

After the success of the Lofoten Islands raid, there was a lull in UK-based Commando operations. Keyes had now built up another amphibious striking force to replace that which he had raised for *Workshop* but which had then been sent to the Middle East as Force Z. Then, in July, as a result of Spanish sabre rattling, which seemed to indicate that they were preparing to enter the war on the Axis side, a plan was put in train to seize the Canary Islands. Codenamed *Puma* and later *Pilgrim*, the force drawn up consisted of two Royal Marine Brigades, Army troops and Commandos, which were assembled at Inveraray under Major General Robert Sturges Royal Marines. The Commando element was to consist of Nos 1, 2, 4, 9 and 12 Commandos, along with a troop from No 6 Commando and 101 Troop also from No 6. This force was designated Force 110, and command of it was now transferred to Lt General Sir Harold Alexander, the GOC Southern Command.

For Keyes this period was one of mounting frustration, which had begun with the cancellation of *Workshop* and what he saw as the dissipation of Layforce in the Middle East. Now, although Director of Combined Operations, he was not allowed the opportunity for which he hankered so much, command of a major amphibious operation and so repeat his success at Zeebrugge in April 1918. Furthermore, he remained convinced that such an operation, against Sardinia, Sicily or Pantellaria, could be decisive in the Mediterranean. As it was, he blamed the Inter-Service Committees, especially the Defence Committee, of obstructionism. The naval representatives on these committees and the Admiralty really drew his venom. Yet, he never seemed to appreciate that the Royal Navy's losses in surface ships during the Battle for Crete and their commitment to having to keep open the supply line to Malta, now under continuous air attack, meant that they did not have the resources to support such an operation.

As it was, Keyes became even more disgruntled at the end of August when the Chiefs of Staff decided, after representations from the commanders involved, that at least part of Force 110 would have to be sent to West Africa in order to provide the necessary training in the right geographical conditions for Operation *Pilgrim*. After some discussion, with Keyes and others, it was decreed by the Prime Minister that part of the force was to be despatched. The unhealthy West African climate and the lack of accommodation precluded the complete force being sent. It was reckoned, however, that the main body could deploy and mount *Pilgrim* if given a month's notice.

Ten amphibious landing ships, including the *Princes Beatrix* and *Queen Emma*, set sail on 15 September, arriving at Freetown, Sierra Leone, on 5 October. This element of Force 110 was codenamed *Journalist*, and *Pilgrim* was changed to *Tonic*. The Commando contribution was four small parties, each of one officer and some 25 other ranks, from Nos 2, 1 and 3 combined, 4 and 9 Commandos under the overall charge of Colonel E.G. Atkinson MVO. They remained, some of the time at Lagos and the rest at Freetown, until February 1942, by which time *Tonic* appeared an unlikely option and they returned home. They carried out amphibious landing exercises, with particular attention to the landing of tanks – A, B, and C Special Service Squadrons Royal Armoured Corps* had been sent complete for this purpose – but had little operational excitement. Indeed, the only major scare came in December. On the 2nd, HMS *Devonshire* intercepted a German raider, who scuttled herself. There were then reports that her crew had been taken off by U-boats and were heading for Ascension Island, which had a very weak garrison. *Queen Emma* and *Princes Beatrix* were ordered there, but, although the Ascension Island garrison reported firing on a U-boat, the operation came to naught.

The Maid Honor

There was another small group of Commandos, besides those in

---

*These had been formed in summer 1941 with the idea of giving the assaulting troops immediate armoured support during amphibious landings. The initial establishment of each was six light Tetrarch tanks and eight Valentine infantry tanks. While B Squadron took part in the Madagascar landings, A and C were disbanded in summer 1942. B Squadron then went on to become the Airborne Reconnaissance Squadron which was to distinguish itself at Arnhem in September 1944.

Journalist, which spent the winter 1941-42 in West Africa. They, however, had a more active time. The origins of this little band go back to B Troop of No 7 Commando during the winter of 1940-41. Commanded by Captain G.H. March-Phillipps MBE RA, with Lieutenant J.G. Appleyard RASC as one of his officers, the troop became part of No 3 SS Battalion on reorganisation. When No 7 Commando was reconstituted to go to the Middle East at the end of January 1941, neither Gus March-Phillipps nor Geoffrey Appleyard went with them. The reason for this was that they had been given another job.

Brigadier Colin Gubbins, who had been appointed to command the London Group of SOE, which was responsible for the control and execution of special operations in Western Europe, needed experts to train the ever growing band of agents which he was recruiting. Sabotage and assassination called for similar skills to those of the Commandos, and it was logical that he should look to the Special Service Brigade to supply him with some of the necessary experts. In January 1941, Gubbins considered, among others, the names of March-Phillipps and Appleyard and both were appointed as 'instructors for Allied troops'. The reason for their names coming to the attention of Gubbins was as a result of a paper entitled *How to Win the War*, which had been written by a member of March-Phillipps' Commando troop, Jan Nasmyth:

> It was an essay really about how the possibility of keeping troops in being in enemy territory by making them independent of any form of human life, either for food or for shelter, so to speak, and next morning Gus came bursting in in full battle order, so to speak, and said to me that my essay described exactly what he had been trying to think of.[6]

Eventually this paper found its way into Gubbins' hands, and he authorised the forming of a small force under March-Phillipps to assist in SOE's cross-channel operations. Rather than rely on the Royal Navy, March-Phillipps had also suggested that a fishing smack be used. This had the advantages of being a good camouflage and also, if it had a wooden hull, it would not be vulnerable to magnetic mines. Gubbins agreed to this and by March 1941 the unit had been formed and was based at The Antelope Inn, Poole in Dorset, with its members being recruited by March-Phillips from the Commando and SOE ranks. Of the founding members, many would have distinguished wartime careers, and would win several decorations for bravery. Sadly, though, few would still be alive in 1945.

The vessel selected was the *Maid Honor*. She was a Brixham trawler of 39½ tons gross tonnage, which had been fished regularly up to 1936 when she was sold and converted into a yacht. In March 1941 March-Phillipps was authorised to requisition her, and she was sailed from Brixham and moored in a quiet part of Poole Harbour.

> Here she underwent an extensive refit. Two crow's nests were fitted to the masts and equipped as Bren gun firing-posts. A fake deck house was also constructed in order to conceal a 2-pounder cannon. Part of the deck was lowered so that twin heavy machine guns could fire through the scuppers and also reinforced with steel plating. In addition there was an attempt to fit a spigot mortar to the deck as an anti-U-boat weapon, but this was abandoned after particles of burning charge holed the mainsail.[7]

With *Maid Honor* came her skipper, Blake Glanville, who taught her new crew how to handle her as well as general seamanship.

The *Maid Honor* Force, as it was called by SOE, was keen to begin operations, but the Admiralty refused to allow the trawler to operate outside coastal waters until a specific operation had been approved. In the meantime, Appleyard won a Military Cross for a cross-channel operation involving the submarine HMS *Tigris* and the collection of French agents. In June, an operation was planned with the Dutch Section of SOE, but the Admiralty refused to sanction it. It was now clear to SOE that Admiralty restrictions made it extremely doubtful that *Maid Honor* could be used at all in home waters. However, in July 1941, an opening appeared.

Axis U-boats were achieving success at this time not just in the North Atlantic but off the West African coast as well. This posed a threat to British sea communications to both the Middle and Far East. It was suspected that the U-boats and their supply ships were lying up in the creaks and rivers of neutral and Vichy French territories. SOE had a section under Louis Franck based at Lagos, and it was decided that the *Maid Honor* Force might be the ideal means of winkling them out, especially since the use of more conventional forces could well further deter the Vichy French territories from joining the banner of de Gaulle and drive Spain into joining the Axis. Consequently, the *Maid Honor* left Poole on 9 August with a crew of five and March-Phillipps as skipper, after Gubbins had personally bid them farewell, while the remainder of the force went out by troopship.

Having called in at Madeira, the *Maid Honor* arrived at Freetown on 20 September. The main party who had arrived at the end of August, was intially based outside Freetown, and met up with March-Phillipps on his arrival. Still ultimately under SOE, they were put under the operational control of C-in-C South Atlantic, Vice Admiral A.U. Willis, although he was advised by Louis Franck. *Maid Honor's* main task was to carry out a discreet search of all possible hiding places from the Gulf of Guinea up to and including Liberia. Indeed, during the last week of October *Maid Honor* carried out a detailed reconnaissance of the Liberian coast.[8] At the end of November they were ordered to leave Freetown for Lagos, and had the frustration of being becalmed ten miles from their haven because of a worn bearing in the engine. In mid January 1942 their moment for proper action came.

On 10 June 1940, the day Italy announced her intention of entering the war on the German side, the 7,561 ton Italian merchantman *Duchessa d'Aosta* entered the harbour of Santa Isabel on the Spanish island of Fernando Po in the Gulf of Guinea. For the next eighteen months the British Vice Consul there sent regular reports on her and two smaller German vessels, the *Likomba* and *Bibundi*.[9] Apart from occasional indications that they were preparing to sail, all three ships remained in harbour. Nevertheless, there was concern that they could be used for re-supplying U-boats, and this led SOE to evolve a plan for capturing them. In view of Spain's neutrality, it had to be a covert operation, and the obvious people to carry it out were the *Maid Honor* Force. Initially the Foreign Office was very much against Operation *Postmaster*, as it was called, and the British Embassy in Madrid was particularly worried over possible Spanish reactions. The Foreign Office did, however, eventually relent.

Much of the detailed planning for the operation was carried out by a member of the Franck Mission, Leonard Guise. He even went so far as arranging for the ships' officers to be present at a party given ashore by a Spanish doctor on the night in question. Since *Maid Honor* herself was unsuitable, he obtained two local tugs, the *Vulcan* and the *Nuneaton*, whose crews volunteered with alacrity, as did some members of the Nigerian Civil Service. The party, accompanied by Guise, left Lagos on 11 January and arrived off their objective four nights later. As to the outcome, the Chiefs of Staff were merely informed in their daily situation summary that on 18 January the corvette HMS *Violet* had intercepted the *Duchessa d'Aosta* some 230 miles south-west of Lagos and was escorting her back to port.[10] The South Atlantic War Diary reveals little more, save to say that the *Violet* had been ordered to patrol the Gulf of Guinea as a result of newspaper reports and radio broadcasts that Free French warships had seized an Axis warship in the Spanish port of Fernando Po.[11] What actually happened was very much more dramatic.

The plan called for the tugs to arrive at Santa Isabel at midnight Spanish time, when the harbour and town lights would be doused. In the event, they arrived an hour too early. Leonard Guise:

> . . . there was a very tedious time of waiting. Gus was all teed up and he wanted to go in, and there was for one moment a rather sticky little scene when we on *Nuneaton* could hear Gus quite loudly disclaiming that he'd every intention of going in and to hell with it. Gus himself struck me as completely intrepid, almost to the point of overdoing it, because . . . this was not really a military operation. It was a burglar's operation and burglars don't go in shooting. But Gus gave the impression that he much preferred to do a job when he did go in shooting.[12]

Gus March-Phillipps did calm down, and at midnight, with the lights now out, in they went, and he made for the *Duchessa*. Desmonde Longe, who was with him, recalled:

> We ran up the little ladder from the well-deck on the promenade of this merchant ship, chased along the gangway. By this time we had a knife in one hand and a pistol in the other. The first thing I knew was something between my legs, and I went for a burton, and I thought it was a panicking Italian, or something or other. In actual fact it was a pig, because the Italians had two or three pigs on the deck at the back.[13]

They quickly captured the crew and placed charges on the mooring cables, thereby cutting them, and *Vulcan* towed her out through the narrow channel to the open sea against a severe cross current. *Nuneaton* under Graham Hayes went alongside the *Likomba* and captured that as well, along with the smaller *Bibindi* tied up with her, and they were towed out to sea. As both tugs got clear of the harbour:

> Pandemonium reigned ashore. Immediately after the detonations were heard the anti-aircraft guns went into action and blazed into the sky, the explosions having been mistaken for bombs from raiding aircraft. It was not until daylight came that it was realised on the shore that the steamers

had gone in the night. It was as well that the 6 in. guns covering the harbour had not opened fire because the most powerful gun aboard the tug was a Bren.[14]

March-Phillipps and Appleyard in the *Duchessa d'Aosta* duly met up with the *Violet,* but Hayes, after numerous problems with his prizes, eventually received a tow from a merchant ship and a destroyer and arrived at Lagos before March-Phillipps and Appleyard. The official reports on this operation were not released for many years,* but the *London Gazette* of 24 July 1942 did announce the awards of the DSO to March-Phillipps, a Bar to the MC to Appleyard and an MC to Hayes. Shortly after *Postmaster,* the *Maid Honor* Force sailed back to England. Sadly, however, *Maid Honor* herself had to be left in Lagos. She was reconverted to a trawler and sold to the Sierra Leone Government, but fell a victim to tropical water worms. As for the *Duchessa d'Aosta,* she was sailed back to Greenock, arriving there in July 1942. She was handed over to Canadian Pacific, re-named *Empire Yukon,* and undertook many voyages across the Atlantic, to South America, Egypt, Mombasa and Australia before the war was over.

Small Raids 1941
The frustrations of this period for the Commandos left in the United Kingdom are only too understandable. They found themselves constantly training for operations which were then cancelled, and many began to wonder whether they would ever be used in action. Apart

---

* Henrietta March-Philips's 1974 BBC radio documentary about her father, *The Quest for Gus,* did shed some new light, but she struggled to get it aired for fears that it might affect relations with Spain, still under General Franco's dictatorship. The *Maid Honor*'s log is to be found in the F. C. Perkins papers held by the Imperial War Museum. The Foreign Office files on Operation *Postmaster* were originally not to be released into the public domain until 2017, but were made available by the Public Record Office (now the National Archives), Kew, London, in the 1990s. Since then further light has been shed through the release of the SOE reports on Operation *Postmaster* and personal files of the *Maid Honor* Force under Class HS at Kew. A recent and most comprehensive account of the operation, which draws on these new sources, is Brian Lett, *Ian Fleming and SOE's Operation Postmaster: The Untold Top Secret Story* (Pen & Sword, Barnsley, 2012), although the Ian Fleming connection is not proven.

from Churchill's initial dislike of small raids, another problem had been the shortage of landing craft. In the late summer of 1941, though, a change of heart began to take place.

On the night of 27/28 July 1941, just over a year after the first two small raids against occupied territory, Operation *Chess* was mounted. This was in response to a Defence Committee decision on a policy of small raids to test the German defences on the French coastline. It was mounted by a party of sixteen men from No 12 Commando under command of Second Lieutenant P.H. Pinckney and the target was Ambleteuse, just north of Boulogne. Their task was to carry out a reconnaissance and, if possible capture a prisoner. They were to be allowed one hour ashore. Operations were to be supervised by Colonel Atkinson, Deputy Commander of the SS Brigade, and the Vice-Admiral Dover, from where it was to be mounted. Postponed on the previous night because of unfavourable weather reports, the party set out in two ALCs, which were towed by a motor launch (*ML 104*). While Pinckney and ten men would land, leaving the remainder as a beach party in the one ALC, the other ALC, which had been taken as a reserve, lay 200 yards offshore. They landed just before 0200 hours, but already realised that they had been spotted, hearing whistles from the cliffs. Pinckney recounts what happened next:

> There was only 30 or 40 yards of sand at this stage of the tide and then a cliff of wet mud 20 feet high and unclimbable at that point. The tide at high water would have reached this cliff. Although a scaling ladder was available in the ALC it seemed best to work right-handed along the sand until a way up the cliff could be found and then strike back along the clifftop towards the village.
>
> Some 200 yards down the beach a possible place to climb the cliff was discovered. Two men and myself got up with difficulty, and found wire on the top. I sent the men to investigate this . . . I remained to get the other men up the cliffs. At this moment a starshell was fired over the ALC from the cliff top, and firing broke out. There was no time to get the men up the cliff, so we quickly returned along the sand. An MG was firing from the cliff edge directly above the boat. We got beneath this and threw grenades up. This silenced the MG. Tracer was being used by this MG and two others on either flank. I then re-embarked my party.[16]

There were no casualties to Pinckney's group, but the engine of the ALC was damaged, which meant a difficult trip back and they had to be towed into Dover. There were also two fatal casualties among

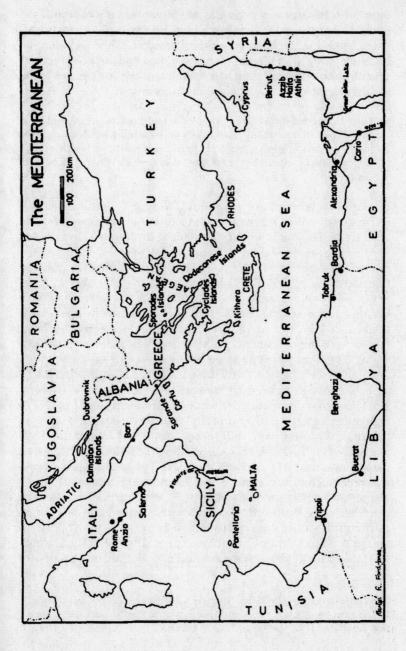

those who had remained on the ALC. One was a stoker and the other, Commander Sir Geoffrey Congreve DSO,* who died from a bullet wound in the back. As on the Lofoten Islands operation, he had gone along as an observer. The operation had not been very successful, although something had been learnt of the defences in the area. Nevertheless, as Colonel Atkinson recorded:

> Later I inspected the ALC which had a few bullet marks, then visited some of the men of the raiding party. They were cleaning weapons and resting. They were in good spirits and interested in what they had done, and hoped it was of value. They considered they were lucky to get off without casualties.[17]

In August there were two operations. The first, Operation *Gauntlet*, did not involve the Commandos, but a force of Canadians, who had been trained in amphibious operations at Inveraray. They sailed to Spitzbergen, some 600 miles from the North Pole, destroyed the coal mines there, to prevent them falling into German hands, and evacuated some 2,000 Russian miners and their families to Archangel. Then, on the night of 30/31 August, it was the turn of No 5 Commando. *Acid Drop* consisted of two simultaneous operations, each carried out by a party of one officer and fourteen men. Their targets were the beaches at Hardelot and Merlimont, west of Boulogne. The aims were the same as for *Chess*, but no enemy were encountered during the thirty minutes that each party was allowed ashore, although some useful lessons were learnt. No 5 Troop of No 1 Commando mounted an operation on the night of 27/28 September, again with the same aims and also making two separate landings, but there were differences. Instead of towing the ALCs across the Channel with MLs, the Raiding Craft Carrier HMS *Prince Leopold* with four ALCs aboard was used. The landing places were also very much further apart. While Lieutenant Scaramanga's party was to land at Pointe de Saire, near St Vaast on the east coast of the Cherbourg Peninsula, Captain Davies's force had Courseulles, north-north-west of Caen, as its target. They sailed from Spithead, and at a point in mid Channel transferred to their ALCs, which were towed to the shore by motor gunboats. Scaramanga's party got

---

*His father was General Sir Walter Congreve, who had won a VC at Colenso in 1899, and his elder brother Billy was killed on the Somme in July 1916 and, having already won the MC and DSO, was awarded a posthumous VC.

ashore in St Vaast Bay, and eventually ran straight into a German bicycle patrol. The Commandos' reactions were quicker than those of their opponents and they opened fire with their Tommy Guns, killing three and scattering the remainder. By now their time ashore was almost up, and they returned to the ALC with one corpse, having been fired on by a machine gun, which luckily caused no casualties. They were too late to make the rendezvous with either their MGB or the *Prince Leopold*, and returned to Portsmouth under their own steam, arriving back there at 1600 hours.

Davies's party had problems of a different sort. As they were making their landfall, Davies himself realised that they were heading for the wrong target, a conspicious turreted house indicating St Aubin, 3½ miles east of Courseulles. With time getting short, they decided to land in any event in order to snatch a prisoner. As the last of the men were leaving the ALC, there was a hail followed by a burst of gunfire. Davies immediately ordered an attack on the machine gun, which entailed climbing up a 10 ft promenade wall and getting through two coils of dannert-wire. As they were negotiating these, a second and then a third machine gun opened up, and there was no option but to withdraw. This was carried out under heavy fire, with one man being wounded. Once aboard the ALC, however, two men were found to be missing but there was nothing that could be done, and the ALC moved fast out to sea, successfully meeting up with its MGB which towed it back to Portsmouth.

Although these raids had not succeeded in their object of bringing back a live prisoner, there is no doubt that they were a tonic to morale, which had suffered from the inactivity since the Lofoten Islands operation in early March and both the Commandos and Royal Navy had learnt valuable lessons.

GHQ Home Forces and Commando Operations

Although immediately after Dunkirk it had been official policy to create and maintain an offensive spirit in the troops in the United Kingdom, even though they were very much on the defensive, offensive operations had remained mainly the province of the Commandos. True, attempts had been made during the winter 1940-41 to train two complete corps in amphibious operations at Inveraray, and part of 1 Corps did do this. The departure of Layforce and the Glen ships, together with the formation of Force 110, however, put paid to this because it tied up all the suitable craft. General Sir Alan Brooke, C-in-C Home Forces, considered this an unsatisfactory state

of affairs, even more so because of the complaints from his subordinate commanders that many of their best men were vanishing into
the ranks of the Commandos. In August 1941 he had requested the
Chiefs of Staff that he be given sanction to carry out raiding operations on the coast between Ostend and Cherbourg. While the Chiefs
of Staff were sympathetic, they told him that he must consult with
Keyes first. Then, in September 1941, he spent three days with Keyes
at Inveraray, but, as he later recorded:

> The whole of my visit to Roger Keyes was on his part to try and con-
> vince me that our Commando policy was right. He failed to do so, and
> I remained convinced until the end of the war that the Commandos
> should never have been divorced from the Army in the way they were.
> Each division should have been responsible for maintaining a divisional
> battle patrol capable of any Commando work that might be asked of it.[19]

Another, who felt even more strongly, was General Sir Bernard
Paget, Brooke's Chief of Staff and successor as C-in-C Home Forces.
Writing, after the war, to one of the Official Historians, he said:

> The operations undertaken by the Commandos were largely a waste of
> effort and could have been better done by a unit of the Field Army ... There
> was during the war a regrettable and dangerous tendency to ignore the
> normal organisation of the Army which had been carefully thought out
> in peace and on which training was based, and to substitute for it *ad hoc*
> organisations such as 'Jock Columns'* and Commandos. This very nearly
> led to our defeat in North Africa.[20]

Clearly, lack of resources and Churchill's own passion for the Commandos precluded Home Forces setting up their own widescale organisation. Brooke therefore tried to get agreement for Commandos to be
affiliated to divisions, but *Pilgrim* prevented this. Southern Command,
or at least V Corps, which was based on the South Coast, did, however,
manage to set up a raiding organisation of sorts. The driving force
behind this was the Brigadier General Staff (BGS), Brigadier (later
Field Marshal Sir Gerald) Templer. In the latter half of 1940 he had
commanded 210 Brigade based in Dorset, and had created what he
had called a 'Special Service' section in each rifle company.

---

*All arms groups, usually based on a motorised infantry battalion which operated in
the Western Desert during 1941. They were named after Brigadier Jock Campbell VC
DSO MC.

... the general idea was that it should form a mobile patrol of cut-throats or, as the Brigadier said with relish, 'thugs', to deal summarily with any small – or for that matter – large – band of enemy troops landed from the air or by sea, if in the latter event they should succeed in penetrating through the beach defences. These men were specially equipped for speed, silence and destructive ability. They were picked men – there were plenty of volunteers but only the most eligible men were chosen – who received special training in fieldcraft and the use of their particular weapons, which included Thompson sub-machine guns a number of which had just been issued to each company.[21]

Now, in V Corps, he managed in November 1941 to set up a detachment at Warsash of the V Corps School of Instruction. Based in HMS *Tormentor*, the V Corps School of Raiding ran courses for units throughout the Command and tied in to a small extent with No 12 Commando. Unfortunately, with only four ALCs and some armoured Eureka boats available, their activities were limited and could not be spread to the other Commands. In the meantime, Brooke was tasked by the Chiefs of Staff with investigating the feasibility of mounting a major cross-Channel raid somewhere on the coast of Occupied Europe in spring 1942. He set up two paper exercises, one a study of the enemy-held coastline in order to select an objective, and the second to study the mechanics of mounting the operation. Paget, who succeeded Brooke as C-in-C Home Forces towards the end of November 1941, reported back to the Chiefs of Staff in February 1942. In view of the likely German opposition and the limited amphibious resources, he did not consider such an operation, which was codenamed *Sesame*, feasible before September 1942. This was accepted, although he was directed to continue planning for it.[22] This led indirectly to the Dieppe Raid of August 1942.

Enter Mountbatten

If General Sir Alan Brooke had failed in his attempt to get the Commandos tightly under his control by affiliating them to divisions, he did, in September 1941, succeed in gaining some influence over them. It was agreed by the War Cabinet and Chiefs of Staff that from now on amphibious operations would not be mounted from the United Kingdom without the authority of GHQ Home Forces. At the same time, Keyes was given a new directive and title of Adviser Combined Operations. Churchill wrote personally to Keyes to explain the thinking behind this:

My Dear Roger,

I hope that you will find yourself able to come to an agreement with the Chiefs of Staff upon the modification of your original directive. Your title of 'Director' does not correspond to the facts. Special operations once decided upon in principle must lie in the hands of the commanders chosen, who have to back them with their reputations and their lives. I am convinced that excursions from this country to the continent, unless entrusted to specially chosen commanders, must have behind them the authority and resources of GHQ Home Forces. In both cases the responsibility for advising the Defence Committee and the War Cabinet can only lie with the Chiefs of Staff. These are facts which must be accepted.

It seems to me that very large spheres of important and interesting work will be open to you as Adviser under the new arrangement, and that some of the causes of friction in the past will be removed. I should find it very hard to resist the advice of all my responsible experts. I trust therefore that you will fall in with the plan that has now taken shape.

Yours very sincerely,

Winston S Churchill[23]

Keyes bridled at this, and Churchill had no option but to replace him. Keyes now wrote a brief history of his time in office, pointing out that his title of 'Director' had, in any event, been a misnomer, in that all his suggestions had fallen on deaf ears. He accused the Admiralty, in particular, of being obstructive, believing that they wanted to do away with Combined Operations altogether. He had raised two striking forces, the first of which had been frittered away in the Middle East, while the second was emasculated, as much of its shipping was tied up in *Journalist*, and, in any case, was now positioned 1,300 miles away from its objective, the Canaries. He had now been offered instead 'the Chairmanship of an Inter Service Committee with the title of "Adviser". As my advice had been persistently ignored, I declined this as a substitute for my appointment of Director of Combined Operations, which has now terminated.'[24] His final flourish was to write to the Prime Minister, expressing his fears that the Special Service Brigade would be broken up. Having failed to interest Brooke and Alexander in schemes to 'beat up' aerodromes in Occupied France and to clear the Cherbourg Peninsula of Germans, he was convinced, now that 'all raiding operations are the responsibility of the C-in-C Home Forces . . . you will get no interest taken in Home Waters other than small reconnaissance raids, for a very long time to come, if ever.'[25]

While Keyes had done much to set up Commando forces on a sure footing, the tragedy was that he was really too old for the job. At the age of 68, his mind was still living the events of twenty years before, when he had had operational command. Since he had always considered himself a man of action, he saw no reason why he should not command operations in this war. He also believed that, with the Prime Minister being an old friend, he could influence him, but this proved not to be so. The result was that he became increasingly dogmatic and ruffled more and more feathers.

Because Combined Operations involved all three Services, it was clear that Keyes' successor would need to be, above all else, a diplomat. He also needed to be a younger man. Churchill therefore selected Lord Louis Mountbatten for the post. Apart from being a member of the Royal Family, Lord Louis was a very professional naval officer, who had recently highly distinguished himself when in command of the destroyer HMS *Kelly* in the Mediterranean. True, as a Captain RN, he was junior in rank compared with those with whom he would have to deal, but his record and personal qualities more than compensated for this. He took up his new post as a Commodore, but was, in March 1942, promoted Vice Admiral, as well as being given the honorary ranks of Lieutenant General and Air Marshal. At the same time, his title was changed to Chief Combined Operations (CCO) and he was made a member of the Chiefs of Staff Committee. His energy, enthusiasm and determination soon began to percolate down through the ranks of the Commandos.

Mountbatten was determined to build up to larger scale raids on the coasts of Occupied Europe, but the first operation mounted was one already planned during the Keyes era. This entailed the destruction of a German battery at Houlgate.

Operation *Sunstar* was to take place in two phases. For the first, *Astrakan*, two pairs of canoeists were to check the beaches and defences, prior to the main raiding party going in some nights later. The canoeists came from 101 Troop of No 6 Commando, which was now based at Glencoe in Scotland under Captain G.C.S. Montanaro RE. They had spent the summer of 1941 assisting the Royal Navy in destroying mines, and this was to be their first operation. On the night 12/13 November they were launched from an ML. Unfortunately, one canoe, with Lieutenant K. Smith and Corporal Woodhouse, overturned in the surf, and both were captured. The other, with Corporal Ellis and Private Lewis, managed to land and confirm that the beach was suitable for ALCs, but missed the rendezvous with the ML and had to paddle their way back to Dover.

Ten days later, on the night of 22/23 November, one hundred men of No 9 Commando made a successful landing, but found that they did not have enough time to carry out their attack. They then experienced much difficulty in contacting the ALCs, which had drawn too far off the beach, to come in and bring them off. This aroused the enemy, but No 9 managed to get away with no casualties. All in all, it was a frustrating raid and demonstrated that much still needed to be done to perfect both planning and execution of raids.

Mountbatten had, however, already set about reorganising the Combined Operations structure so that it would be more effective. For a start, he greatly enlarged the planning side. For all but the smallest raids, the outline plan would be submitted to the Commander-in-Chief in whose theatre the operation was to take place. It would then be cleared through the Chiefs of Staff. A force commander would then be appointed, and he would be responsible for drawing up the detailed plan, which would then once more be cleared by Mountbatten through the Chiefs of Staff. The first opportunity to try this new system out came in the last few days of December.

Anklet and Archery

Mountbatten turned his attention first to Norway, which had been left in relative peace since March 1941. Much of the reason for this lay in the Prime Minister's enthusiasm for a major operation against Norway with a view to relieving pressure on the Russians and helping to safeguard the convoys to Murmansk. Seizing Trondheim, which was what Churchill wanted in October, was clearly not feasible, but, at least if Commando raids could be mounted, it would do something to tie down German troops and prevent them being sent from Norway to the Eastern Front.

The first operation was abortive. On 9 December No 6 and half of No 9 Commando set sail in the landing ship *Prince Charles* to raid the town of Floss. Unfortunately, a grenade accident caused casualties and the Senior Naval Officer then had doubts over the accuracy of his navigation. The operation was therefore called off. Undeterred, planning went ahead for a more ambitious operation. The object of this was to destroy German military installations at Vaagso. On 6 December, Rear Admiral Burrough and Brigadier Charles Haydon were chosen as the naval and military commanders, and selected to carry out *Archery* were No 3, two troops of No 2, a medical detachment from No 4 and a party from 101 Troop, mainly because of their expertise in demolitions. There was also, as for *Claymore*, a Norwegian detachment. By 15 December the raiding forces had been assembled and rehearsals were carried out.

Indicative of the more imaginative thinking now being gener-ated at Combined Operations HQ was the fact that a large scale diversion was planned under the codename *Anklet*. This involved 300 men of No 12 Commando, who landed on the Lofoten Islands on 26 December, catching a German garrison replete with Christ-mas fare by surprise. They remained there for two days, and might have stayed longer if a German bomb had not scored a near miss on the cruiser HMS *Arethusa*, the flagship.

Vaagso Island itself lies on the northern side of the entrance to the Nordfjord, and the precise target was the town of South Vaagso. This is dominated by the island of Maaloy, which was thought to be well defended. The Commandos were broken down into five groups. One would land well to the north of South Vaagso to pre-vent German reinforcements from being sent there, one would deal with South Vaagso itself, and another would take care of Maaloy, while a fourth would land at Hollevik south of the town to capture a strongpoint there. The fifth group would be maintained as a float-ing reserve. Apart from having the support of naval gunfire, RAF Bomber Command Hampdens and Coastal Command Blenheims would drop smoke bombs to provide cover, and other Blenheims and Beaufighters would be overhead to ward off the Luftwaffe.

With the Commandos in the two landing ships *Prince Leopold* and *Prince Charles*, the force set sail from Scapa Flow on Christmas Eve and, buffeted by westerly gale, made for Sollum Voe on Shetland. Here 24 hours were spent repairing the damage to the ships, as well as giving the troops the opportunity to have their Christmas dinner. They sailed again in the evening of the 26th and made landfall at 0700 hours next morning. While the Royal Navy bombarded the batter-ies on Maaloy and the RAF laid their smokescreen, the Commandos transshipped to their ALCs and made for their objectives. One land-ing craft was unfortunately hit by a phosphorous bomb dropped by an aircraft hit by German fire, which caused a number of casualties, but the rest pressed onwards. The Hollevik group seized their objec-tive without any trouble and were soon called upon to reinforce the party attacking the town itself, which was led by John Durnford-Slater, who was in overall command of the landing forces. The naval bom-bardment had succeeded in its objective on neutralising the guns on Maaloy. Major Jack Churchill, second-in-command of No 3 Commando and armed with claymore and bagpipes, which were his 'stock in trade', and the troops commanded by Captains Peter Young and A S Ronald (later killed during the *Torch* landings in North Africa) managed to get ashore without being fired on and quickly reduced the garrison. Ronald then successfully cleared his second objective, the factory at Mortensen. The cut off group, which landed well to the north of the town to prevent reinforcements being sent to it, also experienced little difficulty.

South Vaagso itself proved to be tougher than anticipated, especially since the Germans there were in greater strength than expected – a number having arrived on Christmas leave. Not only did Durnford-Slater have to call upon the Hollevik group, but also Peter Young's troop, which came across from Maaloy. Furthermore, Brigadier Haydon decided to also commit his floating reserve. Street fighting is invariably a tedious and costly business, as one of Peter Young's men later wrote in the Combined Operations journal *The Bulldozer*, an early Mountbatten innovation:

We had to get through the streets and warehouses where snipers were doing their stuff and holding our troops up.

The orders were to go through the town and make contact with some other troops. Our Captain led the attack here, and although it was slow as we had to go from house to house, we were able to spot and shoot the snipers who were doing the damage.

One of our sergeants received three shots in the back from a sniper who had let us pass. We opened fire on this sniper's window and settled him. We dashed to the next house. There was a German here who was a tough fighter. When the captain put his head round the door, the German fired and so did the captain.

Both missed and we threw grenades, a lot of grenades. The Hun just came to the door and dropped two stick grenades near us. One of our officers who had already been wounded through the shoulder went in after him with a Tommy gun. The Hun shot him, but he was able to walk out.

One of my own section dashed in and sprayed a magazine of 'Tommy'. The Hun shot him through the thigh and then let him get away. We decided to burn him out. We threw in Petrol, set fire to it and went on our way, leaving one man to deal with the Hun when he eventually appeared. . . .

From here on we fought from house to house, with several casualties, until we finally reached the other end of the town. We then made contact with the other troops and the whole town was cleared out and the battle was over.[26]

The force, with the short Arctic day drawing to a close, was re-embarked by 1445 hours. They brought with them 98 prisoners and four Quislings, along with some Norwegian volunteers. They also left behind widescale destruction. It had not been without cost, however, with seventy Commando casualties, including 17 killed, and the Navy suffering two killed and six wounded.

Nevertheless, *Archery* meant that, for the Commandos at least, 1941 ended on a high note and did much to establish Mountbatten's reputation as CCO. It also had far-reaching results in forcing the Germans to deploy additional troops to Norway and from now on Hitler could never be sure that the Allies would not mount a major invasion here. For another group of Commandos, though, the year had been one of further frustration.

CHAPTER THREE

The Middle East Commandos
1940-1

In July 1940, while the first Commandos were being organised in the United Kingdom, GHQ Middle East Land Forces (MELF) received instructions from the War Office to do the same on a limited scale. The Commanders-in-Chief of the three Services saw that there was scope for Commando operations in the form of amphibious raids on the coasts and islands of the Eastern Mediterranean in enemy hands and also, perhaps, long range operations behind the Italian lines in North Africa. At the same time, Colonel Macleod, Commandant of ISTDC, was sent out to set up a Combined Training Centre at Kabrit on the Bitter Lakes.

Responsibility for the organisation of the Middle East Commandos was given to G(R) (Research) Branch of GHQ and one officer working there, Lt Colonel George Young RE, was invited to raise the first of these Commandos, No 50. It was to be formed from volunteers from units stationed in the Middle East. One of the earliest to join was Lt Colonel (then Captain) Stephen Rose, Royal Fusiliers, who would later become second-in-command. His battalion had been in Egypt for nine months, having come from India, where Stephen Rose, who was a young company commander, had spent much time big game shooting and trekking.

Since our arrival in Egypt, we had been in various desert camps near the pyramids west of Cairo and at Alexandria. We had taken part in numerous exercises involving movement across the desert in motorised columns as part of boxlike formations containing other brigade or divisional units.

We dug weapon pits by the score and filled them in again before moving on. Though I might have been wrong, I thought there was very little scope for individual initiative and enterprise. Everything about tactical training for desert warfare seemed to be in a straitjacket of procedure which could not be deviated from. I had always had a streak of non-conformism with ideas of my own, and when volunteers for Commandos were asked for, I felt that this was perhaps my line of country, especially as names of volunteers were not to be withheld. Consequently, I was interviewed in Cairo by Lt Col G.A.D. Young RE, Commanding Officer designate of 50 Middle East Commando, at the end of July, and reported for duty at Geneifa near the Great Bitter Lakes a few days later. With me went six NCOs and Fusiliers of my battalion, including Fusilier George Williams, who was to become my orderly and bodyguard and spend 4½ years as a POW after being captured on Crete.

My brother officers in Middle East Commandos were very much kindred spirits. To mention but a few at company commander level, there were Harry Fox-Davies and Ken Harmon of the Durham Light Infantry, Alec Brodie and Jack Monteith of the Black Watch, Graham Taylor of the Leicesters, Bill Burton, York and Lancasters, and Michael Borwick of the Royal Scots Greys. All of them had either been decorated for bravery or were to be later, during their Commando service, including Colonel George Young, our CO.[1]

Although No 50 Commando was largely made up of high quality pre-war soldiers, it did have one unusual characteristic in having some seventy Spaniards on its strength. These were Spanish Civil War veterans, who had fled to France after Franco's victory and had then found themselves serving in Syria, but, on the fall of France, had escaped to Palestine. Major R.L. McGibbon, a Canadian serving with the 2nd Royal Leicesters, volunteered for No 50 ME Commando and found himself, possibly on account of his French and Arab language ability, commanding them.

The Spaniards were from very mixed social and economic backgrounds – one was a captain in the Royal Spanish Marines, another had been a shepherd, some had lived for years in France, while others had never left their villages until the Spanish Civil War arrived. Most had never heard of Communism or Fascism until they found themselves fighting in the ranks of whichever side was in power in their area at the time. More than half of them had been wounded, usually by German mortar shells during the Civil War. They were very frightened that if the Germans captured them they would automatically be shot as communists. None of them believed in the Church – one only had to hear what the Church had done to them to understand why – and many had been involved during the Civil War in pillaging Church property or even raping nuns. Yet when they spoke of that type of thing it all seemed quite natural, an everyday story.

They were all very proud of being members of the Queen's Royal Regiment* and hoped (and believed) that they were or would become British citizens.

---

*They were enlisted into the Queen's Regiment for records purposes.

As soldiers they varied, just like anyone else. Some were very tough minded, good troops. One or two were poor. Considering the language difficulties, most of them picked up instruction in drill and weaponry very fast, and beat our British troops in competition. We gave all commands in English, and one would always hear a murmur in the ranks after each, as they ensured that they all knew what was wanted. Initially our British troops did not like the Spaniards – they were nervous of them and always wanted to avoid night exercises with them. In the dark, the Spaniards could keep awake and absolutely silent, whether moving or lying still. British troops tended to be somewhat noisy and got themselves 'captured' by silent Spanish patrols time and again. Because of the language problem they tended to stick together and shared among one another. It was hopeless to fine a Spaniard for a 'crime' – the others simply made it up to him. Off duty they were as noisy as monkeys, all talking at once all the time. Yet on parade they took a great pride in their turnout.[2]

If No 50 ME Commando had an unusual strain in it, No 51, the next to be formed, had an even more unique background. Its origins owe themselves to a remarkable man, Lt Colonel H.J. 'Kid' Cator MC. As a very young officer he had won his MC serving with the Royal Scots Greys in France during the First World War, but retired shortly afterwards to help on the family farm in Norfolk. In September 1939 he rejoined his regiment, and served with it as a rather elderly subaltern in Palestine on internal security duties. In early 1940 it was decided to form indigenous companies of the Auxiliary Military Pioneer Corps – the 1939 successor to the Labour Corps and shortly to become the Royal Pioneer Corps – in the Middle East. Henry Cator was invited to raise the first of these in Palestine, and it became No 1 Palestinian Company AMPC, with an establishment of 500 men. What was singular about it, in view of the conflict between Jew and Arab at the time, was that it was a mixed unit, and Cator realised from the start that the only way to make the two races get on with one another was to forbid any form of segregation, and this undoubtedly worked. Before February was out and after being inspected by General Sir Archibald Wavell, Commander-in-Chief Middle East, who was clearly impressed with it, the company found itself en route for France where it was employed on the lines of communication of the BEF at Rennes.

Once in France Cator soon began to agitate for his company to be given a more distinctive title in order to give its members *esprit de corps*. He had a major advantage here in that he was socially very well connected, from the Royal Family downwards.* Before he was able to achieve anything concrete, however, the German invasion of the Low Countries took place. Throughout May and early June, No 1 Palestinian Company remained in its 'backwater' relatively unaffected by the momentous events which were taking place elsewhere in France. Then, with a growing German threat against the Rennes area, they found themselves being made responsible for some of the defences, which gave them a more active role. As Cator wrote in his diary: 'The men are in great trim, ready for what they may be asked to do . . . The Palestinians are now like lions longing for the kill.'³ The evacuation of Rennes began on 15 June, and, describing the embarkation at St Malo, Cator commented on his men: 'The men are grand, and I have learnt to love them and admire them and am very proud to command them.'⁴

No sooner was he back in England than Cator began to lobby for his command to be made into a fighting unit. At one point he '. . . had tea with the King and Queen . . . I had the opportunity of having a real heart to heart talk with the King about the Palestinians. He also said he would see Lord Lloyd [Secretary of State for the Colonies]'.⁵ In the meantime, the company found itself defending part of the English coastline against possible German invasion, firstly in north Devon and then at Clacton. Finally, it was moved to Camberley in Surrey. Eventually, Cator obtained agreement to take his unit back to the Middle East, although just before they left at the beginning of August he was invited by Lord Keyes to join the Commandos in England but declined, preferring to remain with his Palestinians. They arrived at Suez in mid-September, and Cator immediately went and saw Wavell, who agreed that he could select 300 Palestinians as the nucleus for another Middle East Commando, and No 51 was officially formed on 15 October 1940, with Cator in command. This was to be followed on 1 November by the formation of No 52 under command of Lt Colonel Fox-Davies DLI. This was recruited, like No 50, from volunteers from British units then in Egypt. Unfortunately, Commanding Officers were by now becoming somewhat irritated by continued calls on their men, and some took the opportunity to unload their 'bad hats' on No 52.

In terms of training:

---

* His family's estate was near Sandringham, the Royal Estate in Norfolk and he knew the Royal Family personally.

The rigorous training in 50 Middle East Commando was the same for all ranks. There were no concessions for officers of any rank. It was they who truly set the pace. Commando officers had to be tough, resolute and superbly fit themselves to lead men who had been selected for their physique and keenness to join.

For my part, I sometimes wondered what I had let myself in for, such was the pace. We had to learn new skills like rafting, boat work, explosives and demolitions, sabotage techniques, even camel riding and management. We covered long distances on foot with dried food and very limited water, lying up in the heat of the day and moving by night. We worked up to a standard requirement of 30 miles in 24 hours over a period of three days.

I remember wrestling with an extremely tough Spaniard. We both had bleeding knees and elbows from our encounter on hard gravelly desert. The whole unit were watching. It did not matter who won. Much more important was the fact that all officers took part in such training and were seen to be as fit, tough and aggressive as the men they were commanding.[6]

No 51 ME Commando went even further in their endurance marching as Colonel Cator's diary records:

50 miles cross country endurance test. The men of 51 ME Commando did remarkably well, Lapraik's* section setting up what I should imagine to be a record by doing 50 miles in 15 3/4 hours. About 30 miles of this trek was over very rough 'jebel' country, both hilly and rocky. The average was about 18½ hours. This endurance test was carried out in full marching order and all personnel were limited to one full water bottle. We started in the heat of the day at 2 pm. The C-in-C General Wavell heard about this march and told me he thought Lapraik and his Arab troops' time must be just about a record for the British Army under the conditions it was carried out in. My time was 18 hours.[7]

Amphibious training was even more primitive, as Lt Colonel Keymer, also of No 51 Commando, relates:

As soon as we heard that we might do beach landings, we borrowed life boats from ships anchored in the Great Bitter Lakes and practised rowing. No one knew anything about rowing, except one rather light weight

---

*Ian Lapraik was later to go on to have a very distinguished career with the Special Boat Squadron in the Mediterranean. See Pitt, Barrie *Special Boat Squadron* (Century Publishing, London, 1983). He also won an MC with No 51 at Amba Alagi in May 1941. (See pages 83-4)

Arab whom we put as stroke. As soon as we started to row – I was just behind him – muscles appeared all over his back and he slaughtered us! On further enquiry it transpired that he had been a fisherman on the Sea of Galilee![8]

These lifeboats and whalers were provided with wooden bungs and mallets in order to plug leaks made by bullets holes – very much a relic of Gallipoli. Like the early United Kingdom Commandos, great stress was laid on individual initiative and personal responsibility. Colonel George Young: 'Basically I thought, and still do, this was a good idea, but it needs a very high degree of personal performance by each and everyone'.[9] No 50 Middle East Commando, being the first to be raised, were somewhat luckier than No 52, in that their volunteers were generally of a good standard. As for No 52, Colonel David Smiley, who was a company commander, recalls:

Men were termed as 'Raiders'. There was no saluting, no saying 'Sir', no calling to attention on parades, and no marching in step. Some of the worse disciplined took advantage of this with disastrous results. When discipline had almost ceased to exist, normal army discipline was reintroduced with resulting improvements.[10]

Henry Cator, who had formed No 51 from an already active unit rather than a mix of volunteers, would have none of this:

I was very angry as Colonel Adrian Simpson who was Chief Staff Officer of G(R) – R standing for 'Research' – Branch of GHQ MELF issued a directive regarding how to train Middle East Commandos. One of the orders was that to encourage the men to think for themselves and act on their own initiative, it was a good idea to 'slacken up' on normal battalion or regimental discipline. 'For example if an other rank was talking to an officer, with a pipe in his mouth, he should not be expected to remove it.'

I remember telling Colonel Simpson that such ideas and tactics would *NOT* be practised in No 51 Middle East Commando.[11]

It must be remembered, though, that these units were experimental and the Commando philosophy called for much greater self-reliance and self-discipline than in a normal battalion. Nevertheless, after initial teething problems, discipline in the Middle East Commandos was as good as in any normal unit.

In contrast to the Commandos in England, there was no billeting system, simply because the facilities did not exist and the Middle East Commandos were all based at Geneifa. Apart, too, from the obvious difference of tropical uniform as opposed to battle dress, the Middle East Commandos adopted their own distinguishing marks. They acquired their own particular brand of Commando knife, the 'fanny', which had a 7-inch blade and a handle incorporating a knuckleduster. The idea for this came from the Cairo Police Museum,* and a cap badge based on it was designed and worn by all Middle East Commandos. Another difference to the United Kingdom Commandos was that the bush hat was adopted as the official mode of headdress.

Early Operations

In September 1940, after three months of glowering at the enemy across the frontier wire, with occasional armoured car raids by the Western Desert Force, the Italians began their long awaited invasion of Egypt. In the event, it proved an anti-climax. They advanced a mere sixty miles to Sidi Barrani and then halted and set about constructing a number of fortified camps. At the time, the British were hopelessly outnumbered and Wavell felt that little could be done but to husband his slender resources against the day when the Italian Army would present a more positive threat to Cairo and the Suez Canal. Nevertheless, the defence was not to be entirely passive and the Italians were kept on their toes by a number of raids across the lines.

In this context it was natural that raids on the North African coast behind the Italian lines should also seem attractive. Consequently, in mid October No 50 Commando was warned off for a raid on the seaplane base at Bomba. Two destroyers, HMS *Decoy* and *Hereward*, were to be used to transport the Commando and their captains were closely involved in the planning. The idea was that the Commando should land at midnight, destroy the huts and tents of the Italian garrison and 'beat them up' with grenades and automatic fire, while Royal Navy motor boats destroyed the anchored seaplanes. Much detailed preparation was carried out, including building a replica of the layout of Bomba on the shore of the Great Bitter Lakes. Then, after repeated rehearsals, the destroyers embarked the Commando on the night of 27/28 October and set sail, aiming to arrive at Bomba

---

* Before acceptance, the fanny was tested on beef carcasses in the RASC Ration Depot at Abbassia!

the following night. Unfortunately, the Italian invasion of Greece on the 28th dramatically altered the situation in the Eastern Mediterranean and the destroyers were ordered to return to Alexandria immediately.

> The cancellation of this, its first operation, was a complete anti-climax for 50 ME Commando, after three months of intensive training. It was a great disappointment to all ranks, although it was later realised that there was a good reason for this sudden cancellation. However, there was a significant drop in morale and it required considerable effort to rebuild this to its former high, level.[12]

The abortive Bomba operation was to characterise so many of the Middle East Commano operations during the next six months.

For No 50 Commando, however, a change of scene helped considerably towards restoring morale. In the event of a threat to the Eastern Mediterranean it had been agreed at the beginning of the war that French troops should be responsible for defending Crete as the Greeks were not prepared to admit British troops there. With the fall of France and the Italian attack on Greece, Crete, with its fine harbour at Suda Bay making it easier for the Royal Navy to protect the Malta convoys, was put in the British lap. The Italian threat to the Suez Canal, the Vichy French in Syria and the Italian overrunning of much of East Africa left Wavell's forces even more stretched than hitherto. No 50 Commando was therefore ordered to Crete on 25 November. Battle Dress was issued, which was the first time that many, who had by now spent some years in the East, had seen it. The fact that they were transported there by the battleships *Warspite* and *Valiant* and the heavy cruiser *York*, with the aircraft carrier HMS *Illustrious* and a strong destroyer screen as escorts, made them feel that notice was being taken of them, although the ships were sailing to meet up with the rest of the Mediterranean Fleet at Malta. Once on Crete they found themselves as part of 14 Infantry Brigade, and, in general, received a warm welcome from the islanders. By now Lt Colonel P. Symons RE had taken over command, with Lt Colonel Young being posted across to command the newly formed No 52 Commando, Lt Colonel Fox-Davies having fallen sick.

It was now the turn of No 51 Commando to suffer the frustrations of raiding on the coast of Libya. On 9 December 1940, the Western Desert Force launched itself under General O'Connor on a major raid (*Compass*), which would eventually culminate in the Battle of Beda

Fomm in early February 1941 and drive the Italians out of Cyrenaica. On 5 December, after a conference with General Wilson, GOC British Troops Egypt, on the previous day, 'Kid' Cator presented himself on board HMS *Warspite*, the flagship of Admiral Cunningham, C-in-C Mediterranean, for further planning of an operation which entailed landing near Buq Buq to cut the water pipeline which ran from Capuzzo to Sidi Barrani. It was aptly codenamed *Cator*. Early on the 10th, the Commando left Alexandria aboard HMS *Hereward*, with a subsidiary party in Lighter *X.39*, which had seen service at Gallipoli and whose task it was to land munitions for the 7th Armoured Division at some place beyond Sidi Barrani. The main party was to land by whaler that night, but a very heavy sea was running, which caused much seasickness and made the transfer to the whalers too hazardous. The operation was therefore postponed, and No 51 ME Commando spent the next day watching naval bombardments of Italian shore positions. The weather remained rough, and it was therefore decided to cancel the raid, the Commando arriving back at Alexandria early on the 12th. A week's waiting on immediate stand-by followed. Then, on the 19th, the Commando was taken by sea to Sollum, where they began to prepare for an operation against Bardia, but this was cancelled as the Western Desert Force had not advanced far enough. Because of the lack of troops, the Commando was now committed to providing labour for the docks at Sollum and then guarding Italian prisoners at Mersa Matruh.

In mid January they returned to Geneifa, and were shortly afterwards warned of a move which would give them a more active part in the war. They were to be following in the footsteps of No 52 ME Commando.

East Africa
In July 1940, the Italians had seized the frontier ports at Gallabat and Metemma and threatened the Soudan. In August, they turned their attention to British Somaliland and drove the small British garrison out of the colony. At the beginning of November, Brigadier (later Field Marshal The Viscount) Slim's 10 Indian Infantry Brigade attempted to recapture Gallabat and Metemma, but was frustrated by overwhelming Italian air superiority. Both sides then settled down to a period of small scale action in this area. With Operation *Compass* now in full swing in the Western Desert, troops were still very stretched, and it was decided in December to reinforce the Soudan by the 4th Indian Division and the so far only uncommit-

ted Middle East Commando, No 52. They arrived at Port Sudan on 20 December 1940, and were placed under command of Brigadier Mayne's 9 Indian Infantry Brigade, which had just taken over from Slim's brigade in front of Gallabat.

No 52 Commando set up a base camp on the banks of the Atbara River about three miles behind the front line. From here they began a number of reconnaissances of the Italian left flank, but little was seen of the enemy. It was clear, however, that the commanders and their staffs on the ground had little concept as to how the Commandos should be used.

> This was all the more unfortunate since the local conditions and general topography could scarcely have been better suited to its purposes. Both sides confronted each other in approximately brigade strength at the end of a ninety mile road L of C passing through thickly covered bush country. Both roads were virtually undefended and indefensible, and offered a target, which could well be considered as made to order for the Commando, and for which it was both physically and psychologically well prepared.[13]

In mid January, however, came the opportunity for a more Commando-like operation. The idea was that, while the 2nd West Yorks put in an attack on the Italian positions in the Gallabat-Metemma area, No 52 Commando with two companies was to penetrate the Italian rear area through their open left flank and lay an ambush on the Gondar-Metemma road, their main line of communication. Colonel David Smiley, then a troop commander in No 52:

> On the night of January 19th we marched down the banks of the Atbara river to Knor Gumsa about 15 miles behind the Eytie lines. We then lay up all day and went again that night. Our object was to get on the only main road which led from Gondar up to the Eytie positions around Metemma. We crept past several camps and even through the middle of a mule coy. Eyties were singing, the sentries idle, and we even heard women's voices – confirming the stories that the Eyties had women right up by the front lines. We blundered on to the road sooner than we expected and just as a supply column was coming down it. We had no time to get into position, were challenged and on getting no suitable reply, were fired on. Then things became delightfully confused and everyone fired at everyone and my own Company Headquarters was shot up from behind and my runner Bateman hit in the leg. We also successfully shot up the supply column and spare mules bashed about in all directions and we could hear the groans of the wounded. We even caught one mule.

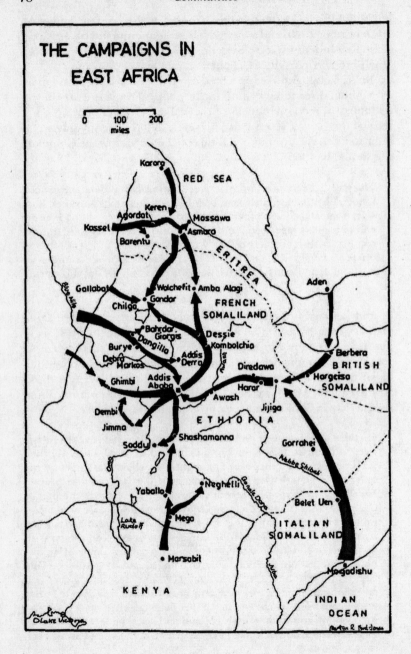

THE CAMPAIGNS IN
EAST AFRICA

0   100   200
miles

Karora

RED SEA

Keren
Agordat
Kassela   Massawa
Barentu   Asmara

ERITREA

Gallabat   Walchefit   Amba Alagi   Aden
Chilga   Gondar   FRENCH
                    SOMALILAND
Bahrdar
Giorgis
Burye   Dangilla   Dessie
Debra   Kombolchia
Markos   Addis   Berbera
         Derra
Ghimbi   Diredawa   BRITISH
Addis   Hargeisa   SOMALILAND
Ababa   Harar
Dembi   Awash   Jijiga
Jimma   ETHIOPIA

Soddu   Shashamanna   Gorrahei

                    Webbe Shibeli
Yaballo   Neghelli
         Mega   Belet Uen

Lake   ITALIAN
Rudolf   SOMALILAND

Marsabit

KENYA   Mogadishu

                    INDIAN
                    OCEAN

Lake Victoria   Merton R Ford-Jones

However, as we had roused the whole neighbourhood Colonel Young gave orders to withdraw. One of my men, Raider Flood, had been killed and one badly wounded. We put the wounded man on the captured mule, but he died in a few hours. We crept back past the same camps – this time challenged by sentries in all directions. We fired on them and were fired on in return. One Eytie sentry was killed by a Commando with a blow on his head from the knuckleduster part of his fanny. We marched by compass all through the night and hit the river at about first light. It was then discovered that one of my Sergeants – Harrison – was missing. It had not been reported to me earlier due to one of those muddles where some people thought he was in front and those in front thought he was in the rear. He was never heard of again, although some men say they heard a lone shot about half an hour after we had started our withdrawal, which may have been him. We got back dead tired and not at all happy over the operations . . .[14]

The main lesson learnt was that two companies were too large a force to control for this type of operation. There was also a distinct lack of intelligence on the enemy dispositions. Nevertheless, it did serve to increase Italian nervousness in the area.

Patrolling continued for the rest of the month and there were a number of clashes with the enemy. These took place at very short range because the tall elephant grass severely limited visibility and both sides suffered casualties. The main problem for No 52, however, was malaria and some sixty of the total strength of 500 went down with it and had to be evacuated. One of the more hair-raising occupations was the daily officers' patrols designed to attract Italian fire in order to establish that they were still in position and had not withdrawn. On 1 February, when it was discovered that forward positions had been evacuated it became obvious that the long awaited withdrawal had begun. No 52 were part of the follow-up forces, and had the satisfaction of 'liberating' stocks of Chianti and Italian food when they came across the recent location of HQ 24 Colonial Brigade. But, because they lacked their own transport, it was felt that they would be of little use in the pursuit and they were ordered back to Gallabat. From there, with no other transport available, they marched to Gedaref, ninety miles in three days, thus achieving the Middle East Commando yardstick, which was a good indication of their fitness. They stayed here for two weeks before beginning their long journey back to Egypt.

With the Italian evacuation of Gallabat, attention now turned to Eritrea, where General Platt with 4th and 5th Indian Division had launched an offensive in the third week of January. At the end of that month No 51 Commando arrived at Port Sudan, and then, after a tedious stay at Gedaref, where they had a brief meeting with No 52 Commando, who were on their way back to Egypt, were ordered into Eritrea. They joined Beresford-Peirse's 4th Indian Division there towards the end of February. They were immediately tasked to carry out reconnaissance patrols of the country west and south of Keren. Cator quickly realised that the occupation of water holes was the key to survival, and concentrated on seizing as many as possible as he pushed his troops closer to Keren. In order to transport stores, he commandeered camels, and hence the initial training which the Middle East Commandos had had with these beasts was put to good use. Cator described his tactics as follows:

> My main object is to keep pushing on, and never, if possible, to allow a day to pass without making fresh ground, at the same time consolidating the defence of the valley as we advance. I always have to remember the danger and possibility of being cut off from the rear, the enemy having slipped in through some lateral pass. The Italian troops have one big advantage over us, though to date they have shown no initiative: they know the country and we do not. They are also more mobile, some being mounted.[15]

They had a number of brushes with the Italians. Lt Colonel Keymer describes a typical one:

> The ridges were about 1000 feet above the valley floor, so patrolling was pretty energetic. We estimated that we did 100 miles a week of this sort of stuff for four weeks between the end of February and the end of March 1941. My party reached a ridge before dawn with a higher point to the right overlooking the valley we had come up from and up which Cator was to move. I left Lowe and the men on the ridge and went to the top with Steve Zavin – nothing but a precipice down into the valley. One Italian soldier appeared and I got Steve to cover him as I stopped him. It took him a long time to understand that I was the enemy, but I took his rifle, bandoliers and satchel of those rotten banger hand grenades off him and told him he was a prisoner. Having relieved him of his encumbrance, he shot off back into the darkness defiladed from Steve and me, who was carrying all his kit! This stirred up a hornet's nest and his friends came at us from down on the left and also when we reformed the men from along the ridge ahead. We had a good session with grenades, hanging on to them after we had pulled the pins out as seven seconds was too long. The bangers they threw at us were ineffective. We were in an awkward position

on a narrow ridge with our backs to a precipice, so we gave them a final salvo of grenades and ran straight through them. I had to come off the ridge across some open ground to another position, so I led the retreat walking, as I feared that the men would bolt if left on their own. Stopping them disappearing was like keeping a dog to heel. It got fully light after this and we had a right angle of enemy positions ahead of us in some rather exposed rocks. There was one fellow with an LMG with whom I had fun. He was firing at a gap in the rocks we wanted to cross. He was too rhythmic and I slipped a man across the gap in his pauses between bursts and he never hit one of us.

I had Urgar and Kramer on my LMG and the rock ahead and the ground on either side was becoming spattered, but they never shifted. I couldn't see the gun at about 450-500 yards as I had lost Cator's X 10 field glasses. I found them and got Kramer to fire a burst at the hill. We saw the strike and I corrected him and that was the end of that Italian gun crew. They made one or two attempts during the day to attack us, but we snuffed them out before they got going.[16]

However, not all these brushes were as successful at this:

After leaving us on March 3rd, 1941, Henry Frost took his troop back to Kilo 129 post haste. The men were already very tired before starting on this long trek back and I gather were never given a chance to have a proper rest when they got there. They were attached to the 11th Bde and on March 4th were sent up to one of the Sikh Battns. Here they were given the task of scaling up the very steep gulley running S. from Beit Gabru and harassing the enemy positions at the top if they existed, also dealing with any O.P's they might see. They set out with about 2 days rations and what water and ammunition they could carry. They climbed the face of the gulley during the early part of the night; the climb lasting three hours. Henry gave them a rest at the top and pointed out their objective, a saddle in between two heights, which looked like the U of the backsight of a rifle. They moved on again about 10.30 p.m. All went well for a short distance. Suddenly, after this, they were challenged. Henry was then heard to say 'Our presence is known, the game's up, go for them.' He and his 30 men then charged the enemy position. They soon found themselves up against wire and this in the dark. Somehow or other they got through it and swarmed the position, killing all the occupants, about 10 in number. They then reformed and found they themselves had suffered no casualties, apart from cuts and tears from the wire. They next moved on to the top of some high ground half right, and took up a position there awaiting daylight. Henry was then hoping to see what his next best move would be. As dawn was breaking they were suddenly fired on by Breda and Rifle fire; then an action started which lasted nearly 50 minutes. It soon became evident that the enemy were trying to close in on them from three sides. Mortars were brought into play and their position became very 'tricky'. Two men, Ulrich and Weinstein, were hit, Weinstein being killed outright. The fighting had by now got to close ranges. The men had thoroughly got their blood up and were fighting splendidly and showing great steadiness. The enemy's advances had now been checked by our Rifle and Bren gun fire, a modest estimate of enemy dead being at least 30. Henry now realised he was not a strong enough force to hang on, and also ammunition was running short. He therefore gave orders to Randel and Millard to retire with their men while he and Sgt. Heath remained back to give covering fire with their Tommy guns. As soon as the men had reached the crest of the ridge and were under cover, he and Sgt. Heath started to fall back themselves. A short distance back, they found Randel, with Ulrich, trying to help him out, one of his legs appearing paralysed from his wound. Henry and Randel between them started to drag the man away. Sgt. Heath giving covering fire. They had gone about 5 yards when they were caught in another burst of fire. Ulrich received another bullet which killed him, and Henry was hit in the leg. Heath and Randel then turned to help Henry. A second or two later Henry got hit again in the body and Randel in the foot, Sgt. Heath getting a graze on his left arm and the hilt of his 'fanny' saving him from being hit in the side above his hip. Henry was by now down and appeared to be dying. He gave orders to Randel and Sgt. Heath to leave him and get out of it as best they could. Sgt. Heath again gave covering fire, until his Tommy gun jammed, at the same time giving Randel a hand. They had about 25 yards to go to reach cover and having achieved this, they looked back to see Henry nearly surrounded by oncoming Italian black troops. He had propped himself up and was firing what was left in the magazine of his Tommy gun, this was his last effort in defiance before they saw him fall back as if dead.[17]*

Nevertheless, the Commandos' enterprise tricked the Italians into believing that they were faced by a significant force and enabled the thrusts from the north and west towards Keren to be linked up. Interestingly, the bush hat came into its own as a means of deception in that it was hoped that the Italians might believe that they were faced by Australians, although there is no evidence that they were taken in by this. The main attack at Keren began on 15th March, and No 51 continued its offensive activities, forcing the Italians to keep their forces dispersed. The fighting remained tough, and it was not until 27 March that Keren finally fell. Four days before this,

*Captain H.S. Frost, Cheshire Regiment, was later posted as missing presumed killed in action on 5 March 1941.

Cator had been wounded in the leg by artillery fire and had been evacuated, his place being taken by his second-in-command, C.D. Miller of the 10th Hussars.

After the capture of Keren, Asmara, the capital of Eritrea, quickly fell and the Italians withdrew southwards into Ethiopia, concentrating in the mountain stronghold of Amba Alagi. No 51, who had had a well earned rest after Keren, played a leading part in the capture of this formidable position.

The task given to them was to capture a feature called Commando Hill. Lt Colonel Miller:

> This feature rose perhaps four thousand feet above the valley and water course along which the road ran to the Falaga Pass and the Italians' main position. It was probable that the Italian pack battery which completely commanded the road obtained their observation from this hill. It was in a sense the key to the Falaga Pass position, as the road, which was the only approach to the enemy positions, skirted this hill and no attack could be made until this hill was in our hands . . . The Hill was so precipitous and rough that movement at night appeared difficult, while to climb slowly upwards by daylight would have been an impossible task in the face of enemy fire. To add to the difficulties of the operation, the upper part of the hill consisted of a cliff, which it was by no means certain could be climbed except by daylight.[18]

A patrol sent to try and find a path up the north face ran across the enemy and were forced to withdraw, with two men captured. It also discovered that this approach was dominated by machine gun fire from a further hill just to the north of Commando Hill. Miller therefore decided to made a frontal attack by night, and this was fixed for the night of 30 April/1 May 1941. Miller again:

> Artillery fire was directed onto the forward positions on April 29th where three enemy positions were observed. Being out of range of small arms fire and not yet fired on by our guns, the enemy were lounging about enjoying the sun . . . This fire caused these parties to run for cover. The first difficulty was to get onto the starting line unobserved . . . since the only possible chance of success was if complete surprise could be achieved. A winding wadi was the most obvious line of approach but a reconnaissance by day showed it to be too broken to be made use of by night. A useful reconnaissance by Captain Lapraik found a more direct route, though this lay in full view of the enemy. For this reason the approach had to be done at dusk, but while there was yet light to find the way.

Artillery support was to consist of 4 3.7, 4 25 pdrs and 4 6 in Hows and was to consist of a concentration on the enemy positions on the forward slopes of the hill with the object of preventing the enemy reoccupying them or, if they had already done so by night, to cause them to retire and allow the climb to take place without opposition. It was hoped that the previous artillery fire would not cause them to suspect an attack, especially as the mountain was so steep that the enemy probably regarded it as impossible to attack.

At dusk the Commando left their rear harbour and climbed Village Hill. Arriving at the top, a pause was made to allow the light to thicken. In the light of the afterglow, assisted by a three days' old moon, the advance was made to a small green spot by the banks of a stream. Here the Commando drank and rested from 7.0 pm to 11.0 pm.

At eleven the advance . . . continued . . . the difficulty of the ground and the darkness of the night making it impossible to adopt any other formation except single file. Progress was very slow and touch was often lost, but as often regained. With numerous pauses the climb continued. At 12.30 am that artillery opened with a crash and for half an hour the previous enemy positions on the forward slopes were subjected to heavy fire. At one moment a mass of rock was detached by the shelling and rolling down a thousand feet passed through the Commando with a roar like that of an express train. By chance it passed through a gap in the ranks . . . without causing any casualty. The Commando closed up again and continued. At first light a position beneath the final cliff was reached and the unit was in striking distance of success. Captain Lapraik and Major McClure succeeded in gaining a foothold on the top and were promptly engaged by the enemy. Captain Lapraik made use of his revolver and the Commando managed to establish itself on the flat top of the mountain.

An Italian observation post was surprised and captured, and the officer in charge warned that the Commando would be driven off before nightfall. Accordingly, defensive artillery fire was called down in front of the position, which enabled No 51 to consolidate without having to cope with an immediate counter-attack. Now reinforced with a company of the 3/12 Frontier Force Regiment, the Commandos held on under heavy small arms and artillery fire.

That evening Miller was given a fresh task. He was, with Skinner's Horse, to make a feint attack on the Falaga Pass in order to draw the enemy's attention away from the main attack on Amba Alagi. While Skinner's Horse attacked the left hand side, No 51 were to take the right.

The Commando moved forward under cover of the dark and, after skirting the slopes of Commando Hill, arrived beneath the objective. Artillery fire was called down but the Very lights were not seen . . . Skinner's Horse attacked first and were unsuccessful and had to withdraw. On this, orders were sent to us to withdraw even if we succeeded in gaining our objective, as otherwise we should have been cut off with the enemy on three sides of us. The advance commenced with No 3 Troop on the right and No 2 Troop on the left, with No 1 Troop in the centre in reserve. Time was given for the flanking troops to get round. At once heavy fire was met with and though No 2 and 3 Troops gained a footing on their objectives, they were unable to maintain them and orders were given to retire. Captain Low and Captain Milford Cotton, the troop commanders of Nos 1 and 2 Troops, were both wounded and the retirement commenced. The country was steep and thickly covered with bushes and it was extremely difficult to get our wounded away under heavy machine gun and mortar fire. It was, however, eventually done and no wounded were left behind. We regained the position on Commando Hill by dawn. . .

Almost immediately, No 51 was ordered to get round the enemy's right flank, and moved to a position called Green Hill, which was held for two days. They were now reduced to a strength of two officers and fifty Palestinians, but were told to take some Italian trenches, against which an infantry company had previously suffered 70% casualties. Luckily, the Italians had by now had enough and asked for an armistice. This was signed on 17 May, and the Duke d'Aosta, the Governor General of Italian East Africa, and 5,000 men surrendered.

Undoubtedly, No 51 Middle East Commando had played a very significant part in these operations, and, in summary, Miller wrote to 'Kid' Cator:

We have been whisked from Brigade to Brigade and called on for tasks which I think would be considered difficult by any troops in the world. We did one attack which appeared harder than it turned out and were congratulated by Division on 'a splendid achievement'. In another night operation we got two troops onto the objective and were driven off, but I think we did our job as it was only a demonstration to concentrate more of the enemy on the opposite flank of our main attack.[19]

The rainy season now came, which put a brake on operations, and No 51 Commando spent the next few months at Adi Ugri between

Adowa and Asmara. One interesting job which they had was to provide escorts for Major (later Major General of Chindit fame) Orde Wingate, who was at that time working among the Abyssinian patriots, who were being organised by Brigadier D.A. Sandford DSO's Mission 101. Then, at the end of November 1941, with the surrender of Gondar, at which No 51 ME Commando was present, Italian resistance in Ethiopia ceased. In December the Commando returned to Geneifa, which it had left almost a year before, but only to face disbandment.

The Dodecanese

While Nos 51 and 52 Middle East Commandos were busy in East Africa, No 50 had remained on Crete, being responsible for the defence of the eastern end of the island. They did try to continue to train for amphibious operations, but were often frustrated by the fact that the Royal Navy base at Suda Bay was on the other side of the island, and the Commandos lacked transport. Nevertheless they did what they could using local fishing boats, and it was as well that they did so since a more active role was gradually evolved for them.

With the agreement by Churchill and the Chiefs of Staff at the beginning of 1941 that operations against the Dodecanese should now take place, Cunningham began planning. While it had been laid down that the seizure of the islands, especially Rhodes, the largest, should not take place until Force Z had arrived and married up with 6th Division, which had been earmarked for these operations, Cunningham considered that it was dangerous to do nothing. With No 50 ideally placed geographically on Crete, he decided on a reconnaissance of the beaches of the island of Kasos, the nearest Dodecanese island to Crete. This was with a view to landing coastal guns there which could dominate the Axis airfield at Scarpanto and both sides of the Kaso Straits. Cunningham had had this in mind for some time but only with the arrival of the Luftwaffe at Scarpanto in January 1941 did the Chiefs of Staff agree that it should go ahead.

The first took place on the night 16/17 January when part of No 50 Commando embarked on the sloop HMS *Derby* and attempted to make a landfall on the south coast of the island. *Derby*'s improvised davits and the poor state of the requisitioned small boats combined to make a landing impossible, with several boats in danger of sinking. The fact that she was a coal burner and had noisy metal decks also made her very unsuitable for Commando operations. The party was therefore re-embarked. A second attempt was made a month

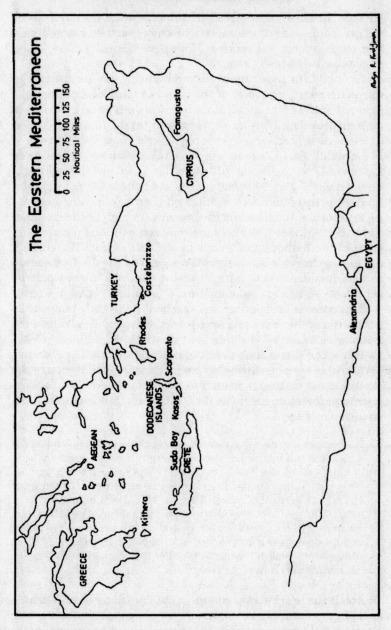

The Eastern Mediterranean

0 25 50 75 100 125 150
Nautical Miles

TURKEY

Castelorizzo

Rhodes

Scarpanto

DODECANESE
ISLANDS

Kasos

Sudo Bay

CRETE

AEGEAN

Kithera

GREECE

CYPRUS

Famagusta

EGYPT

Alexandria

later, on the north coast, but again with little success. A naval officer did get ashore to do a beach reconnaissance, but then a large Italian gun emplacement was spotted. HMS *Derby* hoisted a large Italian flag and sailed back to Crete.

Cunningham now turned his attention to the eastern end of the Dodecanese, especially to the island of Castelorizzo, which he believed would make an ideal motor torpedo boat base, as well as perhaps providing a further stepping stone for the attack on Rhodes, which has now been agreed as the objective of Forze Z when it arrived in the Middle East. Consequently, No 50 Commando were embarked in their old friends *Decoy* and *Hereward* and sailed just after midnight on the night of 23/24 February. They had no idea of their objective until the sealed orders were opened on board. Even then, there was no information to be had on the enemy's strength or the lay-out of his defences. Indeed, all there was were some pre-war picture post-cards of the harbour and a copy of an Italian chart. The concept for the operation, codenamed *Abstention*, was for the Commando to seize the island, hold it for 24 hours, after which they would be relieved by an infantry battalion from Cyprus, and return to Crete.

The coast of Castelorizzo was reached in the early hours of 25 February and the destroyers were guided towards Niftis Point at the harbour entrance by a leading light shown by the submarine HMS *Parthian*. The Commando then began to disembark. The ten whalers available were insufficient to land all at once, and in view of the air threat the destroyers wanted to be away by dawn. The landing operation therefore had to be slick. A.C. Darby, who was in the first wave, remembers:

> It is important to note that the steersman guiding us to our landing was a naval cox'n. I was in the leading boat with him and others followed in blind faith in the Navy's navigation. We progressed slowly until we noticed dark shapes of buildings looming on either side of us and some-one said: 'Where the bloody hell are we? Niftis Point is supposed to be uninhabited.' Almost immediately we were challenged in Italian from the shore and small arms fire fell around us. Our Naval cox'n, with the singular aplomb of a long service sailor shouted 'Dig deep with those paddles, you bastards!' Swinging the tiller hard over, he headed us at a fair rate of knots back to the *Decoy*.[20]

By now it was nearly dawn, and the apparent failure to land as indicated by the returning boats still full of Commandos influenced the Senior Naval Officer to abort the operation, and he began to hoist these boats aboard. Half of them were still missing and when they did arrive, they only had their oarsmen and coxswain aboard. Clearly, then, a landing had taken place, but at the wrong spot. In view of this, Commander E.G. McGregor RN in *Decoy* signalled *Hereward*, to the relief of the Commando, that the landings would continue. These went smoothly, and the Italian garrison was quickly driven back to Paleocastro Fort above the harbour, which surrendered in mid-morning after being attacked by one company supported by fire from the river gunboat HMS *Ladybird*. The Commando had suffered few casualties and had inflicted 13 on the enemy as well as capturing 35 prisoners.

Now began the business of organising the defence of the island, but this was made more difficult by repeated attacks by Italian aircraft based on Rhodes. Luckily, they ceased at dusk, but not before the *Ladybird* had been hit and forced to return to Cyprus, and the Commando, with guards, pickets and patrols detailed, settled down to snatch much needed rest.

> The Commando HQ Staff intended to sleep in the Customs House offices with a sentry group outside. All were very tired and slept from about 2030 hours. Suddenly at 2100 hours a dazzling light lit up the whole building and harbour area outside. It was thought that the enemy had dropped parachute flares and were about to do some precision bombing. The very strong light beam unmistakably came from a warship now coming into the harbour entrance. From the time of being roused to the discovery of where the light came from and the firing of the first 4.7-inch shells was all a matter of seconds. The CO, 2ic, Adjutant, MO and orderlies were all out of the building like lightning but not before two armour piercing shells had ploughed through the walls and ceiling bringing down mounds of rubble. Several more followed.[21]

It took time to reorganise and in the resultant confusion the Italian destroyer put some people ashore who evacuated some Italian civilians and prisoners who had escaped. The rest of the night was spent on the alert against an Italian attempt to regain the island.

In the meantime, in view of the air situation, it was decided to delay the landing of the relief force from Cyprus until that night, but attempts to inform the Commando of this by wireless failed. Luckily, the air attacks during the second day were less intense, and the Commando busied itself in reorganising the civilian administration of the island, and this was much welcomed by the local population. A peaceful night followed, but the relief force still did not arrive, having gone to Alexandria, since the escorting destroyers were now short of fuel. Again, the Commando did not know of this change of plan, and the third day of their stay on the island did not bode well.

> . . . . there was little food left and not very much ammunition as we had expended a great deal shooting at aircraft. Not enough for a sustained defence against a strong counter attack should one be mounted. The bombers and fighters came over as usual, but seemed to know exactly where the Commando was on the island.

Then:

> At 1000 hours on this third morning, 27th February, a breathless runner reported that two destroyers had been seen close to the Turkish coast heading in our direction. Commando HQ had failed to see the Very light signals fired by one of the beach patrols because of the bright sunlight and the height of the cliffs. The two destroyers came round the headland close in shore. At first it was thought that at last they were our ships. But Commander Nicholl RN who was attached to the Commando, pronounced at once that they were Italian although they flew no colours. This was a most unexpected surprise and caught everyone quite unprepared with parties of men all over the place – patrols, fatigue parties and groups of men going into the town to fill their water bottles from one of the cisterns. The ships came straight into the harbour, landed troops who infiltrated along the causeway towards the cemetery position. They also made for the high ground up near the Fort. Some vigorous bren shooting by Commando patrols made them extremely cautious, but in return they had 4.7-inch shells, Breda LAA shells, and the machine gun fire. The Italian counter attack was supported by many bombers dropping showers of 40lb anti-personnel bombs and dive machine gunning by CR42 fighters.
>
> The Commando had been caught on the hop and the situation demanded considerable self control and leadership from all officers and NCOs. The battle was very intense with enemy naval and air forces against us and no way of retaliating effectively. We had no support weapons of any kind, only small arms carried by each man apart from the bren guns. All ammunition had to be carried round the men's necks in cloth bandoliers. We had no tools to dig in and difficulty finding water. At this stage the appearance of our own destroyers and some Fleet Air Arm fighters could have saved the day.
>
> At midday the two separated Commando companies, one at the Cemetery and one at Niftis Point covering the landing beach, were forced to withdraw to the nearby highest ground. This was not due to enemy pressure but to consolidate our position so as to avoid being over-

looked by freshly landed enemy troops making their way along the cliff top. The enemy landing force included a detachment of mountain artillery. The move cleared us from a very unhealthy spot below the cliffs along the coastline, where bombing and machine gunning was intense and we were all at the mercy of the Italian destroyers which were now circling the island looking for targets.[22]

As darkness fell, the situation looked grim, but the Commando was determined to hang on, certain that the Royal Navy would arrive. A.C. Darby:

When darkness fell that night I was given a number of men to form a buffer between the enemy and our own defensive position and I spread my men out at regular intervals about 200 yards in front of our lines having begged as many grenades and as much ammo as could be spared. By that time we were very short of ammo and damned hungry. During that dark period of loneliness – we were spread very thin on the ground – I wriggled forward some way until I could hear muted enemy voices and, having decided that there was no future in hanging around at that point, withdrew to my small 'buffer'. Not a very constructive action on my part but at least I knew the exact location of some of the opposition. Shortly afterwards one of my group reported signals from the sea and I sent back a runner with the information, but I believe our HQ had already made contact with our own ships carrying the Sherwood Foresters – three days late.[23]

The Sherwood Foresters, escorted by the 3rd Cruiser Squadron, had sailed from Alexandria at 0800 hours on the 27th and had finally arrived off the island just before midnight. The Commando HQ managed to make contact with the relief force by means of signalling with matches and an electric torch.

At a conference held in HMS *Decoy* it was decided not to land the Foresters, who turned out to be only in company strength rather than the battalion expected, and to evacuate the Commando. This was achieved, although some scattered patrols could not be contacted in the darkness. Some were captured next day by the Italians, while others tried to swim to the Turkish mainland, a few making it to be eventually repatriated, but others drowned. On the afternoon of 1 March the Commando arrived back at Crete.

Churchill, after hearing of the fiasco, expressed his displeasure in no uncertain terms, especially over the Royal Navy's failure to prevent the Italian counter-attack, and a Board of Inquiry was convened, although its findings were not published at the time. What is clear, however, is that the operation was ill conceived and much of the blame for this must be laid at Cunningham's door. Unfortunately, No 50 Middle East Commando, who had had no say in the planning and had done all that had been asked of them and more, attracted opprobium in some quarters. This was very much as a result of the Royal Navy's lack of understanding of their capabilities and limitations.

No 50 Middle East Commando spent only a few days back in Crete. They then returned to Egypt, joining No 52 back in Geneifa.

The first nine months of the Middle East Commandos' existence had been as frustrating as it had been for those raised in the United Kingdom. The difference was that the the latter had been kept in the public eye, especially as a result of the Vaagso raid, while the efforts of the Middle East Commandos had gone largely unnoticed. On the other hand, they had had more opportunities for action, but, where they had been used in their proper role as fast hitting raiding forces coming in from the sea, the operations had proved abortive because of circumstances beyond their control.

As for the activities of Nos 51 and 52 Middle East Commandos in Sudan, Eritrea and Abyssinia, prolonged campaigning was not what they had been organised for, although they undoubtedly made the most of the opportunities for action given to them. No 51, especially, did play a very major role in the victories at Keren and Amba Alagi. Unfortunately, being merely attached to various formations meant that they seldom received the recognition due to them. Now, with Layforce about to arrive in the Middle East, their own separate identity would become submerged, and their achievements quickly forgotten.

CHAPTER FOUR

Layforce and After

With the decision to mount an operation to capture Rhodes, Keyes' idea of forming a Special Service brigade in the United Kingdom and despatching it to the Middle East in the fast Glen ships *Glengyle* and *Glenroy**, was taken up by the Chiefs of Staff. Consequently, as has already been described, Force Z was constituted under Lt Colonel RE Laycock. Consisting of Nos 7, 8 and 11 Commandos, A Troop of No 3 Commando and Courtney's Folboat Section, it sailed from the Isle of Arran of 31 January 1941. That it was formed in a hurry is clear from the fact that Laycock was only officially appointed to command the force on the day that it sailed, and the Brigade Major of the Special Service Brigade, remarked to him on that very day: 'You appear to be going to command a force of over 100 officers and 1,500 ORs with one staff officer, a note book and eight wireless sets which nobody can work.'[1]

Sailing round the Cape, Force Z arrived at Suez on 7 March, just after the *Abstention* débâcle. Here GHQ MEF, having received orders to this effect from the War Office two weeks before, told Laycock that his force was to be called 'Layforce' forthwith and that, for security reasons, no reference was to be made to the title 'Commando' or that the force had any connections with the Royal Navy. It was also to be placed under command of 6th Division (Major General J.F. Evetts). Three days later, Layforce disembarked at Geneifa. No 52 Middle East Commando was already there, having returned from the Soudan, and No 50 Middle East Commando also joined from Crete at much the same time. Both these Commandos were now to be amalgamated, with Lt Colonel Young of No 52 taking command, Lt Colonel Symons being posted to an engineering job, and placed under command of Layforce. In order to delete all references to Commandos, Layforce was now made up of four 'battalions', as follows:

---

*The third Glen ship, *Gleneam*, set sail a few days later for the Middle East carrying elements of Mobile Naval Base Defence Organisation (MNBDO) I, which had been raised by the Royal Marines in 1940 in the context of capturing and protecting naval bases.

A Battalion – No 7 Commando (Lt Colonel Colvin)

B Battalion – No 8 Commando (Lt Colonel Daly)

C Battalion – No 11 Commando (Lt Colonel Pedder)

D Battalion – No 50/52 Middle East Commando (Lt Colonel Young)

It must be stressed from the outset, however, that these battalions bore little resemblance to an ordinary infantry battalion, lacking both heavy weapons and transport.*

Preparations for the Rhodes operation now got underway, Courtney's Folboat Section carrying out a daring reconnaissance of the island.† But then, on 6 April, the Germans invaded Greece and Yugoslavia and the operation was quickly called off. In the Western Desert, too, the tide was turning against the British. Rommel, who had arrived in the desert in February, launched an offensive at the end of March, driving back the Western Desert Force, which had been seriously depleted by the need to send troops to Greece. By 11 April he had reoccupied Cyrenaica and captured Bardia and Sollum.

As a result of this, the role of Layforce was quickly changed, and it was given the old Middle East Commando task of the previous autumn, raids on the North African coast behind enemy lines. On 11 April Layforce was ordered to carry out a reconnaissance of the Western Desert coastline, operating in raiding parties of 200 men. Next day they sailed to Alexandria in preparation for this, but then, on the 15th, the orders were amended. Immediate raids were now to be carried out against Bardia and the coast road near Bomba.

In the event, the Bomba operation was cancelled, and A (7 Cdo) Battalion was selected to carry out the Bardia raid. The overall aim was to harass the enemy's lines of communication and inflict as much damage as possible on his logistic installations. Four beaches were chosen and these were to be assaulted simultaneously from *Glengyle*'s ALCs. The whole operation was to be carried out on the night of 19/20 April. Although the approach went smoothly, problems began to occur prior to landing. For a start, no guiding light

---

*The War Office did rule later in April that Layforce should be designated Nos 50, 52, 53 and 54 Middle East Commandos with a nucleus for a fifth commando if necessary. Confirmatory orders for this were, however, never issued.[2]

†Courtney was awarded an MC for this and Lt Commander Clogstoun-Willmott RN who actually inspected the beaches, the DSO.

could be seen to direct the landing craft onto the beaches. This was the responsibility of Layforce's Folboat Section under Roger Courtney. They had taken passage in the submarine HMS *Triumph*, which was unfortunately attacked by friendly aircraft en route, making her late on the objective.

Nevertheless, the landing craft were lowered on time, but difficulty was experienced with the release gear on the davits, and one ALC could not be launched. Even so, the various detachments were only some 10-15 minutes behind schedule when they hit the beaches. However, some found themselves on the wrong beach, which caused confusion. Luckily, there were no enemy about, and so the landing was unopposed. The detachments then set about their various tasks, but intelligence proved faulty, with several installations proving not to exist, or incorrectly located. A bridge was blown and an Italian tyre dump set on fire, but with time pressing little else was achieved. There was also tragedy when an officer was mortally wounded by a jumpy Commando sentry. The re-embarkation took much longer than expected, and one detachment, which returned to the wrong beach, never made it; some 67 men were later reported prisoners. Another ALC broke down, but eventually managed to make a landfall at Tobruk. It was not an auspicious beginning, but then, on the other hand, several valuable lessons were learnt for the future.

There now followed a period of intense frustration. Orders were given for hasty operations to be mounted, only to be cancelled again at the last moment. Layforce continually found itself under new masters, and amid this confusion morale inevitably suffered. When A (7 Cdo) Battalion finally vacated the *Glengyle* at the beginning of May, an inscription was found on one of the troop decks which read: 'Never in the whole of history of human endeavour have so few been buggered about by so many'.[3] As Laycock himself said in a lecture on his return from the Middle East at the end of 1941:

> ... I think most of us imagined that conditions in the Middle East would be very different and that the old practice of working up to fever pitch for abortive operations was a thing of the past. I can assure you however that this was not the case and that the situation was, if anything, even more exasperating.[4]

In mid May, however, there was a redeployment. A (7 Cdo) and D (50/52 Cdo) Battalions were placed in general reserve, while C (11

Cdo) was sent to Cyprus in order to strengthen the defences there. This left B (8 Cdo) Battalion, which was based at Mersa Matruh, as the only part of Layforce which still had a specific commando role.

Crete

On 20 May 1941 the Germans made an airborne assault on Crete. Within forty-eight hours they had secured an airhead at Maleme and were bringing in reinforcements. The garrison under General Freyberg had been caught by surprise, having been expecting a sea-borne invasion, and within a few days the German force had grown from 3,000 to 22,000 men. The only way which the attack could be defeated was through the recapture of Maleme, and GHQ MELF saw this as an ideal task for Layforce. The original plan was for them to land at Castel Selino on the south side of the island and then move north, taking the German around Maleme in the flank and rear. This would, however, have meant a cross-country march of some fifty miles and supply problems. Another proposal was to land on the west coast near Kastelli, which would reduce the marching distance to twenty miles. On the other hand, in view of the adverse air situation, the approach and landing would have to be done at night. This would be difficult to achieve because of the longer steaming time and was therefore ruled out, the first plan being selected.

Early on 23 May, A and D Battalions sailed from Alexandria in three destroyers, arriving off Selino Castelli that evening. Unfortunately, the seas were very rough, too much so to lower the boats which would take the Commandos ashore, and the Senior Naval Officer decided to return to Alexandria. Nevertheless, an advance party made up of 200 men of A Battalion, who had gone on ahead, did manage to land at Suda Bay on 24 May while the remainder arrived back at Alexandria late that same evening. It was now decided the main body should also be landed at Suda Bay, and they were re-embarked in the fast minelayer HMS *Abdiel*, which had taken the advance party across, and set sail early on the 26th. At the time, General Freyberg still believed that there was a good chance that Crete would hold, and Layforce was optimistic when it sailed.

Major (later Major General) F.C.C. Graham, Brigade Major of Layforce, recalled in a post-war account:

The passage to Suda was, most remarkably, completely uneventful and at approximately midnight on the 25th [actually 26th] May the ship crept up to the mole at the Western end of the Bay; all was quiet and only distant gunfire and occasional flashes of light from the direction of Canea marred the peacefulness of the night.

No sooner had the ship anchored than boats from the shore began to come alongside and just as the Brigade Commander, myself and other officers were bidding farewell to the Captain of the minelayer, the door opened and a bedraggled and apparently slightly hysterical naval officer burst in. In a voice trembling with emotion he said:

'The Army's in full retreat, everything is chaos. I've just had my best friend killed beside me. Crete is being evacuated!'

Cheerful to say the least of it, and something of a shock to the little party of Commando officers armed to the teeth and loaded up like a Christmas tree, who stared open-mouthed at this bearer of bad news.

'But we are just going ashore,' I faltered.

'My God', he said, 'I didn't know that and perhaps I shouldn't have said anything.'

'Too late now, old boy', I said. 'You can at least tell us what the password is.' But he had forgotten it!

We had no time to stay and check up on his story, which in any event was likely to be unreliable in view of the state of his mind.

Disembarkation started at once and, as soon as we were ashore, we were met by a young officer from the A Battalion advance party who had been sent to give us the 'form'. He brought grim news; Maleme had fallen; the garrison was retreating towards Sphakia on the south coast; the Commandos were to cover the retreat; there was no transport, probably no food and probably no ammunition; the Brigade Commander was to report at once to General Freyberg.

There did not seem to be one bright spot in this little tale of woe!

The Brigadier discussed with me, on a small scale map, the position which we should take up and we agreed that the hills astride the main road from Canea to Sphakia were the most suitable delaying line. This line would be held by A Battalion while the other battalion, D, would go further inland to form another 'firm base' on the Sphakia road. After this decision was made the Brigadier said: 'Well, Freddie, you better get off now as it's a good long hike and it looks as if it is all up hill. Use your discretion about dispositions and administration when you get there – Good Night' and with that he disappeared into the night.[5]

The Brigade Major realised that the two most important items were food and ammunition, and ordered everyone to load themselves up with these. With no transport available, the rest of the stores which they had brought with them were thrown into the harbour. George Williams, late of No 50 Commando and now with D Battalion:

Some supplies were slung ashore and we were told to break the boxes and carry as much as possible with us. I didn't know at the time that there were tins of chocolate or I'd have loaded up with that. As it was I crammed about a dozen tins of bully beef inside my shirt (I didn't even eat the stuff). That was to become a load I was thankful to get rid of later. We marched forward and turned left onto the road heading in the same direction as the retreating men. It was a disorganised rabble and was impeding us a bit. We overtook four men struggling up hill with a stretcher laden with ammunition boxes. Sgt. Major Howland said: 'Come on, lets give these blokes a break.' He collared two other men and we took over. With a wooden handle taking the weight on our shoulders we carried on. That road just went on and on. We'd covered quite some distance and were looking for someone to give us a break with the load but no help was forthcoming. Those stragglers could have made light work of that load. Just a few minutes each, four at a time and it would have been nothing. But they weren't having any.[6]

D Battalion halted and took up positions shortly after dawn on a ridge some six miles east of Suda Bay, while A Battalion was given orders to hold its positions until 0430 hours next morning. Throughout the day, Layforce was subjected to repeated air attack. In the afternoon, a suitable position was found for D Battalion to cover the withdrawal. This was astride the Sphakia road just north of the village of Babali Hani, some twelve miles south of Suda Bay. There was, however, a rub in that one company was ordered to remain in the battalion area, just where the Suda-Sphakia road turns south. This was unsatisfactory in that it could be easily outflanked from the west, but in spite of Colonel Laycock's protests, General Weston, now commanding the rearguard, was adamant. The Spanish Company of D Battalion, now some 110 strong with a mix of the original Spaniards of No 50 Commando and British, was detailed for the task, leaving four companies to hold the main position.

At 0230 hours, the last of the stragglers had passed through A Battalion and they then began their withdrawal, passing through the Spanish Company, and taking up an intermediate position at Stylos, three miles south of Beritiana. Major McGibbon, commanding the Spanish company, received a welcome reinforcement during the night in the shape of a New Zealand Maori platoon, which volunteered to stay with them. Nevertheless, with the dawn came the inevitable German attack, which was preceded by a mortar bombardment. Heavily outnumbered, the defenders did what they could to hold the Germans up. McGibbon was then badly wounded, and ordered the company and Maoris to withdraw. He remained where he was and was made prisoner. It was now the turn of A Battalion, as Sergeant Charles Stewart relates:

> Captain [Jocelyn Nicholls RA] receives orders from Major Wylie who was in command to take and clear enemy troops off side of hill, where they had a good command of the road and were harassing the movement of troops and transport. With L/Cpl Kerdal, I acted as leading scout, safely reaching the top of the plateau, spot enemy but give our presence away to save two sub-sections A and B going into a dip which the enemy had under cover of fire; the result was I very nearly caught one myself. I turned my tommy gun on him. The cat was now definitely out of the bag; a blue Very Light goes up – we soon discover it is the signal for a mortar to fire on the slope that we had come up, but their shots dropped from anything up to fifty yards from us. Captain moves up and I shouted to him the position of the enemy, ordering the men to fix bayonets. He led the attack on top of the plateau with his tommy gun; I grabbed hold of two Bren gun men, instructing them to use them as tommy guns. We made our way round the opposite flank, hoping to run into them, but on arriving round found that they had descended on the other side. I saw the skipper, who immediately informed me that he thought we had lost a few men. While talking, one of Gerry's potato-mashers burst quite near us; luckily no one was injured.
>
> Next, one of the enemy who had got separated from his comrades and knew we were quite near, began shouting 'Englander'. Enraged by the loss, as we thought then, four cut around the rocks to get him, but owing to the heavy heather growth we could not see him. Returning, I discovered that one man had been killed and three wounded, one seriously, that being the PSM [Platoon Sergeant Major], who was shot through the left lung. The Captain at this moment was in a precarious position as the evacuation was still in progress. He suggested carrying the wounded men down to the road in the hope of getting a vehicle of some sort; fortunately we caught one leaving with ammunition, which conveyed them to the dressing station some fifteen miles away. While the Captain went to report our latest adventure to Brigadier Laycock, I mustered the troop underneath an olive grove about fifty yards off the road.[7]

The Germans were temporarily driven off, A Battalion being helped by two I tanks of 7th Royal Tank Regiment,* and the New Zealanders. In spite of this they were in grave danger of being cut off. Laycock and Graham used one of the tanks to get back to D Battalion,

* A half squadron of Matildas had been sent to Crete prior to the invasion.

while A Battalion attempted to disengage as best it could. A large number of them were, however, rounded up and captured by the Germans. With A Battalion now scattered, Laycock organised his force into a single unit based on D Battalion and, in conjunction with the commanders of 4 and 5 New Zealand and 19 Australian Infantry Brigades, decided to modify his original plan of falling back through successive battalion positions, going firm at Babali Hani instead.

By now D Battalion was ready and waiting. George Williams again:

> I was sent forward with three other men to man a look-out post; it was just forward of us but on the top of the hill among a clump of four or five trees. From here we could see quite a long way up the road along which any mechanised vehicles would have to travel. Eventually the first that came into view were Jerry motorbikes and sidecars. Our signallers passed this message back with mirrors. There was a church tower some distance over the other side of the road from which a sniper later did some deadly work. But I think someone was there already and had spotted our signals, because just after this they started peppering us with mortars. They soon got the range and were becoming quite deadly. The corporal then gave the order to get back to HQ. We started to come downhill. The mortar fire shifted and a sniper opened up. It then became a race downhill to the nearest cover, which was one of the many stone walls round there. Running downhill and leaping made for fantastic strides, some of which must have been about ten foot long, or at least they felt like it.[8]

A.C. Darby found himself covering the exposed right flank of D Battalion's position with his section:

> The ground was very hard with little chance of digging in effectively, but we constructed small stone sangars on the forward slope of our part of the rise and waited for Jerry to test our mettle. Later that day we could see enemy troops in the distance, some on motor cycles, but none of our weapons had the range to hit them: nor did I wish to reveal my position at that time. As enemy troops came up against our main defences astride the road the noise of battle swelled and we gradually became aware of small groups trying to filter round our position, of which most of them were unaware as we lay concealed and quiet. As some of them started up the slope I gave the order and we opened up. A number fell: the others ran back into cover and shortly afterwards all hell broke loose. A star shell was fired in our direction to guide the Stukas and they practically fell out of the sky at us until the ground trembled. I think if anything the

mortars were more frightening. The whole of our small area was plastered with them until smoke from the burning shrubbery hid us at times from one another.[9]

The first German attack against D Battalion's defences was made up by two battalions of the 5th Mountain Division. This was repulsed after about an hour. There was then a pause while the Germans brought up two additional battalions and in mid afternoon they made a determined attempt to get round the battalion's left flank. This was beaten off after some fierce fighting and with help from the Australian 2/8th Infantry Battalion, which was positioned in the rear of D Battalion. Other desultory attempts were made to break through, but by dusk it was clear that the Germans had had enough for the time being. D Battalion had managed to achieve this at a cost of three killed and fifteen wounded only.

The evacuation was now well underway, and D Battalion were given orders to begin to withdraw at 2100 hours. This they did, company by company, with no interference from the enemy. Freddie Graham:

> Then began the weary march across the mountains to the Sphakia assembly areas; by this time we had been relieved of our rearguard duties and a brigade of the New Zealand Division had taken over. The Commando assembly area was in a deep gully to the east of and some 3½ miles distance from the Sphakia beaches and here we arrived after an exhausting march, the chief features of which were heat, thirst, hunger and Stukas. As soon as we had had some rest it became urgent that we tried to find General Freyberg and get some orders – there was only one way to do this, one of us had to go and find him. The Brigadier set off first with the Intelligence Officer [Captain Evelyn Waugh] but returned some hours later exhausted and unsuccessful. I took up the hunt. Twelve miles I walked on that warm summer's day with only a spoonful of jam and 'iron ration' to sustain me! At last a kindly cavalry officer sitting in a derelict armoured car and admiring a wound in his leg and half a bottle of gin in his hand gave me the necessary clue and a swig of gin and I found GHQ. Although swaying on my feet with weariness I was able to gather from the gist of General Freyberg's orders that the Commandos, now only 3 or 400 strong, would take up position round the beach and cover the evacuation of the other troops.[10]

This occurred on the 30th, and on the following afternoon, General Freyberg having left the island on the previous night and handed over command to General Weston, Layforce received their final orders. They were to hold their positions long enough to cover the withdrawal of the other fighting forces, but to withdraw themselves to the beaches only on General Weston's orders. It quickly became clear, though, that this was to be the last night of the evacuation – the Royal Navy was losing too many ships to be able to continue it for any longer. That evening, before leaving himself, General Weston dictated the orders for surrender to Freddie Graham and then departed. However, he gave permission for Laycock, Graham and Waugh also to embark on the grounds that Layforce still had two other battalions, one in Cyprus and the other in Egypt. Laycock himself, satisfied that all fighting troops had been evacuated and that only stragglers were left gave orders for D Battalion to make its way to the beach, and handed over responsibility for the capitulation to Lt Colonel Colvin* of A Battalion.

D Battalion got down to the outskirts of Sphakia in good order, but was prevented by the rabble of stragglers from getting to the beach where Laycock, his headquarters, and some Commandos with them caught virtually the last boat to leave. For D Battalion and the remnants of A Battalion the orders to evacuate came too late and they were left stranded. In all 23 officers and 156 other ranks of Layforce were evacuated, although a few more managed to get across to North Africa in commandeered craft during the next few weeks. As for those who remained, A.C. Darby:

> . . . I was told we had written orders to surrender. I was sitting under a large boulder watching Sphakia beach being continually hit by Stukas. One young officer nearby was in tears, not for himself but for his weary men. I smashed my Tommy gun against the rocks in a fury of disgust. I was 25 years of age and four years of my youth were to be wasted in POW camps.[11]

It had been a sad business for Layforce, especially for those former members of No 50 Middle East Commando in D Battalion, to whom it came as the culmination of seven months of frustration – Bomba, Kasos, Castelorizzo and now Crete – during which they had never had the chance to be masters of their own destiny. As for Laycock, he noted after he got back to Egypt that Layforce was totally inequipped to carry out the role given to them in Crete, lacking the heavy weapons and transport that such a task required. Nevertheless, he did

---

*Eventually it was Lt Colonel Young, who actually negotiated the surrender.

pay particular tribute to Colonel George Young* for his foresight in insisting on training his battalion on normal infantry, rather than specialised Commando lines. The main problem had been that the enemy had fought by day, but rested by night, while Layforce had been starved of rest by the need to move at night because of the air threat. In terms of casualties, however, the latter was ineffective; many more were caused by mortar and sniper fire.[12]

Litani River

C (11 Cdo) Battalion of Layforce, having moved from Alexandria to Palestine in mid April 1941, sailed from Haifa for Cyprus at the end of that month. May was spent in Nicosia and Famagusta, and then they sailed back to Palestine. The reason for this was the decision to invade Vichy French Syria. De Gaulle had been agitating since March for the British to take this step, but Wavell, as stretched as he was with campaigns in North Africa, Abyssinia and Greece, as well as the need to hold on to the islands in the Eastern Mediterranean, managed to initially dissuade Churchill. Then, on 1 May 1941, came the pro-Fascist revolt in Iraq led by Raschid Ali, and the besieging of the RAF's vital airfields at Habbaniyah. It then became clear that Admiral Darlan, Vichy France's Foreign Minister, had promised the Germans the use of facilities in Syria, and Churchill began to agitate for Wavell to occupy the territory. Although by the end of May the revolt in Iraq had been crushed, Wavell was now too concerned about Crete to give Syria much thought. He did however, warn General Wilson, GOC Palestine and Transjordan, to prepare for such an operation, and a week after the final evacuation from Crete, the invasion began.

General Wilson's plan involved three thrusts. While the main body, 7th Australian Division, advanced towards Damascus and Beirut from Palestine, two other forces would invade from Iraq, one towards Palmyra and the other along the Euphrates. For the brigade taking the coast route to Beirut there was a serious obstacle just north of Tyre, the Litani River, which ran east-west along a narrow gorge. It was therefore decided that C Battalion should land on three beaches north of the river, and then seize and hold crossings over it until relieved by 25 Australian Brigade, which was allotted the coastal line of advance. C Battalion put to sea in the *Glengyle*, and the intention was that they should land at dawn on 8 June, the

---

*Lt Colonel Young was later awarded the DSO for his gallantry on Crete.

main advance having begun a few hours earlier. The weather, as it had done so many times in the past, now deteriorated. In spite of representations to the *Glengyle*'s Captain that it was worth the risk of losing an ALC rather than sacrifice surprise, the latter decided that conditions were too rough. There was no time to return to Suez and the ships hove to off the coast, the enemy now well aware that a landing was to be made.

Next morning at 0400 hours, with a setting moon behind them and a rising sun to their front, the battalion landed. The northernmost party landed under command of Captain George More, the Adjutant. Lieutenant McGonigal,* OC No 4 Troop, tells what happened:

> We landed in two ALCs — one sub-section under 2Lt Richards and three sub-sections under myself. 2Lt Parnacott was with me. We crossed the beaches with a few stray shots above our heads and no casualties, and made due east to the road. 2Lt Richards' party had not joined us. We crossed the road about 300 yards south of the enemy MT [Motor Transport] whose personnel took no notice of us. Gaining the rising ground, we saw the remaining troops of our fighting party engaging the MT on the road. As long as possible we gave them supporting fire from the rear. Then, when they had captured the trucks, we pushed northwards along the hills towards Kaffa Badr bridge.
>
> On the road running east from this bridge we engaged one armoured truck, and an armoured car. The truck we destroyed and the car escaped to the east. Some twenty enemy retiring to the north were engaged by our small arms at 300 yards with good effect, and then 4 Troop combined with Captain More's party in the capture of the French guns and trucks in the long valley which runs due east from the Kaffa Badr bridge. Capt More consolidated the position and placed 10 Troop on the high ground above the Kaffa Badr bridge and 4 Troop on the hills overlooking the valley some 500 yards east of 10 Troop.
>
> We occupied this position till about 4 o'clock in the afternoon, and set up a very temporary RAP [Regimental Aid Post] and had under our care a large body of prisoners. During this period we saw small bodies of the enemy to the eastward, all of these retiring northwards, and a French reconnaissance plane made repeated flights over us in the early afternoon. We could hear the sounds of 10 Troop on our left engaging enemy AFVs on the main north road and about four o'clock six armoured cars appeared on the road running to our east about 1400 yards away. These AFVs engaged our area with two pounders or some similar gun, and

---

* He was later to become a founder member of the SAS, but was lost on the SAS's first raid, against airfields in the Tmimi-Gazala area in November 1941.

medium MGs. They inflicted heavy casualties on our French prisoners. It had been impossible, owing to the flat nature of the ground around the road, to put any anti-AFV obstacle on the road and so, on the approach of the AFV I withdrew my main body, consisting of one section of 4 Troop and some dozen men from Nos 1, 7 and 10 Troops whom I had formed into another sub-section. One sub-section and two anti-tank rifles stayed in our area and were driven out by the AFVs some fifteen minutes later. We reformed in the hills and with 3 sub-sections and two anti-tank rifles we moved to the support of 10 Troop. During the action with the AFVs many French prisoners were killed attempting to disarm our men or escape.

One sub-section was now sent to hold a main ridge covering our rear and the main road about 500 yards south of No 10 Troop and with the remainder of the troop I reported to Capt MacDonald and placed myself under his orders, this force being meantime augmented by a section of 8 Troop. Capt More arrived and took command of this fighting party. Capt More ordered a withdrawal on the Litani River direction, using the ridges as bounds, and 4 Troop and 10 Troop alternated as forward troops. The enemy were bringing heavy but inaccurate fire to bear on us and, as far as can be checked, we suffered no casualties during the withdrawal.

Eventually Capt More held a conference and it was decided to try and cross the River where it entered the sea. For this purpose we held a position till an hour after darkness and then it was found that 10 Troop and 4 Troop had retired in the direction of the high ground eastwards. It was by this route that most of 4 Troop got out of the fighting area and crossed the River above the main bridge. The remainder of Capt More's fighting party descended to the beach, where eventually we were caught by enemy MGs and suffered seven casualties, including 2Lt Parnacott killed. We eventually succeeded in surrendering, movement forwards or backwards being impossible. Next morning the French commander handed his post over to Capt More and we rejoined the main body of the Commando under Major Keyes.[13]

The centre party led by Colonel Dick Pedder himself, made for the redoubt covering the bridge at Kafr Bada, intending to capture the bridge before the French could demolish it. The enemy began to put up increasing resistance and Pedder was killed. His officers became casualties as well and it was left to RSM Fraser to capture a nearby barracks, thus preventing the enemy from reinforcing the redoubt. The third group, under Major Geoffrey Keyes,* Royal Scots Greys, the second-in-command, which was supposed to combine with Dick

---

* Son of Sir Roger Keyes.

Pedder in seizing the bridge, was unfortunately landed south of the river. As Laycock later said of Keyes:

> Had he been less 'Commando-spirited' he might well have maintained that it was impossible for him to carry out the task allotted to his detachment and have been content to advance across the river with the main body. Actually, however, he succeeded in finding a boat and getting across the river with one other officer and 14 other ranks against heavy opposition. This small party succeeded in capturing the redoubt on the far side which materially helped in the subsequent action of that main body.[14]

Unfortunately, though, the bridge was blown with the Australian advance guard within fifty yards of it. This explains why C Battalion was forced to spend the night amid the enemy. After a night attack, the Australians managed to get across, with their Sappers building a pontoon bridge. Next morning they relieved C Battalion and George More's party found themselves captors rather than captives, with their original captors surrendering to them.

The battalion had suffered 123 casualties, a quarter of its strength, but had acquitted itself well. Keyes now took over command and on 1 July they found themselves back in Cyprus again on garrison duty.

Disbandment of Layforce

Although B (8 Cdo) Battalion had remained at Mersa Matruh during this period, detachments of it were sent to Tobruk, which was put under siege by Rommel on 13 April 1941. The original intention had been that they should make a series of raids on German lines, culminating in a link-up with a relieving force. But Wavell, as stretched as he was at the time, was in no position to go back onto the offensive in the Western Desert and hence no such force was forthcoming. The detachment thus merely remained in barracks in the harbour area for three weeks and then returned to Mersa Matruh by sea.

Such was the shortage of manpower that Wavell decided that Layforce, or what was left of it, was an expensive commodity, especially as the Royal Navy, with its high losses in ships, was unwilling to co-operate in further amphibious operations for the time being. He therefore gave orders in mid June that Layforce, apart from C Battalion, which would return to garrison duties in Cyprus, was to be disbanded. Then, before this could be put into effect, Wavell was replaced by Auchinleck, but he, too, felt the same way. Thus, on 1

August 1941, Layforce ceased to exist. Most of those whose regiments were then serving in the Middle East returned to them. Others, especially the survivors of No 7 Commando, went under Captain Jocelyn Nicholls,* the senior surviving officer of the Commando, to eventually form Mission 204 which was designed to assist the Chinese forces in Burma. Others volunteered to join David Stirling, a No 8 Commando officer, in a new unit, the Special Air Service.

One party of No 8 Commando, however, found itself temporarily exempted from the disbandment. Captain Philip Dunne, Royal Horse Guards explains:

> A party of volunteers was called for to return once more to Tobruk. They came from the 8th Commando. I was with the advance party under command of Captain Mike Kealy of the Devonshires. The party consisted of five officers and 70 other ranks. I was second in command and the three subalterns were Lewis, of the Welsh Guards, Langton of the Irish Guards and Alston of the Royal Regiment of Artillery.†
>
> When we got to Tobruk and repaired to the Headquarters of General Morshead, we were told that no Special Service troops were to be sent there. We pointed out that we were Special Service troops and had arrived as an advance party. We were then told that General Morshead was at that moment at GHQ Cairo, discussing our fate. Some days later the decision to disband the Commandos was reached and we were told we were no longer in Colonel Daly's command.[15]

They were now attached to the 18th Indian Cavalry (Mechanised) and spent much time going on patrol with them.

> About ten days afterwards we received orders to carry out a raid on the Twin Pimples, a strong point consisting of two small hills close together, held by the Italians, which commanded the forward positions of the Indian Regiment. Before the attack we carried out a number of reconnoitering patrols, native Indian officers and men helping us. They were very good indeed.
>
> All the officers went out on these patrols, so as to be thoroughly familiar with the ground. The plan was to get through the Italian forward positions, then their main positions to the left of the Twin Pimples until we reached the main road, or rather track, up which their supplies to the position came. We would then move along the track and take the Italians in the rear. Three minutes before we were due to enter the

---

* He was to be killed in Burma on 11 May 1942.
† Kealy who had commanded A Troop of No 3 Commando later joined the SBS, and Lewis, Langton and Alston the SAS.

position the Indian Regiment would carry out a diversion by opening an attack on one of the forward Italian positions. This raid took place on the 18th July 1941. We moved through our own forward positions in single file, a distance of 1200 yards from our forward positions to those of the enemy. The party consisted of three officers, Mike Kealy, Lewis and myself, the 40 men led by an Indian officer. Half the party was armed with Tommy guns, each man carrying six flat magazines [as opposed to drum magazines], and half with rifles and bayonets. All had, I think, 6 grenades. Every third man had a ground sheet worn bandolier fashion and to be used as a stretcher. The attack was due to start at 1 a.m. and we, therefore, left two hours earlier at 11 p.m.

On quitting our forward positions we moved off in battle formation Mike Kealy in the centre, Lewis on his right and myself on his left, each with our party. To each party two or three Australian sappers were attached, whose job it was to blow up any ammunition dumps or mortars we might find.

It was dark, but darkness in the desert is never as great as in England. The officers knew the ground; we had reconnoitred it, and we walked briskly and it was like an English summer evening and very pleasant. We all kept fairly close, about 15 or 20 yards separating each group of the party. We moved in complete silence, being particularly careful not to betray ourselves by coughing. We were all wearing rubber boots. The silence was very well kept throughout the approach. We went through the Italian forward positions and then through their main defensive lines, consisting of a number of slit trenches. I shall never know if they were manned or not, because we heard nothing from them and were very careful to make no noise. We eventually reached the track, which we could recognise by the wheel marks of cars. We got through a bit too soon and lay down to wait. I took the opportunity to go over to Mike Kealy and check our final move. I whispered close into his ear. I remember we compared the time on our watches.

We waited about five minutes then we started off along the track at more than right angles to our advance and as we got near the rear of the Twin Pimples the diversion arranged for started. As soon as the Indians began to fire, the Italians fired back and shot off Very lights. Two minutes afterwards we were challenged by an Italian sentry 30 yards away. We immediately formed up in a line and went forward firing our Tommy guns and rifles.

It was a bit uphill and there were a lot of stone walls about three feet high, which were, I think, some sort of above-ground rifle pits. I remember jumping a slit trench. We got into the position though we did not see very well in the darkness. Slit trenches and dugouts, some of them being disused corn caves, very deep and quite impervious to fire, others were made of sandbags. I saw an ammunition dump which was being dealt with by sappers and at least one three inch mortar. The fight lasted about three or four minutes. In order that we should not fight each other in the dark the recognition sign was the word 'Jock' and I heard 'Jock . . . Jock' being cried out in the darkness. The Italians rushed into the dugouts and we bombed them out of them. Then they rushed back again clutching each other and screaming. They did not, however, surrender and were most of them killed by the bayonet and hand grenades.

As soon as the sappers had done the demolitions the pre-arranged signal, a blast on a whistle, was given and we began to withdraw. The plan was to move right handed for about quarter of a mile and then turn and make straight for our own lines. We were to be guided towards them by an Indian officer who would stand in one of the forward positions and fire a white Very light every quarter of an hour.

The withdrawal, of course, was the tricky part. We all shouted to our men. I shouted to No 6 Troop; Mike Kealy to No 8 and Lewis to No 4. It was a night of brilliant stars and in order to check our direction we got the north star over our left shoulder as we came back. We had reckoned that after about quarter of an hour the Italians would certainly put down a barrage on the Twin Pimples. This is exactly what they did. We were only about a hundred yards away from the position when they began to plaster it. They fired everything they could both at it and at us; mortars, heavy machine guns, firing explosive bullets and ordinary machine guns. Our first casualty was Corporal Maynard of No 6 Troop. He was a very good fellow and was hit in the shoulder by an explosive bullet. We gave him morphia, put him on a ground sheet and got him back, but he subsequently died. We had four other casualties, only wounded. One of the Guardsmen got back unaided, with one arm broken and a bullet in his leg.

I think the success of the attack, which everyone thought would entail heavy casualties, was due to the careful reconnoitring of the ground beforehand. This, in its turn, was due to the skill of the Indians, who taught us such a lot.

We only took one prisoner and he was wounded and died I think before he could be interrogated. In consequence Lewis took out a reconnoitring patrol a day or two later and captured a live prisoner, the only one to be found in one of the forward posts of the Italians.[16]

There was also an attempted operation to destroy enemy aircraft on two landing grounds in the Gazala area. Under the supervision of Captain Jock Haselden, an Arab specialist with G(R) Branch HQ MELF, the plan was for Arab guides to lead Second Lieutenants The Lord Jellicoe and Mather and Lance Corporal Hole by foot through the defences to Tobruk and then on to the objective. On 15 June, the day before the operation was to be launched, the chief guide, who had just returned from a reconnaissance in connection with another operation, reported that he considered that the enemy defences were too strong to infiltrate. The other guides, on hearing this also declined to take part. Because the raiding party was dependent on them for finding food and water – to carry sufficient of these and the necessary explosives would have been too great a load – it was decided to postpone the operation and try another method of approach. Eureka boats were selected, and having studied the Axis deployment, it was decided to land at a point west of Gazala. Lance Corporal Easter now joined the party and the new plan reflected two two-man teams being used, one for each of the landing grounds. At the end of the month three attempts were made to make a landing, all without success. On the first two the landing place could not be identified and on the final one they were engaged by a shore battery north of Gazala. The operation was therefore abandoned. Another frustration, but even so it did not deter Lord Jellicoe from joining the Special Air Service and eventually commanding the Special Boat Squadron in the Mediterranean with great distinction.

C Battalion had spent the month of July 1941 in Cyprus, where they frequently found themselves under enemy air attack. They were relieved at the beginning of August and returned to Alexandria, and thence to Amiriya. Here they, too, received orders to disband, and began to disperse. Laycock himself had returned to England in July to plead for the Commandos in the Middle East to be kept in being. The result was a minute from Churchill to the Chiefs of Staff:

> I wish the Commandos in the Middle East to be reconstituted as soon as possible. Instead of being formed by a Committee of Officers without much authority General [sic] Laycock should be appointed the DCO with his forces placed directly under Admiral Cunningham, who should be charged with all Combined Operations involving sea transport and not exceeding one Brigade. The Middle East Command have indeed maltreated and thrown away this valuable force.[17]

He followed this up by speaking personally to Auchinleck about it at Chequers on 2 August. Two weeks later he changed his mind and decreed that the Middle East Commandos should be under Auchinleck's rather than Cunningham's control. In the meantime, Laycock returned to the Middle East, albeit still as a Lieutenant Colonel. This did not prevent the formal disbandment of C Battalion becoming fact on 1 September and, indeed, it was not until 11 October that GHQ at Cairo held a meeting to discuss what could be resurrected from the remains. At the time there were left Stirling's unit (L Detachment SAS);* No 51 Middle East Commando, then still in Abyssinia, the remnants of Layforce, with Laycock himself once more present, and the Special Boat Section. Roger Courtney's determination had, in mid 1941, gained the sympathy of Admiral Maund, now Director of Combined Operations at Alexandria, and the SBS was working very much under him, carrying out sabotage operations and dropping agents on enemy coasts in the Mediterranean, using submarines, both Alexandria and Malta based, for their transport.

One other Commando unit which was not considered by the meeting was the Cyprus Commando. This had been formed at the end of June 1941 from men of the Cyprus Regiment with British officers and NCOs. It consisted of five squads each of eleven men and its role was to operate behind enemy lines in the event of an invasion of the island. It was short-lived and ceased to exist after the beginning of January 1942.

In the event, the meeting decided that a reconstituted Middle East Commando was to be organised as follows:

HQ and Depot Troop (at Geneifa)
No 2 Troop (L Det SAS)
No 3 Troop (British remnants of Layforce)
Nos 4, 5 Troops (Palestinian ex 51 Cdo)
No 6 Troop (SBS)

Laycock was given overall command. No 3 Troop, consisting of some sixty all ranks under Geoffrey Keyes, was very much built around C Battalion and insisted on calling itself No 11 Commando, its original title. It was shortly to become involved in one of the most dramatic raids of the war.

The Raid on Rommel's Headquarters
By October 1941, Auchinleck was, under continuous pressure from Churchill, drawing up plans for a counter-offensive designed to relieve Tobruk and drive Rommel out of Cyrenaica. To sup-

*The origin of this title lay with Dudley Clarke, who now had responsibility to Wavell for deception schemes. He had created the fictitious 1st Special Air Service Brigade, to make the Germans believe that there was an airborne formation in the Middle East. When he heard that Stirling was actually intending to carry out parachute training, it was too good an opportunity to miss in making the deception more convincing.

port *Crusader*, as the operation was codenamed, the Middle East Commando was given two tasks. L Detachment was to raid landing grounds in the Gazala-Tmimi area, while No 11 Commando was to penetrate further to the west. Its target was a number of headquarter installations in the Cirene area. Specifically these were Rommel's house and the German headquarters believed to be at Beda Littoria, the Italian HQ at Cirene and the Italian Intelligence Centre at Appollonia. In addition, they were to sabotage telephone and telegraph communications in the area. The attacks were to be carried out on the night 17/18 November, the eve of the launching of *Crusader*.

Although the actual raid was to be under the command of Keyes, Laycock was responsible for the overall supervision of *Flipper* as it was called. His plan was to divide his forces into four detachments, one for each of the objectives. They would be transported in the submarines *Torbay* and *Talisman* to a suitable point on the coast, but landed by rubber dinghy three nights before the operation was to take place, and then meet up with Jock Haselden and three other officers from G(R) Branch, who would act as guides. They would then move by night, lying up by day, make a daylight reconnaissance on the 17th and then attack at midnight that night. The submarines would be waiting to collect them from the fourth to sixth nights after the original landings had been made Laycock:

> I had originally intended to sail on Torbay with the SNO [Senior Naval Officer], but, as Capt GLENNEY 11 Commando, who was to have commanded the dets in TALISMAN, went sick at the last minute, I decided to transfer to TALISMAN, since, for security reasons, insufficient information had been passed on to this junior officer before sailing and Lt Col KEYES, who was the only other officer conversant with all the details, was accommodated in TORBAY.[19]

The party left Alexandria on the evening of 10 November and arrived off the beach four days later. That evening signals were received from Haselden, who had been infiltrated through the enemy lines by the Long Range Desert Group and then, dressed as an Arab, had made his way to the rendezvous. That night the party landed, although not without difficulty. The heavy seas made the dinghies difficult to control and, of Laycock's party, only seven men and himself got ashore. For the rest of the night and next day, the party lay up in a nearby wadi.

Laycock was now in a dilemma. He could either wait for *Talisman* to land the rest of his party, which would mean delaying the attacks, or organise a modified programme. In the event, because of the importance of co-ordinating his operations with the launching of *Crusader*, he chose the second option. Keyes was to attack Rommel's house and HQ, while Lieutenant Cook was to sabotage communications at the crossroads south of Cirene. Haselden also agreed to help out by cutting communications on the El Fridia-Slonta road. Laycock himself decided to remain behind at the RV with the reserve ammunition in the hope that the rest of his party would arrive. The detachments set off on the evening of the 15th amid torrential rain. Haselden, however, had told Laycock that he understood that Rommel and his staff officers lived in a house at Sidi Rafa and not at Beda Littoria. This was subsequently confirmed by friendly Arabs as they got near the objective, which was therefore switched. Lt Colonel Keyes detailed his party as follows:

> He himself [Keyes] with Capt CAMPBELL and Sgt TERRY were to enter and search the house. The remainder of his detachment, less a party of 3 ORs detailed to put the electric light plant out of action, being disposed so as to prevent enemy interference.
>
> 5 ORs were to watch the exits from the guard tent and car park.
>
> 2 ORs were posted outside the nearby hotel to prevent anyone leaving it and 2 ORs were placed on the road on each side of the house. The remaining 2 ORs were left to guard whichever entrance Col KEYES used to gain access to the building.
>
> All parties were in position just before midnight and a recce was made of the house. Unable to find a way through the back premises or windows, Col KEYES' party walked up to the front door and beat upon it, Capt CAMPBELL demanding access in German. The door was eventually opened by a sentry who was set upon but could not be overpowered silently and was therefore shot by Capt CAMPBELL which aroused the HQ and vicinity.
>
> Two men tried to come downstairs from the first floor but thought better of it being met by a burst of fire from Sgt TERRY's Tommy gun. No one attempted to leave the rooms on the ground floor but the lights in them were turned out.
>
> No enemy emerged from the guard tent or the Hotel but two Germans carrying lights appeared running towards the house where they were shot by our sentries.
>
> KEYES and CAMPBELL started to make a search of the ground floor but the occupants of the second room they entered were waiting for them and Lt Col KEYES who had opened the door, was met by a burst of fire

and fell back into the passage mortally wounded.

Sgt TERRY emptied 2 magazines of his Tommy gun into the darkened room and Capt CAMPBELL silenced the party by throwing in a grenade and slamming the door. Together they carried Lt Col KEYES outside where he died almost immediately. While he was attending to him, Capt CAMPBELL was hit by a stray bullet which broke his lower leg.

On the whole the enemy seems to have been taken completely by surprise and put up little resistance. Two German Staff Officers are known to have been killed and others wounded, whilst several soldiers were killed and wounded. It is however particularly unfortunate that General ROMMEL himself was absent attending a birthday party in Rome. A few shots were heard at some distance from the house, but as they did not come from the direction in which our own troops were posted, it is hoped that the enemy were shooting at each other.

Capt CAMPBELL, who was now lying wounded outside the house, ordered Sgt TERRY to concentrate the detachment and tell them to throw all their remaining grenades through any available windows before retiring to their operational RV preparatory to withdrawal to the beach. Capt CAMPBELL, realising that a superhuman effort would be required to carry him back over 18 miles of precipitous country entailing a descent of some 2,000 ft, ordered himself to be abandoned.

In the meantime the party who had attacked the electric light plant had been partially successful. Although they failed to demolish the dynamo completely, as the match head strikers for the charges had been rendered useless by the torrential rain, they nevertheless succeeded in putting it out of action by exploding a grenade on the armature.[20]

Jack Terry and seventeen others managed to get back to the RV and meet up with Laycock and his base party of three, but nothing more was heard of Cook and his group of six men.

On the evening of the 18th, *Torbay* hove to off the beach and made contact with Laycock using her Aldis lamp. Unfortunately the seas were too heavy to attempt to get off the beach in the dinghies, which had been hidden while the operation was taking place. The submarine thus agreed to return the following night and managed to get a boat ashore with food and water. Next day, having set up a position of all round defence at dawn, the party began to notice increasing enemy activity in the area from midday onwards. Firstly, Arab 'Carabinieri', then small bodies of Germans and finally Italians were spotted.

Fire was opened on the detachment and, after a couple of hours, Laycock was forced to abandon his position, with one officer, Lieutenant Prior, wounded in the thigh. He ordered his party to break up into groups of not more than three men each. They were to either make for the alternative beach, where *Talisman* would be waiting, go to the Slonta area in the hope of being picked up by the LRDG, or hide in the wadis north of Cirene until they had definite news of the progress of the main offensive. Laycock himself set off with Terry and eventually got back to British lines on Christmas Day after 41 days in the desert.* The remainder were all made prisoner or were killed by hostile Arabs.

It later transpired that the house which Keyes had raided had never been used by Rommel, although he had at one time used the one at Beda Littoria, and it was merely a logistic HQ. In any event, Rommel was in Rome and did not get back to North Africa until the 18th. As for Laycock, within a week of arriving back in friendly territory he was ordered back to England to take over command of the Special Service Brigade. *Flipper*, although unsuccessful, did, however, produce the first Commando Victoria Cross, which was posthumously awarded to Geoffrey Keyes.

Aftermath in the Middle East

Laycock's place in command of the Middle East Commando was taken by Lt Colonel J.H. Graham. By now No 51 Middle East Commando had finally arrived back in Egypt and were disbanded, although some of their members were absorbed into the Middle East Commando, as had been previously decided in October. The character of the Commando was now changing. Early in 1942 it was reorganised into squadrons, and more and more of its work came under the direction of SOE. Indeed, the title 'Commando' was only retained partly as a cover for its activities and partly to satisfy Churchill's wish to retain Commandos in the Middle East. In the North African desert they worked mainly with the LRDG, and indeed one squadron was transferred to this force. Another squadron, 'B', operated on

---

*To while away the boredom during their wanderings, Laycock read the only book he had with him, *The Wind in the Willows*, to his companion. Jack Terry's first words on reaching safety were supposed to have been: 'Thank God I shan't have to hear any more about that bloody Mr Toad!' Also, on Laycock's arrival at HQ Eighth Army a signal was sent to Oliver Lyttleton, the Minister in Cairo, stating 'Feel it would interest C-in-C and Minister to know that Laycock arrived today at 9.20 p.m. for his Christmas Dinner'. The reply was: 'Please state why Laycock was one hour 20 minutes late for his Christmas Dinner.'

the Syrian-Turkish border, preparing for covert operations should the Germans overrun Turkey. Then, with Rommel's offensive after Gazala, which drove the British right back to el Alamein, much of the unit, which was now called 1st Special Service Regiment, found itself manning defences in the Delta. Morale dropped as those who had volunteered for it increasingly felt that they were being misused. Stirling, whose SAS activities were expanding, also felt that same way and, when Churchill visited the Middle East at the beginning of August 1942, showed him a paper arguing that all special operations, apart from those of the LRDG, should be brought under his control. Churchill agreed to this and that was the end of the Commando presence in the Middle East, special operations becoming the province of the SAS.

Auchinleck did, however, begin to raise other Commando units in the Middle East in the early part of 1942. One of these, the Libyan Arab Force Commando under Lt Colonel Vladimir Peniakoff, and better known as Popski's Private Army, did very good work behind the German lines during 1942. Steps were also taken to raise a Commando squadron from Pathans serving with Indian formations in the Western Desert and to train an Afridi battalion in India for commando operations in North Africa. But these came to nothing. One other small unit raised at the same time was the Special Interrogation Group. This was made up of Palestinian German linguists who had been members of No 51 ME Commando. They, too, were designed to operate behind enemy lines, but wearing German uniforms and being equipped with Afrika Korps vehicles and weapons. They came under the command of Jock Haselden, but most were unfortunately killed, including Haselden himself, during the disastrous raid on Tobruk in September 1942, having infiltrated through the Italian lines and then been surrounded when they attempted to fight their way out again after the failure of the amphibious force.

'I am afraid that the history of the Special Service Troops out here in the Middle East has been a sad one,' wrote Dudley Clarke to a friend in MO9 in July 1941.[21] As we have seen, it remained that way, in spite of Churchill's insistence on a stay of execution for the Commandos in the Middle East. The Middle East Commandos, Layforce and their successors had suffered from a number of problems. Lack of intelligence, lack of appreciation by higher commanders as to what they were designed for, hurried and slipshod planning and confusion as to who should direct them – Royal Navy, Army or SOE –

together with the general growth of private armies at a time when high quality troops needed to be retained to compensate for casualties in regular units, all contrived to give them an undeserved bad name.

Furthermore, it must be remembered that the Commandos in the United Kingdom were the only units there that were carrying out offensive operations during this time and had a priority in getting equipment. The Middle East Commandos, on the other hand, had to compete with the forces fighting in the Western Desert, East Africa, Greece and elsewhere in a theatre where equipment was already short. Often temporarily attached to formations, they never received due recognition for their efforts. Yet, their experiences and more expecially the lessons learnt from them would not be forgotten by Laycock when he took command of the Special Service Brigade in the United Kingdom at the beginning of 1942.

CHAPTER FIVE

The Mountbatten Era
1942

At the beginning of 1942 Bob Laycock succeeded Charles Haydon as Commander Special Service Brigade, the latter going, on promotion, to become Mountbatten's deputy. For the UK Commandos, unlike their compatriots in the Middle East, 1941 had ended on a high note with the success of *Archery* and *Anklet*. Mountbatten had firmly implanted his personality on Combined Operations, and there was a feeling that 1942 would be a busy one, with less of the frustration that had marked so much of 1941.

Yet, the first operation of 1942, although very much in the character of a Commando small raid, was not mounted by the Special Service Brigade, nor, for that matter, was it anything to do with HQ Combined Operations. Operation *Curlew* was carried out by the staff and students of the V Corps School of Raiding, or, as it was more usually known for security reasons, Detachment V Corps School, Warsash. The detachment was commanded by Captain F.H.P. Barber, who had formerly been a company commander in the 7th Wilts, and the original idea was that each cadre, would, as a culmination of its four week course, carry out a small raiding operation. It had been originally intended that *Curlew* should be mounted in December 1941 at the conclusion of the first course, but unfortunately the escorting MGBs, one of whose skippers, Lieutenant Dunstan Curtis RNVR, will feature many times later in this book, were not available. The operation was therefore postponed to the following month. Pat Barber:

> Raids needed meticulous planning and rehearsal. Once an objective had been selected there was the photography by the RAF of long stretches of the French coast in order to get the most up to date information, and detailed interpretation of the aerial photographs by Intelligence and, in particular, by Major J.S. La Trobe Bateman (G2 Intelligence 5 Corps). Then the agreement of the Royal Navy to provide landing craft and escorts on the selected dates. There were not more than six nights per month when conditions of moon and tide would be suitable. Ideally there should be no moon, most of the voyage across should be performed in

darkness, the landing should take place soon after low tide in order to avoid the R-boats becoming stranded on a falling tide, and on the return voyage all the boats needed to get as far away as possible from the French Coast before daylight.[1]

This demonstrates something of the complications that surrounded any cross-Channel raid from now on, and the limiting factors explain why to mount them was easier said than done.

The object of *Curlew* was to discover the layout of the local defences in the area of the little village of St Laurent, which some two and a half years later would be the centre of *Omaha* beach, and 'gain experience in operations of this nature'.[2] It was to be commanded by Pat Barber himself, who would take with him one of his three NCOs, while the remainder of the force would be made up of the second course, three officers and ten other ranks from the 15th Welch Regiment. Brigadier Templer personally briefed all involved, and the force set out on the night 10/11 January 1942, but soon had to turn back because of bad weather. Twenty-four hours later, they tried again. The party made their trip across the Channel in MGBs, towing two R-boats, to which they transferred once close to the objective. As to what then transpired, Pat Barber wrote in his official post-raid report:

> The landing was made at the correct spot at 0100 hours* on the 18th, January 1942. There was a heavy surf which brought the Eureka in closer to the water's edge than had been expected, and which almost knocked the soldiers over as they waded towards the shore. The Beach Head party took up its position near the water's edge, and the patrol set out. The temperature was below freezing point. I accompanied the patrol, my duty being to determine the exact spot at which we landed, and then to give orders to the patrol Commander (Captain P.W. Kempson) as to his future action. We moved across about 250 yards of sand, the beach containing one furrow with about 6 inches of water in it, and then came upon snow covering the shingle. This was unexpected. I wondered whether to abandon the operation, but finally decided that I must at any rate determine where we had landed. The snow as about three inches deep, visibility up to 400 yards. We crossed the shingle, which was about 15 yards broad and came upon a narrow sand dune ridge fringing the coast . . . According to the aerial photographs some form of wire obstacle

---

*This was 1¼ hours behind schedule, and since C-in-C Portsmouth had given strict instructions that they must complete re-embarkation by 0300 hours, their time ashore was very limited.

was to be expected at this point. In actual fact, the only obstacle found was a single strand of barbed wire at the point where the shingle and sand dunes met. This wire proceeded eastwards but was fastened to a wooden frame about 18 inches square, covered by wire netting and standing a couple of inches off the ground. I examined this carefully, being uncertain whether it was some sort of booby trap, but was unable to determine anything. We proceeded on the patrol as indicated on the map, recognising and fixing our position. It was then 0145 hours. I then decided that in view of the snow and that there was only one hour to go, Captain Kempson would investigate as far as the house, which could clearly be seen some 400 yards to the east, to see whether there was any wire or sign of defences, whilst I returned to the Beach Head party having completed my share of the patrol. I now consider this plan to have been unambitious, but I accept all responsibility for it, feeling as I did owing to the lightness of the night and the tracks made in the snow, our chances of remaining undetected were slight. I rejoined the Beach Head party at 0155 to be joined a quarter of an hour later by Captain Kempson whose report accompanies mine. As far as I know, none of us had been spotted by the enemy and we had seen no signs of him.

I ordered the men to return to the R-boat but it immediately became apparent that this would not be easy. One man was knocked clean over by an incoming wave, and lost his Tommy gun which we were unable to find. Meanwhile the kedge line of the R-boat snapped and the boat was thrown broadside onto the beach. The soldiers endeavoured to refloat the boat but had to give in as legs and arms became numbed and useless from the cold. A white Very light was fired towards the boat apparently from the position on the scarp to the east of valley X. The enemy must have heard the engine of the Eureka as it endeavoured to pull off Soon after this the engine failed altogether (probably owing to a life-line being caught around the propeller). Our signals to the support Eureka were successfully understood, and it came in close. Several attempts were made to wade out to it but by this time legs and arms were so numb that no one was able to reach it. On one occasion Captain Kempson and Sergeant Fox rescued a man who had become completely exhausted, and a little later Sub. Lieutenant Turnbull did the same thing. A second Very light was fired at about 0325, this from the direction of the locality to the east of St. Laurent. All felt that this time at any rate we had been spotted, but no fire was opened and at 0340 the boats left the beach under tow from R-93. Our escape was little short of miraculous.*

---

*The Post-Raid Report was headed '*Exercise* CURLEW'. Pat Barber was very tired by the time he returned to Warsash and, in fact, got the Naval Intelligence Officer in HMS *Tormentor* to write the report for him as he dictated it. Being part of Home Forces, he was so used to heading reports 'Exercise' that in this case he thinks that it just slipped out as force of habit. Surprisingly, none of the agencies, including V Corps and COHQ, to which it was sent, spotted this.

Although the operation was not militarily successful, it proved to be a considerable fillip to morale for the troops in V Corps. Pat Barber:

> The fact that a raid had taken place and that more were expected to follow not only increased the enthusiasm in HMS *Tormentor* itself, but also greatly inspired the troops who came on the succeeding courses. No raid was planned for February, but in March we received orders for Operation *Canter* to be carried out under my command by personnel from 2 London Scottish and 8 Royal Welch Fusiliers (Courses 3 and 4). This was to be a fighting patrol with the object of ascertaining the layout of the local defences at Grand Hameau des Dunes and of bringing back a prisoner. There followed considerable interest among senior officers. Major General Dowler GOC 38 Div visited us, and the CO of the London Scottish was so enthusiastic that he volunteered to go on the raid as a member of the fighting patrol. Then, at the last moment, we heard to our disappointment that the Royal Navy had too many other commitments and were unable to provide the necessary ships.
>
> The problem was a shortage of MGBs. These magnificent crews and boats were operating at full stretch doing normal routine patrolling in the Channel. In addition they were used as escorts on raids. Furthermore at COHQ in London plans were being made for an intensive programme of large-scale raids during 1942 and HMS *Tormentor* with its protected waters and extensive boat-repair workshops was to play an increasingly important part. This meant that there would be fewer opportunities for 5 Corps troops to take part in raids, although they would still be trained in boat-drill and landing exercises – and in order to enable more troops to have this training the length of the courses was reduced from four weeks to a fortnight (with an extra fortnight in the event of a raid).[4]

The V Corps School of Raiding would mount no more raids, although Pat Barber himself would take part in the Dieppe Raid. They did, however, act as enemy to Major John Frost's company of 2nd Parachute Battalion in preparation for their famous attack on the radar station at Bruneval. The school was closed down in September 1942 when V Corps moved to Scotland to begin preparing for the North African landings.

There was another and this time, unofficial Home Forces operation a few months later. In mid-April 1942, the Prime Minister's office received a letter addressed personally to Churchill, which was written by a Sergeant P. King of the Army Dental Corps. He wrote that, frustrated in his efforts to transfer to a combat unit, he and another soldier, Private L. Cuthbertson, intended to strike their own blow against the Germans by crossing the Channel with the intention of causing £50,000 of damage to military installations and killing 50 Germans and Nazi sympathisers. By the time that Downing Street had received the letter, the two men had already gone absent from their unit, the Army Dental Corps School of Instruction at Aldershot, with two pistols and 41 rounds of ammunition. Nothing was heard from them for two months. SOE, however, were alerted, as were SIS.

In early July the two men were court-martialled, and their story came out. They had set out for Plymouth, sleeping rough and surviving on little food. Eventually, by 2 May, they had arrived on the Cornish coast, where they hired a motor boat with seven gallons of fuel and set off across the Channel. Landing near Cherbourg, they climbed a cliff, but then heard German voices and decided to try elsewhere. At this point their fuel ran out and a storm blew up, and they drifted in the Channel for the next fifteen days before being sighted by an RAF aircraft. They were then picked up by a destroyer and taken to hospital.

Although found guilty, the story had a happy ending in that King, now reduced to the ranks, was posted to the Commando Depot and Cuthbertson, who was awarded 28 days detention, to the Durham Light Infantry, thus achieving their original ambition.[5] King* joined No 4 Commando, regained his stripes and won a battlefield commission in Normandy. He finished the war as a Lieutenant with the MC.

Enter the Royal Marines

Up until the beginning of 1942, the Royal Marines had had a frustrating war. Although amphibious operations were very much a traditional role, financial stringency between the wars had led the corps away from this to a more defensive posture. The formation of the RM Brigade in January 1940 was in an effort to made amends for this, but, as we have seen, it was not ready in time to carry out amphibious operations in Norway, and as a result, the Army seized the amphibious initiative. True, ships' detachments of Royal Marines did see action in Norway, and small parties fought in the defence of Calais in May 1940. The first operational opportunity

---

* Because he had to be a member of a combatant corps before he joined the Commandos, he elected to transfer to the Duke of Cornwall's Light Infantry on the grounds that it was from Cornwall that he had set out on his unofficial raid.

that the RM Brigade had was in the abortive expedition to Dakar in August 1940, and in that same month it was decided to form a Royal Marine Division by splitting the existing brigade into two and raising a third from scratch. Two of these brigades, 101 (3 and 5 RM Bns) and 102 (1 and 2 RM Bns, 8 Argylls), spent much of 1941 in Scotland standing by for *Pilgrim*, while the third, 103 (7, 8, 9 RM Bns) remained non-operational in Wales.

With the occupation in Crete in autumn 1940, it was decided in January 1941, to send the MNBDO there and raise a second one. It arrived at Suez towards the end of April, and part, under Major General Weston, fought in the Battle for Crete, with many, like Layforce, who came under Weston during the closing stages, being made prisoner. The remainder of MNBDO I remained in the Middle East, and one battalion, 11 RM, did carry out a small raid on the island of Kupho off Crete and the disastrous operation against Rommel's rear at Tobruk in September 1942.

With the RM Division still languishing in the United Kingdom, and the prospects for *Tonic* fading, Mountbatten believed that here was a ready source for new Commando units, especially since the War Office was clearly opposed to drawing off further Home Forces volunteers to raise additional Army Commandos. The Admiralty agreed that a Royal Marine Commando could be formed from volunteers from the RM Division, and in mid February 1942 it came into being at Deal in Kent, with Lt Colonel J. Picton Phillips RM* as the Commanding Officer. One item of note was that it did include an Army element, as a section of 8 Argylls was allowed to volunteer for it.

Achnacarry

Up until 1942 each Commando had been responsible for training its own men. Inevitably this meant that there was a marked variation in standards and, in order to put Commando training on a more formal footing, Brigadier Charles Haydon decided that it should become centralised. The place selected for this was Achnacarry, a country house and estate and home of the Chief of the Clan Cameron of Lochiel, situated some fourteen miles from Fort William in Invernessshire. Initially called the Commando Depot and, later the Commando Basic Training Centre, it came into being in February 1942. To command it, Haydon selected Major C.E. Vaughan MBE The Buffs, who had been Admin Officer of 3SS Battalion and then

---

* He had been Adjutant of the ISTDC before the war.

Second-in-Command of No 4 Commando. From now on, apart from initially the early Royal Marine Commandos, all Commando troops would do the Achnacarry course.

One of the early students to pass through Achnacarry was Captain Joe Nicholl MC, later of No 2 Commando, and he has left a very vivid account, written in the third person, of what it was like:

As always the telegrams had arrived late, and so did Joe. It was about 6.30 on a pleasant evening that the train slowed into the wayside halt which went by the name of Spean Bridge. A single utility was waiting in the station yard and Joe was the only passenger to alight. The driver merely inquired if he had any luggage, and without more than a perfunctory reply to Joe's bombardment of questions, drove him along the hump-backed road through glorious Highland scenery (or so it seemed to Joe on that evening). The road ran for about 7 miles past the long strip of the Inverness Canal and the browning tints of the woods in the foothills, somewhere beneath Ben Nevis. Achnacarry itself was simply the Castle belong to Campbell Cameron of Lochiel, partly gutted by fire, but still typically Scottish Baronial in architectural style.

The atmosphere in the Mess was one entirely new to Joe. There was a notable lack of interest in any newcomer. The Adjutant was hearty and disinterested, but even more hearty was the Commandant, the more rigid disciplinarian, Colonel Charles Vaughan. Outside, the training was continuous. It was extraordinarily exhilarating, just because it was different. Anything novel was tried out, and if a failure discarded. The Officers were as the men for training, and were attached to the different Sections of the different training troops. The only exception was that when drilling on the square, the Officers were expected to assist the Guards Sergeants by remaining aloof and decorative, but not interfering in any way. For P.T. all were stripped to the waist, wearing only denim trousers and boots and gaiters. The exercises were designed to strengthen muscles, rather than simply to get fit. Joe had to learn to handle a length of Scots pine in such a way that, with 8 men underneath, it could be thrown over the head to the other arm. In fact, the team spirit came to be accepted, whether they realised it or not.

Everything had a purpose. Unarmed combat was not just an attempt to learn judo in 3 easy lessons. Nothing was taught that couldn't be learnt and practised by the weakest or dimmest – and put into practice on the toughest. A Toggle rope bridge was an astonishing contraption. With the aid of anything up to 40 of these lengths of rope with an eye at one end and a small smoothed stick at the other, attached together, a three-span bridge could be made and fitted across a swiftly-flowing burn. It was perhaps difficult to see how use could be made of this contraption in warfare, but doubtless there were those who put it into operation.* The trickiness of trying to cross with full equipment and rifle slung around the neck, while hanging on to the guide ropes or pressing them apart as the body swung dangerously, was only fully appreciated when watching someone else doing it.

The Death Slide consisted of wire stretched across the stream from 20ft up in one tree down to a low tree stump on the other side. On the Courses with Joe were a crowd of police who had been allowed to volunteer for Commando work after a very short spell in the ranks. They were first rate material, and were to make some of the finest Commando soldiers, but some of them found the rapid foot movement something entirely new, and something for which they were physically unsuited. So the tenacity with which they stuck to it was all the finer. . . . The Speed March was an organised attempt to get a Troop a distance of 15 miles in three hours. It was not a race, but it was deemed a failure if any member of the Troop had to fall out. All were fully equipped and carried rifles or tommy guns. The unfortunates who had been selected to carry the Bren guns were usually helped by others in the Section, or by the Officer, who in any case was expected to be that amount fitter than his men and to set a good example. Eventually this almost became a 'moral obligation'. As a team exercise it was first rate, as well as being planned so that an average rate for each mile was kept up, and any dropping below that meant picking it up again later on. Those Troops which went off too fast to begin with, nearly always found themselves staggering in in a long staggering line. And as often as not Charlie Vaughan was there to see that no Troop returned through *his* gates in anything but perfect Guards' formation. The route to Spean Bridge and back (7½ miles each way) was impossibly hilly, but it did mean that a swift walk up the inclines left the Section the joy of trotting down the other side. Only it did 'throw you into your boots so', as one Policeman expressively put it.

The 'Opposed Landing' was a timed exercise from the boat house. Four Goatley boats, each containing a Sub-section of 7 or 8 men paddled themselves out into the loch and aimed for the shore about a quarter of a mile away. Rifles, etc., were piled in the bottom of the boat, and the paddlers sat on the wooden-slatted canvas sides at their peril. Arms only were to appear over the sides – and if more appeared, then stentorian shouts reached the craft from the shore, and a burst of MG fire came from Bren guns firing on fixed lines. The tracer bullets were made to hit the water unhealthily close to the craft.

As they came close to the shore grenades were hurled into the shallow water and smoke canisters or grenades ignited. Into those shallows the leading men jumped, and then pulled the craft in until all could jump clear. Then began a wild race. Machine Gunners rushed the Brens

---

* Incidents of this are described later in the book.

forward on to a mound, and fired at white metal plates on the opposite hill. The assaulting troops ran round the trees into a quagmire to get into position.

When the gunners had hit sufficient plates, Instructors yelled at the party to assault. Rushing, squelching, scrambling up the sodden ground, they reached a flat stretch. At the further end there were more plates. 'Get flat! Fire!' With the breath knocked out of them, they tried to hold their aim and hit these pestilential plates. 'Hit them!' Still those bounding white objects stood. At least they could rush forward to bayonet a row of straw-filled sacks. 'In, out. Hit 'em as though you meant it!'

Immediately there was a shout, 'Get back. The white Very's gone up!' Down they slithered, stormed and shouted at, to the beach, linked up with their Bren gunners and pushed out into the Loch. In came the grenades again – and as they paddled frantically away, the Brens, firing on fixed lines, opened up again. (It was fascinating feeling the tracer near enough to splash the paddles (sometimes even to splinter them, or knock them out of their owner's hands), and watching the ricochet whining away into the distance, or seeming to strike into the hillside of heather on the other isde of the Loch. But reality came back on the second attempt, when the previous time had to be beaten, and every thought was eliminated except the struggle to get that ungainly, wretched craft through the water at greater speed. Fortunately this was Joe's final one, because on the very next one there occurred one of the only fatal accidents of the Course. One was was killed and another wounded when their boat sheered off course into the fire of that Bren.

Abseiling was a new 'sport' to be learnt. A party climbed to the top of the baronial tower of Achnacarry House, and found a rope firmly attached to a ring in the floor. The rest of the rope was paid out over the edge of the parapet. Merely to look over that edge down to the tarmac of the drive 40ft. below, made Joe feel quite, sick. He watched the Instructor wrapping the rope round him to demonstrate. With no head for heights this was sheer murder – but like all the other items in the Vaughan circus, it had to be done. Joe wrapped the rope round; gingerly he tried to take the strain, and then lowered himself over the side very carefully until his feet were against the outside wall and his free hand grimly holding the parapet. 'Let go with your left hand and hold the rope in front of you. Right, now let go the right hand and pay out the rope behind you. Lean out! You can't fall!' Never had he felt less like obeying the Instructor. After an eternity of moving down by little jerks, a voice yelled, 'You can jump now'. Tensed for the big jump, and too terrified to look down he fell the last four feet to the ground! He was shaking all over.

'Me and my Pal' provided a real team effort. Armed with Tommy guns with full magazines and two grenades, two men would start for the first 'mock-up' of the front of a house. As one man moved, the other watched. As soon as one of the carboard figures appeared, pulled out at the tug of a wire by an Instructor, 'Jack' had to fire. Then 'Bill' would rush forward, break the imaginary glass of the window with the butt of his Tommy gun, and throw an imaginary grenade. He waited 2 seconds, and then hurled himself over the window-sill, with Jack following closely. As they came out on the other side, Jack sprinted across to the wall, covered by Bill. Here it was a bit tricky for one to keep an eye on the other while he scrambled over the wall. Then came 'grenade confidence'. Each had to throw a 4-second grenade, and watch it land in the ditch below before taking cover. The first throw and glimpse was always very rapid. The second became almost casual.

Towards the end of the month, and all too soon, came the attack on Feddon. In Field Service Marching Order and with twenty-four hours rations in bulk, all Troops marched out for the Highlands. It was sleeting, and there was snow on the hills they were heading for. Commando soldiers were not expected to wear great-coats, so it was a question of a multitude of sweaters, and a gas-cape on top. By mid-afternoon Feddon was sighted by someone out in front. Joe's Troop was painfully in reserve. They sat down, huddled together behind their gas capes. Every now and then they were told to move. At last a blast of wind bit into their faces, and they marched up the saddle leading into the narrow gulley that housed Feddon. It proved to be a stone hut or so, long disposed of as a human habitation by the monthly attacks of weary Commando soldiers in training. They sat down to eat the cheese from their ration, – the only part that didn't need cooking. Then it was on and on.

When the night came down, Joe fondly believed they were lost. In every direction there stretched the bare hillsides. But as the moon came out they could see, far below them, the waves of a Loch – the question was, which . . . ? Fortunately, too, the stars appeared to give a line of direction. At last someone decided on the true position, and the march continued. They found a dis-used quarry about 4 miles from Achnacarry, and in the early hours of the morning settled down to getting warm and dry by the light of a bonfire. Each officer and man held his dixie with a slab of steak in it, to the flames. Some got burnt to a cinder, others could only get theirs half done, but every one had to lump it, because the rain was already damping the flames, and there was a danger of the gas-capes catching fire. For a couple of hours everyone lay down until it was time to march back and in through the gates of Achnacarry at 9 o'clock. There had to be a certain amount of fiddling and dawdling, as no-one was allowed in before then.

The rest of the morning was free, but there was an attempt at a cross-country run in the afternoon. The following morning brought Charlie Vaughan's *pièce de résistance* – the All-in Boxing competition. Each Section of each Troop had to provide 7 men. They were graded very casually according to height and weight, but as there were no scales, it was pretty vague. The ring was set up round a patch of grass, and Col. Vaughan solemnly took his place behind a table, with a red and a green flag in front of him. The seven unfortunates from two Sections were lined up against each other. A gong was hit and the two heavy weights got through the ropes and waded into each other for 1 minute. Then the gong was struck again, then the Col raised a red or a green flag to signify the winner, and the next two went into battle. . . .

The next day the Course ended. There was no formal Passing Out. About two or three men had had to be R.T.U. [Returned to Unit] because they were physically unfit. The remainder were given 7 days Leave before joining their Commandos.[6]

Saint Nazaire

When the Germans overran France in summer 1940, one of the major benefits which accrued to them was the ability to use the French Atlantic ports in order to wage an unceasing attack against Britain's vital supply line with North America, the Atlantic. The focus of their campaign quickly switched from the Baltic to France, and the U-boat bases at Brest, Lorient, La Rochelle, St Nazaire and Bordeaux were established. There was also the threat to Allied convoys from German capital ships, but crucial to having them based in the French ports was the dry dock at St Nazaire, the only one of its size capable of taking major warships. If this could be destroyed, it would do much to deny the French ports to German capital ships.

Early in 1942 it was agreed that this should become a Commando target, and Lt Colonel Charles Newman of No 2 Commando was selected to command the raid. He began his detailed planning in February, having been given two objectives – destruction of the dry dock and also inflicting as much damage as possible to the U-boat installations and the docks in general. The best way to achieve the first, it was decided, would be to ram and destroy the dock gates, and for this an old destroyer, one of the fifty 'four stackers' which the United States had given the Royal Navy in exchange for bases in the Caribbean in autumn 1940, HMS *Campbeltown* (ex USS *Buchanan*), was offered up by the Admiralty.

The general destruction required would also need specially trained demolition parties, and it was decided that, while No 2 Commando would provide the main force of 100 men, with responsibility for neutralising the defences in the docks and providing close protection to the demolition parties, the latter would be formed from volunteers from Nos 1, 3, 4, 5, 9 and 12 Commandos. A further problem to be solved was the fact that St Nazaire is situated on the estuary of the River Loire, and the only deep channel approach to it was known to be covered by four coastal batteries. Otherwise it was a question of overcoming the mudflats, only possible at high tide with very shallow draught craft. Therefore, instead of using ALCs launched from landing ships, motor launches would be used instead. Sixteen of these were made available, together with one MGB and an MTB, all under command of Commander R.E.D. Ryder RN.

In early March, the Commandos, who had been doing their training in Scotland, boarded the *Princess Josephine Charlotte* and sailed round the west coast of Scotland to the Cornish port of Falmouth, which had been selected as the mounting base. An elaborate cover story had been created that the force was designed for antisubmarine sweeps, and that the Commandos were being sent overseas – items of tropical kit were purposely left lying about. A dress rehearsal was carried out against Devonport dockyard, which bore some resemblance to St Nazaire. This was not a success, but invaluable for all that. For the Commandos, confined as they were to the ship for reasons of security it was a time of increasing tension. From the diary of Captain Bertie Hodgson of No 2 Commando:

March 24th Feeling really 100% fit now. Saw 2 Hunt Class destroyers and HMS *Campbeltown* arrive during the evening – a welcome sight too. Busy after dinner, orders, demolition charges to be made up. Slept like a log and dreams not too horrible for a change – I've reached the excitement stage at the moment. I wonder how long it will last!

March 25th Great Activity – dumps for stores to be made ready for loading on to ML – completed Operations Orders for the group. I do hope they will work out OK, there's a lot to think about. . . . Off jobs in the afternoon, such as checking ammunition, stores, food, etc. – for the journey.

Became more and more active as the evening drew on, eventually finished final Orders at 12.30 feeling rather tired but full of beans. Everybody has been in great form and worked like blacks, particularly CO [Newman], Major Bill [Copland] and the RSM [Moss], all darned well in need of leave – like me!

March 26th Holy Communion at 7.30 with Naval Chaplain on Fore-Deck, sun shining from East and tankers passing up and down alongside the ship. Rather enjoyed the whole scene and during service wondered why people wanted to take Communion on such occasions as these, it must be because one finds some sort of help and satisfaction out of the ceremony. I rather like it I admit, and soothing. I was wondering if it really did make any difference to talk to God and ask for a safe return, probably not, but nevertheless it's a wee bit comforting.

After breakfast more rushing around and packing up, etc. A rousing speech by Charles Newman which put morale up to 100% – he really is a fine chap and all of us realise how much he has done to make the job a success. If anyone has been patient, helpful and charming the whole time, it was he. Just before parading on deck some letters arrived on board with medical orderlies from HQ at Ayr. . . .

We left the PJC (*Princess Josephine Charlotte*) about midday in 'R' boats*, all the crew wishing us 'bon voyage'. Boarded ML 10 [447]† and fixed up stores, weapons etc. After two false starts, eventually sailed out of Falmouth in glorious sunshine. Well, here it is – the day we've been waiting for for two years for most of us. . .

Busy in the afternoon handing out grenades, ammunition, etc. Everyone in high spirits all the time. I feel more confident now than I have ever felt during the last fortnight, but I still pray that we are allowed to touch land and have a scrap – if we don't the men will go crazy poor devils.

Very smooth water, good dinner, sardines and bully beef stew. Clear moon and sky and, after talking to Lieutenant Briault (commanding the ML) went to sleep at about 11 o'clock.'

The flotilla sailed on through the night and by dusk on the 27th were beginning to close in on the French coast. One engine of *ML 447* then packed up, and Hodgson and his party had to transfer to *ML 446*.

Awful scramble to get stores, etc, transferred. We lost some distance but attempted to catch up. We spent about one and three quarter hours looking for them vainly (the rest of the flotilla) – it has been one of the most horrible occasions in my life. Watching till the eyes ached, somehow I couldn't believe I could be cheated of this job at the crucial moment. We have at last sighted the MLs and hope to get back in position for the attack. Lovely moon and conditions perfect. Have now really arrived in position as before. Submarine and destroyers left behind.

Here we go 'nearer St Nazaire to thee'. I feel so relieved now that most of my apprehensions and fears have gone. . . .'

Sadly, these were the last words that Hodgson ever wrote. His ML came under heavy fire and he was killed, along with most of those with him, before they could get ashore.

---

* Eurekas.

† '10' was the operational number given to this ML for the raid. She was actually ML 447.

The flotilla itself was led by Newman and Ryder in *MGB 314*. Following them came two MLs armed with torpedoes, and then the *Campbeltown*, commanded by Lt Commander S.H. Beattie RN, with Copland to direct the Commando landing, two assault and five demolition parties, and a 3in mortar group. Behind them came two parallel lines of MLs carrying further assault, demolition and close protection parties. With the fact that *Campbeltown*'s funnels had been cut down to make her resemble a German torpedo boat, the use of a German speaking Petty Officer and knowledge of the German naval code, the flotilla managed to negotiate the channel and get close to the docks with only desultory fire from the Germans. This was also helped by an attack mounted by RAF Bomber Command. Then, as *Campbeltown*, now steaming at maximum speed, approached the dock gates, fire broke out in earnest. Lieutenant S.W. Chant of No 5 Commando, who was commanding one of the demolition parties on board *Campbeltown*:

A light cannon or heavy machine gun fired over us from our port bow and was joined in quick succession by Bofors type gun heavy machine guns and coastal batteries of 6" guns. The fire lasted between five and ten minutes. At that time four MLs very quickly blew up. The 'CAMP-BELTOWN' was repeatedly hit by all types of shells including three direct hits from the 6" guns. Two hits were on the bows which rapidly caught fire, one blew the 12 pounder gun off the bows killing all the crew. Some of the Oerlikon gun crews were also killed. I was lying amidships on deck abaft the aft funnel. Several of the Army personnel were wounded and some killed. I would estimate that total number of casualties during the run in at 75% of those on deck, most of these being wounded, though this did not mean that they were out of action. The noise from our own Oerlikon was terrific; they were firing just over our heads. I sustained two shrapnel wounds in the right arm and left leg and these slowed down my movements. This was generally the case with those wounded who were not too incapacitated to move at all. The next thing I realised was our hitting the boom. This was signified to me by a slight shudder of the ship and a moment later we came to an abrupt stop and there we were jammed in the middle of the Dry Dock gates.[8]

Campbeltown struck the gates at 0134 hours and the main task had been achieved. Now it was the turn of the demolition parties.

Charles Newman and his headquarter group were put ashore, but RSM Moss's group, which was supposed to secure the position on shore selected for the HQ group, failed to land, their ML being blown up and all killed. While the surviving assault parties began to tackle the German gun positions, the demolition parties went about their work. Lieutenant Chant:

> We climbed from the bows down some scaling ladders already lowered by the crew of the 'CAMPBELTOWN' and jumped on to the Dry Dock gate. We then ran like hell to the Pumping Station where we found that Captain Roy's party had killed the crews of the guns on the roof and was in the process of destroying the guns . . . I went on to tackle the big steel door barring our access to the interior of the Pumping Station.
>
> We blew this in with a slam type ready-made 4oz plastic charge, then I entered the Pumping Station with Lieut Hopkins who had left the 'CAMPBELTOWN' with me. He accompanied me to the impellor pumps 40ft below . . . .
>
> The impellor pumps were made of heavy iron castings and the charges laid at the most delicate and intricate parts of the machinery which were most difficult to replace. These charges were in turn connected from the four main and two subsidiary pumps to two parallel connecting fuses. This task completed. I sent all my party but Sgt Dockerill upstairs to warn the neighbouring troops that the explosion would take place in 90 seconds. I then pulled the two percussion igniters attached to the main fuses and raced upstairs with Sgt Dockerill. I retained Sgt Dockerill with me in case my wounds would prevent me from firing the charge. He helped me all the way up the stairs. I think there were about 8 flights and we had great difficulty in keeping to the staircase due to the fact that the building was in complete darkness. All we had in the way of light were small torches attached to our webbing equipment.
>
> We raced outside and lay on the ground about 20 yards away . . . in the open on concrete paving. A few seconds later the explosion took place and with sufficient force to break glass windows and blow outwards the concrete blocks which had been placed there by the Germans to reinforce the building against bomb damage.[9]

Two other demolition parties succeeded in wrecking the Winding Station and the other gate into the dry dock, but, because of casualties, the remaining teams failed to reach other gates and bridges which had been earmarked as demolition targets. The various parties now began to pull back towards the outer dock in order to re-embark in the MLs, firing increasing in intensity. Chant:

> Running alongside the Old Entrance, I saw an ML which had taken on board Lieut Smalley and his demolition party drawing out into mid-stream, hard astern. It was being hit by heavy fire from all quarters and

did not stop when I shouted to it to take us on board as well. I susb-
sequently heard that it blew up in midstream and Lieut Smalley and
some others were killed; the remainder swam ashore and were taken
prisoner.

Chant and his party now made their way to Charles Newman's HQ,
who said:

> 'This is where we walk home. All the boats have been blown up or are
> gone'. He called all officers to him and an all-round protective screen
> was formed by the troops. This was about 0245. . . We then numbered
> about 70 officers and men all told, of whom at least 60% were wounded.

It was decided to fight into the town and then try and break out into
the countryside beyond. They were making good progress in the
face of constant German opposition, when daylight caught them,
and they were forced to go to ground in a café. There they were
discovered and made prisoner.

Chant, who had been wounded once more and been unable to
carry on, had his wounds dressed by the Germans.*

> There were at this time a great number of German officers and high
> party officials crossing over into the dock area in cars, all of whom
> stopped to look at us and I was asked by a German officer through an
> interpreter who was a German sailor, 'How the hell did you ever manage
> to get up here?' I replied 'We just got here' and the German said, 'Well
> it beats us how you managed it.' The surprise of the Germans was most
> marked.

This was intensified, when towards midday, 5 tons of explosives concealed with a time fuse in *Campbeltown*'s bows went up, killing many
of those who had come to inspect the damage. Further confusion
followed in the late afternoon of the next day when two delayed
action torpedoes fired by the two leading MLs during the initial
approach also went up.

Only the supporting destroyers, five MLs and the MGB made it
back across the Channel. The human cost, too, had been high. The
Royal Navy suffered 85 killed or missing, with a further 106 captured,
while out of the 241 Commandos who took part, 59 were posted as
killed or missing and 109 captured. This did not include the many

---

* Because of his wounds, he was repatriated at the end of 1943.

who were wounded. Yet, for good reason has Operation *Chariot* been dubbed 'the greatest raid of all'. The bravery of those who took part was recognised by no less that 83 awards for bravery, including five Victoria Crosses. These were awarded to Beattie, Ryder and Newman, and posthumously to Sergeant Durrant of No 1 Commando, and Able Seaman Savage, both for manning guns on board the MLs until the last. A further 51 officers and men were Mentioned in Despatches. In addition, the dry dock was out of action until the end of the war, and, indeed was not repaired until the Fifties, thus effectively preventing the Germans from maintaining capital ships on the Atlantic coast.

The success of St Nazaire encouraged the mounting of a similar, although smaller scale operation at the beginning of June 1942, Operation *Foxrock*. This involved 100 all ranks of No 12 Commando, who were given the mission of destroying lock gates, a railway bridge and other installations at St Valéry-en-Caux at the north of the Somme Canal. They set out on the night of 1/2 June, but wireless intercepts indicated that German aircraft had spotted the force when it was 25 miles south of Dungeness and they turned back. No second attempt was made since attention was now concentrated on Dieppe.

There was no pause for breath after St Nazaire. At the beginning of April it was the turn of 100 members of Nos 1 and 6 Commandos under Lt Colonel Will Glendinning. They embarked in the *Queen Emma* and *Princess Beatrix*, fresh back from West Africa. They were disguised as Spanish merchantmen, but had the support of five destroyers. The object was to land at the mouth of the River Adour, by Bayonne, and attack military and economic targets and destroy merchant shipping. After cruising off the Spanish coast, they attempted a landing on 5 April, but found their approach blocked by a sand bar. *Myrmidion* was therefore aborted and the party returned home without incident. Then, a few days later, on the night of 11/12 April, in Operation *JV*, Captain Montanaro and Trooper Preece Royal Tank Regiment of 101 Troop paddled their canoe into Boulogne harbour and succeeded in blowing up a German tanker, which had previously been damaged in a torpedo attack by *MTB 45*, with limpet mines. This they achieved even though their canoe had sprung a leak and indeed they were picked up at the moment of sinking by *ML102*. For this Montanaro was awarded the DSO and Preece the DCM. Sadly the Germans, believing that it had been the work of the French resistance, executed one hundred Frenchmen as a reprisal. At the end of the month 101 Troop was merged into the newly formed No 2 SBS under Roger Courtney, who had returned from the Middle East in December. This was initially based at Ardrossan-Saltcoats.

The final operation in April was *Abercromby*. The target for this was Hardelot village, and the object was to reconnoitre the beaches, capture prisoners and inflict as much damage to the defences as possible, including the destruction of a searchlight battery. Selected for it were 100 men of No 4 Commando and 50 from the Canadian Carlton and York Regiment under the overall command of Major The Lord Lovat, 2ic of No 4. The first attempt on the night 18/19 April had to be aborted because rough weather caused the ALCs, which were being towed by MGBs, to take in water and the party returned to Dover. The weather also prevented another attempt on the night 20/21 April, but the next day saw an improvement and that night the party set out again, planning to make two landings. For the first time a new type of landing craft was used, the Landing Craft Support (LCS), which was armed with two machine guns and a mortar, and was designed, as its name suggests to give fire support to the landing parties.

The northern landing by Lord Lovat's own group was achieved without any enemy opposition, and it was only when they reached the sand dunes above the beach that searchlights, Very lights and parachute flares were seen. The Canadians, however, because of a navigational error which brought them to a position north rather than south of Lord Lovat's landing, failed to get ashore. As for Lovat's party, the deep sand in the dunes, combined with a mass of wire entanglements, resulted in slow progress. Machine guns opened up from the flanks and fire from the two LCSs partially neutralised them, but although the Commandos came across several bunkers, none was occupied. Indeed, only three Germans were encountered, but the Commando sentry challenged too early, allowing them to escape before they could be dealt with. Lovat sent out a fighting patrol to attack the searchlight battery, but, although they successfully located it, that old enemy time meant that they could not carry out the attack, and the party withdrew and re-embarked without incident. As Lovat wrote in his report:

> The German troops located in the area seem to have been badly trained and put up a very half-hearted resistance. Those in the sand dune area, even assuming that our initial landing came as a surprise, had ample time to regroup their defences and organise a strong

counter attack or bring up light machine guns to harass the final re-embarkation. From the number of lights seen it was more than apparent that there was a considerable amount of military activity afoot in the area, yet all patrols reported that although they covered a great deal of ground in which they found bunkers and pill box defences recently occupied, yet in no case (except for a certain amount of dropping fire) did they come across any real determined opposition. The impression of the raid as far as I was concerned was that we had been lucky not to be shot up from the commanding high ground to our North and from the tops of the sand dunes all along the coast during the re-embarkation.[10]

There was now a pause in the raiding programme as far as the UK based Commandos were concerned, but several thousand miles away No 5 Commando were taking part in the first of the major Allied landing operations, which would now increasingly become the main Commando role.

Madagascar

Churchill had first thought of Madagascar as a possible naval base in early December 1941. With the Japanese invasion of Malaya, the loss of Singapore in February 1942 and the resultant incursion of Japanese submarines into the Indian Ocean, the island assumed more importance. The greatest fear was that the Vichy French, who held it, would allow the Japanese to use the port of Diego Suarez in the north of the island as a naval base, which would pose a grave threat to the convoys bringing reinforcements to the Middle East. Consequently, in early March, plans were hastily drawn up for its capture and the operation was given the name *Ironclad*. Rear Admiral Syfret was appointed Force Commander, with Major General Robert Sturges, who had been commanding the RM Division up until then, the Land Force commander. 29 Infantry Brigade (Brigadier (later Field Marshal) Frankie Festing) was selected as the main assault formation, with No 5 Commando (Lt Colonel Sanguinetti) being placed under command. On 23 March, the force sailed, with the assault troops in the hastily converted transports *Winchester Castle*, *Duchess of Atholl* and *Sobieski*, as well as the assault ships *Keren* and *Karanji*, which No 5 Commando knew well from the previous year's training.

After they arrived at Durban on 22 April, there was a short pause for breath and final preparations were made for the landings, which were to take place on 5 May. The plan was for the main assault to be made on two beaches on the north-west coast and then for 29 Brigade to strike north-east across country in order to seize Diego Suarez. No 5 Commando's task was to make a silent landing a few hours before the main assault went in in order to neutralise two artillery batteries. This they did, achieving complete surprise and capturing some 300 prisoners with only very light casualties. Then they joined in the capture of Diego Suarez, which, after a brief naval bombardment, fell two days later. It was hoped that this might lead to the capitulation of the rest of the French forces on the island, but this did not occur and a further series of amphibious operations took place in September, once Diego Suarez had been made fully operational and reinforcements brought in.

These were to consist of landings at Majunga and Tamatave, on the west and east coasts respectively, and then an advance on the capital, Tananrive. A number of feints were also to be made at various points. One of these involved No 6 Troop, who landed from the destroyer HMS *Napier* with a party of soldiers at Morandava in order to deflect enemy attention away from the Majunga landing. The fort here was quickly occupied and the French flag hauled down. This was then seized by the wife of the Commandant, who to the Commandos' amazement proceeded to wrap herself in it. One Commando, who was a fluent French speaker, as well as being a good mimic, then proceeded to imitate the Commandant in a telephone call to the capital, pretending that a larger force had landed than was really so, but was caught out when the French staff officer at the other end asked him the name of the Governor's eldest daughter. Nevertheless, Majunga, which also involved No 5, was secured on 8 September, and the advance against Tananrive started.

On the 18th, after the Vichy French had rejected British armistice terms, came the landing at Tamatave. Here the Commando was embarked in four destroyers, which opened fire on the port after a French refusal to surrender. They put the Commando ashore on an isolated quay and, after some spasmodic street fighting, the garrison gave in. Tananrive was entered on the 23rd, but there was still resistance in the south of the island. For a while, one party of No 5 Commando under the Second-in-Command found themselves operating on horseback, but then it was decided to leave the final subjugation to other troops. Not until 5 November did resistance finally cease, but by that time No 5 Commando was just arriving back in the United Kingdom.

In spite of the time taken to finally subdue the French on

Madagascar, the operation, mounted as it was from a base 9,000 miles away, was successful. This was espcially so from No 5 Commando's point of view. They had spear-headed the landings, had the opportunity to use their initiative and could now finally consider themselves operationally experienced.

Enter the RN Commandos

Ironclad was the first of the major British amphibious landings. One vitally important aspect, which was quickly realised, was the need to control the landing of craft, troops and supplies on the beaches themselves. This had been a Royal Navy responsibility from the outset, but the original concept was that these landing parties should be affiliated to a particular assault ship. Thus, for *Ironclad*, the five or six parties which took part were known as the *Keren* party, the *Karangi* party etc. Just after the amphibious force had sailed for Madagascar, however, COHQ decided that the beachhead units would be more effective if organised in a different way. Also, since their members required at least some of the Commandos' skills, as well as a clear understanding of how they operated, they should undergo specialised training.

Therefore, in the spring of 1942, the RN Beachhead Commandos began to be set up. In order not to confuse them with the Army or Royal Marine Commandos, they were given letter designations, using the Services' phonetic alphabet of the time. First to be formed were *Charlie, Dog, Easy, Fox* and *George*, while those involved in the Madagascar operations were termed *Able* and *Baker*. In the event, *Baker* existed just as a paper unit, since there were only sufficient personnel in Madagascar to form one RN Commando. Each was commanded by a lieutenant commander or lieutenant, who was the Principal Beachmaster, and had three sections each of two officers, Beachmaster and Assistant Beachmaster, a petty officer and 17 ratings, which was later increased to 22.

They had their own training base at Ardentinny in Scotland, which was entitled HMS *Armadillo*. John Hill, who was to join *How*, describes something of the way in which they were prepared for their specialised and very vital role:

> There is little point in going through the manual of Commando training nor of reciting the litany of endurance; aching muscles, sleeping in wet clothes, and never, never enough sleep. It is all old hat now. Sufficient to say we were hardened, body and soul, by a gang of sadists posing as Training Staff . . . .

Together with the landing craft crews we exercised invasion drill along the shores of Loch Long at Blairmore, Coulport and Strone; sometimes speed-marching overland to Ardkinglas on Loch Fyne, to do beach drill with the Army. Sometime in April [1943] we were warned of a night exercise, due in a week's time, in which battle conditions would be simulated. When the day came we trooped aboard the landing craft at Ardentinny and as we three had not as yet been allocated to any Beach Party, we were each put on a different LCI to take part and learn.

As the signal rocket curved upwards, exploding against a black, moonless background, the craft moved off, one at a time and as silently as possible, in line ahead, keeping station about fifty yards astern of the preceding LCA.

The fireworks started as the small fleet passed Gairletter Point. Bren guns hammered a hostile greeting from the shore, their tracers arching in a graceful parabola over the line of boats, but not too far over. Pretty but not impressive seemed to be the general opinion, but when a fast motor vessel began to dart among the LCAs chucking thunderflashes and plastic percussion grenades into the landing craft, people became a little more tense. Someone in the boat ordered everyone to keep their heads down as the Gunnery Officer's launch was close alongside. We all obeyed. Then I remember a blinding flash and, perhaps a few seconds later, awoke to find myself flapping up and down on my belly like a salmon. Blinded and semi-conscious I lay there until we reached the shore, where, without exception, everyone leaving the boat stumbled over me in their rush down the ramp. The last man, bless his heart, cursed, looked down, and then helped me ashore where he left me in charge of the Beachmaster. Full consciousness returned as someone shone a torch in my face and it appeared there was a ring of giants gazing indifferently down upon me as I struggled to rise. A sort of rumbling chorus advised me to stay where I was till the Doc came. It transpired that the shapes belonged to Charles Vaughan and some of the Achnacarry staff who were attending the exercise as observers. Doc Bonner spent most of that night picking bits of plastic grenade out of my face, plus two small steel balls from my shoulder. God knows where they came from.[11]

By the end of 1943 no less than 22 RN Commandos had been formed, of which the last, *William*, was an all Canadian unit. They were to serve in every theatre of war from now on, and play a leading role in all amphibious operations.

Later in 1942, the RAF formed Servicing Commandos, whose task was to service newly captured airfields. Although they wore the Combined Operations flash, they were very much more under the Air Ministry, and COHQ had little responsibility for them.

No 10 (Inter Allied) Commando

No 10 Commando, as was explained in Chapter One, was originally to have been formed from troops in Northern Command, but there were not sufficient volunteers forthcoming at the time, and it was left in abeyance. By early 1942, however, there was a build up of agitation from the free forces of the countries of Occupied Europe stationed in Britain to form Commando units, very much because they saw them as a valuable adjunct to their own armed forces. There was also the advantage that these men, speaking the language and knowing the countryside, would be invaluable in both raiding operations and during the liberation of their respective countries when the time came. Indeed, the Dutch had already formed their own Commando troop towards the end of March 1942. Its members did the Achnacarry course in April and also carried out attachments to various Commando units.

In June 1942, No 10 (Inter Allied) Commando was formed, with Lt Colonel Dudley Lister, who came across from No 4 Commando, being appointed to command it. The first troops formed were French, Dutch and Belgian, and these were quickly followed by Norwegian and Polish troops. As far as their status was concerned, this is spelled out in a letter from Mountbatten to General Sikorski, commanding the Free Polish forces:

> I am glad to confirm that your soldiers will be commanded by Polish officers during their training and in action, but the organisation of the Inter-Allied Commando as a whole will come under direct command of a British officer, Colonel Lister. I shall be glad to send him round to see you, or any of your staff, whenever you like. It is agreed that they will be available to go on any other duties you might desire provided you inform me in sufficient time. The Commando Troop will, of course, remain open to your inspection or to inspection by any of your officers whom you may wish to nominate at any time.
>
> I hope that you will agree that the Troop may wear the word 'Commando' on their shoulders as is the case of all other soldiers in the Commandos. This will, of course, be in addition to your own national badges, etc. . . . . The troops will be paid by the Polish Government and will be governed by Polish Military Law. They will be equipped with British equipment but will be permitted to wear their national dress as desired.[12]

The establishment of each troop was set at four officers and 83 other ranks. The Commando Headquarters was based at Harlech in

North Wales and, as the troops formed, they were each allocated a town nearby. Not surprisingly, there were administrative complications that had to be overcome:

> The French and Belgian names had been difficult enough, the Dutch little more so, and with the arrival of the Norwegians it seemed that the ultimate limit in this respect had been reached. But the Polish Troop! Nominal roles were the order of the day, and such things as Guard Orders had to be typed in all languages, so the state of the HQ typists may well be imagined. Three or four consonants in a row were quite common, and unpronounceable, and we found ourselves addressed in countless languages . . . .
>
> Considerable confusion was caused, too, by the varying badges of rank amongst the different troops. The French Officers had straight gold bars across their shoulders, taking the place of 'pips' on British Commissioned Officers, and they carried an additional rank of 'Aspirant', which, broadly translated means 'aspiring to the rank of Officer', and though not commissioned he was treated as a 2/Lt. Next came their Sergeant Major, who was simply glorious in his gold braid and might have been supposed to be at least a Rear Admiral. The NCOs, however, simply had a piece of red tape sewn on the front of their battle dress blouse, between the second and third button. The Dutch had effected [the] British system, except for their officers, who carried their 'pips' on the collars of their blouses . . . . The Belgians also had adopted the British system. The Norwegians, however, showed this commissioned rank on their collars, while the NCOs had tapes on their cuffs.[13]

There was, however, one unique troop in the ranks of No 10 (IA) Commando, X Troop, later No 3 (Miscellaneous) or the 'British' Troop. This was made up of 'enemy aliens', mainly pre-war German and Austrian refugees, with some Czechs, Danes, Hungarians, a Russian and a Rumanian. All could speak perfect German, and the particulars of many were known to the Gestapo. Almost all had been interned at the beginning of the war and then, on release, had been allowed to join the Pioneer Corps, from which they were permitted to volunteer for the troop. It was formally raised on 11 July 1942 around a Pioneer Corps Sergeant and six Pioneer Corps privates who had come from Military Intelligence in the War Office. Its commander was Captain (later Major) B. Hilton Jones RA, and he explains the extraordinary lengths that were gone to in order to provide his men with a watertight cover:

. . . the men, and their families, had obviously to be guarded against the possibility of identification as Germans either at home or, above all, on capture by the enemy. This necessitated the issue of 'false' numbers, names and regiments, false personal histories, false next-of-kin, false mail facilities etc; and this in turn involved a tortuous procedure whereby all of it was kept secret from the normal army pay and record offices without disturbing the normal administrative channels. Such extra 'tit-bits' as attachment to another unit, overseas service, and the legalisation of 'false' names by ACI [Army Council Instruction] in 1943, simply added to the complications; and it was a long time, with (it must be said) on the whole the helpful and willing co-operation of the War Office departments concerned, before the jig-saw could be fitted together and all contingencies prepared for.[14]

Eventually, No 10 (IA) Commando would be organised as follows:

British Headquarters
No 1 (French) Troop
No 2 (Dutch) Troop
No 3 (Misc) Troop
The Belgian Tp HQ
No 4 (Belgian) Troop
No 5 (Norwegian) Troop
No 6 (Polish) Troop
No 7 (Yugoslav) Troop
No 8 (French) Troop
No 9 (Belgian) Troop
No 10 (Belgian) Troop

All went through the Achnacarry course and wore the '10 Commando' and Combined Operations flashes and, as we shall see, would fight in all the British operational theatres of war.

Dieppe

The reason for the pause in cross-Channel operations after April 1942 was because both Home Forces and Combined Operations HQ were deeply involved in the planning of an operation, which would be on a much larger scale than anything mounted so far. The background to it lay in the debate between the US and British Chiefs of Staff on the overall conduct of the war, which had surfaced during the first of the major Allied conferences, *Arcadia*, which had been held in Washington in December 1941. While both sides agreed that priority must lie in the defeat of Germany first, rather than Japan, there were differences over how this should be done.

Both the American and British planners agreed that an invasion of the Continent would have to take place, and that the Russians must continue to contain the bulk of the German armies in the East. The mounting base for the invasion was to be the United Kingdom, and a build up of US forces there, under the codename *Bolero*, would be a prerequisite. At the time of *Arcadia*, though, the British wanted first to clear North Africa of the enemy, and with Auchinleck's *Crusader* offensive going well, believed that this could be done by a US landing in French North Africa, which would meet up with the Eighth Army in Tunisia. By February, however, with Rommel having counter-attacked, *Gymnast*, as it was called, was obviously not feasible, but while the British considered that it should merely be postponed, the Americans wished to cancel it altogether. Instead, they argued for a cross-Channel invasion in autumn 1942 (*Sledgehammer*). The British Joint Planning Staff, using the worst case of Russia on the verge of collapse, also supported this plan, seeing it in terms of a bridgehead established in summer 1942 in order to relieve pressure on the Eastern Front. Brooke, who had been appointed Chairman of the British Chiefs of Staff Committee in early March, thought it suicidal. Instead, the cross-Channel offensive should take place in 1943 (*Round Up*), once sufficient resources, both men and material (especially shipping) had been built up. Marshall, Brooke's 'opposite number' in the USA, acceded to this, and they agreed that *Sledgehammer* would only be considered if the Russians were near to collapse. Yet, the Russians themselves were now pressing hard for a second front to be created.

American and Russian pressure, together with the need, for which Mountbatten in particular was agitating, to explore the problems of an opposed landing on the coast of France through a practical trial, led Churchill to conclude that at least something must be done. The alternative to *Sledgehammer* was a major raid, and two such schemes already existed on paper. One, *Imperator*, envisaged the use of four divisions and was quickly dismissed as being too similar to *Sledgehammer*. The other, *Rutter*, involved a 'hit and run' raid on Dieppe, and had been under active consideration by both COHQ and GHQ Home Forces since March. Mountbatten formally presented the plan to the Chiefs of Staff on 13 May and it was accepted. It was laid down that it should take place in July. The troops taking part were to come from Home Forces, and since General Montgomery's South-Eastern Army was deployed opposite Dieppe, it was logical that they should be selected from his command, and he chose 2nd Canadian Division.

The original plan called for a frontal assault on the town itself, to be carried out by infantry supported by a battalion of Churchill tanks, while parachute units were to neutralise the German batteries on the headlands either side of the port. There would be a preliminary air bombardment by RAF Bomber Command, while RAF Fighter Command, in the hope of drawing up the maximum number of German fighters and inflicting damage on them, would provide air cover during the landings.

The first rehearsal, Exercise *Yukon*, took place on 11-12 June and was a disaster, but a second, ten days later, which was attended by Mountbatten and Paget, went better, and on 1 July Montgomery wrote to Paget to say that he was satisfied. The operation would take place on 4 July or the first possible day after that when the weather was favourable. Unfortunately, there was now a spell of bad weather, and on 7 July the operation was called off.* At this stage Montgomery wanted it cancelled for good, since all the troops taking part had been briefed and there was a danger of compromise. Mountbatten and Paget, on the other hand, were still keen that it should be mounted, and it was agreed that it should be postponed until August.

There were now a number of amendments to the plan. For a start, the codename had been changed to *Jubilee*. The preliminary air bombardment had been dropped because of fear of excessive French civilian casualties. Furthermore, uncertainties over the weather meant that there was no guarantee that the airborne operations would be successful, and it was decided to use the Commandos instead, with No 3 and 4 Commandos and the Royal Marine Commando being chosen.

As for Montgomery's fears, he was right in that from early July the Germans had been expecting something to happen. On the 9th, Hitler had written that, as a result of the success of the current German offensive on the Eastern Front,

.... England may be faced with the choice of either immediately mounting a major landing in order to create a Second Front or of losing Soviet Russia as a political and military factor. It is highly probable, therefore that enemy landings will take place shortly in the areas of C-in-C West

---

*This was not before the V Corps School of Raiding had taken part in a series of diversions by embarking in R boats, and, escorted by MTBs, sailing by night towards the Brittany coast.

. . . in the first place, the Channel coast, the area between Dieppe and Le Havre, and Normandy, since these areas can be reached by enemy fighters and also because they lie within range of a large proportion of the invasion craft.[15]

The Germans also obtained information from traitors within the French resistance that the British were showing particular interest in Dieppe, and accordingly, apart from maintaining a high level of alertness, evolved a deception plan to make the British believe that the garrison was very much weaker than it was. This was swallowed by MI6. The concentration of invasion craft and interception of radio traffic also served to confirm German suspicions. Nevertheless, *Jubilee* was now rescheduled for 18 August. In the meantime, Montgomery was ordered to a new command, the Eighth Army, which was licking its wounds after the protracted battle of First Alamein, which had stopped Rommel's drive to the Suez Canal.

The main landing on the seafront of Dieppe was to be carried out by two battalions, each landing on a separate beach, and supported by the 14th Canadian Tank Battalion. Immediately east and west of the town were two coastal batteries, codenamed Rommel and Hindenburg, which would be taken care of by a further two battalions, assisted by the Royal Marine Commando. Further east lay the Goebbels Battery at Berneval, which was to be the responsibility of Durnford-Slater's No 3 Commando, while to the west of the Hindenburg Battery, No 4 Commando, in which Lord Lovat had now replaced Lister in command, would take care of the guns at Vasterival and the Hess Battery at Quiberville. In addition, five members of X Troop and a detachment of the French Troop under Lieutenant Vourch of No 10 (IA) Commando would also take part. In all, some 6,000 men were to take part, including 1,000 Special Forces.

On 17 August the troops embarked, with the tanks being loaded onto LSTs under the cover of smoke. The aim was expressed as: 'The 2nd Canadian Division will seize Dieppe and vicinity. Occupy the area until demolition and exploitation tasks are completed. Re-embark and return to England.' The weather again prevented sailing that evening, but on the next night the force set off, arriving off the beaches, after having negotiated a suspect minefield, at 0330 hours on the 19th. Accompanying Nos 3 and 4 Commandos were fifty men of the 1st US Ranger Battalion, who had been trained at Achnacarry, and were now based in the Hebrides.

No 3 Commando was being carried in R-boats, now known as Landing Craft Personnel (Light) (LCP(L)), and was escorted by a Landing Craft Flak (LCF), with two 4-inch guns, and a Steam Gunboat.

Pat Barber, Commandant of the V Corps School of Raiding:

For security reasons the Commandos were billeted at Seaford and were not allowed to be seen in Warsash, and the Navy were not allowed to be seen in Seaford. I was, therefore, appointed as liaison officer between Commander Wyburd* and the Commandos as I could come and go without causing comment in either place. Seaford was full of holiday-makers. The port of embarkation was Newhaven. The Eurekas had already sailed round there by night and were hidden from aerial view in the Hide, a covered area just upstream from the harbour. 3 Commando and some Canadian troops arrived during the late afternoon of 18 August in order to embark. There was a good deal of congestion in the street near the small harbour, and apprehensive speculation among civilians who watched them.

I sailed with Commander Wyburd and Lt-Col Durnford-Slater in SGB [Steam Gunboat] 5 (Lt Hummel RNR) the Command ship in the left flank. We departed at dusk on a lovely summer's evening with our flock of Eurekas in formation behind us. It all seemed so peaceful.

I travelled on the bridge and was asked to man a Browning machine-gun in case of emergency. The Steam Gunboat was larger than an MGB and had a funnel from which occasionally would belch forth a volley of sparks in a most disconcerting manner. Each time this happened an absolute tirade of abuse from the Captain would pour down the speaking tube to the engine room and then all would be peaceful for a time. It was after one of these unnerving explosions of sparks, accompanied by the inevitable outburst of abuse, that there followed a loud report and there high above us was a large parachute flare drifting very slowly down towards us illuminating the SGB and the trail of Eurekas behind us with a very bright light whilst all around us was a deep pitch blackness. Until you have actually experienced it you cannot imagine how naked and vulnerable you feel. Then all hell was let loose. I can remember watching the tracer coming at me and wondering as I fired the Browning machine-gun in reply, whether there would be time to duck for each tracer and pop up again and fire a few shots before the next one–vain hope! We had been spotted by a German flak ship which was escorting a small convoy along the French coast. The SGB was quickly put out of action and more than half those on board became casualties. Later it was towed home. The Eurekas were scattered in all directions, some sunk, some put out of action, some reached the beach and were taken prisoner.[16]

---

* In overall command of the R-boats based in HMS *Tormentor*.

As a result, only five out of the twenty landing craft actually reached their correct beaches. Four of these under Captain Wills, the same officer who had sent the cheeky telegram to Hitler during the first Lofoten Islands raid, hit Beach Yellow 1 below the Goebbels Battery and, accompanied by four French Commandos, fought their way ashore. Unfortunately, the Germans were able to prevent them getting near the battery and slowly forced them back to the beach. In the meantime, the tide had gone out leaving the landing craft stranded on the rocks. Few got away, including only one member of the RN beach party.*

The one landing craft to hit Yellow Beach 2 fortuitously had Major Peter Young, now 2ic of No 3, on board. Young's party managed to get up the cliffs using a steep gully, and then advanced to engage the battery. There were only eighteen of them, but by engaging the battery with careful deliberate fire from the flank, they managed to distract the gunners to such an extent that one gun traversed through 180° and began firing inland. Realising that it would only be a matter of time before reinforcements arrived, Peter Young withdrew his party, unfortunately suffering one man wounded on a mine on the way back, and, fighting a classic 'leapfrog' rearguard action, they successfully re-embarked in the LCP (L).

The Royal Regiment of Canada, which was responsible for the Rommel Battery, was hampered from the start in that its landing craft formed up behind the wrong gunboat. The twenty minutes lost in sorting out the muddle proved fatal. They were caught in searchlights as they approached the beach, and it was daylight by the time they landed. The result was annihilation and only 60 out of their strength of 543 were eventually rescued from the beach. It was much the same story with the main landings with the Essex Scottish and Royal Hamilton Light Infantry being caught in a murderous crossfire as they came ashore. Of the tanks, 24 managed to get ashore, of which six got over the sea wall, but were soon destroyed. The reserve battalion, the Fusiliers Mont-Royal, was now committed, but the result was the same, with no one able to get off the beaches under the intense fire.

It was now the turn of the Royal Marine Commando, who had been kept offshore as a further reserve. General Roberts, commanding the 2nd Canadian Infantry Division, decided to use

*They came from *Dog*, which suffered such severe casualties that it was disbanded, but eventually reformed in July 1943.

them to reinforce White Beach, being unaware from the garbled reports he was receiving of the true situation on shore. The Royal Marine Commandos had been transported across the Channel in fast French motor boats, called *chasseurs*, and the gunboat HMS *Locust*. They now transferred to landing craft, and Captain P.W.C. Hellings DSC RM, commanding A Company, takes up the story:

> The Commando started to move toward the shore, it being about 1130 hours. Smoke was provided by the chasseur, who accompanied us within 500 yds.
>
> Shell fire was opened up on the boats almost immediately, at about 4000 yds, increasing in intensity as the range shortened . . . . The range was shortening and rifle and LMG fire was becoming apparent, the chasseur being no longer able to support the force owing to the depth of water . . . .
>
> The MLC in which we had embarked had done the main landing and was in need of repair, one engine being out of commission and the deck of the MLC was washing down with water. Owing to one engine being out of commission and the other very hot, steering was difficult, and our speed reduced which resulted in an ever increasing distance between boats. Just prior to reaching the shore and whilst in thick smoke we completely broke down, which my have been the result of a near miss or the overheating of our engine. The engine was started after about 2 mins and we proceeded on toward the shore out of the smoke in time to see the Colonel's MLC and an ALC containing Capt Devereux and one platoon and Major Houghton's ALC arrive under heavy mortar and MG fire. Fire was intense and any attempt to reach the houses would have been most hazardous. Colonel Phillips stood up in his MLC and waved the remaining boats to return to the protection of the smoke. One ALC was extracted, the Colonel's MLC turned broadside on and I believe from survivors caught fire.
>
> My MLC at this stage received a hit close to the stern which finished any attempt at steering, leaving us some 300 yds off the shore. Smoke was used in quantity and we were able to increase the distance by about 300 yds before the engine finally went.[17]

They were later picked up by a chasseur, which took them back to HMS *Locust*. The Commanding Officer, who had put on white gloves so that everyone could see his signals to withdraw, was tragically killed, while Major Houghton, the Second-in-Command of the Commando was wounded and taken prisoner.

It was a sad and frustrating operational debut for the Royal Marine Commandos.

As for the role played by No 10 (IA) Commando, Francis Vourch's French Troop detachment was split into three. Five members were attached to No 3 Commando, Vourch and six to the Royal Marine Commando, and the remainder to No 3 Commando. Their main task was to obtain information from and carry out any necessary liaison with the local population. Also taking part were seven members of X Troop of No 10. Their task was even more specialist. They were to accompany Captain P.J. Harratt and other SOE members to the Town Hall and German headquarters in order to snatch any documents of value, as well as a new type of respirator which the Germans were believed to have. In addition to this the X Troop men were tasked with selecting up to twelve civilians for evacuation back to England at the end of the operation and also for distributing propaganda leaflets. Also accompanying the party were a radar expert, MEW representative, and two SIS members.[18] Their role was also gathering intelligence – technical, economic and general – but they achieved little success.

This mixed team was split among two Landing Craft Tank (LCT 13 and 14), and was to be supported in its dash to the town centre by some of the Churchills. It met with no success. Those tanks which did manage to disembark were destroyed before they could get off the beach and the party itself was trapped. Some managed to escape by swimming to other landing craft, but the remainder were killed or captured. Of the five X Troop members, one was killed on the beaches, one wounded, but got back to England, as did one other. As for the remaining two, they were captured, but then disappeared without trace. It is probable that the Germans, having discovered that they were refugees from Nazism, either sent them to a lingering death in a concentration camp or summarily executed them. The lives of X Troop members were always in greater danger on capture than those of other Commandos.[19]

Thus No 10 Commando's first taste of action was as sobering as that of the Royal Marine Commandos, especially for X Troop, which had only formed just over a month before. Those members of the French Troop who were attached to No 4 Commando did, however, enjoy some measure of success. Indeed, three were to be decorated for their services, two with the *Croix de Guerre avec étoile* and one with the Military Medal, No 10's first British award for gallantry.

On the extreme right flank of the landings, No 4 Commando achieved the only clearcut success in *Jubilee*. Their target was the battery of six 150mm guns by Varengeville-sur-mer. Lord Lovat had been given his task in mid July. Having studied the problem, he concluded that to use the whole Commando would lead to complications, involving more landing craft or possibly two lifts. He therefore selected just four out of his six troops. The plan he evolved was for two landings. While his Second-in-Command, Major Derek Mills-Roberts, landed with 88 men on Orange 1 beach and engaged the battery with small arms and mortars from a wood some 300 yards away, he would take the remainder across Orange 2. They would get into position to the rear of the battery and attack, while the enemy's attention was distracted by Mills-Roberts. During late July and early August, they carried out several rehearsals at Lulworth Cove in Dorset, which had a similar cliff configuration.

No 4 Commando embarked in HMS *Prince Albert* and arrived at the point where they were to transfer to their landing craft on schedule. Mills-Roberts's party quickly got ashore, and, using Bangalore torpedoes to clear away the wire defences, got up the cliffs and into the village of Vasterival, which was found to be unoccupied. A fighting patrol then set off to cut the telephone lines leading from a lighthouse in between Orange 1 and 2 and which the Germans were known to be using as an Observation Post (OP). The remainder of this troop, under Captain Boucher-Myers, then moved forward and occupied a prominent double crossroads in order to prevent any counter-attack from the west. Mills-Roberts took his remaining troop, commanded by Captain Dawson, through the wood and spotted the German battery, and then opened fire. Soon they were engaged in a desperate fire fight with the Germans, with casualties mounting on both sides.

Meanwhile, Lord Lovat's party had landed under mortar and machine gun fire, although the support given by LCSs offshore helped to neutralise this to some extent. They overcame the pill boxes on the beach, but suffered some casualties from mortar fire and then doubled alongside the River La Saane before turning eastwards towards the battery, from which direction the sounds of heavy small arms fire could be heard. As they approached, they ran into a group of Germans debussing from a truck prior to counter-attacking Mills-Roberts. In the fighting that followed, Captain Pettiward, one of the troop commanders, was killed, Lieutenant Macdonald mortally wounded and other casualties suffered. At this moment, Acting Major Pat Porteous, who was acting as liaison officer between the two groups, came forward. As the citation for the Victoria Cross which he was subsequently awarded said:

> Major Porteous . . . was shot at close range through the hand, the bullet passing through his palm and entering his upper arm. Undaunted, Major Porteous closed with his assailant, succeeded in disarming him and killed him with his own bayonet thereby saving the life of a British Sergeant on whom the German had turned his aim.[20]

After this intensive hand-to-hand fighting, the Commandos managed to get forward and secure the ditch which was to be their start line for the attack on the battery.

Mills-Roberts now laid down an intensive machine gun barrage and fired smoke from his 2in mortars, while Spitfires of 129 Squadron strafed the battery. Lord Lovat fired a series of white Very lights to signal Mills-Roberts to stop firing, and the Commandos charged, led by Major Porteous and Captain Webb. Again, from Porteous's citation:

> . . . the larger detachment was held up, and the officer leading this detachment killed and the Troop Sergeant Major fell seriously wounded. Almost immediately afterwards the only other officer of the detachment was also killed. Major Porteous, without hesitation and in the face of a withering fire, dashed across the open ground to take over command of this detachment. Rallying them, he led them in a charge which carried the German position at the point of a bayonet, and was seriously wounded a second time. Though shot through the thigh he continued to the final objective where he eventually collapsed from loss of blood after the last of the guns had been destroyed.

The Germans were cleared away from the guns, and the demolition party set about destroying the guns and the underground magazines. Once this had been done, the time for withdrawal came. As with Peter Young's party, the success of this was brought about by skilful fire and movement and the use of smoke, through smoke generators, which covered their re-embarkation on Orange 1.

The efforts of Nos 3 and 4 Commandos provided the only rays of light in an otherwise dismal picture. This had been not without heavy loss. No 3 lost 117 killed, wounded or missing out of 420 who took part and No 4 Commando 45 out of 265. In addition, the Royal Marine Commando suffered 76 out of 370, the US Rangers 13 out of 50 and No 10 Commando 6 out of 18. As for the specialist intelligence gatherers, their casualties were never included in the official reports. Indeed, so classified was their work that there is no specific mention of what they did.

For the Canadians, who left a third of their numbers behind, *Jubilee* was a pill that provoked much understandable bitterness, and they felt that they had been used as mere cannon fodder. The controversy has lasted to this day. While the Royal Navy felt that they were lucky to get away with just one destroyer sunk, although there was a heavy toll of landing craft, and the RAF congratulated themselves on having drawn the Luftwaffe into battle, claiming to have shot down 170 aircraft, albeit at a cost of 106 of their own, there was no getting away from the fact that in the short term the operation had been a failure.

Yet, there were benefits that came out of it. For a start, the idea of building the amphibious assault on the Continent around the immediate capture of a port was now definitely ruled out. Many other valuable lessons in the conduct of an opposed landing were also learnt and, if nothing else, it demonstrated to the Germans that they could not afford to relax their guard in the West in order to reinforce in the East. Finally, it proved that *Sledgehammer* was not a viable concept, and that no invasion could possibly be mounted until well into 1943. This, as we shall see, gave added strength to the British argument for *Gymnast.*

Small Scale Raiding Force

On 19 February 1942 Mountbatten approached the Chiefs of Staff with an idea of forming a permanent group of fifty men as an 'amphibious sabotage force' equipped with two large MLs, which would operate directly under him.[21] This was approved some four weeks later. Mountbatten saw *Maid Honor* Force, at that time on leave in South Africa, as being ideally suited for what he had in mind, but they were still under the control of SOE. After some negotiation, it was agreed that while SOE would continue to administer and finance them, they would be under CCO's operational control, although no raids were to be mounted without SOE agreement, and *Maid Honor* Force was summoned home. Although usually known as the Small Scale Raiding Force (SSRF), the unit was given the cover name of No 62 Commando, and was known as 'Station 62' in SOE circles. Based at Anderson Manor, three miles north of Bere Regis in Dorset, they soon found that the two MLs, although they could carry a reasonable number of men, were too slow, and so they were given their own Motor Torpedo Boat, *MTB 344*, which was specially adapted to their needs and fondly became known as 'The Little Pisser'. One problem though, was that she was unmanageable in more than a Force 4 wind.

It was not until August that the SSRF began to carry out operations on behalf of CCO.* After one attempt, *Barricade*, which had as its objective an anti-aircraft gun site north-west of Pointe de Saire south of Barfleur, was mounted on the night 14/15 August. Unfortunately, the eleven raiders landed at the wrong place, but nevertheless ran across Germans, definitely killing three, and possibly inflicting further casualties. They also brought back useful information on the defences in the area. Then came Dieppe, in which the SSRF does not appear to have been involved. In September, however, the SSRF carried out no less than three operations.

The first of these, on the night 2/3 September, was highly successful. Codenamed *Dryad*, the target was the lighthouse on Les Casquets north of the Channel Islands. Ten officers and two other ranks took part, and they anchored *MTB 344* some 800 yards away

---

*According to Admiral Hughes-Hallett, the reason for the delay in mounting an operation was because of March-Phillipps' inability to write an operation order in a form that would inspire the confidence of C-in-C Portsmouth under whose direct control the naval side of the raiding operations off this part of the coast was.[22]

One account[23] mentions the SSRF training for an attack on the *Tirpitz* in her Norwegian fjord. They were to be taken by submarine and there use a machine somewhat like an underwater bicycle to get them to the ship, on whose hull they would plan limpet mines. The *Tirpitz*, however, was then moved to another fjord which had unfavourable currents and the operation was aborted. This was confirmed by Tom Winter and Peter Kemp to the author as one of the many ideas which Gus March-Phillipps had.

and then landed using a Goatley Boat. Graham Hayes and one other officer were left in charge of the boat, while the rest of the party clambered up an 80ft cliff.

> Coiled Dannert wire was met and climbed through on the way up the cliff, and the gateway was found to be blocked by a heavy knife rest barbed wire entanglement, but a way was found over the Western wall and the whole party made the courtyard unchallenged. At this point the order was given for independent action and the party split up and rushed the buildings and towers, according to a pre-arranged plan. Complete surprise was obtained and all resistance was overcome without a shot being fired.
>
> Seven prisoners, all of them Germans, including two leading telegraphists were taken in the bedrooms and living rooms. The light tower, wireless tower and engine room were deserted, although the generating plant in the engine house was running, and the watch, consisting of two men, was in the living room. The rest were in bed, with the exception of two telegraphists who were just turning in. A characteristic of those in bed was the wearing of hairnets, which caused the Commander [March-Phillipps] to mistake one of them for a woman.[24]

The radio was then destroyed, documents and Codebooks seized, and the party, with prisoners, some still in pyjamas, made their way back to the waiting Goatley. Geoffrey Appleyard unfortunately twisted his ankle during the descent, and Captain Peter Kemp injured his leg while re-embarking, but otherwise there were no casualties, and much information was gained from the prisoners after the return to Portland.

Five nights later, a party on *MTB 344* carried out a reconnaissance of the lie Burhou in the Channel Islands, but then, on the night of 12/13 September, tragedy struck. The idea behind *Aquatint* was to land east of St Honorine, which is positioned just to the east of what would become *Omaha* Beach, scale some cliffs, which seemed possible from a study of air photographs, and then approach the village from the rear and attack the first house or strongpoint containing Germans and attempt to snatch a prisoner. Unfortunately it was a very dark night and they could not identify the spot where the cliff was climbable. March-Phillipps therefore decided on a landing, which was again by Goatley boat, at St Honorine itself. As the party of eleven made for the shore, lights were seen on the cliffs, but after they landed, those still aboard *MTB 344*, including Appleyard who, in spite of his ankle injury, had gone along as navigator, heard sounds of small arms fire. This continued for some fifteen minutes, and was then joined by grenades, Very lights and machine gun fire. Tony Hall was one of the landing party:

> . . . hardly had we landed when we saw a German patrol coming along, and from what I remember from it . . . our job on that occasion was to get prisoners, and I remember grabbing hold of one chap, a goon and dragging him down to the beach, and he kept saying the whole time 'Nicht Deutsch, Nicht Deutsch, Czechish, Nicht Deutsch, Czechish', and I was sort of saying 'oh, we'll sort that out in the boat, you know', then somebody came up and clobbered me from behind.[25]

Then, after about another 15 minutes, there was machine gun fire in the direction of *MTB 344*.

> At about this time a shout of 'come back' was distinctly heard ashore on the right, and what was thought to be the landing craft could be seen on the beach on the right, broadside on and carried up above the high water mark, almost under the sea-wall. No-one was seen near it, and no attempts were being made to launch it. A voice was heard on the shore, thought to be that of Major March-Phillipps and thought to be hailing the MTB but the message could not be distinguished. Immediately afterwards Captain Hayes' voice was heard hailing Captain Appleyard (on the MTB) by name, and, when a return hail was made from the MTB, a message was shouted which could not be definitely made out, but which was thought to be an order to the MTB to withdraw and leave the landing party which was unable to re-embark off the beach as it was brightly illuminated and enfiladed by machine gun fire.[26]

A gun now opened fire on the MTB and so the anchors were cut and it made out to sea, or at least limped as the starboard engine had been put out of action by a bullet. Once things had quietened down on shore, the MTB came in again, but this time she was spotted by German patrol vessels, who opened fire. There was no option but to abandon efforts to rescue survivors of the landing party and *MTB 344* made her way back through a minefield and back to base.

From German radio broadcasts over the next couple of days,

it transpired that three of the party were definitely dead.* One of these was identified as Gus March-Phillipps, who had been drowned while attempting to swim out to the MTB. All the others, apart from Graham Hayes were taken prisoner, although André Desgranges, a Frenchman who had been a founder member of *Maid Honor* Force, eventually managed to escape and made his way to England, via Spain and became an SOE agent. Company Sergeant-Major Tom Winter, too, in company with an SAS officer, managed to escape from his camp between Bremen and Hamburg in April 1945, both disguised as French soldiers. They ran into the Guards Armoured Division and Winter guided them to liberate his camp. He had, like other SSRF members, been given a code by MI9, responsible for escape and evasion, for use in writing letters home, and in this way had been able to feed SOE with information during his captivity. He also, when in a camp in Poland, frequently broke out in order to give the Polish underground instruction in explosives, and was decorated by the Poles for this.[27] As for Hayes, he managed to get to Spain with help from the French underground, but there was arrested and handed over to the Germans. After nine months' solitary confinement he was shot in July 1943. For the remainder of the SSRF:

> we had been prepared for casualties, but not for such a catastrophe as this. The death of the gallant idealist and strange, quixotic genius who had been our commander and our inspiration, together with the loss of so many good friends, all in the space of a few hours, was a crippling calamity which nearly put an end to our activities. Indeed, it probably would have done so but for the energetic reaction of Appleyard, who refused to let our grief for our comrades arrest his determination to avenge them.[28]

Both COHQ and SOE were fully aware of the value of SSRF and were keen to keep it in being. Indeed, it was recommended immediately after *Aquatint* that the SSRF be quickly brought back up to strength and that Appleyard be appointed to command. Furthermore, a projected raid against Sark should be carried out as soon as possible for the sake of morale.[29]

---

*Gus March-Phillipps, Sergeant A. Williams, The Queens Regiment and Private R. Leonard (alias Lechniger) Pioneer Corps, lie buried in the village churchyard at St Laurent. March-Phillipps's gravestone states that he was killed in action on 12 September 1942, while the other two gravestones indicate that Williams and Leonard were shot on 13 September 1942.

This was mounted, as Operation *Basalt*, on the night 3/4 October under command of Appleyard and once again using *MTB 344*. A party from No 12 Commando had by that time joined the SSRF. The raiding force consisted of seven members of the SSRF and Captain Philip Pinkney and four men from No 12 Commando. *MTB 344* hove to off the southern end of the island, the intention being to scale the steep cliffs of Pointe Chateau. Unfortunately, the first landing was made on a small rock island off the point and the party had to be re-embarked and try again, this time successfully. The first 150 feet of the climb was tough, and not helped by shale and loose rocks, but after that the gradient became easier. Sent on ahead was Second Lieutenant Anders Lassen, a Dane and veteran of *Maid Honor* Force who was fast making a name for himself, in order to check on a suspected machine gun post, which he did not find. The party then moved north and attacked what they thought was a Nissen hut and radio mast; it turned out to be a flag pole and butts of a range. They then reached a group of cottages, Petit Dixcart, but these were found to be empty and so they pressed on further to a house called La Jespellaire, which was believed to house Germans.

Here again the main party remained behind under cover whilst the three-man reconnaissance party made a tour of the house and outbuildings, one of which contained a horse, and tried all the doors and windows on the ground floor level. These, however, were all found to be locked, but some French windows were found on the SE side of the house, which appeared easy to force. The body of the party was then called up and a quick forced entry was made into the house at 0150 hrs by tearing open the French windows.

Inside they found a woman, Frances Pittard, daughter of an RNVR Captain and recent widow of the island's retired medical officer. She was able to give the raiders much information on the German deployment on the island. She declined, however, an invitation to return to the mainland with the Commandos, in spite of her vulnerability to reprisals, on the grounds that she had lived in the Channel Islands all her life. Most pertinent of the information which she gave was the fact that there were Germans living in the annexe of the nearby Dixcart Hotel.

The whole party then entered the annexe and a thorough search revealed the presence of five Germans, all sleeping in separate rooms. Their clothes were searched for weapons, pay books, papers etc likely to prove of value, and the prisoners were then taken out of the house to be assembled under cover of the trees nearby. In the darkness outside the house one of the prisoners, seeing an opportunity, suddenly attacked his guard and then, shouting for help and trying to raise an alarm, he ran off in the direction in which it was known there were buildings containing a number of Germans. He was caught almost immediately, but after a scuffle again escaped, still shouting, and was shot. Meanwhile, three of the other prisoners, seizing the opportunity of the noise and confusion, also started shouting and attacking their guards. Two broke away and were shot immediately. The third, although still held, was accidentally shot in an attempt to silence him by striking him with the butt of a revolver. The fifth prisoner remained quiet and did not struggle. There were answering shouts from the direction in which the prisoners had attempted to escape and sounds of a verbal alarm being given.

With its one remaining prisoner the party managed to get back to the shore, got out to *MTB 344* and entered Portland Harbour at 0630 hours.[30]

From the SSRF's point of view it had been a very successful raid, and just the fillip to morale that they wanted. There was, however, one unfortunate aftermath.

Although Appleyard was certain that all four prisoners who had attempted to escape were shot, a German communique issued two days after the raid implied that at least one of the prisoners had escaped. The German High Command declared that they had been illegitimately roped and that two had been shot while resisting this. They compared this to a similar alleged barbarity which had taken place at Dieppe and others elsewhere, which included using prisoners to clear mines in Libya and the gagging and binding of prisoners captured in the Lofoten Islands raid.

On the 9 October, Berlin announced that 1376 British prisoners,* officers and other ranks, had been fettered, and accusation and counter-accusation flowed between the two governments. The British now manacled the same number of German prisoners in Canada in retaliation. Eventually, after requests from the Swiss Government, these were released on 12 December, but the Germans refused to

---

*Tom Winter and other members of the SSRF captured on *Aquatint* were among those fettered.

unshackle theirs until the British Government had given an assurance forbidding the binding and shackling of prisoners under any circumstances. Furthermore, although kept secret by the Germans at the time, on 18 October Hitler issued his infamous 'Commando Order', which is reproduced below:

The Führer	SECRET
No. 003830/42 g.Kdos.OWK/Wst	F.H. Qu. 18.10.1942
	12 copies
	Copy No. 12.

1. For a long time now our opponents have been employing in their conduct of the war, methods which contravene the International Convention of Geneva. The members of the so-called Commandos behave in a particularly brutal and underhand manner; and it has been established that those units recruit criminals not only from their own country but even former convicts set free in enemy territories. From captured orders it emerges that they are instructed not only to tie up prisoners, but also to kill out-of-hand unarmed captives who they think might prove an encumbrance to them, or hinder them in successfully carrying out their aims. Orders have indeed been found in which the killing of prisoners has positively been demanded of them.

2. In this connection it has already been notified in an Appendix to Army Orders of 7.10.1942 that in future, Germany will adopt the same methods against these Sabotage units of the British and their Allies; i.e. that, whenever they may appear, they shall be ruthlessly destroyed by the German troops.

3. I order, therefore:–

From now on all men operating against German troops in so-called Commando raids in Europe or in Africa, are to be annihilated to the last man. This is to be carried out whether they be soldiers in uniform, or saboteurs, with or without arms; and whether fighting or seeking to escape; and it is equally immaterial whether they come into action from Ships and Aircraft, or whether they land by parachute. Even if these individuals on discovery make obvious their intention of giving themselves up as prisoners, no pardon is on any account to be given. On this matter a report is to be made in each case to Headquarters for the information of Higher Command.

4. Should individual members of these Commandos, such as agents, saboteurs, etc., fall into the hands of the Armed Forces through any other means – as, for example, through the Police in one of the Occupied Territories – they are to be instantly handed over to the S.D.

To hold them in military custody – for example in P.O.W. Camps, etc., – even if only as a temporary measure, is strictly forbidden.

5. This order does not apply to the treatment of those enemy sol-

diers who are taken prisoner or give themselves up in open battle, in the course of normal operations, large scale attacks; or in major assault landings or airborne operations. Neither does it apply to those who fall into our hands after a sea fight, nor to those enemy soldiers who, after air battle, seek to save their lives by parachute.

6. I will hold all Commanders and Officers responsible under Military Law for any omission to carry out this order, whether by failure in their duty to instruct their units accordingly, or if they themselves act contrary to it.

(Sgd) A. Hitler

*

HEADQUARTERS OF THE ARMY	SECRET
No.551781/42g.k. Chefs W.F.St/Qu.	F.H.Qu. 19.10.42.
	22 copies
	Copy No. 21.

The enclosed Order from the Führer is forwarded in connection with destruction of enemy Terror and Sabotage-troops.

This order is intended for Commanders only and is in no circumstances to fall into Enemy hands.

Further distribution by receiving Headquarters is to be most strictly limited.

The Headquarters mentioned in the Distribution list are responsible that all parts of the Order, or extracts taken from it, which are issued are again withdrawn and, together with this copy, destroyed.

Chief of Staff of the Army
(Sgd) JODL

Commandos, as we shall see, would soon fall victim to this order. As for the Channel Islanders themselves, German retaliation, which included deportation of a number, among whom was Frances Pittard, to the Continent for a time, did provoke an understandable feeling of resentment towards Commando raids.

Nevertheless, in spite of the furore over the binding of prisoners, Mountbatten was so impressed by the performance of the SSRF that in the middle of October, with SOE agreement, he resolved to increase its strength to four troops. With SSRF HQ remaining at Anderson Manor, the out-stations were to be at Scorries House, Redruth, Cornwall, at Lupton House, Dartmouth, Wraxall Manor, Dorchester and Inchmery, Exbury in Hampshire. In addition, the naval craft available to the SSRF were increased and *MTB 344* was joined by CMB (Coastal Motor Boat) Nos 103 and 104, and 312, 316, 317 and 326, all of the 14th Flotilla. The expansion of the SSRF was to be achieved by retaining a permanent cadre of 'originals' and drawing on Special Service or Regular Troops on temporary attachment for operations. Since the organisation had become so much larger, Major Bill Stirling, brother of David, was posted into SOE, in which he had been previously, as Commander SSRF in the rank of lieutenant colonel, with Appleyard as the operations commander. The greater Royal Navy involvement meant that responsibilities had to be more closely defined than hitherto, especially since on 12 October, Force J had come into being. This covered the ships and small craft which had taken part in *Jubilee* and which had been kept together ever since. This gave a brigade's worth of amphibious lift, and 102 RM Brigade was the first formation to be allocated to it. The headquarters of Force J was established under Captain J. Hughes-Hallett RN at the Royal Yacht Squadron, Cowes, Isle of Wight under the title HMS *Vectis*.

While raids were to be carried out under the 'unified command' of Stirling, they were to be under the 'general operational control' of Hughes-Hallett. Stirling was to submit proposals for raids direct to Mountbatten, which indicated that the SSRF was still being given a fair degree of latitude. However, a copy was to be sent to Hughes-Hallett, who was to obtain clearance from the Naval C-in-C in whose area the operation would take place. Intelligence was to be the responsibility of COHQ. Stirling was at liberty to appoint a naval officer from what was now called the Small Scale Raiding Flotilla as Force Commander for a particular raid, should he so wish, provided he obtained agreement from Hughes-Hallett.[32]

The first operation under the new organisation took place on the night of 11/12 November. By that time No 12 Commando had contributed to the SSRF three separate parties under Captains Pinckney and Rooney and Lieutenant Gilchrist, who had each brought six NCOs from their troops. Pinckney's party had already taken part in *Basalt* and it was now the turn of Rooney. Peter Kemp, Brian Reynolds and Sergeant Nicholson were given the responsibility of training them for the raid, although, given No 12's experience in small scale raiding, Peter Kemp found that:

Rooney, a powerfully built, self-confident officer, who knew his men intimately and commanded their implicit obedience, had little to learn from me. In fact, apart from pistol shooting and movement at night, he and his men knew more about the business than I.[33]

The object of *Fahrenheit* was a reconnaissance of the defences, attack on the signal station and seizure of prisoners at Pointe de Plouezec on the north Brittany coast. The raid was to be commanded by Kemp and was mounted in *MTB 344* from Dartmouth. The signal station was correctly identified, but having reached the top of the cliffs the party found themselves in a minefield. Rooney and one man then went and checked the station, finding it protected by wire and sentries. They also looked at a pill box, which was unoccupied, and cut the cable from this station. The minefield restricted anything other than a frontal assault, and so, split into three, the raiders got to within ten paces of the wire. The two sentries were seen to be very alert, and the party waited for 15 minutes in the hope that they would move away. Peter Kemp:

> Out of the corner of my eye I saw Rooney make a slight movement; then I heard a distinct metallic click as he unscrewed the top of his No 6 grenade. The sentries heard it to; they stopped their conversation, and one gave a sharp exclamation. I sensed rather than saw Rooney's arm go up, and braced myself for what I knew was coming. There was a clatter as one of the sentries drew back the bolt of his rifle; then everything was obliterated in a vivid flash as a tremendous explosion shattered the silence of the night. The blast hit me like a blow on the head. From the sentries came the most terrible sounds I can ever remember: from one of them a low, pitiful moaning, from the other bewildered screams of agony and terror, an incoherent jumble of sobs and prayers, in which I could distinguish only the words '*Nicht gut! Nicht gut!*' endlessly repeated. Even in those seconds as I leaped to action I felt a shock of horror that those soft, lazy, drawling voices which had floated to us across the quiet night air could have turned, literally in a flash, to such inhuman screams of pain and fear.

Both sentries were finished off with Tommy gun fire, and Rooney's party then moved forward past an empty guard house, and waited for the remainder to come out of the station itself. Two did, one after the other, and both were shot. The other occupants were now returning fire, and, in view of the time factor, the fact that reinforcements were likely to be on their way, and the difficulty of getting any casualties incurred back down the cliff, Kemp decided to break off the action. The party successfully re-embarked and returned to Dartmouth.

Four nights later it was the turn of Gilchrist's party of No 12 Commando to be inducted. This time Colin Ogden-Smith was raid commander. *Batman* entailed a reconnaissance of coastal defences and the taking of prisoners in the Omonville area on the north-west corner of the Cherbourg Peninsula. Poor visibility caused difficulties in identifying the correct beach, and then a strong breeze blew up, resulting in a choppy sea, which would have made a landing difficult, and hence the operation was aborted.

Batman was to be the last SSRF raid mounted in 1942, although further operations were planned. The weather had now worsened and made these too risky to be carried out. There was, too, a growing conflict of interests over the activities of the SSRF. While Mountbatten was content to allow Stirling a very free rein in the planning of operations, SOE were becoming concerned over the danger of them cutting across their own activities. Although agreement on a new SSRF charter was achieved in mid-December, Mountbatten realised, as he indicated to the Chiefs of Staff on 22 December, that his raiding operations on the Norwegian and Brittany coasts, to which he gave priority because they were comparatively lightly defended, were in competition with MOI (SP), the military cover name for SOE, and the Secret Intelligence Service (SIS) (MI6). It was this lack of co-ordination which, as we shall see in Chapter Seven, would eventually bring about the demise of the SSRF.

Operation Torch

The idea of an invasion of French North Africa had been first seriously considered by the Allies at the *Arcadia* conference. While President Roosevelt was very much in favour of it, seeing it as an early opportunity to demonstrate to the American people that the United States was actively engaged against the Germans as well as the Japanese, his planners considered it more important to build up men and materiel in Britain for a direct invasion of the Continent of Europe. A furious debate raged during the first half of 1942 and, finally, at the end of July, Roosevelt decreed that the invasion would take place under the codename of *Torch*, by the end of October. Some hectic detailed planning now followed.

General Dwight D. Eisenhower was appointed to command the operation and his staff decided that there should be amphibious landings at three places, Casablanca, Oran and Algiers. The first two would be made by Americans only, with that at Casablanca being made by troops coming direct from the United States. Algiers would be seized by a mixed force of British and American and this landing, along with that at Oran, would be mounted from the United Kingdom. Included in this force were Nos 1 and 6 Commandos. However, before the landings could be carried out, there were vital tasks to be done by other Special Service elements.

One of the most crucial factors in the planning was whether the French troops would oppose the landings or not. A meeting was therefore arranged by Robert Murphy, the US Consular-General in French North Africa, between General Mast commanding the Algerian Division and the Allies represented by General Mark Clark, the Deputy Commander-in-Chief of *Torch*. Mark Clark and his party were put ashore on the night of 21/22 October at a point 75 miles west of Algiers from a submarine. The responsibility for getting them from the submarine, HMS *Seraph*, to the shore was given to No 1 SBS, which was now part of Stirling's 1st SAS Regiment. Three members, Captains G.B. Courtney, (brother of Roger Courtney who had pioneered the Folboat concept) and R.P. Livingstone and Lieutenant J.P. Foot took part in this successful operation, which led to Mast agreeing that French resistance would only be at the most little more than a gesture. Two weeks later, No 1 SBS was involved in a similar operation, to rescue General Giraud from Vichy France. A distinguished soldier, who had made a spectacular escape from a POW camp after the fall of France, it was hoped that, once *Torch* had taken place, he would be able to rally the French in North Africa to the Allied side.

Another element which also had a vital role in the success of *Torch* was what would become the Combined Operations Assault Pilotage Parties (COPPs). The origins of this lay in the reconnaissance of Rhodes carried out by Lt Commander Nigel Clogstoun-Willmott RN and Roger Courtney in March 1941 (see Chapter Four). Since then, Clogstoun-Willmott had carried out one more similar reconnaissance on Kupho Island off Crete, which was raided by Royal Marines in the summer of 1942. The *Torch* planners recognised early on the importance of a proper beach reconnaissance and the need to guide the invasion craft onto the correct beaches. Consequently, Clogstoun-Willmott was summoned back to England and in early September 1942 began to organise parties for this. He gathered together some young naval officers and SBS canoeists and, having flown to Gibraltar, detailed reconnaissance on the *Torch* beaches was carried out during the last part of October. Then, on the night 7/8 November, five teams were sent ashore from submarines to do the actual marking, using infra-red beams to mark the flanks and red torches the centre of the beaches.

It was not until well into October that Nos 1 and 6 Commandos, now commanded by Lt Colonels T.H. Trevor and I.F. McAlpine respectively, were told that they were to take part in *Torch*. The original plan was for their efforts to be co-ordinated by a small headquarters under Colonel Will Glendinning, now Deputy Commander of the SS Brigade, and two other officers, including Randolph Churchill. It was then decided that they should be integrated with the American forces, in particular the 168th Regimental Combat Team of three infantry battalions, an artillery battalion and supporting elements. These were merged with the Commandos at company level. What it did mean was that Nos 1 and 6 Commandos would be split among three ships, with No 6 in the *Aawatea* and No 1 divided between the *Otranto* and *Leedstown*. The preparations were somewhat hectic. Henry Brown of No 1 Commando recorded in his diary on 13 October:

> Early morning proceeded with full kit to Dundee station to join other chaps. Train left station at 0715 hours and proceeded via Perth, Glasgow to Stranraer. Here we boarded the channel steamer for Larne (N Ireland) which we reached after darkness. After unloading kit from steamer to train we proceeded to Belfast. Once more stores were unloaded, this time onto waiting transport. I went by march route with the rest to the docks; it was pouring with rain and we got well and truly soaked. Here we embarked on USS *Leedstown* just before midnight. On seeing my office stores properly stored I went to my sleeping quarters. These I found to be very comfortable when compared with most of the quarters available for soldiers. Nine men had to sleep in the same bunk.

They left Belfast next day, and then cruised at sea for five days while plans were laid for an amphibious exercise. This gave the opportunity for the Commandos to get to know their American counterparts as well as the US style of life on board. They found the rations to be rather too rich, but appreciated the endless ice cream and cigarettes. They carried out a practice landing at Inveraray, and then anchored off the Isle of Arran, finally setting sail in convoy for North Africa on the 26th. While at sea, they had plenty of time, with the aid of models and maps to study the tasks ahead of them. They were equipped with US helmets and Garand rifles because it was felt that the French would be more likely to surrender quickly to American rather than British troops, since the destruction of the French fleet at Mers-el-Kebir, the port of Oran, by the Royal Navy in July 1940 still rankled.

Half of No 1 Commando, under Tom Trevor himself, was to land at Cap Sidi Ferruch, some ten miles west of Algiers, and capture the fort there. This they achieved with no casualties, the garrison surrendering without a shot being fired. Among the prisoners were found the German Armistice Commissioners, along with the German Ambassador and his family. They then went on to seize the airfield at Blida.

No 6 Commando were to capture Fort Duperre, on the west side of the Bay of Algiers, but their day did not go as smoothly. For a start, the crew of the *Aawatea* were only imperfectly trained in handling landing craft and these were clumsily lowered, leading to the loss of some. Craft were sent from other ships to take the troops off, and the result was further confusion, and only a fifth of the craft met up with the motor launch which was to lead them to the beach. Engine problems and leaks also caused many to straggle and the first of them reached the beach two hours late. By this time the garrison was well alerted and the craft were illuminated by searchlight and subjected to artillery and machine gun fire. Poor navigation also added to their problems and few hit the right beach. One party under the Second-in-Command, Major A.S. Ronald, landed in the most heavily fortified part of Algiers harbour and all were killed, including Ronald, or captured. Eventually, the remainder made their way to Fort Duperre, but could make no impression against it with the light weapons which they had, and only after an air strike had been called down upon it did the garrison surrender.

The third party, the other half of No 1 Commando, under the Second-in-Command, Ken Trevor, cousin of Tom, also had an adventurous time in their efforts to capture Fort D'Estrée and the Batterie de Lazaret on the east side of the Bay of Algiers. Henry Brown:

At 0030 hrs we left USS *Leedstown* by landing craft and all craft then got into position for the move inshore. We were about seven miles off shore when we left the *Leedstown*. The boat which was to lead us inshore was soon contacted and we set off. There was a very heavy swell which tossed the small craft about a great deal. When about three miles off land the lights of the streets and houses of Algiers came into view. Our boat made its way to the east side of Cap Matifou (this is a point on the east side on the Bay of Algiers). When only a couple of miles off land a large battery of guns opened up and fired out to sea, a searchlight was also being used, however, as our boat came under cover of a hill the light did not shine on us. All boats formed up approximately ½ mile off shore and then moved in to land in formation.

At about 0312 hours our boats touched land and we commenced to disembark. There was a great swell and the surf on the North African shore is very heavy. Before all the men had got out of the boat a great wave came and lifted it clean out of the water on to the sandy shore, here it stayed as it was impossible to get it off. This by the way happened to most of the landing craft. We carried on and found we had landed in a slightly different place that was originally intended, it turned out to be the village of Ain Taya. However, orders were given and the Commando moved to its respective objectives.

I moved off with Headquarters and we proceeded in the direction of Cap Matifou to attack Batterie de Lazaret. Long before we reached the Batterie firing could be heard; this turned out to be one of our Troops attacking. We carried on along the road without opposition apart from having to duck from time to time due to tracer bullets proceeding in our direction. Dawn was now breaking and for the first time we were able to see what kind of a country we had invaded.

I carried on and soon came in sight of the Batterie which seemed quite a fine Fort. When about 300 yards from the Fort we had to take cover as French naval personnel in the Fort started to snipe at us. We endeavoured to set up the mortar so that we could shell the place, but every time we got up out of our lying positions bullets passed us in their dozens, we therefore stayed put for a while. I was then called upon by an officer to take the mortar cart and move it behind a shed some 200 yards away, but as soon as I got up bullets started flying once more. I asked for covering fire from our men which the officer gave permission for. I then ran very quickly to the shed with the truck; this enabled the chaps to set up the mortar and fire on the Fort. Time was getting on and the Fort would not surrender. An attack was put in by one of our Troops but it did not succeed; one of the men was killed and seven wounded.

We then called by wireless to a destroyer out at sea to come in nearer land and bombard the Fort; this it did but not enough time was given for us all to get out of the line of fire. At 1100 hours the bombardment commenced and we were caught right in the middle of it. Casualties occurred and one chap close to me lost his arm. Most of the local civilian population ran out of their houses when the firing started and really got very scared but nothing could be done for them. Time was getting on and still the Fort would not surrender. Attack by dive bomber was then asked for and we proceeded to evacuate the local population for the period this attack was to take place. During this time Algiers was attacked by German bombers but most of the bombs dropped by them were seen to drop in the bay.

The attack by English dive bombers was carried out on the Fort and then we again stormed the Batterie. This time they gave in and we entered during the afternoon. Most of the men were found to be very scared and it was evident that if it hadn't been for the French Commandant in charge of the Fort, they would have given in many hours before. All the troops then moved to La Perouse to find accommodation for the night which was coming quickly on. We broke in to a large house and after making a drop of tea and making something to eat we bedded down for the night. The wounded were made as comfortable as possible in a house close by.[35]

In spite of the problems which they had encountered, both Commandos had succeeded in capturing all their objectives, and were glad to hear next day that armistice negotiations had begun. There was now a few days' pause, while preparations were made for the next phase, the advance into Tunisia. In the meantime, one blow to many in No 1 Commando was the sinking of the *Leedstown* during an air raid on the evening of the 12th. Unfortunately she still had their kit on board, and it was to be some time before they would have anything more than what they had gone ashore in.

One other Commando, No 9 (Lt Colonel Ronnie Tod) was indirectly involved with *Torch*. They were sent as a reinforcement to the garrison at Gibraltar at the beginning of November in case of any retaliatory Axis moves through Spain. They remained there until early March 1943, when they returned to the United Kingdom, No 3 taking their place.

No 30 Commando

Another unit which made its operational debut during the *Torch* landings was No 30 Commando. It had been noted that during the campaigns in Yugoslavia and Greece, the Germans had made use of special intelligence gathering teams, the *Abwehrkommando*, who advanced with the forward troops, or sometimes ahead of them, and entered captured enemy headquarters to seize documents. This caught the attention of Commander I.L. Fleming RNVR (later Ian Fleming of James Bond fame), who was then working as Personal Assistant to the Director of Naval Intelligence (DNI), Admiral Godfrey. He put forward an idea for the formation of an 'Offensive Naval Intelligence Group', which was supported by DNI, and plans began to be laid for such a unit to be employed in *Sledgehammer*.

Another thinking along similar lines was Major W.G. Cass, The Buffs, then working as a staff officer in MI5. He had discussions with GHQ Home Forces, but they were negative in their reactions, considering that the existing Field Security Sections should be able to take on this task as an extension to their normal intelligence gathering role. Admiral Godfrey now approached the Joint Intelligence Committee (JIC), with the suggestion that an inter-service unit be formed. The War Office initially reflected the GHQ Home Forces view, and the Air Ministry considered that this was a task which could be carried out by the RAF Regiment without participating in a new organisation.

Eventually, however, DNI's persistence won through and it was agreed that such a unit, with RN, RM and Army elements should be raised. It came into being under the cover name of 'Special Engineering Unit' on 30 September 1942 and was placed under the control of CCO. Initially appointed to command it was Commander 'Red' Ryder VC RN of St Nazaire fame, with Major Cass as 2ic and Ian Fleming to represent DNI's interests. Three troops were formed – No 33 (RM), No 34 (Army) and No 36 (RN or 'Technical').* Selected to command No 33 Troop was Captain H.O. Huntingdon-Whiteley RM, a first class athlete and linguist who had taken part in the Dieppe raid with the RM Commando. The establishment of the troop was set at two officers and twenty other ranks, with the latter being selected from among volunteers for the RM Commandos, mainly those who had been in Huntingdon-Whiteley's platoon at Dieppe. The Army Troop had a slightly smaller establishment of two (later four) officers and twelve (later twenty) other ranks. They were chosen personally by Major Cass from those serving in the Commandos, but this was not without its problems:

> An immediate limitation as regards personnel became apparent. Special Service Brigade could provide men of first class character, good education and intelligence and of the highest physical capacity, but linguistic talent was lacking. Such men as had talent plus capacity were inevitably marked for promotion and could not be made available. The choice of suitable and entirely reliable personnel was of prime importance. This took a little time, but finally a very high standard of character and capacity was reached. It is worth noting that no less than 10 other ranks were young police officers between the ages of 23 and 26.

To command the troop, Major Cass chose Captain J. A. Ward RA, an experienced officer who had been with the Field Security Police in France during 1939-40 and then had joined No 3 Commando, taking part in both the Lofoten Islands and Vaagso raids.

While both Nos 33 and 34 Troops were placed under the admin-

---

*No 35 was held open in case the Air Ministry might change its mind over RAF participation. It never did.

istration of the Special Service Brigade, the Admiralty was not prepared to countenance this for No 36 Troop, their only exception
at this time being Royal Navy chaplains and surgeons serving with
the Royal Marine Commandos. In the end, therefore, the troop was
put on the strength of HMS *President 1* 'for duty outside the Admiralty with CCO (Special Engineering Unit) outside COHQ'[37], which
was a subtle way of saying that although No 36 Troop was operating
under CCO, the Admiralty, especially DNI, wanted to retain control
of it. The RN troop was, however, somewhat different to the other
two. For a start, its original establishment was just five officers, with
no ratings. It was also involved purely with technical intelligence,
and its officers attended numerous courses on sea mines, torpedoes,
electronics, hydrophones and asdic gear and the internal layout of
submarines. Its Commanding Officer, Lt Commander Q.T.P.M.
Riley RNVR was personally selected by Commander Ryder. Before
the war he had been heavily engaged in Polar exploration, and had
joined the RNVR on the outbreak of war, but had been temporarily
transferred to the Scots Guards for the projected expedition to Fin-
land in 1939, which never materialised. He had served with Gubbins
in Norway, and then been a flotilla officer with Combined Operations before going off to be a winter warfare instructor in Iceland.

Training for the unit as a whole was very comprehensive. Besides
general Commando skills and weapon handling, it covered enemy
mines and booby traps, the handling of explosives, demolitions and
counter-demolitions and recognition of enemy uniforms and equipment. Parachute training and small boat work also figured, as well
as recognition of enemy documents, search techniques, including
safe cracking and lock picking, prisoner handling, photography and
escape techniques. Although the unit was initially based at Amer-
sham in Buckinghamshire, the troops were each responsible for
their own training, which did lead to some unevenness in standards.

The first assault intelligence operation was, in fact, mounted
before the unit was formed. DNI had tasked the RM Commando
with the seizure of a German HQ in Dieppe during *Jubilee*, and
Huntingdon-Whiteley had formed a special section from his platoon
for this purpose. Unfortunately, it suffered along with the rest of
the Commando, its landing craft being hit and most of its members
spending several hours in the water before being picked up. *Torch*,
however, gave an ideal opportunity to put the concept into practice.
Training, of course, had at this stage hardly started, and so an *ad hoc*
section was formed, No 33 Section. It consisted of six Royal Marines

under the command of Lieutenant D.M.C. Curtis DSC RNVR, who had joined No 36 Troop from Coastal Forces, taking part in both the St Nazaire and Dieppe raids, and winning his decoration for the latter. Paul McGrath was a member of this select band:

We were going to enter Algiers harbour, make for the French Admiralty building, blow a few safes, pinch all the secret papers we could find and if Admiral Darlan was available, take him as well. There shouldn't be any shooting as the Americans had done a deal with the French who had agreed to capitulate as soon as they saw the Stars and Stripes. We were not entirely convinced but it sounded quite hopeful.

Nevertheless, I checked my armoury again. I was equipped with a Thompson sub-machine gun which fired .45 snub nosed bullets from a magazine which held twenty-eight of them, a .45 Colt semi-automatic, a fighting knife and a half dozen 36 grenades not yet primed.

For the remaining days prior to docking at Gibraltar we gave unarmed combat lessons to the Americans who reckoned that we were pretty rugged guys and they were glad we were on their side! We fired our guns at tins thrown into the sea, did our press-ups and fine tuned ourselves for the Algiers job.

At Gibraltar we were all kept below decks during daylight as it was feared that the spies for the other side might twig the operation. Eventually, we transferred to the *Malcolm*, a British destroyer flying the Stars and Stripes as it was agreed that the French would not fire on the American flag! The *Malcolm* was an old ship with two funnels, or smoke stacks to the Yanks, and as we raced through the Med. they belched out and occasionally choked us with acrid smoke.

As the light faded we settled on the port side of the funnels. Our gun magazines were full and grenades primed. Beneath us the steel deck was throbbing with life as the stokers drove the ship flat out towards our target, Algiers. In front of us we could see her sister ship the *Broke* but she was soon lost in the darkness. We were some five miles off the North African coast which twinkled with the lights of the towns and villages and as I lay on the deck with the tommy-gun nestling in my arms I had a happy thought that D.C.* might be right and that there would be no killing.

That thought became the first casualty when I saw the lights on the coast behind us go out. Almost immediately all the other lights were being switched off and it gave us a tight feeling in the gut. We were not being made welcome! Two or three searchlights beamed out to us but they passed over us as we were low on the water and a difficult target to pick up. However, our position was known and some shore batteries opened fire. We huddled on the hot deck and the memories of all the

*Lieut Dunstan Curtis.

fire we had endured at Dieppe made us twitchy as we knew what a high explosive shell could do to the nerves.

Fortunately the shells hit the water several hundred yards off target and soon we were out of range of that battery. Clearly, the gunners had not seen the Stars and Stripes; anyway, how the hell could they we asked. The night was moonless, a little cloudy and the stars were faint. As we turned the western point of the Bay of Algiers, D.C. who had been talking to the *Malcolm's* skipper decided that we should be on the starboard side of the funnels to facilitate our exit from deck to quay. As we settled into our new positions having squeezed out a few Yanks, we were caught in the full glare of a searchlight. Almost immediately the shore batteries to whom we were a clear target opened fire. 'Christ', I thought trying to dig into the deck, and then another thought which had sustained me before. 'You will be alright'.

The first shell hit the ship on the port side of the funnel killing outright some forty American soldiers. Our change of position had saved us. Of course we were unaware of the number of dead but we knew from the sound of the explosion that it had been a big shell and as the deck of the destroyer was carpeted with scores of American soldiers there just had to be a lot of casualties. And so it was.

The French gunners, presumably firing over open sights, struck the ship again and again and soon it was listing badly and moving slowly in the water. There were shouts from the naval gunners, 'Let's shoot back at the bastards!' And 'Take down that fucking flag and run up the white ensign!' And then another cry went up 'Throw the ammunition overboard!' The ship was blazing with several fires one of which was immediately behind where we were hugging the deck. I turned my head and saw that several crates of mortar bombs were alight. We had to work fast or we would be killed by our own explosives and that wasn't a happy thought. Reaching for our fighting knives, Corporal Whyman and I levered ourselves off the deck, rushed over to the blazing mortar bomb crates and after much hacking at the ropes and cursing and swearing we threw them all into the sea.

The ship was a shambles of wreckage, material and human. Even so, I learned later from D.C. that the skipper wanted to make another attempt to crash the boom into the harbour. It was not possible and we limped out to sea and finally beached on the coast some five miles west of Algiers.

Our party had escaped unhurt except for a small shrapnel nick to my left hand which the ship's doctor had dealt with after the shooting. It was now early morning and although we had no information as to whether the French were still fighting the decision was made to march to Algiers. We got there without incident, although a bit weary after the road march in hot weather, to say nothing of the night's activities. Under D.C.'s guidance we made for a villa perched on top of the west side of the hill which overlooks Algiers. It turned out to be the Italian Armistice Commission H.Q. and the occupants were not looking for trouble. We took their weapons and their cook prepared us a delicious Italian meal after which we viewed our prisoners with a little less belligerence![38]

This meal was very welcome as No 33 Section did not reach the Villa El Djenna until 0930 hours on the 9th. Later that morning they handed over the premises to the Field Security Police, and spent the next day helping arrange the release of Allied prisoners taken by the French. On the 11th, they joined the Field Security Police in searching the German Armistice Commission's quarters in the Hôtel Aletti, which ended up in a glorious party that evening with the Americans. Next day, however, Curtis heard that some members of the German Armistice Commission had been captured near Sidi Ferruch and that documents had been found on them. After extensive enquiries he traced the papers to the office of the US Army Intelligence and was able to inspect them. On the 15th, the section returned to Gibraltar, but Curtis and two of his party then returned to Algiers, where they spent another two weeks carrying out a detailed search of enemy headquarters.

Although the landing had been very much tougher than expected, *Torch* did prove that the Intelligence Assault Unit had a very worthwhile role to play, and Curtis took much comfort in the fact that they beat the Field Security Police to the Italian Armistice Commission by a clear two hours. From now on the unit would play an important role in all Allied operations in NW Europe and the Mediterranean, but not without some frustration.

Further Expansion

Before the end of 1942 two additional Commandos were raised. The first of these was provided by the Royal Marines, and marked another step in what would be eventually recognised as their logical right to be the amphibious force specialists. However, instead of calling for volunteers from the Royal Marine Division, it was decided to convert an existing battalion to the Commando role. Thus, on 10 October 1942, the 8th Battalion, which had been part of 103 RM Brigade in Wales, became B (RM) Commando under Lt Colonel P.W. O'H. Phibbs RM and moved to join what was now A (RM) Commando on the Isle of Wight. These titles, however, only lasted a matter of a few weeks and they became 40 and 41 (RM) Commandos respectively. After Dieppe No 40 (RM) Commando, now commanded by Lt Colonel J.C. Manners RM, made up the gaps in its ranks from volunteers, and Major Jeff Beadle was one of these:

> My total experience of the Corps at this time consisted of Recruit Training in the traditional hub of the Chatham Division, a brief period as a Corporal with a Boom Defence Detachment on the Thames and Officer Training. The relaxed mode of dress – cap, comforter and leather jerkin – less rigid discipline, living out in billets and roadside Troop Parades contrasted sharply with barrack life, blue sea service uniforms and ceremonial drill. This came as a cultural shock to a newly commissioned officer. Nevertheless, it quickly became apparent that the spirit, morale and discipline were exceptionally high. The only penalty for misdemeanour or failing to measure up to the stringent standards demanded was RTU – Return to Unit.
>
> The Commando had faced heavy opposition in its first action and there was a feeling that there could be plenty more of the Dieppe-type operation to follow. Training was therefore directed towards improving fitness and perfecting fighting techniques. Platoon and Troop training was interspersed with unit exercises, with particular emphasis on night landings and assault on coastal batteries.
>
> Troops exercised on specific tasks allotted to them – such as cliff haulage or beach demolition. The knowledge gained was then passed on to the remainder of the Unit. Some ranks marched north to try their hand at the Achnacarry course, whilst others attended specialist courses run by the Corps and Army.
>
> Training was not without its trial and error, but the incentive was always to be better than the next man or platoon. One aimed for realism and the use of live ammunition helped considerably towards this end. Fitness was of paramount importance and the daily speed march, run against the clock, would end with a plunge into the sea in fighting order when the opportunity presented itself. Local garrison troops provided an enthusiastic enemy opposition, with tough inter-service rivalry, leading at times to the odd bloody nose.[39]

It must be stressed that, unlike with all newly joined Army Commandos, and, indeed many who had been in the Commando ranks for some time, the Achnacarry course was still not mandatory for the Royal Marine Commandos at this time.

The other new Commando, No 14, was raised for more specialist employment. Since the Vaagso Raid, there had been no Special Service activity against Norway, mainly because of German reprisals during the winter 1941-42, but Churchill was constantly turning his attention here, fully realising that here was another area in which German troops could be kept tied down. There was also the thorny problem of Norway's wealth of natural resources, and the need continually to deny the Germans their use. It was with the latter in mind that Operation *Musketoon* was mounted in September 1942. The object was to destroy the power station at Glomfjord, south of Narvik, which supplied an aluminium plant in the area.

Selected to carry out the operation were Captains G.D. Black MC and J.B.J. Houghton MC with eight other ranks of No 2 Commando, along with two Norwegian corporals who were working for SOE. They set sail from the Clyde in a Free French submarine on 11 September, arriving off Glomfjord four days later. Having landed and hidden their craft in moss, they then had a difficult approach march over mountainous and glacial country, but nevertheless arrived in sight of the power station on the 18th. They now lay up and made plans, and made their attack on the night of 20/21 September. They achieved complete surprise and managed to place charges on all five generators, but, as they withdrew and the charges were beginning to go up, they encountered Germans and were forced to split up. In the ensuing mêlée, one of the Norwegians was mortally wounded, a British soldier killed and the two officers also wounded. The wounded and four others were captured, but the other Norwegian, Corporal Christiansen, as well as Guardsman Fairclough and Private Twigg, and Lance Sergeant O'Brien managed separately to reach the Swedish frontier and were eventually repatriated. As for the prisoners, they were the first to suffer under Hitler's Commando Order, Captains Black and Houghton being shot by firing squad.

The story of this was only pieced together when the survivors arrived back in England. In the meantime, Mountbatten considered that for operations of this type, especially in the inhospitable Norwegian winter, troops were needed who were physically acclimatised. Consequently, he ordered the setting up of North Force. This was organised in October 1942 and was built round Captain F.W. Fynn's troop of No 12 Commando, which was sent to Lerwick in the Shetlands under the title of Fynn Force, with a cover story of Royal Marines engaged on hardening training. In mid-November they were joined by Lieutenant Risnes and ten men of the Norwegian troop of No 10 (IA) Commando, and on the 22nd of that month left Lerwick in an MTB for their first operation, a reconnaissance, but were stopped by a German patrol boat south of Bergen and forced to return. Undeterred, another group set out on the evening the first party returned to Lerwick. This time they succeeded in anchoring in a small fjord, where they remained for two days, stopping local water traffic and interrogating the Norwegians they came across, before returning home.

This was only a start, for Mountbatten was convinced of the need for Arctic specialists from any source. In a minute to the Chiefs of Staff dated 5 November 1942 on winter operations in Norway, he wrote:

> I have under consideration the establishment of two or three small advanced bases on islands or reefs on the Western Coast of Norway from which attacks on shipping by canoe, and winter raids on important inland targets in Norway by small raiding parties, could be carried out.
>
> 2. It will be appreciated that the success of this type of operation is dependent upon the personnel selected having considerable skill and experience in living and operating in conditions of extreme cold. Provided they are thoroughly skilled, particularly as skiers, operations which would not otherwise be feasible in winter could be carried out with every chance of success.
>
> 3. In order to mount these raids it will be necessary to collect a pool of about 15 officers and 40 other ranks who are expert in operating in Arctic conditions. If the operations are to take place this winter the collection of this Force must be carried out now as a matter of urgency.
>
> 4. The supply of such officers and men, and especially other ranks is extremely limited, [and] it would be necessary to draw on all three services and the Allied contingents to collect sufficient suitable personnel.[40]

The Chiefs of Staff agreed and six days later No 14 Commando began to form under the command of Lt Colonel E.A.M. Wedderburn Royal Scots. It was organised into two troops – No 1 with nine officers and 18 ORs specialising in small boat operations and No 2 with six officers and 22 ORs as cross-country skiing specialists. Included in its ranks were some Canadians and members of the RNVR.

There was at the beginning of October 1942, a proposal for yet another Commando to be raised. On the 5th, Lord Lovat wrote directly to the Prime Minister asking that his own family regiment, The Lovat Scouts, become a Commando unit with a special role:

> I am confident that I am on the right lines. I have not destroyed any aeroplanes in this war but I have killed quite a lot of Germans. With

a few really good men I think there are definite possibilities of doing something on 'Stirling's' [sic] lines on the Occupied Coast Line.*

Both Churchill and Ismay initially thought that, since The Lovat Scouts were then in the reconnaissance role with an independent infantry brigade in Caithness, they would make a very good addition as a replacement for Layforce. Whether they envisaged sending the Lovat Scouts to the Middle East, though, is not clear. There was, however, a snag, whch was pointed out by the War Office. The Lovat Scouts were only 450 strong, and it was certain that a proportion would not be up to Commando entry standards, and the danger was that the regiment would lose its unique character. Lovat saw the sense in this and the idea was eventually dropped.[41]

Operation Frankton

As 1941 had ended on a high note with the Vaagso raid, so did 1942, but with a very different type of operation and another specialised unit of whom no mention has been made up until now. Its origins were similar to those of the SBS and, like the latter, it owed its existence to one man. Captain H.G. Hasler RM, known to all as 'Blondie', had distinguished himself as a landing officer in the Norwegian campaign, being made an OBE and winning the French Croix de Guerre. Like Roger Courtney, he had much pre-war small boat experience, and while serving with the MNBDO on Hayling Island in autumn 1940, he wrote a paper suggesting that enemy shipping in harbour could be destroyed by using canoes carrying powerful charges and manned by divers. The canoe would be placed alongside the ship, the charge exploded, and the canoe scuttled. The Admiralty considered it impracticable, and so in spring 1941 Hasler tried the idea on COHQ, also suggesting beach reconnaissance as another role. Again, especially with the SBS in existence, the reaction was negative.

On 19 December 1941, Italian 'human torpedoes' penetrated Alexandria harbour and badly damaged the battleships *Queen Elizabeth* and *Valiant* with delayed action charges. This caused some consternation and even Churchill himself began to agitate for similar tactics to be adopted. COHQ now remembered Hasler's paper, and

---

* Stirling's original concept for the SAS was the destruction of enemy aircraft on the ground.

he was posted to the Combined Operations Development Centre (CODC), which had taken over from the old ISTDC, to develop suitable boats. For this he was given two men from the SS Brigade.

Initially, Hasler concentrated on producing an 'explosive' motorboat along the lines of an Italian model which had been used in a successful attack on Royal Navy shipping in Suda Bay in March 1941, and a similar, but abortive operation against Malta, during which the Italian boats had been captured. This craft was known under the cover name of a 'Boom Patrol Boat'. Canoes, however, were never far from Hasler's mind, and he proposed that they should be used in conjunction with the Boom Patrol Boats, using them to find ways through any surface obstructions which might hinder the latter. This was agreed by Mountbatten, and the Royal Marine Boom Patrol Detachment (RMBPD) was formed, its name partially a cover, but also representing the fact that one of its tasks was to patrol the defensive boom outside Portsmouth harbour. Hasler set up his headquarters in Southsea, and recruited his officers from the RM Small Arms School at Gosport and his men from the RM Auxiliary Battalion at Portsmouth. The organisation was two sections, each of six 2-man canoe teams. Instead of using the SBS Folboat, Hasler, wanting something more robust for the heavier loads which they would have to carry, developed the Cockle, which, rather than being completely dismantled like the Folboat, was merely collapsed onto the hull.

Of increasing concern during 1942 were the activities of the German blockade-runners, which brought back essential raw materials from the Far East. Bordeaux was known to be one of the principal ports used, but lying ninety miles up the Gironde, it was a difficult target. Air attack, mining and a standing submarine patrol were dismissed and, in September 1942, COHQ decided that only the use of the RMBPD stood any chance of success, and Hasler was called in to join the planning team. He proposed that three canoes be dropped by submarine at the mouth of the Gironde (this was subsequently raised to six) and that, lying up by day and paddling by night, they could make their way to the harbour. Here they would attack limpet mines to the merchantmen, withdraw, scuttle their canoes and then make their way overland to Spain. It seemed fraught with difficulty, but, after several rehearsals, from which valuable experience was gained, Hasler believed that it could succeed.

The force was divided into two. In A Division were *Catfish* (Hasler and Marine Sparks), *Crayfish* (Corporal Laver, Mne Mills) and *Conger* (Corporal Sheard, Mne Moffatt), while B had *Cuttlefish* (Lieutenant

MacKinnon, Mne Conway), *Coalfish* (Sergeant Wallace, Mne Ewart) and *Cachalot* (Mnes Ellery and Fisher). At 2000 hours on 7 December they disembarked from the submarine HMS *Tuna*, (Lieutenant R.F. Raikes DSO RN), but suffered an early casualty as *Cachalot* damaged her hull when being passed through the submarine's hatch. As they entered the estuary of the Gironde, they became caught up in a tide race, and *Coalfish* disappeared without trace, with its crew presumed drowned. They then encountered a second and heavier tide race and *Conger* capsized. Hasler told the crew, after towing them for a distance, to make for the shore, but both were later found to have drowned. Their troubles were not yet over. Coming across four anchored Chasseur-type boats, they were forced to proceed with caution and adopt a more widely dispersed formation. Once clear, Hasler discovered that *Cuttlefish* was missing, but there was nothing that could be done but to go on. At 0630 hours, they attempted to land, but were foiled by submerged stakes on a shingle line, and daylight was breaking when they finally found a suitable spot in which to rest up, having covered 23 nautical miles. They camouflaged the canoes and took cover in some low scrub. It was not, however, an undisturbed day, as Hasler relates:

> A considerable number of small fishing boats had begun to issue from the CHENAL DE ST VIVIEN, and now headed towards our beach. At the same time, a number of women appeared walking towards us along the shore. We took cover as well as we could, but it became hopeless when a number of boats landed on the beach and the fishermen began to light a camp fire and make preparation for breakfast within a few yards of us.
>
> We were soon observed and had to explain that we were British and that our presence was not to be revealed to anybody. Some of the party seemed quite unconvinced and declared that we were Germans, but we pointed out that in any case it would be to their advantage to say nothing to anybody on the subject and shortly afterwards the women returned to the village and the men to their boats. At about 1600 hours some of the women returned for a further chat, but as we were otherwise undisturbed it seemed as if they had followed our instructions.[42]

Apart from some difficulty in relaunching the canoes, the next night's paddling was uneventful, although it became very cold, with splashes of water freezing on the cockpit covers. They found a place to lie up at the first attempt, and their only concern was when a herd of cows was released into their field. They were now faced with a problem. On the night of the 9th/10th there were three hours of flood tide, followed by six hours of ebb, and then a further three of flood. They thus had to pause while the tide was in ebb, and so they had to halt on an island in the middle of the river. This, however, meant that their plan to attack on the following night was not possible because they were behind schedule. Hasler therefore decided to establish an advanced base this night and then make his attack early on the night of 11/12 December, thereby allowing several hours of darkness for their withdrawal. They found a suitable place at 2300 hours on the 10th and, after a night's rest, spent the day preparing the limpet mines and sorting out their equipment. The plan was for *Catfish* to cover the west and *Crayfish* the east side of the docks. The time fuses on the limpets were set at 2100 hours and 15 minutes later both canoes embarked on the final lap.

Catfish got past the entrance to the basins without difficulty, except that it was necessary to keep about a cable offshore owing to a good many lights on shore, particularly around the lock gates . . . eight limpets are believed to have been placed as follows:-

> 3 on a cargo ship of about 7,000 tons.
> 2 on the engine room of a Sperrbrecher.*
> 2 on the stern of a large cargo ship of about 7,000 tons.
> 1 on the stern of a small tanker.

Owing to the necessity for a later start it was not possible to examine more than half the length of the target area before the tide began to ebb and it became impossible to proceed any further in silence. Whilst *Catfish* was a little distance from the side of the Sperrbrecher in the act of turning to go down stream, we were seen by a sentry on deck, who shone a torch on us. Fortunately, we were able to get back close to the ship's side and drift along with the tide without making any movement. The sentry followed us along the deck, shining his torch down on us at intervals, but was evidently unable to make up his mind as to what we actually were, owing to the efficiency of the camouflage scheme. We were able to get into a position under the bow of the ship where he could no longer see us, and after waiting there about five minutes everything seemed quiet, so we resumed our course down stream. The attack on the second large merchant ship was rather spoilt by the presence of a tanker alongside her, and the fact that the tide was now running so strongly that I considered it unsafe to get in between the bows of the two ships; this forced us to attack the stern end only. After all the limpets had been placed *Catfish* withdrew down the river without further incident. Whilst having a short rest in mid-stream near the south end of the ILE DE CASEAU we were

*Fast patrol boat used for laying mines.

rejoined by *Crayfish* who was also on her way back, having completed her attack. This meeting was purely by chance and it was decided to continue in company until the end of the withdrawal.[43]

Corporal Lever had experienced no problems with sentries and had placed eight limpets in all, five on a large cargo ship and three on a smaller liner. The two crews continued down stream and then landed, a ¼ mile apart, at 0600 hours. This was the last that Hasler saw of *Crayfish* and her crew. Both now scuttled their canoes and set off on foot.

Back in England, the first news heard on the operation was a German High Command communiqué on 10 December which announced that a sabotage squad had been caught at the mouth of the Gironde and eliminated. On the 21st, DNI received a message that two merchant vessels, *Dresden* and *Alabama*, and three others had been damaged by mysterious explosions. Nothing else being heard, all ten canoeists were officially posted as 'Missing believed killed'. Then, on 23 February, a further message, this time from Hasler himself, came via SOE giving very brief details on the three canoes which had been lost en route to the target. A week later, he and Sparks arrived back by air from Gibraltar having been passed down through a French Resistance escape organisation. It later transpired that five merchantmen had indeed been damaged, although, being empty at the time, the damage was not as extensive as it might have been. As for the others, apart from those drowned, Wallace, Ewart, Laver, Mills, MacKinnon and Conway were all captured and became further victims of the Führer Order on Commandos. For their gallantry Hasler was awarded a DSO and Bill Sparks a DSM, while Albert Laver and William Mills received posthumous Mentions in Despatches.

CHAPTER SIX

The Mediterranean
1943

Tunisia

After the *Torch* landings and the subsequent armistice with the French, the next stage was the advance into Tunisia. Before this could be done it was vital to seize ports with amphibious operations along the coast. On 11 November 1942, Bougie was seized by 36 Infantry Brigade and next day No 6 Commando captured the port of Bône, while the 3rd Parachute Battalion seized the airfields, having been dropped from US C-47s. The Commandos relieved the Paras on the airfield, and on the 14th came the first German reaction, when the Luftwaffe attacked, but was fended off using Oerlikon guns taken from damaged ships in the harbour. That evening a squadron of Spitfires arrived. Six days later No 1 Commando arrived from Algiers to join No 6. During all this time Bône was subjected to constant air raids, both by day and night.

On 21 November, No 6 Commando were ordered to move to Tabarka, sixty miles to the east. They went by train, covered by a solitary Spitfire, which had to keep returning to Bône to refuel, and during one of its absences tragedy struck. Two Fwl90s strafed the train and the Commando suffered 43 casualties, including 11 killed. The Arab driver had fled, and a Commando had to drive the train to La Calle, a small port west of Bône, where the next few days were spent unloading stores from ships. Two troops, under Captains Murray Scott and Robinson, were sent to the Tabarka area to check on a suspected tank harbour, which proved to be a dummy, but they did have some brushes with the Germans. They got back, having inflicted casualties at no cost to themselves, but what those who took part remembered most was the intense cold inland from the coast. No 1 Commando now moved by landing craft on the 26th to Tabarka, and No 6 was ordered, on the same day, to Sedjenane.

The overall situation at this time was that what was now the British First Army under Lt General K.A.N. Anderson, but represented by little more than 78th Division, was advancing into Tunisia on two axes, with its ultimate objective as Tunis. 36 Brigade was taking the northern route from Tabarka via Sedjenane and Bizerta, while 11 Brigade took the inland and more direct route via Béja and Sidi Nsir. In the meantime, the Germans were steadily reinforcing by flying troops in from Italy and Sicily and what was about to take place were a series of meeting engagements. Indeed, the 6th Royal West Kents, who had helped the Commandos secure Bône, had already had a brush with Kampfgruppe Witzig at Djebel Abiod on the 17th, but the Germans had withdrawn once the rest of 36 Brigade came up.

The advance from Sedjenane was led by the 8th Argylls, who had been transferred from the RM Division to 78th Division earlier in the year. Some ten miles east lay two features, which were nicknamed Green Hill and Bald Hill by the CO 8th Argylls. These stood astride the road to Mateur, providing an ideal ambush position, something which the Germans had been quick to realise. The inevitable happened, and the Argylls had to pull back having suffered heavy casualties. On 30 November, No 6 Commando was ordered to attack Green Hill, while the 6th Royal West Kents went for Bald Hill. This was to be a straight forward infantry attack, which did not require specialist Commando skills, and was to be the first of many operations in which the Commandos would have to perform as ordinary infantry. There was little time for reconnaissance, and at 0400 hours Captain Mayne and No 5 Troop put in a feint attack, while Nos 3, 4, and 6 Troops under Captain Coade attacked from the north and west. Lack of air and little artillery support compounded the problem and, in spite of a battle which went on all day, the Commandos could make little impression on the German defences and were forced to retire. The attack by the Royal West Kents was a similar story. No 6 Commando suffered the loss of another eighty casualties, which, with no reinforcements available, meant reorganising it into four troops. Four days later, Lt Colonel McAlpine was evacuated sick, and the second-in-command, Major McLeod, took over temporary command until Derek Mills-Roberts arrived out from England on 13 January.

Meanwhile, No 1 Commando had not been idle. They were given a task more suited to their training, an amphibious landing at Sidi el-Mouhjad, some fifteen miles west of Bizerta, in order to turn the enemy flank. They embarked, with four US 168 RCT troops under command, from Tabarka on the night of 30 November in nine LCMs and four LCAs, and, after an uneventful voyage, landed in the early hours of the following morning. It was a very wet landing, but the

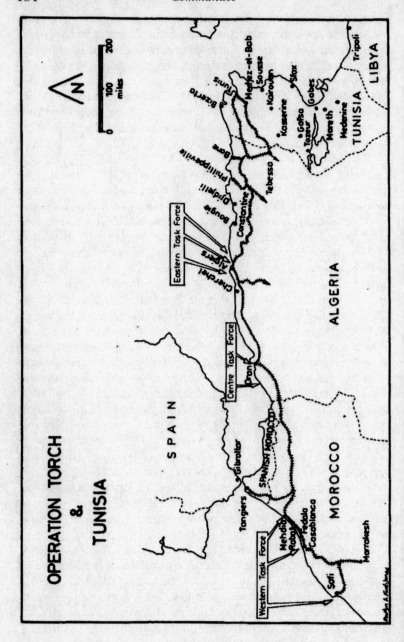

only casualties were some donkeys, which had been brought along to carry the mortars, an Army Film Unit sergeant's camera equipment and a wireless set. The troops then advanced inland and set about disrupting the Axis lines of communication.

> From now on until three days later the Commando not only dominated this area and denied the use of the road [Bizerta-Sedjenane] to the enemy, but they sent a troop to keep under continuous observation the aerodrome at Sidi Ahmed, about seven miles to the north-east of Douar Faoudja. During those three days the Commando also occupied an area of some 125 square miles, inside which they moved with complete freedom, and were able to destroy any enemy transport attempting to use the road. . .
>
> All this was accomplished in the face of considerable topographical difficulties, none of which could have been suspected from a preliminary study of available maps.
>
> Near the roads the countryside is open and easily accessible to tanks, but only in their immediate neighbourhood. Off the road the Commando was able to advance only about two miles in every hour during the hours of daylight and at half rate at night. The hills and valleys are covered with tall Mediterranean heather, rising miles [sic] at a time to a height of at least seven feet. Higher up the mountains the scrub is lower but the going no less difficult. The easiest method of progression is to imitate the goat and move on hands and knees, for these animals, which roam the hills in profusion, have forced their own tracks through the undergrowth. What tracks for human beings the country does provide are hard to find even on a large-scale map, and normal movement is impossible without the aid of a local guide.
>
> Trustworthy guides are difficult to find . . .[1]

Indeed, on three occasions local Arabs gave away troop positions to the Germans, and there were several brushes with the enemy, culminating in what was virtually a pitched battle. Another limiting factor was rations. Each man was supplied with two tins of stew, half a tin of bully beef, three bars of chocolate and two packets of biscuits to last him for the complete operation. Some managed to supplement this with chickens and eggs, but it was shortage of food more than anything else which forced the Commando to withdraw to Cap Serrat. As with No 6 Commando, casualties had not been light, with sixty British and 74 American, and on reorganisation No 1 was reduced from ten to six troops.

Both No 1 and No 6 Commandos now found themselves helping to hold the line, which was by now very stretched with too few

troops. These verses by Leslie Greenslade of No 1 Commando give
something of their activities:

> We were spread out to work in the mountains,
> And our Xmas was spent amongst mud,
> But our NAAFI supplied us with beer and fags,
> But they couldn't supply us the pud.
>
> The rumour of going home had faded,
> As they moved us from front to front,
> And the rains were falling so heavy,
> For patrolling we thought we'd need punts.
>
> We now come to a mountainous sector,
> Where patrols have become a routine,
> All round a strong-point called Green-hill,
> Which is more of a nightmare than dream.
>
> We got swopped from sector to sector,
> From Greenhill to Beja and back,
> The mountains we'd got used to,
> We could tell you offhand every track.[2]

For a time Will Glendinning and his headquarters were able to exercise
some operational control over the Commandos, but then they came
under command of different formations and once again he became
superfluous. Perhaps the most epic action was that fought by No 6 on
26 February, the day on which the Axis launched Operation *Ochsen-
kopf* ('Ox Head'), their follow-up to the Battle of Kasserine, which had
inflicted a 'bloody nose' on the Americans, and aimed to push the
British back in the north. At the time the Commando was operating
with the reconnaissance regiment of 78th Division in the Medjez el
Bab area. Reduced to 250 men, Mills-Roberts was expected to defend
an area of some 75 square miles and could only do this by setting up
a series of strong-points and patrolling between them. One of these
strongpoints was attacked by the crack Parachute Regiment Koch, and
a desperate battle followed as Mills-Roberts sent other troops to the
area. There were some one hundred casualties, but No 6 succeeded
in halting the enemy, who were later thrown back by a counter-attack
made by tank and infantry reinforcements. For this Mills-Roberts was
awarded a DSO to add to the MC which he had won at Dieppe.

Lack of reinforcements from England, which meant that both
Commandos were dwindling in strength, together with the fact that

they lacked the heavy weapons and transport of a normal infantry battalion, resulted in them being finally withdrawn from the line at the beginning of April, before the final decisive battles took place, and they left for England at the end of the month. They had had a hard and frustrating time, but had more than proved that they were capable of operating as normal infantry. An overall lack of Allied manpower had, however, been responsible for their misuse, and it was this factor which was often to influence their employment in the future, especially in Normandy. That their efforts were officially recognised is reflected in this letter from General Eisenhower to Tom Trevor:

Dear Colonel Trevor,

You and the men whom you command have been identified with the TUNISIAN campaign since the very day on which the initial landings were made. Since then you have been engaged actively on the most difficult mountainous terrain of the entire front.

As the time draws near for your departure from this theatre, it is a real pleasure to me to express to you and your gallant men commendation for a job well done. You have exemplified those rugged, self-reliant qualities which the entire world associates with the very name 'Commando'. Please transmit my appreciation to the officers and men of your command.

Sincerely yours,
(Sgd) Dwight D. Eisenhower[3]

Every man in both Commandos was given a copy of this or the similar one written to Derek Mills-Roberts.

No 30 Commando, too, had been involved in the Tunisian campaign. The success of No 33 Section during *Torch* did not go unnoticed, and in February 1943 Dunstan Curtis returned to North Africa, along with Captain Huntingdon-Whiteley, Lieutenant G. McFee RNVR, 17 Royal Marines and a Naval writer (clerk). They were placed under the command of C-in-C Mediterranean, Admiral Cunningham, with the task of operating against naval intelligence targets, their title now being No 33 Troop of No 30 Commando. They based themselves at Bône, and were equipped with three jeeps and a staff car. They soon made contact with another embryo force, Bill Stirling's element of No 62 Commando (see next chapter) and were able to carry out special boat and parachute training with them, and, indeed, a section took part in a small, but abortive raid with them at the beginning of April on the island of Galita.

The bulk of No 33 Troop, set out, at the end of March to pass through the British First Army and met up with the Eighth Army in front of Gabes Gap. It was agreed that they should accompany the leading troops, and to this end they joined the 51st Highland Division for the Battle of Wadi Akarit, which opened on the night of 6/7 April. They were able to search a number of very newly captured positions and had the odd brush with the enemy, suffering one casualty when Dunstan Curtis was slightly wounded during a confrontation with some German tanks. Although nothing of particular interest was found, it was a very useful experience and enabled the troop to perfect its tactics.

Once the Eighth Army had come up against the strong Axis defences at Enfidaville, the emphasis switched to First Army, and No 33 Troop now returned to their area of operations. They were placed under a makeshift organisation called S Force, which was to coordinate all intelligence gathering activities. Thus, No 33 Troop found itself joining the SOE, SIS, Special Investigation Branch (SIB) of the Royal Military Police, Political Warfare Executive (PWE), Civil Affairs and three squadrons of the RAF Regiment. Most of these agencies were non-combatant, and did not expect to enter Bizerta and Tunis, the two ultimate objectives of the campaign, until they had been secured. This, of course, was not No 30 Commando's style, as used as they were by now to entering with the leading troops. Curtis, therefore sought and obtained permission from the commander of S Force to operate independently, with the proviso that any intelligence material captured would pass through S Force before going to C-in-C Mediterranean. Nevertheless, it still did not give Curtis the freedom of action which he had had with the Eighth Army, and No 33 Troop was not able to get into Tunis until after it had been captured. They, did, however, capture the airfield at El Aouina on their own, after a short skirmish, and this revealed some valuable items, and over 250 prisoners were captured by the troop during the period 7-9 May. During the search of Tunis, Huntingdon-Whiteley and half the troops joined the Americans in Bizerta, but found little of value. All important material was sent by air to Algiers.

Although, in sum, the information gathered was not as valuable as had been hoped, No 33 Troop did learn important lessons, which would make their operations much more valuable in future. Others, too, recognised their worth, and this was reflected in a bar to Curtis's DSC, and Mentions in Despatches for Huntingdon-Whiteley and Sergeant Kruthoffer.

Husky

With the *Torch* landings successfully completed and the British First and Eighth Armies slowly beginning to bottle up the Axis forces in Tunisia, the next problem for the Allies was to decide where to strike next after North Africa had been cleared. The British view was that the main clash of arms was currently on the Eastern Front, and that since the Western Allies were not yet strong enough to mount *Round Up*, they should continue to concentrate on the Mediterranean, with the aims of preventing Axis reinforcement of the Eastern Front and knocking Italy out of the war. This could best be done by a series of amphibious operations, first against Sicily and then the Italian main-land. The Americans, on the other hand, were keen to maintain pressure in the Pacific and still wanted to strike directly at Germany rather than operate on the European periphery. They viewed inten-sive amphibious operations in the Mediterranean as a drain on the still limited amphibious assets. The opportunity to debate the issue came at the Casablanca Conference of January 1943. After five days of intensive discussion, it was agreed that the Anglo-American objec-tive would be Sicily (*Husky*) and that in the meantime *Bolero* would continue and *Round Up* be mounted once German resistance had been sufficiently weakened. Planning for *Husky* began immediately.

The plan eventually evolved was for two major landings, by Pat-ton's Seventh US Army on the south-west coast and Montgomery's Eighth on the south-east corner of the island. 1st Canadian Division would land on the west side of Cape Passero, and 51st Highland Division on its tip, while the British 5th and 50th Divisions landed south of Syracuse. As with *Torch*, one of the main concerns of the planners was coastal batteries, in particular some on the left flank of Canadian beaches and those dominating 5th Division's land-ings. This was an obvious Commando task, and it was a question of selecting which Commandos should take part. At the time, March 1943, there were three Commandos in the Mediterranean. Nos 1 and 6 were in Tunisia, but depletion of strength through casu-alties and the fact that they had been in continuous action since early November ruled them out. This left No 3 Commando, which had just relieved No 9 on Gibraltar. They were accordingly sent to Algiers in April. From here they went to Sfax, and then in May to Egypt, where they married up with General Dempsey's XIII Corps and were finally told of *Husky* and their role in it, which would be to land with 5th Division.

It was considered that the Canadian landings would require the

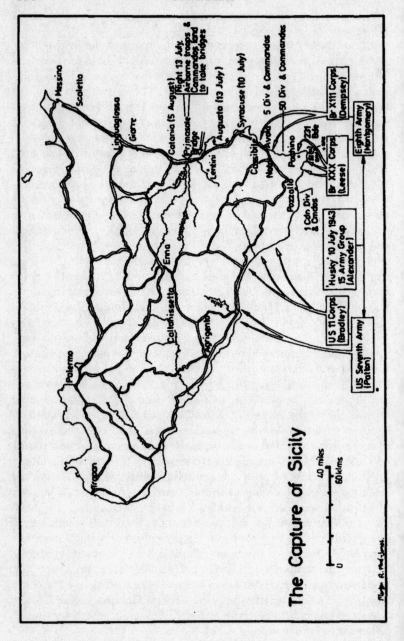

The Capture of Sicily

Messina
Scaletta
Linguaglossa
Giarre
Catania (5 August)
Primasole Bridge
Lentini
Augusta (13 July)
Cassibile
Syracuse (10 July)
Avola
Noto
Pachino
Pozzallo

Night 13 July, Airborne troops & Commandos land to take bridges

5 Div & Commandos
50 Div & Commandos

Br X111 Corps (Dempsey)
Br XXX Corps (Leese)
231 Inf Bde

Eighth Army (Montgomery)

Enna
Caltanissetta
Girgenti
Palermo
Trapani

US 11 Corps (Bradley)

1 Cdn Div & Cmdos

'Husky' 10 July 1943
15 Army Group (Alexander)

US Seventh Army (Patton)

40 miles
50 klms

0

services of two Commandos, and the two Royal Marine Commandos, who were both training in Scotland at the time, were chosen. No 2 Commando was also selected as an initial reinforcement, to be moved to the Mediterranean once transport was available.

The concept of having a Commando headquarters where more than one Commando was involved in operations in the same theatre had not worked in Tunisia. However, with the prospect of up to four Commandos about to operate in the Mediterranean, Laycock argued that a coordinating headquarters would be needed, if Commando interests were to properly represented. In spite of War Office objections, this was agreed, and on 12 April 1943 Laycock set up the SS Brigade Advanced HQ at Prestwick, with Nos 2, 3, 40 (RM) and 41 (RM) Commandos under command. This left the Rear HQ under Lord Lovat at Sherborne in Dorset, with responsibility for Nos 1, 4, 5, 6, 9, 10, 12 and 14 Commandos, the Assault Intelligence Unit, which now had the cover name of No 30 Commando, No 62 Commando (SSRF), No 2 SBS, the COPPs and RM Boom Patrol Unit.

Laycock, and Nos 40 and 41 (RM) Commandos set sail in the transports *Derbyshire* and *Durban Castle* at the end of June. By now, especially as a result of Tunisia, each Commando was organised into five troops of three officers and 62 men each, broken down into two sections, and a Heavy Weapons Troop with two 3in mortars and two Vickers medium machine guns, which considerably enhanced the Commando's firepower. With the Royal Marine Commandos were embarked elements of 1st Canadian Division, with whom Nos 40 and 41 had spent the last half of June in combined training exercises. This enabled a very good relationship to be built up. The plan was to sail to Sicily and on 1 July everyone was briefed on the impending operation. In the meantime, No 3 Commando had been carrying out intensive training outside Suez. They had been placed under command of what was called HQ Middle East Raiding Forces.

When David Stirling took over control of the reconstituted Middle East Commando in summer 1942, it had become 1st SAS Regiment. Stirling himself controlled its destiny single-handed, but unfortunately he was captured at the end of January 1943, while operating behind the Axis lines in the Gafsa area of Tunisia. Paddy Mayne, his second-in-command, while operationally brilliant, did not have the temperament to manage what had grown into a large organisation, especially as it inevitably meant much paperwork. It was therefore decided to break 1 SAS down into the Special Raiding Squadron

(SRS) under Paddy Mayne, and, what had been No 1 SBS, the Special Boat Squadron under Lord Jellicoe. The Greek Sacred Heart Squadron was also brought into the organisation, and appointed to overall command in early March 1943 was 'Kid' Cator. After recovering from his wound received at the head of No 51 ME Commando in Eritrea, he had been running an SOE school at Haifa, and would now coordinate the operations of both SRS and No 3 Commando in support of the XIII Corps landings in Sicily. While No 3 Commando was to land ahead of the 5th Division, Paddy Mayne's squadron was to support 51st Highland Division by seizing a lighthouse and battery on the very tip of Cape Passero. As for Cator's first impressions of No 3 Commando, he visited them in their makeshift desert camp outside Cairo soon after their arrival, and thought them 'a grand lot of chaps and [with] a v good past operational record'.[4]

On 9 July, the day before the Sicily landings, the Commandos were given their final briefing. In the meantime, in fact, ever since February, the COPPists had been busy carrying out detailed reconnaissance of the beaches. COPP 3 had lost three men in February, and COPP 4 had also suffered casualties. Later they had been joined by COPPs 5 and 6, who carried out the final beach marking. Also involved were RN Beachhead Commandos *Charlie, Easy, Fox, George, King, Mike* and *Nan*.

No 40(RM) Commando (Lt Colonel J.C. Manners) and No 41 (Lt Colonel B.J.D. Lumsden) were to land side by side on the left flank of the Canadians, with No 41 on the right. Their main task was the clearance of a number of machine gun nests. The timings called for them to transship to their landing craft at just after midnight, but the weather had turned rough and there was a delay in bringing the landing craft alongside. As this affected the Canadians as well, it did not jeopardise the plan for the Commandos to land first. Nevertheless, it proved to be a rough trip to the beaches. R. Mitchell of No 41 (RM) Commando describes what it and the landings were like:

Now, to the right of the plunging craft, the indistinct shape of Sicily wasn't entirely black. Here and there white fingers of searchlights swing across the sky, probing for the R.A.F. bombers which must now be attacking Pachino. We could hear the drone of aircraft engines high over our heads but no sound of bombing reached us above the continuous roar of the landing craft's engines. The coastline was becoming perceptibly closer and more distinct as we drew nearer to the shore, the height of the seas gradually diminished. By this time the victims of sea-sickness were retching on empty stomachs but, as if by magic, all the groans and gurps stopped when the unmistakable 'Booom' of a medium – heavy gun reverberated across the sea. Anti-aircraft or Coast Defence? We held our breaths, counting the seconds, ears cocked for the tell-tale screams of an approaching shell – but nothing happened. It must have been ack-ack, if Coast Defence, aimed elsewhere. In either case why was one round fired? We couldn't guess the reason but at least the effect upon our sick comrades was lasting. The coast was now a distinct black silhouette less than a mile away and in the calmer inshore waters, flashes of phosphoresence could be seen dancing around the bows of the other craft. As the two columns turned towards the shore for the final run in we were given the order to 'Get down'.

Crouching on one knee I adjusted the Tommy gun sling on my left shoulder and grasped the pistol grip with my right hand. With my left hand I took a firm hold on the neck of a sand-bag partly filled with .303 ammunition which I was to carry ashore and drop on the beach. Not long to go now. The engines were throttled back; and the bullet-proof doors in the bows were swung open. Muscles were tensed ready to spring forward; eyes fixed on the back of the man in front. The officer in command of the craft began quietly calling out the distance to the shore, '500 yards. . . .' '400 yards. . . .' '300 yards. . . .' The only sounds now were the low hum of the engines and the gentle slapping of the sea against the bows as we nosed slowly towards the beach. '200 yards. . .' '100 yards. . .' Abruptly the near silence was shattered by the harsh rattle of a machine gun. 'Ours? . . . or Theirs?' There was hardly time to formulate the thought before we grounded with a slight shudder; the ramp thumped down with a splash into the sea. No time to wonder about the false beaches, barbed wire in the water or mines in the sand. Reaction was automatic. Up sand-bag and run . . . along the craft then down the ramp and into the sea. It reached above my knees and the going was heavy but at least we were on a real beach for there, only about thirty yards away, was the soft sand of Commando Cove.

The machine gun was still chattering away continuously but nothing was coming in my direction. Shadowy figures were splashing through the water beside me – faces indistinguishable in the semi darkness. I had almost reached the sand and had just realised that the cliffs did not look nearly as high nor as steep as expected when I tripped and fell full length into about a foot of water. Almost before realising what had happened I was up again stumbling across the foreshore through deep soft sand. It was a great relief to drop the bag of cartridges and a greater one to realise that what the photographs had shown as steep cliffs were no more than high sand dunes. Scrambling up and over the top I went forward a few yards to what should have been our assembly point and flopped down. Automatically I removed the magazine from the gun in case it had collected some sand during its immersion, pushed it into my pocket and fitted a fresh one from the ammunition pouch. As I was wondering whether the gun's mechanism had been affected, my brain formulated the Instructor's admonition heard many times during training sessions, 'Don't forget to refasten your pouch' – I snapped it shut.[5]

In the event, they landed at approximately 0300 hours, but west of where they should have been and on No 40's beach. They quickly adjusted, however, and set about clearing their objectives, finding the opposition lighter than expected. No 40(RM) Commando also had problems. They lost one LCA, which hit a sandbank, the LCAs of their Q Troop became mixed up with another flotilla, and eventually landed two hours after the main body. The leading LCA of the troop was, however, misdirected by an ML and landed on the right of the Canadians, but those on board eventually joined up with the remainder of the troop. Nevertheless, by 0500 hours, both Commandos had achieved their objectives, killing some fifty Italians and capturing just over one hundred prisoners. Although they had been warned to expect to tackle coast defence guns, as well as machine gun posts, they found no evidence of any, and at 0800 hours they were ordered to move inland and take up defensive positions on the higher ground in order to protect the Canadians' left flank. This was successfully achieved under light sniper fire, although once they were in position they were subjected to long range mortar fire, which was eventually silenced that evening by a 4in mortar from the Seaforths of Canada. Their casualties were light for the day, with No 40 having one killed and 20 wounded, while No 41 had seven killed, including two officers, and 17 wounded. They remained in position for two further days, although they had to rely on Benzedrine to keep them awake during the second night, and were then withdrawn into XXX Corps reserve.

The Special Raiding Squadron, which numbered 270 all ranks, had a highly successful day, and one can do no better than quote from an account by Laycock of what they achieved. It also gives an insight into Paddy Mayne's irrepressible character:

The role of the S.R.S. in the initial assault was to capture and destroy the Coast Defence Btry at CAPE BURRO DI PORCO. The Commander (Major Mayne DSO ex 11 Cdo) was instructed that subsequent action must depend on circumstances. He was given the alternative either of re-embarkation in HMS *ULSTER MONARCH* or of taking on further objectives if considered possible.

It says something for the Commando spirit that the S.R.S. (270 all ranks) actually succeeded in taking three Btrys, many MGs and 500 prisoners. On 10 July the Squadron was lowered in LCA from HMS *ULSTER MONARCH* and *DUNERA*. They touched down unopposed on the right beach at 0320 hours. The 3˝ mortars immediately engaged with the Btry with great accuracy. One troop was sent to stop any enemy reinforcements which might arrive from the west, one Trp to provide covering fire on the Btry while the third Trp carried out the assault.

The Btry position was over-run without much difficulty by 0500 hours. 60 prisoners were taken and some 50 killed or wounded. Four 6˝ guns, three Light AA guns, one range finder and several light and heavy Breda guns were captured. Our casualties were nil. Several airborne Div* personnel, including Brigadier Hicks joined up with the Squadron during the consolidation of the position.

In view of the success of this operation Maj. Mayne decided to advance Northwest to attack another 6 gun Btry some 2½ miles distant which had by now opened fire. The Squadron were therefore ordered to assemble at DAMERIO farm and at 0600 hrs. continued to advance.

The approach to the Btry was impeded by five or six defended farms met with en route. These were protected by MGs and rifles in addition to snipers' posts in concealed positions in neighbouring fields. The enemy were, however, attacked and knocked out in succession and a number of Airborne Div personnel, some of them badly wounded were released from their captors.

On arrival at the vicinity of the Btry the 3˝ mortars at once engaged the gun positions whilst Nos. 1 and 2 Trps attacked with fire and movement which came up against stronger opposition.

Our casualties were however very light (one killed and two wounded) whereas we destroyed or captured five 80mm guns, one large range finder, four 4˝ mortars and several MGs and LMGs.

Major Mayne now decided to assault yet a third Btry at PUNTA DELLA MOLA. He therefore ordered No. 1 Trp to proceed to the assault while the 3˝ mortars engaged a fourth Btry at FARO MAS-SOLIVIERI.

No. 1 Trp successfully accomplished its task capturing and destroying the following equipment:

Three C.D. [Coastal Defence] guns (6"), one 40mm AA gun, two light AA guns, one range finder, several MGs and LMGs and the Bty Commander and all his personnel.

The 3˝ mortars had in the meantime engaged the Fourth Bty with success setting alight to the magazine and blowing up the ammunition. On the completion of their tasks the Sqn RVd at MASSA LACONA farm

---

* 1st Airborne Division, of which Brigadier Hicks' 1st Airlanding Brigade had been tasked with the seizing of the Ponte Grande bridge, south of Syracuse.

and at about 0600 hrs proceeded towards the main road to join hands with the 5 Div. On the way several defended farms and snipers' posts were mopped up. The Sqn finally bivouacked for the night at 2100 hours. Summary of casualties:-

Enemy – 500 prisoners	200 killed or wounded
Own tps – I killed	2 wounded

On the next day the S.R.S. captured 50 more prisoners which were sent back, with those captured previously, under escort of the 5th Div.[6]

Meanwhile, No 3 Commando were also in action. As it had been at Dieppe, it was split into two halves. The first under John Durnford-Slater landed from HMS *Prince Albert* and had the task of taking out a coastal battery north of Avola. They transshipped to their landing craft successfully, but on the run in came under heavy fire when still some 300 yards offshore. Replying with every available weapon, they quickly silenced this and landed dryshod. Captain Ruxton's troop speedily cut a gap in the wire, and the other two troops passed through. Making their way over several stone walls and through much close scrub, they eventually reached their target, which was engaged with 2 and 3 inch mortars, along with Bren gun fire, before the assault went in. By 0600 hours, the battery was in their possession and the guns were spiked at the cost of very few casualties. It had been a text book action.

For Peter Young's party, however, the day was one of frustration. His three troops were in the *Dunera*, along with Cator and his head-quarters element. They were to land south of Avola and soften up some beach defences prior to to the main landing. Unfortunately, the landing craft flotilla leader lost his way in the dark, and they landed on the wrong beach well after daylight. When they eventually found the correct landing place, it was only to meet a patrol from the other half of the Commando. When Peter Young finally met up with Durnford-Slater in the captured town of Cassibile that evening, he was, according to Laycock, 'near tears with rage and disappointment'.[7] Nevertheless, he had some consolation next day, when he accompanied Captain John Lash's troop on a fighting patrol to clear the ground immediately north of Cassibile. In Peter Young's own words:

We received information from an R.A.S.C. Coy. that there had been firing, from the direction of TORRE CUBA during the night, but that, as everything had been quiet that morning, they assumed that the enemy had withdrawn or surrendered. This was misleading for, when the Troop came close to the farm, they came under a well-sustained fire, from at least three Breda guns, not to mention riflemen. At this time, Captain Lash was with HQ and L/Sgt Knowland's sub-section to the right of the road, Lt Buswell to the left of the road, both within 100 yards of the farm. I myself with my runners, was advancing 200 yards from the farm and Lt. Nicholas with his section was somewhere to the east of the road. The engagement lasted for about 15 minutes, during most of that time I was busily engaged crawling backwards on my stomach, to get out of the line of fire of two of the a/m M.G.s. A point of detail as regards equipment to be devised is some better method of carrying hand-grenades than the present one of sticking them on the belt by the lever. I, several times, had to crawl back for mine when I least wished to.

Meanwhile, Captain Lash approached the TORRE CUBA going up the right hand side of the wall bounding the road past the S. W. corner of the farm where there was a concrete post. Every time that he advanced, Lt. Herbert DCM, MM, sprang up and plastered the post with a bren gun from the shoulder. While this was going on the party was sniped ineffectively from their right; from the direction of a glider which had crashed about 300 yards away. Captain Lash threw a grenade at the M.G. post, but missed it. The gunners, however, ran away. Taking advantage of their momentary confusion, Captain Lash, Lt. Herbert DCM, MM, and Trpr Underwood of Sgt Knowland's sub-section (the rest of which for some unknown reason did not take part in the assault) entered the farm followed by CSM Fawcett and wounded about eight Italians and unfortunately one British paratroop, who was a prisoner in the farm. A general surrender ensued. At the same time, Lt. Buswell and L/Sgt Shaw's sub-section, which had advanced through an orchard under a fairly high fire and without any hesitation, effected an entry at the north end of the farm. Tprs Knill and Hough both showed dash by pushing on to the water tower on the seaside of the position, and all resistance was at an end. A little before this, Tpr. Pritchard enabled my HQ. and Lt. Nicholas' section to advance without casualties by coming coolly back to us along the wall indicating which line of approach was clear. In this attack 6 officers and 51 O.R.s of the 206th (Italian) Coastal Div. were taken prisoner and 1 officer and 10 other ranks of the British Airborne Division were rescued. Tpr. Smith was our only casualty. He was wounded a little behind by the first burst. The prisoners were filing away to the rear, I singled out the leader, Captain Covatto, and kept him with me. I would like to say that in my opinion, good troops should hold this position until cannon is brought against it. The farm was more or less secure with strong walls and buildings around it. There was a heavy M.G. at each corner and another in the tower and trenches deep inside the position. The enemy had seen us approaching when we were 3/4 of a mile away through an excellent telescope on top of the water tower, which was about 60ft high. They had previously beaten off smaller fighting patrols from a bridgehead and had captured the parachutists a/m. It is alleged that some of the Italian soldiers said they would not have fought if Captain Covatto had not forced them to do so.

In my opinion the credit for the capture of TORRE CUBA must go to Captain Lash, Lt. Herbert DCM, MM,* and Tpr. Underwood.

The Airborne troops and a few men under CSM Fawcett took the prisoners back to CASSIBILE.

The remainder of the Troop now advanced on TORRE OGNINA. On the way Captain COVATTO indicated to us a mine dump where we passed an Italian strong point which had been evacuated. We then captured TORRE OGNINA without any resistance. The garrison of 1 Officer and 16 other ranks surrendered when Captain Covatto informed them that they would receive no quarter if they resisted or fired. The patrol then returned to CASSIBILE with its prisoners having examined two crashed gliders but found nobody to rescue.[8]

On the 13th, No 3 Commando re-embarked in the *Prince Albert*, but any thoughts that this might be the end of their operations for the time being were quickly dispelled. That afternoon, Durnford-Slater was summoned to a conference at the Naval HQ in the newly captured town of Syracuse. Here he was told by Dempsey that he was to land in the area north of Augusta, and then move inland and seize and hold a vital road bridge over the River Lentini. This was to be carried out that very night, but he was assured that elements of 50th Northumbrian Division, which was attacking the town of Lentini at the same time, would relieve him by first light on the following morning.

Back on board *Prince Albert*, there was a quick briefing and she sailed at 1900 hours. Arriving off the beach 2½ hours later, the LCAs were lowered and the Commandos made for the shore. As on the initial landings, fire was opened on them when they were 300 yards out from the shore and this was returned. Nevertheless, the first flight, with half the Commando, made a good landing, finding a gap in the wire, which the Italian garrison had used to launch a fishing boat in order to supplement their rations. A small beachhead was then secured so that the second flight could land. Both landings were made under intermittent mortar fire, and some 25 casualties were suffered. The Commando then set off for the bridge, engaging a number of small strongpoints en route. Eventually, they arrived, stalked and captured a pill box just short of it, and carried the bridge

---

*Later killed in Normandy.

itself. South-west of it were a number of German troops and vehicles in the orchards, but efforts to clear these met with heavy fire, and so a tight cordon was placed around the bridge and PIATs set up to deal with any transport approaching it. At the same time demolitions found under the bridge were removed. By now dawn was fast approaching, and the PIATs and other weapons began to engage enemy vehicles and machine guns: A heavy tank appeared and began to engage the Commandos, but they had nothing with which to reply to it and merely had to endure its machine gun and main armament fire. Mortar fire, too, was coming down with increasing intensity, and the position was beginning to look precarious, especially since there was no sign of the 50th Division. Shortly before 0530 hours, Durnford-Slater decided that it would be suicide to hold on for any longer and ordered a withdrawal to some hills 800 yards south-east of the position, from which he could still cover the bridge to some extent.

This was successfully achieved, with the troops covering each other back with fire and movement. Once in position, however, they soon came under accurate fire from heavy mortars and 88mm guns using air-burst HE. Casualties began to mount, and with still no sign of their relief, Durnford-Slater gave orders for everyone to split up into small parties and make for a prearranged rendezvous on the coast. There were frequent brushes with the enemy, and often the parties had to lie low for some hours, waiting for night to fall so that they could infiltrate their way through. Peter Young, however, on his own initiative, took a small party back to the area of the bridge and caused considerable havoc among the enemy, as well as collecting together a number of Commando wounded, including Charley Head, the Adjutant. He was also able to bury some of the dead. Eventually, on the 16th, the survivors were collected together, after they had been finally rescued from their predicament by 50th Division.

It might have been thought that this operation was a failure, especially bearing in mind that the Commando had suffered no less that 153 casualties, killed, wounded and missing. Yet, the vital achievement made was ensuring that the Germans did not blow the Malati Bridge, and it was not for nothing that Montgomery decreed that from then on it should be renamed 'No 3 Commando Bridge'. The 1st Airborne Brigade, who had been detailed to carry out a similar operation on the Primasole Bridge, also experienced the same problems, but like No 3, succeeded in removing the demolition charges. Here the fighting to prevent the Germans laying fresh charges and blowing it, was to go on for 48 hours and Primasole Bridge, was to become a proud battle honour for both the Parachute Regiment and the Durhams of 50th Division.

During this time, the other Commando elements had not been idle. The Special Raiding Squadron had re-embarked in *Ulster Monarch* on the 12th and were then given orders by Dempsey to capture the town of Augusta, which it was believed would only be lightly held. They set sail at 1700 hours that evening, but en route met Admiral Trowbridge, who, on asking them what their mission was, warned that Augusta was strongly held and they should not try an assault from the west side of the breakwater, which indeed was what Paddy Mayne's plan was. He therefore hurriedly amended it to a landing on the east side. This was carried out under fire, but, with support from two destroyers and a cruiser, the SRS got ashore with only nine casualties. Resistance then slackened, and the town was captured without much difficulty. It was handed over to elements of the 5th Division next day (13th) and the squadron re-embarked in the *Ulster Monarch* for another task, which would also involve the two Royal Marine Commandos.

The failure to achieve a lightning thrust across the Litani River and onto the Catania Plain, caused in the main by a resolute Axis defence and the fact that lack of transport and the intense heat were creating problems for the advancing troops, prompted Montgomery to alight on a fresh plan to restore impetus to his advance up the east coast of Sicily. He decided to mount a Commando landing north of Catania itself, while XIII Corps thrust towards the town from the south. This was scheduled for the night of 17/18 July. Accordingly, Nos 40 and 41 (RM) Commandos, who had been withdrawn to rest in the Canadian beach area, were ordered to proceed to the port of Syracuse.

There was, however, one problem, as noted by Bruce Lumsden commanding No 41:

> Observing that we were informed that all our kit had returned to England in error and we had nothing but that which we came ashore in, I was somewhat doubtful as to the soundness of such a plan. I contacted what HM ships I could and the ex 7th Bn RM, who found us in the vicinity, receiving every assistance from them. We sailed in destroyers and spent the next evening disembarked in the dock area of SYRACUSE awaiting the arrival of assault ships and experiencing a heavy air-raid during the night.[9]

Next day they embarked in the *Queen Emma, Princess Beatrix* and *Prince Albert* and joined the SRS in Augusta. Here they learnt that, in view of the fact that the enemy had been understood to have reinforced the Catania area, the operation was cancelled. Unfortunately, that night they were subjected to another air raid, and the *Queen Emma* was hit in several places, causing the deaths of fifteen men from No 40 and one from 41, as well as wounding 56 from the former and seven from the latter.

By now it was clear that the remainder of the campaign would be a hard slog, in view of the terrain and strength of the enemy resistance, and Montgomery decided that the Commandos should be placed in reserve in preparation for the invasion of Italy itself. In the meantime, a welcome reinforcement in the shape of No 2 Commando under Lt Colonel Jack Churchill arrived from England. 'They look fit and well and are delighted to be with us. Jack brought his bagpipes and his bow and arrows', as Laycock recorded.[10] As for the other Commandos, although their few first line reinforcements left at Algiers had been summoned, they were still well below strength, especially Nos 3 and 41, and Laycock was already making approaches to General Alexander to seek permission to call for volunteers from the Eighth, Ninth and Tenth Armies then in the Mediterranean and the Middle East.

Preparations for Italy

On 1 August 1943, Laycock and Tom Churchill, his GSO I and brother of Jack, flew to Algiers to discuss plans for the forthcoming invasion. The overall plan at the time was for two major assaults to be made. While the Eighth Army was to be launched across the Straits of Messina in Operation *Baytown*, the US Fifth Army, of which the British X Corps was a part, was to sail straight from North Africa and either support the Eighth Army in the toe of Italy (*Buttress*), or, in a more daring stroke, land at Salerno (*Avalanche*). Both assaults needed Commandos to spearhead them, and Laycock therefore split the SS Brigade into two. While he and Tom Churchill would take Nos 2 and 41 (RM) Commandos off to operate with X Corps, Nos 3 and 40 (RM) Commandos, along with the Special Raiding Squadron, would be commanded by John Durnford-Slater,* with

---

*Although Cator had by rights been second-in-command, he had returned to Egypt towards the end of July to plan for yet another projected invasion of Rhodes (*Accolade*), which did not come off. In any event, it is clear that he and Laycock did not get on personally[11].

Brian Franks, the Brigade Major, and would be under command of XIII Corps for *Baytown*. In the meantime, in spite of Montgomery's edict, the Commandos were stood by for a number of operations in support of the British advance in the east of Sicily, but only one of these, *Blackcock*, which involved No 2 Commando and 4th Armoured Brigade in an operation to assist 50th Division's advance on Scaletta, was actually mounted.

By the end of the first week of August, *Avalanche* had been selected in favour of *Buttress*, and the original idea was for Nos 2 and 41 (RM) Commandos to move to North Africa and sail to Italy from there. This, however, was cancelled, almost at the last moment, and both were to join the *Avalanche* force at sea from Sicily. As far as *Baytown* was concerned, the planning was somewhat simpler in that both Commandos and XIII Corps were already together. Nevertheless, it was clear that updated information was needed about the enemy defences in the toe of Italy, and both Paddy Mayne and Peter Young, commanding No 3 in Durnford-Slater's absence, suggested that reconnaissance patrols should be sent out, to be followed by a brigade size force in order to locate and destroy these defences prior to the main landing. This was the subject of much discussion between Durnford-Slater and Dempsey, and Dempsey and Montgomery. Eventually, it was decided that Peter Young should take a small party across the straits in order to check on the situation in the Bova Marina area. This he did on the night of 26/27 August, and brought back one prisoner, reporting that he had found no evidence of enemy defences.

As a result, Dempsey now decided to land 4th Armoured Brigade, supported by No 3 Commando and the SRS, at Bova Marina with the object of capturing Melito and Reggio di Calabria. However, Eighth Army were unwilling to release the armoured brigade, and Dempsey, with Montgomery's approval, made a fresh plan, *Quicksilver*. No 40 (RM) Commando, along with a squadron of tanks, troop of SP guns and a company of infantry would be brought in in place of the brigade. As a precaution, Dempsey insisted that five more patrols be sent across and that the operation would not be mounted until they had reported back.

Accordingly, on the night of 27/28th, Peter Young sent across five more patrols, each of an officer and six men. Their orders were to radio back any information, and then lie low until the main body, which was due to land the following night, met up with them. When nothing had been heard from them the next day, Peter Young went across in a landing craft to try and contact them, with the understanding that *Quicksilver* would be mounted on the night of 29/30th. In fact, all had run across Italian soldiers in some numbers and were frustrated by the fact that their wireless sets did not work. Young's landing craft stuck on the beach, so he split his party of Commandos and sailors up into small groups and set about trying to locate the others. Unfortunately, his wireless did not work either. By the next day, with nothing heard and indications from a wireless intercept that one patrol might have been captured, Dempsey saw no option but to cancel *Quicksilver*. In the meantime, the other patrols took to the hills, doing what they could to annoy the enemy and keeping on the move. Eventually, most – 44 out of a total of 55 – managed to make contact with the main force in the days after the *Baytown* landings. It had been a frustrating business, but was, like the experiences of Nos 1 and 6 Commandos in Tunisia, proof that the Commandos were more than capable of looking after themselves behind enemy lines and with scanty resources.

Baytown

XIII Corps carried out the *Baytown* landing in the early hours of 3 September, and by 0630 hours both Reggio and Santa Giovanni were secured. During this time, both No 3 Commando and the SRS remained as a floating reserve, ready to carry out any operation at short notice, while No 40 stayed in Sicily for the time being, under command of 231 Brigade. In order to maintain the momentum of his advance, Dempsey now decided to use the SRS to execute a left hook at Bagnara Calabria, this to be carried out early the next day. The 3rd, however, proved to be one of frustration for Paddy Mayne as his landing craft kept breaking down, and this meant that he was 2½ hours late in landing. Nevertheless, the SRS got ashore safely and made their way towards the town, which they took in the face of only light German resistance. They consolidated on the southern outskirts and, although subjected to accurate mortar fire, as well as long range sniping and machine gun fire, remained there overnight, carrying out active patrolling. Next morning, they linked up with elements of 15 Infantry Brigade. Although they suffered seven killed and 17 wounded, they killed 30 enemy, wounded 18 and captured 34, and some of the prisoners admitted that the landing had taken them completely by surprise.

No 40 (RM) Commando had by this time embarked with 231 Brigade in landing craft and moved to Messina, where they were subjected to another air raid, which caused some casualties. Consequently, they moved some ten miles north of the town to a less obvious shelter. No 3 Commando continued to remain in reserve. Then, on the 6th, Dempsey decided to try another left hook, this time to prevent the enemy from establishing any form of defensive line across the thin base of the toe. While 231 Brigade was to make the main assault, both No 3 and No 40 (RM) Commandos would land thirty minutes ahead in order to secure the beaches. These were three in number, and No 3 was given the left hand one, for which they earmarked two reinforced troops, while No 40 was made responsible for the other two. The landings were to take place in the Vibo Valentia area under the codename *Ferry* on the night of 7/8 September. No 3 moved round to join up with 231 Brigade on the afternoon of the 7th, and the force set sail at 1815 hours.

> At 0130 hours the next morning, the convoy had reached the lowering position, and the transfer of men and material from the LCIs to the LCAs began. Some delay occurred in this phase of the operation due to the swell which made the transfer difficult. It is perhaps worth noting that each soldier carried some 50 pounds of weight of equipment, and that even in a calm sea their transfer to the LCAs was no easy task. In any case, the LCAs were not ready to leave for the assault before 0300 hours, and were already late for the landing. More delay was caused on the way in. The navigators, travelling in the LCAs of Force 1 of 40 (RM) Cdo, had relied on seeing the outline of the mole protecting S VENERE Harbour as an indication that they were in fact landing on the right beach. But this mole was extremely low, and in the rough sea and because of the darkness of the night it was impossible to see it. Some 90 minutes were therefore wasted as the LCAs cruised up an down parallel to the shore trying to locate the mole. By this time the LCIs of the main force were coming in, and, in desperation, the LCAs ran into land in small groups on the initiative of the local military commanders. Even then, the main body landed directly after the first LCAs, and simultaneously with the more tardy ones.[12]

Luckily the landing was unopposed, and the beachhead was quickly secured, although No 40 had some trouble from enemy fire from Santa Venere on the left flank, which they succeeded in silencing. Later in the morning, the Royal Marine Commandos were subjected to fire from 88mm guns, which caused some forty casualties, and

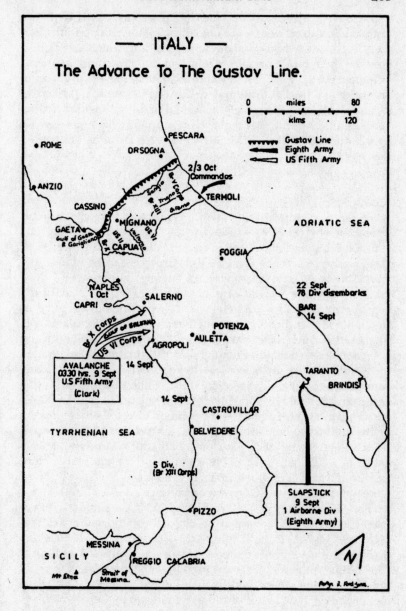

— ITALY —

The Advance To The Gustav Line.

Brigadier R.E. Urquhart,* decided that these must be silenced. Two Commando patrols were sent out to pinpoint the gun positions, and then Kittyhawk fighter-bombers were called in, which successfully knocked them out. A patrol was now sent into Pizza, and ran across a German patrol, forcing it to withdraw after killing ten, at a, cost of one killed and two lightly wounded. The enemy counter-attacked on the left flank, but were beaten back, and desultory shelling continued until 2100 hours that night. Next morning, Pizza was entered once more and a link-up achieved with the 5th Division. This ended the Commando part in *Baytown*.

Avalanche

While *Baytown* was relatively straightforward, the landings at Salerno were to involve the Commandos in some very tough fighting. The main object was to seize Naples, and for this two corps, the US VI and British X Corps, of the US Fifth Army were to be used in the initial landings, with the Americans on the right and the British on the left. While VI US Corps would hold the right flank of the beachhead, the British would turn north-westwards and advance on Naples itself. The direct route, which ran through Salerno and Vietri, passed through two narrow defiles at La Molina and Nocera, and it was decided to land the Commandos at Marina, which dominated the western part of the bay of Salerno, in order to capture a coastal battery there before moving inland to seize and hold the La Molina defile until relieved by 46th Division. Three battalions of US Rangers would mount a simultaneous operation directed on the Nocera defile. In order to help him in his task, Laycock was given a troop of 6-pdr anti-tank guns, six US manned 4.2in mortars and two detachments of a field ambulance. He would also have additional naval gunfire and artillery support available, and was allotted two Forward Observation Officers (FOOs) to control each.

The SS Brigade HQ, No 2 and No 41 (RM) Commandos set sail from Palermo on 8 September, and, apart from one air attack that night, the voyage to the landing area was uneventful. No 2 Commando, with naval gunfire support, made an unopposed landing at 0330 hours on the 9th and, supported by his mortars, Jack Churchill quickly captured the battery, which was found to be undefended. In the meantime, No 41 landed and moved inland to Vietri, which was again found to be virtually clear of enemy. Advancing onto their next

*Later Commander 1st Airborne Division at Arnhem.

objective, La Molina, however, the Royal Marines came up against a PzKw IV tank, which they succeeded in ambushing, killing the crew and destroying the tank with hand grenades. No 2 Commando and Brigade HQ moved to Vietri, and established communications with 46th Division. They learnt that one brigade was now ashore, but was held up on the eastern outskirts of Salerno. No 2, which had two troops operating on the western outskirts was also having problems, and suffered some casualties from two Tiger tanks before they were forced to withdraw under 6-pdr and PIAT fire. The Germans then tried to break through No 2 Commando's positions, but without success. Nevertheless, it was clear that they were not going to give Salerno up without a fight, and No 41 were also experiencing increasing resistance in front of La Molina.

There was also heavy mortar fire on the beaches, which was so intensive that one LCT was hit twice, and the LCAs carrying the Commandos' large packs and ammunition reserves were unable to land. While they were able to draw ammunition and food from the beachhead, the failure to deliver their packs meant that they had to fight during the next nine days with just the light equipment with which they had originally gone ashore. Nevertheless, as night fell it seemed as though 46th Division were now breaking into enemy defences in Salerno and that the next day would see the link-up, and the Commandos' task would be done.

Shortly after first light, reconnaissance elements of 46th Division tried to probe their way through the German defences at La Molina, but without success. It then became clear that the division was coming under increasing pressure from north of Salerno and they unable to spare any troops to relieve the Commandos. Then, at 1000 hours the enemy began to move against No 41 (RM) Commando under heavy machine gun and mortar fire. A small enemy party also got up onto the high ground overlooking Vietri and began to bring machine gun fire to bear on the town. Jack Churchill, controlling operations from the roof of the Brigade HQ building, forced them to withdraw with mortar and Bren gun fire, and then moved his two reserve troops onto these heights. The realisation that every piece of high ground in the area needed to be held if the Commandos were to maintain their positions caused Laycock to ask for more infantry. A Field Company RE was sent to him, but it was not made clear to him that the situation in the beachhead meant supporting arms and services units were being hastily turned into infantry, and consequently he merely held them in reserve in case any sapper tasks should materialise.

Pressure on No 41 continued throughout the morning. Then, in early afternoon heavy shelling on both Vietri and No 41 began, and Bruce Lumsden was wounded, handing over command to Major Edwards. Later, A Troop was heavily attacked, and although a counter-attack by Q Troop succeeded in halting this, the Commando was forced to withdraw some 200 yards. It now became clear that the main threat was to the left flank of No 41, and that although this could be stopped while daylight lasted, there would be little to stop the enemy infiltrating No 2 Commando's positions around Vietri during the hours of darkness. Laycock again asked for more infantry, and this time some was forthcoming, sufficient to relieve No 2's two troops operating on the western outskirts of Salerno, as well as making a further troop available from the Vietri area. These three troops mounted an attack shortly before dusk to seize a ridge overlooking No 41's left flank and this was successful.

The night was quiet and early next day (11th) two more infantry companies arrived to reinforce the SS Brigade. There was little activity and that night both Commandos were relieved and went back into reserve between Salerno and Vietri. Next day, however, the enemy began to exert further pressure on the 46th Division positions north of Salerno, and both Commandos were ordered to re-occupy their former positions. They had been given a slightly narrower frontage than before, but even so casualties had reduced their numbers to little over 300 each, not sufficient to constitute a proper reserve.

Apart from some shelling and mortaring, however, the 12th was relatively uneventful, but at dawn next day No 2 Commando came under attack, and both flanks were quickly turned. Nevertheless, with the help of some excellent artillery support, they held their ground. Laycock ordered No 41 to send a troop to help out, and Jack Churchill used this and one of his own troops to put in a counterattack under his second-in-command, Major Lawrie. Lawrie was killed, but Major Edwards of No 41 took over and the enemy advance was stopped. By 1330 hours, No 2 Commando had managed to get back into its original positions, but, in doing so it had lost 72 out of 316 men. Still, it was to be the last major enemy attack towards Vietri and much of the credit for this must go to the doggedness of No 2's defence.

Both Commandos were now once more relieved, and took up fresh positions in reserve in the area north of Salerno. A very welcome peaceful 24 hours followed, but, in the late afternoon of the 15th, both Commandos were ordered to move to Mercatello, where they would come under command of a brigade of 56th London Division.

Here a grave situation had developed in that the enemy had seized three prominent features overlooking the beachhead and there was a very real danger that he would cut it in half. No 41 (RM) Commando was ordered to attack one of these features, which was now called '41 Commando Hill', while No 2 Commando were to search the valley to the east of it, as far as the second of the features, the 'Pimple'. No 41 launched their attack at 1730 hours, as darkness was falling. They had three Sherman tanks to support them, but one crashed through a bridge shortly after passing through the Start Line, while the other two became bogged down a mile short of the objective. In spite of this, and thanks also to a well directed artillery barrage, the Commando captured the hill with the loss of one killed and two wounded only, and for once the enemy made no effort to counter-attack. As for No 2 Commando, they began their sweep at 1830 hours.

> The moon had not yet risen, and the night was extremely dark. The country was broken and irregular, consisting of terraced vine covered slopes and rocky hillsides. It was country over which silent movement was well-nigh possible, while 41 (RM) Commando's attack on the right was bound to make the enemy in the valley both alert and nervous. Surprise was therefore in any event difficult to obtain. And the advantage of surprise was questionable, for the object of the sweep was to find the enemy and clear him out of the valley, not to creep past him unnoticed. The easiest way to find the enemy in such country and on such a night was to frighten him into betrayal of his whereabouts. At the same time, noise properly used gives confidence at night, and greatly assists control while it prevents separation, loss of direction and position. Considering all these factors, Lieut. Colonel JMTF Churchill MC decided to organise his sweep in six parallel troop columns with himself in the centre with his headquarters. Each column was to keep in touch with its neighbours by shouting 'COMMANDO', and the whole party was to take its direction from the headquarters in the centre. In this novel way the advance was carried out. The troops would be heard crashing through the undergrowth and yelling 'Commando' as they swept forward through the valley. The Germans, unable to see their attackers in the darkness, and overwhelmingly conscious of the wide spread of the advance, were caught like fish in a net, and, for the most part, surrendered without a fight. Moving with commendable speed, the Commandos swept up the valley through the village of PIEGOLETTI* and on to the PIMPLE, and then back through the valley to their start line. At midnight, tired but triumphant, they reached our own lines once more with 136 German prisoners, more than the whole the rest of the Division had taken to date.[13]

---

*In fact it is called Piegolelli, and a contour line running through the name on a badly printed map caused the confusion.

Clearly, it was now essential that the Pimple be quickly seized, and so, with no pause for breath, the Commando set out once more to retrace their steps. Visibility had now improved considerably, and enemy resistance became increasingly strong. Eventually Piegolelli itself was re-captured and a link-up made with No 41, but efforts to capture the hill failed. Two troops suffered heavy casualties in the attempt, including the Duke of Wellington, who was one of the troop commanders, killed, and the survivors fell back to the village. With the coming of the dawn, the enemy began to make efforts to dislodge both Commandos from their positions, but they hung on grimly throughout the day, with a mounting toll of casualties. 138 Brigade of 46th Division was to make another attempt on the Pimple that evening, but this was suddenly changed, and the task was given to No 41. By now time was short and the men very tired. The upshot of this was that a mistake was made in the artillery support planning, and as the Royal Marine Commandos crossed the Start Line they were subjected to a withering barrage from their own side. Casualties were heavy and included Major Edwards mortally wounded. As a result, the attack was called off and the Commando returned to its former positions on 41 Commando Hill. One troop failed to get the order to withdraw and went on to the attack on the Pimple, which it took and held until ordered to withdraw next morning. During the next day the American mortars which had been placed under Laycock's command pummelled the enemy to good effect and prevented him from making any further attacks. Then, on the night of 18/19 September, both Commandos were finally relieved and returned to Sicily to refit.

The Salerno operations had cost the two Commandos almost 50% of their strength. They had been through a severe test of tenacity, courage and endurance, and both had passed the test with flying colours. Indeed, it was largely through their efforts that the beachhead was finally secured. A link-up was achieved with the British Eighth Army at Auletta on 20 September, and, on 1 October, Naples finally fell.

Termoli

On 21 September 1943, Laycock flew back to England to take over from Mountbatten as CCO. He departed conscious of the pressing need to provide reinforcements for the now depleted ranks of the Commandos in the Mediterranean, but while No 2 and No 41 (RM) Commandos were allowed to rest in peace in Sicily, the other elements of the brigade were tasked with another operation. A number of plans had been drawn up in the days after *Baytown* to strike further north on the west coast of Italy, but the speed of the XIII Corps advance quickly made these superfluous, but then, having met up with the Fifth Army, it was decided to switch the corps to the east coast. Consequently, Nos 3 and 40 (RM) Commandos, along with the SRS, were redeployed, arriving at Bari by sea on 30 September. Here they were briefed for Operation *Devon*, which was to take place on the night of 1/2 October.

At this stage, enemy resistance north of Foggia was giving both 78th and the 1st Canadian Divisions problems, and there was cercern that the enemy might well be tempted to take up a defensive position on the River Biferno, from which it would be difficult to budge him. In order to prevent this, the Commandos were to capture the port of Termoli from the sea, thereby outflanking any possible defensive line on the river. It would also enable the lateral road from Naples to Termoli to be opened up, and thus give greater cohesion to, the Allied operations as a whole. Little was known about the enemy dispositions around the port, but it was assumed that they would be little more than the rear echelon of the 1st Parachute Division, which was then facing 78th Division on the coast. What was not realised was that 26th Panzer Division was then on its way to Termoli from Naples, where it had been reorganising after the fight at Salerno.

Durnford-Slater's plan was for No 3 Commando, temporarily commanded by Captain A.G. Komrower as Peter Young was in hospital, to establish a beachhead one mile west of Termoli. No 40 (RM) Commando would then pass through and capture the town and harbour and seize a road junction two miles to the south-west. Simultaneously, Paddy Mayne's men were to move through the eastern side of the town and secure two bridges over the Biferno, where contact would be made with 78th Division, who would then continue the advance northwards. The operation was postponed for 24 hours in order to ensure that the link-up with 78th Division occurred sooner than later, and the force sailed from Bari at midday on the 2nd. Apart from three of the LCIs grounding on a sandbank, which caused some delay while they were extracted, the voyage was uneventful. No 3 Commando made a dry landing and established the beachhead without any difficulty, and Brigade HQ came ashore. No 40 and the SRS, however, experienced a problem in that their LCIs grounded some distance from the shore. Peter Smithson was serving at the time as a young signaller in No 40(RM) Commando:

We had a wet landing and although being 6ft 1in in height, the water came up to my waist. I remember it being a moonlit night and we got ashore quietly and without fuss, some troops carrying boots and socks above their heads to keep them dry. With HQ Troop we made for the railway station where we took some prisoners. It was still dark and the opposition was not great, and I gathered that many of the enemy still slept soundly without knowledge of us being there.[14]

In fact, No 40 had quite a fight for the railway station, with one building nearby being the German headquarters. In the meantime, a troop of No 3 Commando managed to capture a train with steam up and took twelve prisoners. Eventually, by 0800 hours, the town was secured and No 40 moved southwards, while the SRS began to patrol forward to the Bifurno. As for No 3 Commando, they found themselves preventing enemy infiltration into the town, as well as dealing with some determined snipers from the 1st Parachute Regiment. At about 1100 hours, the SRS met up with a patrol from 11 Brigade and shortly afterwards with the Brigade Commander himself. While they were tying up details for the relief, No 40 (RM) Commando spotted enemy transport approaching Termoli from the west, and laid a very successful ambush, destroying nine vehicles and killing and capturing all the reinforcements on board. The SRS also laid an ambush, but although successful, did lose a section. The Commandos then established a perimeter defence around the town, and early that afternoon 11 Brigade arrived. This enabled No. 3 Commando and the SRS to be relieved from the perimeter defence, but No 40 remained where they were until withdrawn into reserve later that night.

At about midday on the 4th, however, Durnford-Slater was asked by HQ 36 Brigade, who had arrived by sea the previous night, to send reinforcements to protect their right flank, where enemy activity was becoming noticeable, and accordingly No 3 Commando were sent to take up positions south-west of the town. Then, a similar request was received from 11 Brigade, and an SRS troop was sent, coming under command of No 3 Commando. Various other adjustments were made, but although it was becoming clear that the enemy was preparing to mount a counter-attack, he made no positive move. Next morning, twelve aircraft attacked the harbour area and an attack began to develop. While other elements came under severe pressure, it was not until the afternoon when tanks began to threaten them, did the Commandos feel it. As darkness fell, the enemy began to infiltrate, and they were forced to give some ground. The situation now quietened down, which enabled a further tidying up of the perimeter defences to be made, with the SS Brigade being given the west side of the town.

Next day brought renewed pressure, but the defenders managed to hold on without giving away too much ground. An additional brigade was brought in by sea that night, but, although this provided considerable additional strengthening of the defences, No 40 (RM) Commando still found themselves engaged next morning in a particularly bloody battle for the possession of a cemetery. Towards midday, however, enemy pressure began to slacken. The London Irish Rifles attacked through No 40 Commando, finally securing the cemetery and other troops enabled the SS Brigade to be withdrawn into the town. Peter Smithson:

> After Termoli was securely in British hands, I met up with other signallers and we entrenched in the basement of a small *Pensione* and found many bottles of wine in the cellar with which to celebrate. I also found a sack of flour, sugar and other ingredients in the basement and so got the stove alight and proceeded to bake some cakes for the lads, and was very excited when they turned out to be some quite enjoyable biscuits, which were gobbled down with relish. That night was the first decent night's sleep for some time.

Termoli, after the early Commando success, had proved to be a very tough battle and the SS Brigade suffered some 130 casualties from its already depleted strength.

Reorganisation
At the end of the Termoli operation, No 3 Commando was sent to Molfetta, a little port on the east coast of Italy between Bari and Barletta, in order to recuperate. The SRS and No 41 (RM) Commando, however, remained at Termoli, although on 8 October they left the command of XIII Corps for General Allfrey's V Corps, which was now taking over the coastal sector. Allfrey was soon made aware of the problems under which the SS Brigade was operating – lack of numbers, limited logistics and the fact that all their less mobile stores were still in Sicily. Montgomery, too, visited Termoli, and it was decided that, apart from one troop of No 40, which would stay there and be available to V Corps for any immediate operations, the remainder would concentrate at Molfetta, which would be made an advanced Special Service base and come directly under HQ Fif-

teenth Army Group. At the beginning of November, the Termoli troop, which had been preparing for an operation which was cancelled, also moved back to Molfetta.

Back in England, the decision had been made, with the formation of additional Royal Marine Commandos and the disbandment of Nos 12 and 14 Commandos (see next chapter), to create an enlarged organisation, the Special Service Group, which would control four SS Brigades, each of four Commandos. At the same time, Laycock had been devoting much attention to the reinforcement of the Mediterranean Commandos. His first step was to send out No 9 Commando under Ronnie Tod, and this was to be followed by No 43 (RM) Commando (Lt Colonel R.W.B. Simmonds RM) at the end of November, once it had completed its training. In return, the SRS, No 3 and No 41 (RM) Commandos returned to England in early November. As for the problem of bringing the other two Commandos back up to strength, No 40 was partially reinforced from the United Kingdom, receiving 100 replacements in November, and obtained the balance from Royal Marines already serving in other capacities in the Mediterranean. The system used for No 2 Commando was different, with General Alexander agreeing that volunteers could be found from the ranks of Fifteenth Army Group. Consequently, officers from No 2 were sent out to visit all the main formations.

Stan Buckmaster, then serving with 11 Infantry Brigade, was one of these volunteers, and had been accepted after an interview with Captain G. Hemming, one of the troop commanders of No 2.

Within a few weeks of our interviews with Capt. Hemming we were on our way to Molfetta. Travelling by train we arrived at our destination at about midday after a somewhat slow and laborious journey that had started the previous evening at Campobasso, by a roundabout route that had taken us through Benevento, across to Foggia and so on through the east coast towns, all of which we had seen before as we advanced up Italy from Reggio. The Italian railways had been almost wrecked.

The weather was fine and warm in this more southerly region, where snow is very rare, but despite the warmth we were still wearing our greatcoats. With kitbags and packs it is easier to wear the coat than attempt to carry it.

Before reporting in at Commando HQ we decided to get a drink and some food, and, as we were looking decided scruffy, to try and smarten ourselves up, before venturing any further. This done, we made our way to the large white school building that housed No 2 Commando. We were met at the entrance by a regimental policeman, whose turnout would have been acceptable in the Brigade of Guards. His expression as we approached was a mixture of pity mingled with amusement. He came part way down the steps at the entrance, then turned and gestured us to follow. Inside, a group of about a dozen men stood chatting and laughing among themselves. The R.P. indicated that we should join them, and this we did. I noticed that they looked a lot smarter than us, and that the majority of them were from the Royal Artillery. Their accents indicated that most were from the London area. None were wearing overcoats.

At this moment the R.S.M. arrived. With his stick under his arm and a clip board in hand he bawled at us to fall in, in single file. 'Spread yourselves out a bit, I want a good look at you lot. Why are you wearing those bloody coats?' 'Because it's bloody cold where we came from, Sir,' answered Cameron. 'Don't answer me back lad, or your feet won't touch the ground!' Then, glancing down at the clip board, the R.S.M. said 'Which one is Cameron?' 'Me, Sir', said Jock, 'I bloody thought so' said the sergeant major. 'Well, I'm a Scotsman too and it cuts no ice with me laddie'. After similar exchanges with a couple of other men, the R.S.M. took another look at the list. 'Which one is Buckmaster?' 'I am, Sir' I replied. 'Do you have a brother in this unit?' 'Yessir'. 'Well, don't think that will do you any favours'.

Eventually we were dismissed with orders to hand our overcoats into the stores.

We spent the rest of the day cleaning up and scrubbing our webbing equipment that would have to be white from now on. It was a Sunday and apart from those with duties to perform the Commando men were free to do more or less what they liked.

There were some more men who had arrived a few days earlier but as they were part of our intake we eventually joined them. Empty class rooms had been set aside for us, and we set our bedrolls down in the spaces allocated to us.

We were then called to the orderly room for documentation and handed in our pay books. Then having completed our kit check and cleaning we were free by early evening, whereupon we went out for a stroll. Strangely enough there seemed to be no serious attempt at blacking the town and as the sky darkened more lights came on in the shop windows. Life for the Italians in Molfetta seemed almost back to normal, and it appeared to me that almost all the townsfolk spent their Sundays strolling alongside the main thoroughfares.

Training started right away after an 6.30 reveille on the Monday morning with a run and a short session of P.T. This only served to remind me of just how much out of condition I really was, and I knew that Cameron was feeling likewise.

Riding motor cycles continually in all weathers and conditions, calls perhaps for a certain ruggedness, but it's hardly likely to maintain a man in the kind of physical shape that was now required. After breakfast we paraded again and the three instructors who were to be mainly responsible for our training and assessment introduced themselves to us. The intake had been divided into two separate groups, each of about twenty men. Our group included two officers Lt. James Coyle and Lt. 'Paddy' Jermyn. For the duration of the course the officers would be treated the same as the other ranks, and would not be permitted to have a batman. They would, of course, take their meals in the Officers Mess but that would probably be the only difference, although on field training they would eat their rations sitting around with the rank and file.

Sgt W.F. Rudge was the senior NCO of the three instructors, a prewar territorial of the South Lancashire Regt, his home town being Warrington. He had won the D.C.M. at Salerno, and had previously served on Malta during the worst of the Island's aerial bombardments and had been part of a small commando detachment assigned to special operations, sometimes involving the use of submarines. He had the appearance of a no nonsense N.C.O., was stockily built, and physically fit, but had an easy going manner. Sgt Jack Aldred was a Royal Engineer who was to instruct us in the intricacies of mines, explosives and booby traps, etc. Quietly spoken, untypical and very mildly mannered.

Cpl Arnold the third instructor was there mainly to assist the two sergeants with the weapons training and map reading etc. But should the sergeants be on other duties at any time, he was perfectly capable of carrying on alone.

Many of us, however, were quite at home with the Bren, rifle, tommy gun and grenades, and most had taken part in major engagements, particularly the infantry and field artillerymen. This was probably the main difference between an intake at home in U.K. and one recruited from the army abroad.

The training programme was full of variety and at no time did we feel that there was too much repetition. Firing practice was carried out at a former Italian Army rifle range a couple of miles outside Molfetta. We would run and walk to and from the range as a preparation for the speed marching that we had yet to undergo. Speed marching was considered to a be a very essential part of commando training as it was the only means of rapid movement that a commando unit could rely on. It comprised a very rapid walking pace with a stride lengthened more than normal, and would go on for a couple of hundred yards or so, until a burning sensation developed along the shins and the muscles at the back of the thighs, then having reached a condition where the muscles were at the peak of fatigue, the order would be given to break into a run. The running would bring immediate relief to the aching limbs and would go on for a further two hundred yards until the same sensation developed at the front of the thighs and at the back of the leg below the knee. Then it would be back to the rapid marching pace and so on, until a distance of about seven miles had been covered in approximately one hour.

The final speed march of the training course would be over a distance of fifteen miles which would be covered in roughly two and a quarter hours, whilst wearing small packs, webbing equipment, etc., and of course as always, weapons, i.e. rifles, Bren guns, 2˝ mortars, the heavier weapons being passed around around the troop so that all took a turn at carrying the additional weight. Many of us dropped out during the early days of training, although here we were fortunate in having a man like Sgt Rudge in charge of the training. 'Tan' Rudge as we were soon to know him (the origin of this nickname was obscure, even to him) was a man with his own ideas of the type of men that would be an asset to the unit, and particularly to those he wanted in his own troop. He had the ability to size up the individual volunteer and obviously had the foresight to see and accept that the majority of the men in his training troop had lived 'rough' in the line, or at least in the forward area, subjected to shelling and mortaring, etc., and that what may have applied to Achnacarry did not necessarily apply here. This in no way implies that the training was in any way less rigorous or strenuous than that back in the U.K., although it must be appreciated that it wasn't possible at this stage to develop quite the same course with the same lay out of equipment such as rope bridges for crossing streams and the like, as the terrain around Molfetta in the province of Bari didn't really lend itself to anything of this nature, being very flat and featureless. However, there were additional hazards of a warmer, humid climate, dusty roads, of which many were surfaced with a very coarse gravel that tended to be rather hard on the feet. Sweat rashes in very sensitive places were quite common, and some of the foot blisters had to be seen to be believed. Rudge had no intention of losing men he knew to be good soldiers, and I am certain his assessment of an individual was based more on the man's attitude, marksmanship, and general all round ability with weapons. He had no time for the moaners, or the 'flyboys' or men with a sloppy turnout, and would watch closely to see how a man fitted in, and how he got on with his comrades. The officers came in for the same sharp scrutiny as the men, particularly on the early morning parade. 'This won't do at all, Sir' or 'With respect, Sir, I am sure you can do better than this', would be the manner in which he addressed them.

After a few weeks had gone by, the first R.T.U.s took place and my own old pal, Cameron, was among them. No reason had to be, or was, given to these men who were now being returned to their units, although one or two had requested that they be sent back. In Cameron's case I believe that it stemmed from his habit of answering the questions that were directed at no one in particular, as though they were addressed to him alone. I knew him to be a good soldier, quite fearless, but possibly too much of an individualist to make a good member of a team. The hardest part for him was probably going back to a unit that had expected him to make the grade.

Paddy McClaughlan on the other hand was already wearing a Green Beret, for as a member of the R.A.M.C. with his first class qualifications as a nurse and first-aider, etc, plus his undoubted experience of battle conditions, the M.O. must have reasoned that there was little or nothing they could teach him. To the medical team he must have been just what the doctor ordered. Probably the only difference as far as Paddy was concerned would be that for the first time he would carry a weapon. In Special Service units medical orderlies all carried side arms, unlike those in the field army who were completely unarmed, so henceforth he would be in possession of a 4.5 Colt automatic pistol.[15]

As for the personalities of No 2 SS Brigade, Tom Churchill, who had been in command since Laycock's return to England, was made Brigade Commander with the rank of Brigadier, with John Durnford-Slater as Deputy Commander. A number of other members of the Headquarters had also returned to England, including Brian Franks, who was to make a name for himself while commanding 2 SAS in France. In his place as Brigade Major came Major J.P.L. Henderson MC of No 2 Commando, while Captain A.L. Blake RM was sent out from England as Staff Captain. At the same time, the brigade was brought back up to strength in terms of equipment. Nevertheless, it was to be some time before it could be considered fully operational. No 9 Commando arrived at Molfetta on 8 November, and was immediately operational, but No 40 was not ready until December and No 2 not until January 1944. As for No 43, they arrived at Algiers on 26 November. It was then decided to give the Commando a further opportunity to train before going on to Italy. Not until the end of December did they leave Algiers, and the rail journey from there to Bizerta was remembered long after by all who experienced it:

We were rather surprised when the train was only four hours late in starting and not much surprised to be informed that the journey was liable to take four days to complete. The cattle trucks which later were to become so well known to all were not the best Christmas homes, but everyone settled in fairly well and resigned themselves to the wearying journey. It was not long before much interest was shown in the fairly large number of chickens, ducks and geese that abound in that part of the world near the line, and the speed with which these disappeared was remarkable; equally remarkable was the way in which they were hidden when caught from the eyes of the officers continually searching the train for them, but immediately the train restarted the air became thick with feathers from these luckless birds. Another little addition to comfort which was soon discovered was the steam escape pipe on the engine, which gave boiling hot water on the turning of a knob, and as a result at every stop those not pursuing chickens were racing up to the engine in search of hot water.[16]

Delayed by a storm at Bizerta, they eventually arrived at Naples in early January. In December, too, No 4 (Belgian) and No 6 (Polish) Troops of No 10 (IA) Commando also arrived in Italy and were placed under command of No 2 SS Brigade.

No 30 Commando and the Italian Landings

While No 33 Troop were in Tunisia, there had been a number of changes in the hierarchy of No 30 Commando. Commander Ryder had been posted to Force J and was succeeded by Major Cass. He was, however, posted to South-East Asia in April 1943, and was replaced by Lt Commander Riley, who had been loaned to No 14 Commando. There were also adjustments in the officers of both Nos 33 and 34 Troops, and, because the latter was one officer over establishment and the former one under, Captain Glanville relinquished his Army commission and joined No 33 Troop as a lieutenant RNVR. Both the RN and Army Troops continued their laid down programme of training during the early months of 1943, but that of the RM Troop was interrupted by the Tunisian commitment, and it was not able to carry out formal intelligence gathering training, although it was generally accepted that it would be employed more in the escort role to the naval specialists.

The Commando was to take part in *Husky*, and to this end Lt Commander Riley flew to Algiers towards the end of June 1943, with the remainder following by sea at the same time. The commitment to *Husky* and other operations meant that the Commando was to be split into small parties. Riley, Huntingdon-Whiteley, who had taken part with eight Royal Marines in the capture of Pantellaria in early June, and nine others would land at Cape Passero, their particular target being the radar stations there. Captain P. Martin-Smith, who had joined No 34 Troop in the spring of 1943 from No 12 Commando, was to take seven of his soldiers to land on the east of Cape Passero, and Glanville, with eight Royal Marines, would follow him and land on D+I with the unit's transport. Captain Belcher, nine soldiers and Lieutenant Phillips RNVR were to move to Alexandria for operations in the Eastern Mediterranean, of which more later.

In the meantime, Curtis had suggested that he and a small party should land by parachute and take up an observation position overlooking the main coastal road leading northwards from Reggio di Calabria and radio back information on enemy troop movements. While the Army planners fully supported *Bantam*, as the operation was called, Cunningham eventually objected since he did not feel that it was fitting employment for a unit owing allegiance to the Royal Navy. Those not involved in any of the above would remain at Bône until the HQ moved across to Sicily.

The initial landings in the Cape Passero area went well and much valuable information and radar equipment was obtained. As for Glanville's party, his convoy. . . .

. . . had been diverted on account of underwater obstructions, to a new beachhead near Porto Palo. The section had accordingly to make its way across country to the rendez-vous fixed for 0900 next morning at the Wasserman tower. On the way, a mobile coast-watcher radar set was found. The crew had all been killed, and the set itself was damaged, by shell fire. Some high grade documents were picked up, however, including a technical handbook on the Wuerzburg (Telefunken) series of radar sets, operators' logs, and on the body of the Officer Commanding the station, a notebook recording courses taken in radar.[17]

A forward HQ was set up in the lighthouse at Porto Palo, and all captured equipment and documents gathered and sorted here before being shipped to Malta on 12 July. There were, however, some imperfections in that some vital technical parts were initially overlooked and only later found by other agencies, while others were not properly guarded and unwittingly destroyed by British troops. There was also the frustration of having to provide guards to prevent looting by the Sicilians in liberated towns. Nevertheless, the Army section did go on to take part in the capture of Syracuse and Augusta, where it was joined by Huntingdon-Whiteley and a mass of material found, although they were somewhat hampered by an outbreak of looting by British troops.

Most of the documents in the port and harbour buildings had been destroyed or had been lost or damaged in the wholesale looting which took place, but much interesting equipment was found, most of it relating to anti-aircraft gunnery, in some cases with the relevant technical handbooks. The search was extended to the batteries and coastal installations on the headland of Agnone where a further selection of generally similar documents and material was discovered. Most of this matter had a negative value, inasmuch as it merely demonstrated the ingenuity and resource displayed by the Italians in endeavouring to develop, in the absence of radar, an effective and dependable apparatus, based on acoustics, to give early warning of the approach of aircraft.

The ashes and charred paper from the underground rooms where the secret work had been done was carefully sorted and every scrap of ash or paper which looked likely to yield valuable intelligence was packed between layers of glass wool (taken from the Italian battery store) in a light fibre suitcase for shipment to Malta.[18]

Another noticeable problem with these operations was that the unit's lack of radio communications meant that information on intelligence targets was often not received in time to take advantage of it, and this was never really solved throughout the campaign.

A party under Martin-Smith and Glanville then took part in the operations around the Primasole Bridge, but, instead of gathering material, found themselves fighting with the 8th Battalion Durham Light Infantry, under whose command they were placed. It now seemed that the Seventh US Army were making better progress in the west of the island, and Glanville and Huntingdon-Whiteley moved across to join them. The Americans agreed that they could take away naval intelligence material, but their progress was initially frustrated by the number of damaged road bridges and lack of precise information on the progress of the advance. Nevertheless, they eventually entered Trapani and identified five naval stores with useful material in them. They did not have the men to guard them themselves, and the Americans were too busy looking after the mass of prisoners. In the end, therefore, they had to use captured Italians. They now moved on to Palermo, where they met up with Riley, and carried out another search there.

In the meantime, No 34 Troop continued to be frustrated because of the dogged defence being encountered by the Eighth Army. However, with the fall of Catania, further tasks came their way, although the search of this town was impeded by a mass of booby traps left by the enemy. They then took part in the advance northwards, to Messina. To get there by road proved impossible because of the destruction through demolitions and shell fire, and an attempt to get through on foot cross-country failed, because of the amount of equipment which needed to be taken. It was therefore decided to land from the sea, but it took some time to obtain an LCT, but they eventually did and landed on the night of 15/16 August. Much time was now spent clearing up the north-east corner of Sicily as well as making plans for No 30 Commando's role in the invasion of the Italian mainland.

No 30 Commando was to take part in both *Baytown* and *Avalanche*, with the bulk of its effort involved in the latter, only Lieutenant Davies RNVR and his RM orderly accompanying the Eighth Army landings across the straits of Messina. Riley, Glanville and Martin-Smith were to lead in the Salerno landings, since Curtis was about to be invalided sick back to England, and Hargreaves-Heap had been detailed to remain with the rear element in Sicily for the time being. Before they set off for Salerno, disaster struck in the form of a fire at the villa which was their HQ, and this destroyed most of their stores. They therefore had to be hurriedly re-equipped by the Army. As for Davies, he found himself navigating a landing craft which had lost its way during the initial stages of *Avalanche*. On landing, he came across no targets of value and was not forewarned of the Taranto and Termoli landings, which would have revealed much naval intelligence. Hence, he moved across to join the others in Salerno on 18 September.

No 30 Commando's landing at Salerno got off to a bad start when the LST in which they were in hit a submerged sandbank thrown up by the craft in front. Efforts to re-float her resulted in damage to the doors and it was not until 1800 hours on 9 September that they eventually got ashore, their vehicles waterlogged. Searches during the next couple of days produced little of value, and the German counter-attack on the beachhead further restricted their activities. Riley therefore decided to investigate other targets in the Bay of Naples area. Their first operation, though, was different from their normal activities in that they were asked by Brigadier Airey, BGS(I) of X Corps to carry out a reconnaissance of the beaches between Castellamare Stabia and Torre Annuziata to investigate the feasibility of a surprise landing there. This was successfully carried out on the night of 11/12 September by Captain Martin-Smith and a mixture of Royal Marines and soldiers, along with a party from No 5 COPP under Lieutenant Berncastle DSC RN: '. . . though strictly outside our sphere, it did under the circumstances prove of value, from a training and also morale point of view, as it accustomed the men – including myself – to small scale landings in conditions likely to be met in the present campaign'.[19] Next came the capture of Capri on 13 September, and this was followed by that of Ischia next day. The No 30 Commando party spent a number of days here, and whereas Capri was quickly handed over to the Americans, they left No 30 in charge of Ischia with a responsibility of restoring law and order. Next target was the neighbouring island of Procida. For this Lieutenant Berncastle's COPP joined No 30 Commando once more, and they were to be responsible for surveying the beaches, harbours and shipping there. Lieutenant Taylor RNVR was to inspect the coastal batteries and get the guns in working order, while Trevor Glanville and his RM orderly would handle the intelligence side.

They landed on the afternoon of 15 September and discovered that the Germans had left, although there was still a force of Blackshirt militiamen there. Furthermore, an American OSS team had landed two nights before, and they were able to provide Glanville with much useful information. The most interesting target was the torpedo works at Baia. Interrogation of an accountant who worked there revealed that Admiral Minisini, the General Manager and Technical Director of the firm responsible, SIC, was being held by the Germans at the torpedo testing range at San Martino. Consequently plans were made to raid this, and it was to be mounted on the night of 17/18 September. Although misleading OSS reports on German E-boat movements and the coastal defences in the area caused some confusion, Glanville, with Martin-Smith, Berncastle and a mixture from both the Army and RM sections set sail in an Italian torpedo boat (MAS). Trevor Glanville:

The MAS sailed towards midnight on the 17th, the sea being calm and covered with a light mist. The craft slid noiselessly alongside the jetty at the range and the landing party were ashore before the presence of the boat was noted (except by an Italian watchman who did not raise the alarm).

A number of Italian workmen were quickly rounded up and interrogated. They undertook to guide a party to where Admiral Minisini was sleeping and also indicated the position of the German LMG posts on either side of the range. The fire support party accordingly trained their weapons on these targets, their orders being to open fire the moment the Germans showed any signs of coming to life.

Admiral Minisini was soon located and interviewed, by Lieutenant Glanville, to whom he declared that he would not move save under compulsion. He was therefore declared a POW upon which the Admiral agreed to come without more ado, except for a request to be allowed to pack his belongings and to be accompanied by his wife. Signora Minisini, who was reliably reported to hold strong pro-German sympathies, was dealt with by Captain Martin-Smith, whose German was perfect. So much so that the Signora was under the impression that she was being removed by the Germans and kept referring to him as 'this charming young Rhinelander'. Eventually the Admiral and his wife, with thirteen pieces of luggage, were embarked in the MAS and taken to ISCHIA, where they passed the night, and next day to Capri.

At Capri next morning Admiral Minisini was interrogated by the Staff of F.O.W.I.T. [Flag Officer's Weapons Intelligence Team] and also by 30 Commando. He explained that all the documents relating to recent Italian torpedo research and to the development of the midget submarine were stored in various places indicated by him in the buildings on or near the torpedo range. He also mentioned that important tests with experimental torpedoes were being conducted by the Germans at the SILURIFICIO WHITEHEAD S.A. FIUME. A signal was therefore sent to the O.C. 30 Commando, suggesting that the underwater weapons specialists should come to ISCHIA as soon as possible.

It was decided, after consideration, that the recovery of the documents mentioned by Admiral Minisini was sufficiently important to justify the mounting of a second raid the same night (i.e. September 18/19). It was appreciated that after the last show there was a considerable risk of the landing party meeting with a warm reception and special precautions were taken to cope with this contingency. It was further decided to carry out a reconnaissance of the country inland from SAN MARTINO, since a signal had been received from C.O.I.S. Med. [Combined Operational Intelligence Section, Mediterranean] indicating the radar and communications centre at LICOLA as an important target. Intelligence reports received from the OSS, however, indicated that the area was strongly defended, although 30 Commando's experiences to date had not confirmed this. It was therefore arranged to make an armed patrol of the area while the buildings on the torpedo range were being searched. An additional objective of the raid was to locate the guns which had been shelling ISCHIA and PROCIDA during the day.

The MAS flotilla had been transferred to CAPRI and was no longer available. Permission was therefore obtained to use LCI(L) 249 (Sub-Lieutenant Webb, RNVR). In view of its relatively low speed of 16 knots and the noise of its exhaust, as well as the usual difficulties of handling these craft, it was decided not to go alongside in the LCI(L) but to tow the landing party in a whaler to a point near the objective and to lay off while they rowed ashore. A fire party of Royal Marines was arranged with LMGs along the upper deck and in the 'chicken coop' to support the four 20mm oerlikons of the LCI(L), should the landing party encounter

Amphibious training, 1940, in Scotland. A Landing Craft Mechanised Mk l.

The toggle bridge being demonstrated by No 2 (Dutch) Troop of No 10 (IA) Commando in the harbour at Portmadoc in North Wales.

Above: Castelorizzo – the harbour.

Right: Charles Vaughan, the Commandant at Achnacarry.

Opposite above: The *Maid Honor* as she looked before the war.

Opposite below: The target of *Maid Honor* Force in Fernando Po, the *Duchessa d'Aosta*, here seen later in the war as the *Empire Yukon*.

Abseiling at Achnacarry.

Achnacarry.

Practising an assault landing.

Left: ABERCROMBY – the raid by No 4 Commando on Hardelot, night 21/22 April 1942. A returning Assault Landing Craft.

Below left: ABERCROMBY – Lord Lovat talking to C in C Dover, Admiral Sir Bertram Ramsay.

Opposite above: MTB 344, the workhorse of the SSRF, in Summer 1943. On the bridge are (extreme left) Rik van Riel, the navigator, a Belgian nicknamed 'The Admiral' by the SSRF, and next to him Lieutenant Russell-Smith, then her skipper (Lieutenant Bourne DSC RNVR commanded her for most of the SSRF raids). The symbols on the front of the bridge denote two E-boats destroyed and eight Commando raids undertaken.

Opposite below: Members of the Small Scale Raiding Force training in Cumberland, Summer 1942. Left to Right: Lord Francis Howard (captured St Honorine, Sep 42), André Desgranges (behind) (captured St Honorine, Sep 42), Jock Taylor, Peter O'Kelly (both fate unknown), Graham Hayes (shot by the Germans, July 1943), Anders Lassen (killed Lake Comacchio, April 1945).

1 SS Brigade going ashore at Ouistreham on D-Day.

Members of 1 SS Brigade move inland on 6 June 1944.

Commandos digging in at Merville, after the capture of Pegasus Bridge by glider coup de main.

Army Commandos with men of 6th Airborne Division shortly after D-Day.

Left: Three well known Commando characters in Normandy – (left to right) Charley Head, John Durnford-Slater and Peter Young.

Below: The run-in to Walcheren – Royal Marine Commandos in their Landing Vehicles Tracked (LVT), in this case Buffaloes, on board a landing craft.

Weasels and Buffaloes coming ashore in the Westkapelle Gap.

Walcheren – Royal Marine Commandos round up prisoners.

Commando Vickers machine gunners give covering fire during 1 Commando Brigade's crossing of the Rhine at Wesel.

Bringing in a wounded man near the River Maas. The polder country, where the river ran above the surrounding country, shows what 4 Commando Brigade's final area of operations was like.

4 Commando Brigade 3in mortar crew in action on the Lower Maas, April 1945.

1 Commando Brigade enters Osnabruck, 4 April 1945.

Lake Comacchio – A German Obergefreiter is ordered to remove the firing pin from his artillery piece.

Lieut Comdr Patrick Dalzel-Job RNVR of the RN Wing, 30 Assault Unit, Germany, April 1945. Note the insignia on his upper arm and the way in which the Commando dagger is worn; he is armed with a captured Schmeisser.

In the jungle near Kangaw.

On Hill 170.

any opposition. The landing party itself was organised in three teams, one to make a preliminary survey of the buildings, then to climb the cliff and reconnoitre the enemy positions, a second to search the positions already indicated by Admiral Minisini and a third to give covering fire in an emergency.

The landing party got ashore without incident, although most of the men were seasick, the whaler having moved a good deal in the choppy sea. The Italian workmen on the range were immediately lined up and placed under armed guards in a room adjacent to the entrance to the tunnel leading to BAIA. The places where the documents were stored were identified and handed over to a search party consisting of Corporal Schermuly and L/Corporal Mayers of the Army section, who undertook a meticulous search of the offices and laboratory. The opportunity was also taken to carry out some useful counter-demolition work.

The patrol party, consisting of Lieutenant Glanville, Captain Martin-Smith, Sergeant Whitby, Corporal Ellington, L/Corporal Blake RM and Pte Edwards (Army section) climbed the cliff to MONTE PROCIDA and for an hour patrolled the whole area. The coastal batteries reported on MONTE PROCIDA were found to be non-existent, although marks on the road indicated that certain of the shells falling on ISCHIA came from self propelled guns specially brought up from the plain. This fact was later confirmed from Italian civilian sources. MG posts were noted at TORRE GAVETA and SAN MARTINO. It was intended to make a further reconnaissance towards LICOLA, but this was precluded by the rising of the moon, the weather being clear. The patrol returned therefore to the torpedo range and after the officers had satisfied themselves that a meticulous search had been made, the documents captured were packed into sacks and the landing party embarked in the whaler and reached the LCI(L) without incident. Once again the Germans had showed no signs of life.

The next morning, Messrs. Taylor and Austin arrived in ISCHIA in order to examine the documents captured from the torpedo range and to interrogate Admiral Minisini.[20]

At this stage No 30 Commando had a base at Salerno harbour with a small group there under Lieutenant Orton, who were awaiting the capture of Naples, and the bulk on Ischia. Recent experience with the unreliability of OSS intelligence in the area convinced Riley that, before operations against remaining targets in the Bay of Naples were mounted, No 30 would have to carry out its own armed reconnaissance first. This became common practice from now on. After investigating a number of targets, some of which entailed landing behind enemy lines, No 30 Commando spent the end of September

in the Naples area. Riley now believed that the Adriatic would provide more fruitful pickings, and visited Malta at the end of September to put forward a plan for setting up an advanced base on one of
the Dalmatian islands in order to make contact with the partisans in
Yugoslavia and cooperate with them in raids on enemy installations.
A main base would be established at Bari or Brindisi. A similar party
should also be based in Corsica for raids on the coasts of Italy and
southern France. His proposals were accepted by the intelligence
authorities, and Riley then went to Brindisi in order to gather information on the situation in Yugoslavia and to select likely targets. Here
Trevor Glanville, who had worked for SOE in the Balkans early in the
war and spoke Serbo-Croatian, joined Riley, and on 16 October they
set out in two MTBs to make contact with the Yugoslav partisans on
the island of Vis:

> The boats were fired upon as they approached VIS harbour, but once
> the party was ashore the nature of the Mission was explained to the
> Town Commandant, a youth with a somewhat chequered career in rela-
> tion to collaboration with the Axis occupying forces. A conference was
> accordingly held with local Partisan Authorities, who guardedly admit-
> ted that there were in the country Military Missions from Great Britain
> and Soviet Russia. They stated, however, that they did not know how to
> get in touch with these Missions, nor, indeed, where they were located.
> 30 Commando's field team was therefore requested to remain on VIS
> until their proposals for operations on the Dalmatian Coast had been
> submitted to Partisan Headquarters, Lieut. Commander Riley, mean-
> while, returned to BARI.
>
> Two days later, Lieut. Commander A.R. GLEN DSC RNVR, arrived
> in VIS bearing a message from Lieut. Commander RILEY, request-
> ing Lieut. GLANVILLE to get in touch with Brigadier F. MACLEAN,
> Head of the British Military Mission to the Jugoslav Partisan Forces,
> who was reported to be at KORCULA on the island of that name. It
> was, therefore, decided that representatives of all the British organisa-
> tions on VIS should proceed to KORCULA and report their presence
> to Brigadier MACLEAN. On October 21, therefore, Lieut. Com-
> mander GLEN, Lieut. GLANVILLE and Captain JED EVANS of MI6
> informed Partisan headquarters at VIS that they proposed to sail that
> night for KORCULA in order to contact the British Military Mission.
> This proposal met with a good deal of obstruction on the part of the
> Jugoslavs, who stated (1) that Brigadier MACLEAN was not on KOR-
> CULA and (2) that it was undesirable to sail anyway, as the Germans
> were reported to be at sea. It was pointed out that the object of the
> MTB's presence was to find the Germans and that the party would sail

forthwith. After some discussion the MTB (Lieut. D SCOTT DSC RN) weighed and arrived at VELIKI OTOK on KORCULA soon after midnight. The Partisans here proved much more amenable and provided a truck to carry the party to KORCULA, which was reached at 0330. Brigadier MACLEAN expressed some indignation that unauthorised persons should have entered his territory without referring to him. It was explained, however, that until 24 hours previously no one of those concerned had been aware of the whereabouts of the Mission or of Brigadier MACLEAN's position as its head.

The nature of 30 Commando's proposed operation was, subject to security reservations as to detail, explained to the Brigadier, who argued that there was a case to submit to Marshal TITO for securing his consent for the cooperation of the Partisans in raids on certain objectives. He also agreed that Lieut. GLANVILLE should cross to the mainland and proceed to Marshal TITO's headquarters in order to explain the requirements of 30 Commando and to endeavour to arrange for the collaboration of the Partisan forces. Meanwhile, the section of Royal Marines was to transfer to HVAR where the headquarters of the Naval section of the Mission was situated. Here, soon after arrival, an enemy AMC [Armed Merchant Cruiser] with an escort of two R boats was sighted sailed toward BRAC. They succeeded in making SPLIT, however, as the RN MTB's were short of fuel and the Jugoslav batteries did not open fire. It is possible that they were carrying some valuable documents.

Lieut. GLANVILLE, accompanied by a Marine PLAXTON, and a Jugoslav guide, accordingly sailed from HVAR in a sardine boat and landed at PODGORA. Thence they hitch-hiked inland to LIVNO in BOSNIA, which was the local Partisan Headquarters. Thence they started by road for JAJCE (TITO'S headquarters), but at BUGOJNO they met Brigadier MACLEAN (who in the meantime had flown to JAJCE) who informed Lieut. GLANVILLE that Marshal TITO had refused to allow 30 Commando to operate in Jugoslavia and that GLANVILLE was therefore requested to return to Italy as soon as possible. The whole party, therefore, returned to LIVNO and in due course returned to BARI by way of HVAR and VIS. It was stated that Lieut. GLANVILLE was unacceptable to TITO and later accusations were made that GLANVILLE had interfered in local politics and had actually made a public speech in favour of General MIHAILOVIC. These stories were quite unfounded and were probably the creations of the Partisan Security Service (O.Z.N.A.), since Lieut. GLANVILLE's activities in Jugoslavia at the beginning of the war would suggest to the O.Z.N.A. that he belonged to the 'Intelligence Service' and was likely to inquire too deeply into local affairs.[21]

This was a disappointing setback, but, as will be related in Chapter

Nine, other Commandos would come to know Vis, Hvar and the other Dalmatian islands, as well as Tito's partisans, intimately during 1944.

While Glanville was attempting to set up operations with the Partisans, Riley had returned to Ischia, where he ordered the Royal Marines there to move to Bari. He then flew to Corsica to set up operations there, and in due course Captain Martin-Smith, along with Captain John Coates, late of No 10 (IA) Commando, and the Army Section sailed there in their own ML, which the unit now had. They were to remain here until the end of the year, but a prolonged spell of bad weather prevented them from carrying out any operations.

During much of this time, Captain Belcher's section of No 34 Troop had been operating in the Eastern Mediterranean. It had been Riley's original intention for the complete troop to be together under Captain Ward, but it was decided at the end of July 1943 that, in view of the number of likely targets in Sicily and Italy, it would be better to retain Martin-Smith's section there, and for Belcher's section to take care of the Levant. Belcher, accompanied by Lieutenant Phillips RNVR, therefore travelled with their men to Lebanon, but no operational opportunities arose until the Italian capitulation.

Churchill's fixation with the Aegean Islands rose again during summer 1943, but a full-blooded invasion of them, built around *Accolade* (the invasion of Rhodes), faltered when the Combined Chiefs of Staff refused to release landing craft for it. Now with the Italians coming onto the Allied side, it was seen as important that the garrisons on these island should be psychologically stiffened in order to forestall the Germans taking over. Consequently, as soon as the armistice had been signed on 3 September, Earl Jellicoe parachuted onto Rhodes and made contact with the Italian commander, Admiral Campioni, and gave him a message from General Maitland Wilson, C-in-C Middle East, assuring him of his support. The SBS and Long Range Desert Group under Brigadier Turnbull, who had taken over from 'Kid' Cator as Commander of the Middle East Raiding Forces, now landed on Castelorrizo, and elements from them visited other islands. Shipping in the form of Royal Navy destroyers and Greek caiques was gathered together and by the end of September 234 Infantry Brigade had been brought in to stiffen the defences. It was at this juncture that Belcher and his section, together with Naval Intelligence specialists, arrived in Leros. They immediately carried out reconnaissance of a number of the neighbouring islands, and then joined Brigadier Turnbull in the hope of being given some intelligence tasks. The Germans now began to react and, on 3 October, seized Kos. This was witnessed by Belcher and his men from the neighbouring island of Kalymnos, and on the night of the 4th they moved back to Leros.

In convoy with several other caiques we made the crossing to LEROS without incident, arriving approximately 0200 hours on the 5th where we unloaded all stores, etc., on the dockside. The L.R.D.G. and the S.A.S. who had also been evacuated from KALYMNOS were already sleeping alongside their kit on the dockside: we also slept beside our kit and Captain BELCHER informed us that we would be awakened at 0430 as there was danger of bombing.

We had just finished breakfast that morning when a reconnaissance plane came over at approximately 0530: we moved away from our kit undercover. At approximately 0615 aircraft were heard approaching: Captain BELCHER shouted 'Follow me lads' and started running towards a shelter. All the men with the exception of McDiarmid and Levy, who were looking for their Bren gun, which had been taken by mistake by a man in the S.B.S. McDiarmid and Levy were running to retrieve their gun and saw bombs bursting in the direction where Captain BELCHER and the men had gone: they had run into a stick of bombs. McDiarmid and Levy took up a position on the side of a hill overlooking the docks, opening fire on the Stukas, with the Bren, which were coming over in waves.

The raid was severe and it was concentrated on the dockside where all the troops and stores were. By this time soldiers were scattered all over the hillside with their Bren guns and it was impossible to go down to the docks during the raid. When the raid eventually ceased we made our way to the docks. We found out that Captain BELCHER, Tpr. McDaid and Fus. Ashton had been killed outright: Cpl Bancroft and Sgt. Wilkinson had been taken to hospital where Cpl Bancroft died twelve hours later. We eventually found McLellan who had been injured in the raid looking for us on the dockside.

Lieut. STEWART of the S.A.S. then took charge of us, promoting Levy, the senior man to Corporal.

In turn, the S.B.S. came under the L.R.D.G.

We were then taken to a position in the hills, after a few days there, Gnr. McLellan and Pte McDiarmid went with the S.B.S. on patrol to guard a stretch of road, and to blow up a bridge if the necessity arose.

Cpl. Levy was sent as a runner to Lieutenant-Colonel Prendergrast of the L.R.D.G. We all remained in these positions for three weeks and were daily bombed and strafed. Cpl. Levy during the three weeks had been endeavouring to contact either Lieut. SOLOMON or Lieut.

PHILLIPS who we knew were on the island: this he eventually did and after the position had been explained we were taken to Navy House to await a ship leaving LEROS. On 25 October we left the island on H.M.S. *HURSLEY* for Alexandria.[22]

This was a sad end to what at the outset had seemed a promising and fruitful role for Belcher's section, and it was particularly frustrating that they were not used on intelligence gathering missions. As it was, the Germans quickly regained control of the islands, with most of the British garrisons being captured. Brigadier Turnbull's men would, however, continue to operate in the area.

Early in November, attention turned to the capture of Rome, which it was hoped would be achieved by Christmas. It was intended to set up another S Force, as used in Tunisia, and it was agreed that No 30 Commando would be included in this, and a number of other operations were planned. Later that month, however, the Director of Naval Intelligence decided that the RM and RN Troops had collected the cream of the intelligence material in the Mediterranean and that it would be better for them to return to the United Kingdom in order to prepare for *Overlord*. There was also concern in his mind that No 30 Commando had, through its unconventional methods of going about its tasks, ruffled feathers in some quarters, and he sent out a senior officer to Bari at the end of November to investigate the complaints. The two troops left the Mediterranean at the end of the year, leaving the remnants of the Army Troop on Corsica.

Final 1943 Operations

Much of the burden of the remaining operations in Italy during 1943 rested on the shoulders of No 9 Commando. A week after their arrival at Molfetta, they were detailed to send troops to carry out a reconnaissance of the islands of Tremiti and Pianosa. No evidence of the enemy was found on either. Then, at the end of the month, they moved to the Naples area, coming under command of the US Fifth Army. Attention in the west was concentrated on the Garigliano and Rapido rivers, on which the Germans were now basing their defences. Initially there was a plan to force a crossing of the Garigliano near its mouth, and it was envisaged that No 9 Commando would support this by making a landing to the north of it. Bad weather, which had brought about extensive flooding, and the marshiness of much of the ground caused this to be cancelled, and the more lightly held Rapido was now favoured. Yet, it was important that the enemy in the extreme west were kept fully occupied. It was therefore decided that No 9 Commando would still carry out an operation north of the Garigliano, but this time it would be a feint attack. It was dependent for its success on the remaining enemy positions on the home bank of the river being subdued, and this task was given to a brigade of 56th Division and 201 Guards Brigade. The operation was also designed to make the Germans believe that a major attack was being mounted by X Corps.

No 9 Commando was given three specific objectives by X Corps, a hill feature, Monte d'Argento, 2000 yards north-west of the mouth of the river, the already destroyed bridge carrying Route 7 over the river and the spit of land north-west of the river mouth, which separated it from the coast – the three making up a triangle. Ronnie Tod's plan was to land halfway along the shore side of this triangle, and then to divide his force into three, one for each objective. Once these had been cleared, each party would then withdraw across the river to the home bank. A rehearsal was carried out on the night of 27/28 December, and two days later it was learnt that 167 Brigade had cleared most of the enemy positions on the home bank, and that 201 Guards Brigade were confident of quickly completing this task. That evening, the 29th, the Commando embarked in HMS *Royal Ulsterman* and *Princess Beatrix*.

> LCAs were slipped 6 miles SOUTH of the landing beach, and were formed to move off at 2130 hours. Two US Navy PT craft escorted and guided the LCAs, but lost their bearing and tried to land the Cdo some two miles SE of the river. However, Lt Col R.J.F. Tod, the CO, observed the navigation lights SOUTH of the river, the WP [White Phosphorus] smoke shells and the shell bursts of our arty conc and decided that the flotilla was too far SOUTH. He came alongside the 2ic's craft and ordered him to move NW up the coast with the first wave, and find a suitable landing place. The 2ic, Major E.W. CLARK, accordingly moved up the coast until he passed the river mouth, and landed 700 yards NW of it . . . at 0035 hrs (1½ hrs late and 1000 yds from the correct beach). At this time, smoke and dust made the shell bursts difficult to see, and there were no distinguishing marks on the coast line. The second wave landed in the same place a few minutes behind the first wave.[23]

One LCA developed a steering fault and did not land, which meant some reorganisation of the three parties as well as having to establish exactly where the Commando was. This was achieved by 0100 hours. Y Force, consisting of 120 men of Nos 1 and 2 Troops, set off under Captain J. McNeil to tackle the hill feature, but the added distance caused by landing in the wrong place, as well as irrigation ditches, mines and wire resulted in slow progress and it took them over two hours to reach Monte d'Argento. Here they split into two and, while one troop attacked the top of the hill, the other cleared houses and blocked the road to the north. It was found that the hill itself was defended mainly by mines and booby traps, and that the enemy were concentrated to the north. They therefore searched the lower ground, and blew up a PzKw Mk III Special tank, which they discovered in a cave. They then began their withdrawal to the river, having killed six enemy and captured four at a cost of four casualties to themselves. As they got close to No 6 Troop's objective, the bridge, they heard the skirl of pipes playing the 'Pwbrrachd of Donald Dubh', which No 6 Troop used as the charge, and McNeil ordered his piper to reply with his troop march 'Green Hills'. In this way the two forces were able to meet up, without firing on one another.*

Captain Cameron led Z Force of Nos 4 and 6 Troops, and like Y Force, found it slow going, not arriving at the bridge until 0500 hours. They then attacked supported by artillery fire and captured a pillbox, suffering no casualties. A message then came through from 201 Brigade stating that the home bank near the bridge was clear of enemy, which proved to be inaccurate, and Cameron decided to cross the river by the bridge. Here, to cross one of the two fifteen foot gaps in the bridge, a toggle rope bridge was made, one of the few times it was used on operations. Once across, they did run into some enemy, whom they made prisoner. In the meantime, X Force, which included the Commando HQ, had cleared the Spit, capturing one prisoner, but had had five casualties to a mine. It and Y Force, which had left Z Force in the bridge area, then crossed to the home bank using DUKWs, US amphibious wheeled vehicles. They had some problems with the latter grounding on a sand bank, but were eventually all back on the home bank by 0730 hours.

Although No 9 Commando had nine killed and 21 wounded in Operation *Partridge*, as it was called, they killed sixteen of the enemy and took 28 prisoners. More important was the fact that the operation, combined with that of 56th Division was taken seriously by the enemy and persuaded him to reinforce this part of the line.

---

*Being originally formed as a Scottish Commando, each troop had its own piper and particular marching tune and charge. This proved invaluable in action for locating troops and rallying them.

The Belgian and Polish troops had arrived at Molfetta on 3 December. Originally, it had been the intention to leave them in North Africa for the time being. It was at Brigadier Churchill's insistence that this was changed, since both they and he were impatient for them to begin operations as soon as possible. Churchill believed that the mountains in the River Sangro area, which were held thinly by both sides, would be ideal for both troops to practise active patrolling and infiltration. General Dempsey, whose corps was holding this area, agreed, and they moved to join 78th Division under Major General Charles Keightley on 13 December. Here they were placed under command of 56th Reconnaissance Regiment. As for the conditions at this time, Tom Churchill:

> Linear distances on the map do not represent actual distances to be traversed between two points owing to intervening hills and valleys. The climate is cold and crisp in fine weather but damp when cloud lies on the hills, which is the case on most days at the present time of the year. Visibility is normally limited to 30 yards but the clouds may suddenly lift for brief periods when a vista of up to 10 to 15 miles is suddenly revealed. The Sangro River at the moment is not in spate and averages a depth of 4ft 6ins and a 9 knot current. It is however liable to flood at any time when it increases in width to approximately 25 yards and becomes unfordable except by highly trained troops using ropes and accepting considerable risk. There are no bridges anywhere on the front now under description. The villages are in ruins having been systematically blown up by the enemy before retiring in order to deny winter quarters to our army. Bridges on roads on our side of the river have been blown by the enemy and only certain vital supply lines have been reopened by us. None of the roads adjoining the FDLs [Forward Defended Localities] laterally and parallel to the Sangro River are open, and all movement has to take place on foot. Supply to the Poles is by mule train.[24]

Neither troop was the slightest put out by these conditions and immediately mounted a very active patrol programme on the far bank of the Sangro. There were frequent brushes with the enemy. The Poles began operations the night they arrived with the object of selecting crossings over the river with a view to searching houses in two villages which were known to be occupied by the enemy on various nights. Tom Churchill:

> While reconnoitring the banks of the River the Poles found enemy 'S' mines on the far side. As it would have been dangerous to have carried

out patrols in this sector by night Captain Smrokowski* decided to operate in daylight the following day. After lying up for the rest of the night
he led the patrol out shortly after noon and proceeded a considerable
distance searching houses etc, until one was reached from which enemy
fire was encountered. Sharp exchanges took place, the Poles bringing all
their weapons to bear on the windows and door of the house. The Germans were pinned to their positions, but to assault the house over open
ground in daylight would have been unnecessarily risky and no weapons
were carried by this patrol which were capable of blowing the walls. During the encounter one Pole was wounded in the leg and was lying in the
open. Under covering fire from the rest of the Troop Smrokowski and
a Polish soldier crawled forward to the wounded man, assisted him on
to the soldier's back and the party crawled back to cover some 150 yards
away. The patrol then withdrew bringing back their wounded man.[25]

As for the Belgians, they began operations the day after their arrival,
and their war diary gives an idea of how they spent Christmas in the
line:

> *23 Dec 1943* In two days it is Christmas.
> Christmas at the front!
> The artillery is very quiet, only some rounds of English medium artillery
> fall in the woods on the hills north of the Sangro. The enemy gives no
> sign of life except towards 1400 hours with a long burst of machine gun
> fire which does not seem to be aimed at us. We learn that during the
> night 21st/22nd about 250 Boche troops attacked the village where our
> Polish friends are. A violent battle lasts all night. Three wounded are to
> be lamented among our friends; the Boche take away their dead, one
> reckons the enemy losses at ten or twelve killed or seriously wounded.
> The English artillery harasses the Boche withdrawal, hotly pursued by
> Polish patrols, without stop. The Brigadier himself [Churchill] followed
> the battle from the Regimental CP [Command Post 56 Recce Regt].
> Towards 1000 hrs Lt Dauppe takes the daily patrol of three men
> down to the Sangro, not seeing any enemy activity. He returns towards
> 1400 hrs with half a large butchered pig and three sheep which will serve
> as the Troop Christmas dinner.
> At 1700 hrs Lt Deton patrols down to the river but is not able to cross
> seeing the pitch darkness and the intensity of the current swollen by the
> recent rain. Lt Memy crosses the Sangro on the right of the sector and
> approaches d'Atteleta without meeting the enemy.
> They both return at 1700 hrs.
> The ground is now extremely difficult to patrol because of the rain

---

* Commanding the Polish Troop.

and the river will soon become impossible to ford. Private Tielemans of Lt Memy's patrol was carried away by the current and only owed his safety to his Mae West. He lost his rifle in the course of his efforts not to be drowned.

24 Dec 1943 Christmas Eve. It rains all the time. Half our little HQ is installed in a little less rudimentary fashion in the one house of the village which is not partially destroyed. The Captain [Danloy] and Lt Dauppe have to take post each night close to the CP of the squadron commander under the tent with weapons, runner and the driver with the Jeep.

Corporal Bekaert goes down towards the river at 1300 hrs with the soldiers Feldheim, Bury and Dryvers for the daily patrol until 1700 hrs along the length of the river which is covered with fog which reduces visibility to 50 or 60m. At 1600 hrs Lt Deton renews his standing patrols with the same sub-section but tries to cross the river and lay an ambush to surprise the enemy and bring back prisoners. Corporal Thonet with the following Privates, Waroquiez, Boulvin, Bury and Jacobs act as a standing patrol this side of the river in the area S Cristo, that is to say where we previously had an outpost. This evening at 2030 hrs A Section had its Christmas Eve dinner and at 2400 hrs Father Corbisier said Midnight Mass at the church of S Pietro.

The Padre distributes the Christmas NAAFI, which consists of 70 Players cigarettes, ¼lb of chocolate, a box of matches and a razor blade. The Captain decides that this NAAFI and a bottle and a half of beer per man will be distributed gratuitously to each as a Christmas present from the PRI [President Regimental Institute] along with the pig and three sheep previously brought back by Lt Dauppe.

'The Christmas Spirit' develops very sweetly. A Section had caught 20 chickens, God knows where, and all morning those men off duty had been working hard killing and plucking these poor beasts for the evening meal. Each officer and each sergeant is able to buy a bottle of Whiskey at the canteen. The Father proposes the first Christmas drink after lunch.

Long Live Xmas, Long Live Father Corbisier,
Long Live the Belgian Commandos at S Pietro.

At 1700 hrs Corporal Thonet (probably our best patroller) takes a 15cwt down to the area of our old outpost with four men to remain there until 0100 hrs as a standing patrol and listening post. Up to his return he noticed no enemy activity and heard no enemy patrols.

At 1745 hrs Lt Deton goes down by the same route to the Sangro with Guevorts' sub-section as a fighting patrol. He follows the river on an 'opaque' night for about 4km and then crosses the frozen river with water up to the waist. About 500m into enemy territory Lt Deton lays his ambush at 2100 hrs and waits silently until 2315 hrs, but nothing comes. It is Christmas night, the Boches stay at home. At 0030 hrs Lt Deton returns with his patrol. He is very cold. During this time Captain Danloy had been present at A Section's Christmas meal. A gigantic meal:

Menu:

Soup, Chicken Salad, Roast Lamb, Christmas Pudding

.... At midnight the Father says Christmas Mass.

25 Dec 1943 Christmas, Christmas! It is not a 'White Xmas' but the sky is full of clouds which pass quickly, promising snow. The tops of the mountains which surround us are already white and the bushes which cover them up to halfway are slowly covered with frost with superb effects and almost unreal in their grandeur and stillness. The guns are very quiet ... just a few salvos of 'medium' are fired at the end of this festive day. The men are happy! Even those who have passed the night lying on watch in their damp battle dress on the banks of the Sangro ... and who have waited in vain ... they think of their loved ones far from the Sangro but close to their hearts ... Adjutant d'Oultrement is ordered to patrol with four men this night on the other side of the river up to a suspect house which he is to search. Sergeant Uydebrouck is to patrol our eastern boundary and the neighbourhood of Monte Cristo (our old outpost), Sergeant Uydebrouck returned before the fixed time because Private Galland of his unit was ill.

Adjutant d'Oultrement says that he has not been able to locate the ford because of the pitch blackness of the night and has contented himself with patrolling our bank of the Sangro.

This evening at 2030 hrs B Section with its part of the HQ section organised their Christmas dinner. Sergeant Delo helped by Acton and Toul have prepared a succulent meal of which the menu is:

Hors d'oeuvre: salmon with salad

Chicken and Onion soup

Beefsteak with boiled potatoes

Pork cutlets with fried potatoes and green salad

Christmas pudding – Christmas Cake – Beer and toasts

Excellent atmosphere. Lt Roman presides. Lt Dauppe represents the Captain. When he thanked B Section for their dinner, Lt Dauppe proposed a toast to Colonel Lister, 'the commander who formed us and who is unhappily not here to harvest with us the fruits of his excellent work in directing our training'.[26]

Both troops would continue this full programme of patrolling and ambushes until well into the New Year.

CHAPTER SEVEN

Towards Overlord
January 1943–June 1944

The problem over the clash of interests among COHQ, SOE and SIS, which had come to a head in December 1942, was resolved by the Chiefs of Staff at a meeting on 4 January 1943, when they decided that priority for small raiding operations would henceforth rest with the SIS, but that where there was a clash of interests with SOE and COHQ, the Admiralty would adjudicate. In general terms, COHQ were banned from raiding the French mainland west of the Cherbourg Peninsula. Although this rather cramped the freedom of action of the SSRF, who had now been joined in No 62 Commando by No 2 SBS, it in no way brought an end to their operations, although many were carried out by the SBS rather than SSRF. Thus, on the night 8/9 January four members of No 2 SBS with two canoes set out in MGBs 111 and 112 to destroy enemy shipping in St Peter Port, Guernsey, but were forced to turn back because of the appalling weather. Many other operations were planned, but the weather forced cancellation.

In the meantime, the long thinly held lines in Tunisia brought about a realisation that this theatre had much scope for amphibious raiding operations, but, apart from the Special Engineering Unit and Nos 1 and 6 Commandos, all the various 'private armies' – SAS, LRDG and Popski's Private Army – were operating on the Eighth rather than First Army front. Accordingly, Anders Lassen and Philip Pinckney were sent out to Cairo on 23 January to discuss the concept of setting up a force specifically designed for amphibious operations on the Tunisian coast. Their ideas were welcomed by both GHQ Middle East and Eisenhower's Headquarters, and on 2 February Bill Stirling relinquished command of the SSRF and set out for North Africa, to form, what would become in May 1943, 2 SAS. Appleyard, too, and some of the other SSRF stalwarts followed two weeks later. They were to soon exert influence at Allied Headquarters, as Dunstan Curtis who was finding it difficult to find gainful employment for No 33 Troop, quickly recognised, and Stirling was of much help to him.[1] The remainder of the SSRF in England were now commanded by Peter Kemp from Anderson Manor, and he himself was now much more under the control of Colin Gubbins than of COHQ.[2]

Although the loss of many of these who made the SSRF what it was did thin its numbers, operations continued. On the night of 27/28 February Captain Porteous vc and Lieutenant Thompson took eight other members of the SSRF in *MTB 344* to Herm. The object of *Huckaback* was to establish whether artillery could be landed on the island in order to support an invasion of Guernsey. This they succeeded in confirming, and the only evidence of any enemy was a notice in the grounds of the château there stating that they were out of bounds to all troops. Nevertheless, they dropped propaganda leaflets in conspicuous places and left the letter 'C' chalked on various walls. Two nights later it was the turn of No 2 SBS again, when two officers attempted to carry out a reconnaissance of Anse St Martin on the north-west corner of the Cherbourg Peninsula. Using *MTB 344* once more, they arrived at a point some 1¼ miles from their objective when two searchlights were switched on, and a number of coastal guns opened fire. While they were deliberating as to whether they had been compromised or not, two suspected patrol vessels were spotted, and it was decided to abort the operation. The conclusion at COHQ was that they had been picked up by radar, the first time this had happened to a raiding party.[3]

The last SSRF operation, *Pussyfoot*, took place on the night of 3/4 April, when ten members set off in *MTB 344* to Herm once more in order to reconnoitre the west side of the island, which Porteous had not been able to do because of lack of time, and, if possible, capture a prisoner. Unfortunately, the weather, as it had been so often in the past, was unfriendly, and they had to return because of a thick fog. By now, with the nights becoming shorter, small cross-Channel raids were seen to be impracticable as the time ashore would be so limited.

Although, by this time the COPPs had also come under the No 62 Commando umbrella, it was decided on 19 April that Bill Stirling's force should be separated from it. With no foreseeable task for it in the United Kingdom during the summer, there was little left for the SSRF to do, and it was disbanded. Some of its members, like Peter Kemp, went to work for SOE, Bruce Ogden-Smith was to distinguish himself as a COPP swimmer. The majority, however, who had been loaned by No 12 Commando, returned to them, as did one or two other SSRF members. These and other members of the SSRF were sent on parachute courses to RAF Cardington, where all SOE agents underwent training in this skill. The former SSRF members also had to go and attend Commando training at Achnacarry. Only then were they permitted to wear the green beret which they had up until then not worn.[4]

As for those who went to North Africa with Stirling, many would not survive the war. Appleyard was killed in Sicily, Colin Ogden-Smith in France, Dudgeon in Italy, Pinckney, who joined the SBS, was also captured and shot in Italy. Lassen's name will crop up again later in the book.

In spite, of the tighter control exerted by the SIS, Commando operations in Norway also continued during the early part of 1943. In order to provide sufficient training to cope with the inhospitable terrain, the Commando Mountain and Snow Warfare Training Camp had been set up at Braemar in Scotland on 1 December 1942. Its first task was to train the members of North Force. By the middle of February this consisted of two troops (B and D) of No 12 Commando, an officer and ten men of the Norwegian Troop of No 10 (IA) Commando, an officer and four men from No 1 (Boating) Troop of No 14 Commando, and an officer and four men from No 30 Commando. However, Lt Colonel Wedderburn considered that the experiment of mixing Canadian soldiers with British and Norwegian sailors in the No 14 Commando troop had not worked in that their outlooks were so different that it was impossible to foster any *esprit de corps*. It was therefore decided to disband this troop but retain No 2 (Skiing) Troop.[5]

Nevertheless, this did not prevent several operations from being mounted from the Shetlands. On the night of 23/24 January, D Troop of No 12 Commando, together with ten men of the Norwegian Troop under Captain Harald Risnes, under the overall command of Major, as he now was, Fynn, attacked the island of Stord off southern Norway, having sailed from Lerwick in a force of seven MTBs of the 30th (Royal Norwegian Navy) MTB Flotilla. The main objective of *Cartoon* was the pyrites mine at Lillebo.

> The operation was highly successful. Owing to navigational difficulties and detours necessitated by enemy air reconnaissance the raiding party got ashore later than intended and carried out their tasks in just under 3 hours instead of 5½ hours as originally allotted.
>
> Enemy opposition was encountered during the landing of half the force on SAGVAAG quay, which was held by a detachment of 20 Germans with two 75 or 105mm guns and two AA guns. These guns were not

manned but fire support was brought to bear on the enemy defences as the MTB closed the quay . . . The remainder of the force was landed unopposed on northern side of bay, (approximately 400 yards away) and covered 2 miles to their objective at LILLEBO in 25 minutes carrying approximately 50 lbs weight of explosives each.

The mine was effectively destroyed by destruction of the hoisting and winding gear, jaw [ore?] crusher, the transformer and compressor houses, and two engines in the railway shed. . .

The silo jaw crusher, conveyor belt, and the 4 guns and ammunition dump all at the quayside were blown up by delayed action fuse, and the whole quay could be seen blazing from 4 miles away as force was on passage back. During the operations ashore 3 of the MTBs proceeded to LEIRVIK to attack shipping in the harbour, but no ships were seen. On the way back a 2,000 ton enemy ship was set on fire and beached in a sinking condition and mines were laid. There was heavy shore gunfire, which was returned by our Naval forces.[6]

In addition, two of the MTBs (625 and 631) shot down a Ju88 on the way back, and three prisoners were taken as well as a quantity of enemy equipment and papers. It was estimated that the mine, which in 1942 had produced 160,000 tons of pyrites, would be out of action for a year. This was done at a cost of one Commando killed and two, together with eight sailors, wounded and three MTBs slightly damaged.

A month later, on 23 February, a small party of sixteen made up from Nos 12 and 30 Commandos and the Norwegian Troop, set sail from Lerwick on Operation *Crackers*, whose object was to attack an observation post and occupy another in the Tungodden area. Rough seas prevented the attack from taking place, but the party manned an observation post for a week undetected, as well as collecting much useful intelligence on local fortifications and Quislings. Then, on 12 March, Lieutenant Rommetveldt, now commanding the Norwegian Commando detachment, and six of his men accompanied two Norwegian MTBs on a foray into the harbour at Floro (Operation *Brandy*).

Arrived early in the morning [13th] off the Norwegian coast near Flora. My men used for guarding the boats and for observation. Stopped a number of Norwegian fishermen. All were allowed to proceed after interrogation. *14 Mar 43* at 2300 hrs proceeded into Floro harbour where two German merchant vessels were torpedoed and sunk. Respectively 5000 tons and 10000 tons. Before entering the harbour, mines were laid at the entrance resulting in the sinking of a German ship of 15000 tons. On leaving the harbour the MTB which my men and myself were in went aground. The ship sustained substantial damage and had to be abandoned. Crew were transferred to the other MTB. . .

We were pursued by a German destroyer and a German armed trawler, but managed to get away in the darkness.[7]

A few days later (19th), a party from No 12 Commando, accompanied by two men of No 5 (Norwegian) Troop went to the Stadt area for another naval operation, but this was aborted after a clash with the Germans on a bridge linking two of the islands, in which the enemy had two killed.

Southern Norway seemed to be a happy hunting ground, but in April came signs that the enemy was significantly increasing his defences. Thus, on the 9th, 70 men of No 12 Commando, with ten men from No 5 Troop set sail for another raid on the Stadt area. Bad weather forced them back, but they made another, this time successful attempt next day. When they arrived off the target area, they contacted a number of locals who told them of new defences in the area, as a result of which they were forced to cancel the operation, especially as the Admiralty would not allow them to attack a smaller target. Finally, on the 29th, an attempt was made by six members of No 14 Commando to attack shipping at Haugesund with limpet mines. Sadly, bad weather meant that they were not picked up the first time round, and three other attempts were made to collect the party, but no trace of them was ever found, although there were rumours that they had been successful against at least one ship. The operation, *Checkmate*, was the last for the Commandos of North Force for some time. Summer in those parts meant little darkness, and the lack of security would be even greater than across the Channel. North Force, however, still remained in the Shetlands in case there should be some new development.

Further Reorganisation

The requirements for the invasion of Sicily had, as was explained in the previous chapter, necessitated the SS Brigade being split into two headquarters in mid April. There were, however, wider issues in the wind. With the realisation that Sicily reinforced the trend begun with *Torch* that Commandos were now about to be used on a much larger scale than hitherto, together with the experience of Nos 1 and 6 Commandos in Tunisia, Laycock believed that the time had now come for a major reorganisation of the Commandos. Accordingly, on 1 April 1943 he sent a paper to Mountbatten entitled *Role of the Special Service Brigade and Desirability of Reorganisation*. He began by pointing out that the Commandos had originally been raised for the primary function of small scale raids, but 'in the new offensive stage of the war the policy of mounting small scale, seaborne raids, with the sole intention of annoying the enemy, is to be abandoned. Such raids as do take place are likely to be on a large scale, of long duration and immediate strategic importance'. There were three options. The Commandos could either be retained in their present form for small scale raiding, in which case it was unlikely that more than three Commandos would be required. They could be disbanded, which Laycock considered a 'disastrous' step in view of their achievements, or they could be reorganised to enable them to 'take the fullest part in the coming battle', in which they could operate independently or 'in conjunction with the Field Force'.

He strongly recommended the last course, and stated that for a start a Holding Commando should be established. The problem of reinforcement of a Commando engaged in prolonged operations had been highlighted by the experience of Nos 1 and 6. It would, of course, be possible to reinforce it by sending drafts from other Commandos, but this would be detrimental to the *esprit de corps* which had been built up in each. The answer was therefore the Holding Commando to which a recruit would go once he had passed the Achnacarry course. Once there, the added benefit could be gained of giving him collective training. He then went on to point out that his present span of command stretched 'from Inverness-shire to the Isle of Wight, and from North Wales to Buckinghamshire', and that he had eighteen subordinate units, many times more than an ordinary brigade. The problem of command and control was even more aggravated when simultaneous operations were being mounted from different parts of the country. He therefore proposed that the SS Brigade be broken down into three Commando Groups, each of three Commandos, while the more specialist units – Nos 10, 30 and 62 – along with the Depot, Commando Mountain and Snow Warfare Camp and Holding Commando be retained under the direct control of the SS Brigade HQ. Furthermore, if the Commandos were to be involved in prolonged operations, especially with the Field Force, then their firepower needed to be enhanced, and they must have the necessary transport and administrative personnel so that they would not incur 'the charge of being "parasites"'.[8]

Mountbatten generally agreed with Laycock's proposals, and put them to the War Office, who accepted them in principle,[9] although General Paget, still C-in-C Home Forces, did not believe that one of Mountbatten's arguments for the proposed organisation, that the Commandos would be required to take part in operations after the initial amphibious assault.[10] Sicily and Italy quickly proved him wrong.

By now Laycock had set off for the Mediterranean, taking with him four Commandos. General Sir Frederick Morgan, who was then responsible for planning the invasion of France, now decided that to support his projected three division assault on France in 1944 he would need four Commandos per assault division, twelve Commandos in all. While General Sir Alan Brooke, the CIGS, had in March laid down a target for nine Army Commandos to be operational by late September 1943 and 18 by 1 April 1944, by July he realised that this was clearly not possible. It would merely lead to further 'creaming off' of those formations earmarked for *Overlord* and reinforcement of all theatres, the practice which had been so unpopular in 1940-1. Yet, there was still the Royal Marine Division, which continued to languish in the United Kingdom, apparently not required in any operational theatre, and neither MNBDO 1, now in India, nor MNBDO 2 in the Middle East, appeared to be doing much. Indeed, it seems at this point, in July, that the CIGS considered that the Royal Marines should take over total responsibility for Commandos. Mountbatten, too, thought that the additional Commandos should be raised from the RM Division and the MNBDOs and obtained the First Sea Lord's agreement to this. This was approved in July 1943, and additional Royal Marine Commandos were to be raised as follows:

No 42 (RM) Commando from 1 RM Battalion (Lt Colonel R.C. de M. Leathes RM)

No 43 (RM) Commando from 2 RM Battalion (Lt Colonel R.W.B. Simonds RM)

No 44 (RM) Commando from 3 RM Battalion (Lt Colonel F.C. Horton RM)

No 45 (RM) Commando from 5 RM Battalion (Lt Colonel N.C. Ries RM)

No 46 (RM) Commando from 9 RM Battalion (Lt Colonel C.R. Hardy RM)

No 47 (RM) Commando from 10 RM Battalion (Lt Colonel C.F. Phillips RM)

These were officially formed on 1 August 1943, and on the 7th of that month the first of them, No 43, moved north to Achnacarry to undergo the Commando course, to be followed in turn by the others.

As for the overall organisation, with the Commandos now dramatically enlarged in numbers, Laycock's original proposal was not far-reaching enough, and it was agreed that it should be modified. Instead of having a Special Service Brigade, a Special Service Group would be set up. Under it would come two Royal Marine Commando Brigades, each of four Commandos and commanded by brigadiers, and one Army Commando brigade under a brigadier, broken down into two groups, reflecting Laycock's plan, of four Commandos each and commanded by colonels. This was discussed in detail at a meeting held at COHQ on 8 September 1943. Four Commandos (two Army and two RM) were already in the Mediterranean, and No 9 Commando, together with two troops of No 10, were about to leave for that theatre, with another Commando due to follow in early October. This meant that 6½ Commandos would be in the Mediterranean. Three or four Commandos would 'almost certainly be' needed in India by December and would have to sail shortly. It was agreed, therefore, that, as a general rule all Army Commandos would serve overseas, leaving the RM Commandos committed to *Overlord*.[11]

Appointed to command the SS Group was Major General R.G. Sturges CB DSO RM, and by the middle of September, the new organisation had come into being. The concept of the one Army SS Brigade was quickly dropped as being impracticable, and instead of the two groups, two Army SS Brigades were set up. The order of battle was now as follows:

HQ 1 SS Bde (Brigadier The Lord Lovat DSO MC) Midhurst, Sussex
No 1 Commando Winchester, Hants
No 4 Commando Seaford, Sussex
No 5 Commando Shanklin, IoW
No 6 Commando Hove, Sussex
No 10 (IA) Commando Eastbourne, Sussex
No 12 Commando Bognor Regis, Sussex
HQ 2 SS Bde (Brigadier R.E. Laycock DSO shortly to hand over to Lt Colonel T.B.L. Churchill MC) Molfetta, Italy
No 2 Commando
No 3 Commando
No 40 (RM) Commando
No 41 (RM) Commando
Special Raiding Squadron

HQ 3 SS Bde (Brigadier W.I. Nonweiler RM) Canterbury, Kent

No 42 (RM) Commando Herne Bay, Kent

No 43 (RM) Commando Ramsgate, Kent

No 44 (RM) Commando temporarily at Achnacarry

HQ 4 SS Bde (Brigadier B.W. Leicester RM) Newton Stewart, Scotland

No 45 (RM) Commando moving from Portsmouth to Ayr, Scotland

No 46 (RM) Commando Troon, Scotland

No 47 (RM) Commando moving from Dorchester to Castle Douglas, Scotland

Directly under SS Group HQ, which was set up at Milford-on-Sea, came No 9 Commando, which was about to move to the Mediterranean, No 2 SBS (Titchfield, near Southampton), the Commando Mountain & Snow Warfare Camp, which had now moved to Lanrwst in North Wales, the RM Holding Commando (Piddlehinton, near Dorchester) and the Commando Depot.

This organisation did not last long for a number of reasons. The marriage between Army and Royal Marine Commandos did not get off to a good start. Major General J.L. Moulton, who was to command No 48 (RM) Commando:

> Now the Army commandos felt and said that the Marines, unlike themselves, were not volunteers, lacked operational experience and were appropriating themselves prestige that they had not won; Marines felt, and usually tried not to say, that, while there was much to admire and envy in the well-publicised efforts and record of the Army commandos, not all of it was above criticism and some of it was positively amateurish.[12]

Robert Sturges realised that if this antipathy was allowed to grow between the two, both would suffer. The concept of keeping both separate when, after all, they were performing the same role, would merely aggravate this. In any event, the Mediterranean was demonstrating that both could work well together in action. Thus, during the closing months of 1943 he worked hard to weld the SS Group together. The cornerstone of this was the mixing of the two types of Commando within each brigade where possible. Thus, by the end of 1943 the new order of battle was as follows:

No 1 SS Bde Nos 3, 4, 6 and 44 (RM) Commandos (Sussex)

No 2 SS Bde Nos 2, 9, 40 (RM) and 43 (RM) Commandos (Italy)

No 3 SS Bde Nos 1, 5, 42 (RM) and 44 (RM) Commandos (India)
No 4 SS Bde Nos 10 (IA), 41 (RM), 46 (RM) and 47 (RM) Commandos (Kent)

The RM Holding Commando and the rump of No 12 Commando had been moved to Wrexham in North Wales, and were merged to form the Operational Holding Commando. Finally, in order to demonstrate to the Army Commandos that he had their interests as much at heart as the Royal Marines, Sturges appointed John Durnford-Slater as his Deputy Commander in the rank of Brigadier. He had also moved his Headquarters to Pinner in Middlesex in October 1943.

Small Scale Raiding - Later 1943

In April 1943 Lt General Sir Frederick Morgan was appointed Chief of Staff to the Supreme Allied Command (or COSSAC) and, with a mixed Anglo-American staff, was tasked with the planning of the invasion of France. One of the first questions the planners had to answer was where the most suitable landing area was, and this entailed accumulating information from every source on the state of the beaches, tides and German defences along the complete coastline of Northern France. Much of that from inside the country was collected from SOE and SIS sources, but as the summer wore on the Germans, conscious that invasion would come at some time, began to restrict severely French civilian movement in the coastal areas, which made information more difficult to obtain. It was therefore decided that COHQ should be brought in to help, and that a number of raids be mounted in the area north of the Seine running up to the Franco-Belgian border, previously a 'no-go' area for the Commandos.

With the SSRF now disbanded and its members dispersed, the only unit with expertise in small scale raiding was No 12 Commando, now commanded by Lt Colonel The Lord Sysonby DSO. At the time, early June, North Force was still in the Shetlands, with a strength of 3 officers and 79 other ranks. The remainder were split into three. Major F.W. Fynn was brought down from the Shetlands to form another Fynn Force (5 officers, 39 ORs), Captain 'Mickey' Rooney, who had, with some of his men, seen action with the SSRF, formed Rooney Force (7 officers, 62 ORs) and Lieutenant Hollins led Hollins Force (3 officers, 19 ORs). A series of raids was planned under the overall cover name *Forfar*, and it was decided that Fynn, in view of the hard experience which he had gained in Norway during the previous winter, should be in overall command of the three forces, and that their collective title should be Forfar Force. Understandably, Sysonby was somewhat put out by this in that it left him with no operational command, and rumours started to fly among his men that the Commando was to be disbanded. On 2 June he wrote to General Haydon, who as GOCO, represented the Army Commandos' interests at COHQ, asking him to explain what the future of the Commando now was. The upshot was that those members of No 12 Commando who were not involved in North or Forfar Forces were posted to Nos 1 and 6 Commandos, with a few to Nos 3 and 9, and, with the Sergeants' Mess wound up at the end of July, No 12 existed little more than in name only, although it survived in this state until the beginning of December.

Also to join Forfar Force were No 2 SBS, and members of No 10 (IA) Commando. Apart from the activities of detachments of the Norwegian Troop with North Force, and elements of the French Troop, which had taken part in the Dieppe Raid, No 10 had been training hard for almost a year, but as yet had no operational experience. They had also been scattered in troop bases about North Wales. On 30 May 1943, the Commando came together for the first time at Eastbourne. Here, both the Norwegian and British Troops were sent on a parachute course, and No 7 (Yugoslav) Troop was formed, but was smaller than the others with only two officers and 14 men. It was, however, small detachments of the British Troop and Captain Philippe Kieffer's French Troop, which were to join Forfar Force.

The *Forfar* raids were planned as follows:

Forfar Beer	Target Eletot, east of Fécamp
Forfar Dog	Target Biville, east of Dieppe
Forfar Easy	Target Onival, south of the R Somme
Forfar How	Target Quend Plage, north of the R Somme
Forfar Item	Target area west of St Valéry-en-Caux
Forfar Love	Target Dunkirk pier

In all cases, the aim was the same, to gain intelligence of the German defences and to capture a prisoner. The first to be mounted was *Forfar Easy*. Two officers and eight men of Hollins Force, led by Hollins himself, set off on the evening of 3 July in *MTB 24*, with gunboats in support and fighter cover. They landed by dory, collected samples of wire found on the beach, and then climbed the cliffs. They laid an ambush on the coast road, but no enemy came into it and, with time running out, they were forced to re-embark. *Forfar Beer*, *Forfar Dog* and *Forfar How* were mounted on the night of 5/6 July. *Forfar Dog* was successful in that the party of two officers and eight men, using a dory launched from *MTB 250*, were able to land and scale the cliffs, but on reaching the top discovered thick wire, which they could not get through and had to return empty-handed. *Forfar Beer* did not get this far. Using the old SSRF craft *MTB 344*, they had to turn back when they ran across an enemy armed trawler. *Forfar How* was also aborted because of the heavy surf.

It was not until the end of the month that another raid was made, when *Forfar Beer* was tried once more on the night of 31 July/1 August. This time both unfavourable weather and the breakdown of the dory prevented a landing. *Forfar Easy* was also mounted again on the same night, but, the need to dodge German E-boats on the voyage across produced navigation problems as well as resulting in too little time to spend ashore, meant that this was also once more aborted. Nevertheless, Fynn remained determined to achieve some success, and three nights later *Forfar Beer* and *Forfar How* were tried once more and *Forfar Love* was mounted for the first time. *How* failed once more because of the surf, although the dory did actually reach the shore. *Forfar Beer* went slightly better, and there was a new innovation in that the party landed on the first night, lay up the whole of the next day in a fold in the cliffs and carried on their reconnaissance the following night before being picked up. Unfortunately, they, too, had no success in capturing a prisoner. *Love* saw No 2 SBS being used in *Forfar* for the first time. Stan Weatherall, then a sergeant and one of the unit's most experienced members, tells the story:

At Dover, on 4th Aug, Capt Livingstone, Lt Sidders, Sgt Salisbury and myself boarded an MT boat with two canoes and left Dover Harbour at 9.30 pm prepared for a job at Dunkirk. It was not an ideal night, as it was a little too light. However, at 11.45 pm we sighted the jetty and pier, so launched the two canoes, one mile from the jetty. Paddled along towards the jetty, but a beach light was shining off the pier end. However, we continued until we were in the beam of the light, and it took us five minutes to get' out of it. The gerries must have spotted us for they swung the light round on us again just as we got into the black-out of the beam. It was useless to proceed any further. We were only a few yards from the jetty, and about 100 yds from the pier end. Capt Livingstone decided to turn back. We expected the enemy to open fire at any second. Why they didn't I fail to understand, for they continued to shine the light on us, and turned it as we turned to escape. The light must have had a fixed arc, for it stopped, and we got out of the beam. Capt L and myself kept in touch with Lt Sidders and Salisbury by Walkie Talkie, and flash light. Our last message to them was 'to steer due north until daybreak then steer west', as we could not find the MTB. Learned afterwards it had been in a scrap with three E boats. The 'Rhud' was pretty choppy, and just after we cleared it, Capt L became violently sick, with taking a bromide tablet in mistake for a benzedrine tablet,* so I had to do the paddling.

It was about 2 am by now. I took over the compass and continued to paddle due north. Capt L went to sleep between his sick spasms. Paddled north until dawn, then turned west. Tried to get in touch with Sidders but failed to. At 8.30 am saw a Spitfire a good way off so lit one of my smoke floats, and fired a very light, but the pilot did not spot us. Capt L still very sick and could not help me paddling the canoe. Was getting tired now. Continued west until 11.30 when I saw two Spitfires, so I lit a smoke candle, and held it on the end of my paddle. The pilots observed us, for they both circled round us for 10 minutes, then one left for Sidders had lit a smoke candle. We now had a Spitfire each. Sidders was about 1½ miles behind, so we turned round and paddled towards each other. We were about 10 miles from the coast of France and 20 to 25 from Dunkirk. Four more Spitfires came on the scene, and they shot up three E boats who were going to pick us up and take us prisoners. A Walrus seaplane came along and landed not far from us, so we paddled towards it, and climbed aboard. We sank the canoes by firing a Spandau at them, took off about 10 minutes later and landed at Hawkinge aerodrome very wet and tired.[14]

The final two *Forfar* operations took place at the beginning of September. *Forfar Beer* was mounted for a fourth time, with the party of ten all ranks again staying ashore for two nights. Among their stores they took a cage of carrier pigeons.

The days were 'packed with little incidents which seemed of immense importance'. Among them was a meeting with a French fisherman, whom they terrified by their appearance, for they 'were dressed in special camouflage suits, our faces painted with black, brown and green stripes, with nets over our heads. He must have thought we were dervishes or sea devils. However, some British chocolate assured him of our bona fides; we had no passports.' The fishermen went away and returned the next day with 'a great pile of postcards of the village with all the German positions marked on them.' Encouraged by this the raiders loosed

---

*The use of benzedrine by Commandos has already been mentioned in relation to Nos 40 and 41 (RM) Commandos and the Sicily Landings. Trials had been undertaken towards the end of 1940 into this drug as a means of keeping troops awake and alert during raiding operations,[13] but it was surprisingly not on general issue to the Commandos.

off five carrier pigeons, each carrying a message asking the motor boat
to postpone its arrival for twenty-four hours. 'To our horror we saw five
peregrine falcons sweep down from the cliffs and bear the pigeons away
to their eyries, messages and all.' About 1930 hours that evening two
German Focke-Wulfs flew several times very low over their heads, but
failed to spot them. Just before they went back to the motor torpedo
boat, which duly arrived, they blew a Bangalore torpedo among the German wire.[15]

Thus, although they failed to get a prisoner, the information
which they brought back was of particular interest to the *Overlord*
planners.

Mounted at the same time, while the *Forfar Beer* party were
ashore, was *Forfar Item*, which was unusual in that it used parachuting
as a means of inserting part of the raiding group, while the remainder used MTB and dory. It was carried out by Rooney Force, most
of whose members were now qualified parachutists. The airborne
party took off in Whitleys from Thruxton on the evening of 2 September, the idea being that they would be extracted by the sea party
in the dory.

> The landing zone was close by the village of Le Tot, west of St Valéry-
> en-Caux. On dropping, however, the party became split into two and it
> took an hour and a half to reunite it. In the meantime the MTB, which
> was to take them back to England, and the dory to take them from the
> shore to the MTB, had deployed and contact was made with them by
> Walkie-Talkie radio. The target was a suspected searchlight position, but
> all that could be found were some binoculars and other observation
> equipment, which were seized, and a signal wire which was cut. The
> Commandos then abseiled down the cliff face to the beach, 'the stiffest
> abseil that anyone had had'[16], but then found that the dory was in fact
> waiting for them some two and a half miles away, just west of the har-
> bour at St Valéry-en-Caux. They therefore had to hump their equipment
> across heavy shingle. The dory itself had been holed in several places
> and by the time it had been made seaworthy once more it was almost
> daylight. Nevertheless, the MTB came in and picked them up and they
> were back at Newhaven by 0645 hours.

Rooney, in his report, considered that the operation would have
been more successful if there had been more training in orientation
in darkness, and recommended that each man should in future be
equipped with some demolition stores.[17] Nevertheless, this seemed
a promising method of insertion, and it was taken up again in the
next series of operations at the end of the year.

These two raids were the last of the *Forfar* series. On 11 September, the Chiefs of Staff decided that, in future, all reconnaissance operations mounted from the United Kingdom should be coordinated by COSSAC, except for those in connection with the Anglo-American strategic bombing offensive, *Pointblank*, and a Reconnaissance Committee was set up for this purpose.[18] Forfar Force was disbanded, and there was a pause in raiding operations until close on the end of the year. In the meantime, attention turned once more to Norway. A fresh unit, Timberforce, was formed, and No 42 and then No 47 (RM) Commando also had to provide a party of two officers and thirty men to act as 'boat guards' to the MTBs of the 30th Flotilla.[19] Timberforce, which was mainly made up of No 5 (Norwegian) Troop, was to mount a number of operations in early 1944, but seldom achieved surprise, finding the Germans very alert. Nevertheless, this in itself was not discouraging, for the threat of an Allied invasion of Norway was one of the major deception plans for *Overlord*.

Plans for the next series of cross-Channel Commando operations were drawn up by COSSAC in November 1943 for mounting in December. There were two types. *Hardtack* operations were, like *Forfar*, reconnaissance operations in the areas between Le Havre and Ostend, the east side of the Cotentin Peninsula and the Channel Islands, with the object of capturing prisoners if possible. *Manacle*, on the other hand, was designed to take out certain enemy strongpoints along the coast. *Hardtack* used the same size of force as *Forfar*, ten all ranks, and the same method of transport, MTB and dory, apart from one operation, which was to be airborne, while *Manacle* employed a complete Commando troop of 60-80 men and an LCI(S).

Major Peter Laycock, brother of Bob, and then 2ic of No 10(IA) Commando, was appointed in overall command, and his force was known as Layforce II to distinguish it from the original 1941 Layforce. As for the forces involved, Laycock had at his disposal Nos 1 and 8 (French) Troops of No 10 Commando, No 2 SBS, who were to provide the dory crews, two officers and 4 ORs, formerly of No 12 Commando and now on the strength of the Holding Commando, for the seaborne *Hardtack* raids, and No 3 (Misc) Troop of No 10 for the airborne operation. For *Manacle* and *Hardtack* 5 three troops of No 4 Commando were to be used under Major R.P. Menday, 2ic of No 4, and not surprisingly his force was known as Menday Force. The force concentrated in the

Newhaven area on 8 December and officially became Layforce II on the 17th. The operations planned for the December dark period, which came at the end of the month, were numerous, and are listed below:

Code Name	Command	Part of Departure	Target area	Military Unit
Hardtack 28	C-in-C Plymouth	Dartmouth	Jersey	French Troop 10 (IA) Commarido
Hardtack 7	C-in-C Plymouth	Dartmouth	Sark	French Troop 10 (IA) Commando
Hardtack 21	C-in-C Portsmouth	Newhaven	Cotentin-Quibeville	French Troop 10 (IA) Commando
Hardtack 24	C-in-C Portsmouth	Newhaven	Cotentin-Varreville	French Troop 10 (IA) Commando
Hardtack 13	C-in-C Portsmouth	Newhaven	Benouville	French Troop 10 (IA) Commando
Hardtack 9	C-in-C Portsmouth	Newhaven	Port Susselle St Valery-en Caux (Airborne)	3 (Mise) Troop 10. (IA) Commando
Hardtack 4	C-in-C Portsmouth	Newhaven	Biville- sur Mer	French Troop 10 (IA) Commando
Hardtack 5	VA Dover	Dover	Onival (rec-cefor Mana-cle 5)	French Troop 10 (IA) Commando
Hardtack 14	VA Dover	Dover	Merlimont	French Troop 10 Plage (IA) Commando
Hardtack 19	VA-Dover	Dover	Stella Plage	French Troop 10 (IA) Commando
Hardtack 11	VA Dover	Dover	Pointe de Gravelines	French Troop 10 (IA) Commando
Hardtack 23	VA Dover	Dover	Bray Dunes	French Troop 10 (IA) Commando
Hardtack 26	VA Dover	Dover	Middelkerke	French Troop 10 (IA) Commando
Manacle 5	VA Dover	Dover	Onivai	No 4 Commando
Manacle 8	VA Dover	Dover	Quend Plage	No 4 Commando

These were, preceded by a 'dress rehearsal' *Hardtack Dog*, which took place on the night of 26/27 November. It was led by Lieutenant

I.D.C. Smith of No 12 Commando, which was then on the point of being finally disbanded, and with a party of nine he revisited Biville, the scene of *Forfar Dog*. Setting out from Newhaven, in 'perfect weather', they transferred to their dory two miles off shore, and approached the landing point. While doing this, their MTB came under fire from coastal guns, and was forced to withdraw to five miles out. Smith then discovered that his kedge was not holding. He sent his rubber dingy in to check on the possibility of landing without a dory kedge, but the dingy was punctured. He decided to risk using the dory without the kedge, and managed to get ashore. They found a way up the cliff, but, with the MTB refusing to come in again, had no time to do anything more, and, relaunching the dory, they successfully met up with the MTB. As far as Smith was concerned, it was essential that the dory had a trained crew to operate it,[20] which his was not, and this was the reason why No 2 SBS were brought in.

As for Layforce II operations proper, a number were cancelled because of the weather or because the Royal Navy found themselves with prior commitments. *Manacle 8* and *Hardtack 13* and *23* did actually sail, but no landing was made because of bad weather. This left *Hardtack 4, 5, 7, 11, 21* and *28* which were actually carried out. The first mounted, *Hardtack 11*, took place on Christmas Eve, and was led by Warrant Officer Wallerand of No 10 (IA) Commando. The landing was successful, but then problems began to arise. In their enthusiasm to get ashore, the French raiders forgot to help push the dory out into deeper water, with the result that the two SBS men could not prevent it being washed aground by the breakers, and it filled with water, which stopped the engine. Nevertheless, they managed to push it out into deeper water and paddled their way back to the MTB. Here it was drained, but efforts to get the engine restarted failed, and so the crew took one of the signallers with them and paddled back towards the shore, having received a wireless message that the party ashore were trying to locate the dory. In order to make the task of the paddlers easier, the MTB had moved closer inshore to reduce the distance. Then, about 15 minutes later the codeword *Maroon* was received on board the MTB, which meant that the dory had been sunk or wrecked. The MTB moved in closer until the depth had reduced to five feet, and spotted three of four swimmers, but none seemed to get any closer and they vanished, although shouts were heard for a time. No sign of the nine was ever found, although the MTB returned on Christmas night in the hope of rescuing any survivors.

In spite of this tragedy, two more operations were mounted on Christmas night, *Hardtack 7* and *28*, against Sark and Jersey respectively. Those on the former were landed on a rocky promontory, which proved unscaleable, while the men on the latter got ashore without trouble and discovered an unoccupied observation post, having skirted a minefield and passed through the deserted village of Egypt. They knocked on the door of an unoccupied farm, but the woman who answered the door was frightened and merely directed them on to another farm. The two men here were also frightened, but they managed to calm one of them down sufficiently to give them much useful information, which included details of a strongpoint in the neighbourhood manned by 15 Germans and about ten Russians. Having been given a glass of milk each, they made their way to the strongpoint. Here they came across a suspect minefield, and time was now too short to find a way through it in order to attack. They therefore moved back to the cliffs and the dory, but unfortunately Captain Ayton of No 2 SBS, the one Briton in the party, trod on a mine and was badly wounded. Nevertheless, they managed to get him on board and he was successfully evacuated.

The night of 26/27 December saw another three raids. Lieutenant Smith returned to the scene of *Hardtack Dog*, now called *Hardtack 4*, with a mix of ex-No 12 and French Commandos. Unfortunately, as the first of them reached the top of the cliff, they saw a German patrol of fifteen men moving towards them in an extended line. Deciding that discretion was the better part of valour, they withdrew to the beach, where they carried out a reconnaissance before returning to the MTB. *Hardtack 5* saw the redoubtable Captain Porteous vc and a party from No 4 Commando carrying out a reconnaissance for *Manacle 5* at Onival. They had one man wounded by an S mine shortly after landing. They located their strongpoint, but found it unoccupied. In all, they spent 4½ hours ashore, but, apart from wire and the odd field telephone cable, saw or heard nothing of the enemy. Finally, Lieutenant Vourch took a party of French Commandos to the Cotentin-Quibeville area on *Hardtack 21*. The most significant aspect of this operation was that the party brought back valuable information on an anti-tank beach obstacle known as Element 'C', which was made of steel girders and weighed some 2½ tons. The last operation in the December dark period took place on the following night and was a repeat of *Hardtack 7*. The party was a mixture of Holding Commando members and French Commandos, and was led by Lieutenant A. McGonigal. This time they succeeded in getting to the top of the cliffs – a 200-foot climb up a sheer rock face – and then found a path. Thick gorse forced them to keep to this, but unfortunately it led them straight into a minefield. Two men were killed and all the rest, except one, were wounded, and the party was forced to withdraw.

Although a brave face was put on it, *Hardtack* during the December dark period was only at best a partial success. Some useful information had been brought back, but no prisoners had been captured, and there had been casualties and frustration suffered by those involved. The latter was especially so for the parachute party of No 3 (Misc) Troop under Captain Hilton-Jones:

> *20th November [1943]*
> The first operational party under Captain Hilton-Jones leaves for Wimborne Minster, Dorset in preparation for the first air-borne 'Hardtack Operation'. The party stays in great secrecy in an empty requisitioned house not far from the aerodrome, gets a couple of practice jumps out of the Halifaxes to be used, but then has the disappointment of seeing the raid called off on the account of adverse weather. For three successive Dark Periods (no moon) this party stood by, the last two times at Bournemouth for 'Hardtack' but the weather defeated them each time, although they once got as far as preparing to emplane.[21]

They were planning to use the same idea as Rooney Force had for *Forfar Item*, with a second party led by Lieutenant George Lane, who was in fact a Hungarian called Lanyi and the first member of No 3 Troop to receive the King's Commission, going in by dory, to collect the parachutists after they had carried out their tasks. In spite of the setbacks suffered, it was intended that *Hardtack* and *Manacle* should continue in the New Year.

The Run Up To Overlord

On 1 January 1944, General Sir Bernard Montgomery arrived back in England from the Mediterranean and assumed command of 21st Army Group, which would be responsible for conducting the *Overlord* landings. He had already seen the COSSAC plan when he stopped over at Eisenhower's headquarters in Algiers, and he did not like what he saw. His basic objection was that the front was too narrow, and that it should be extended eastwards from the beaches north of Caen up to and including the western base of the Cotentin Peninsula, and that the initial assault force should be increased from three divisions to five, each landing on a separate beach. By the end of

January, his concept had been accepted and worked into a detailed plan, involving three British and two US divisions.

As far as the Commandos were concerned, he stated as early as 14 January that he required ten Commandos for the assault, although he reduced this to eight two weeks later.[22] With four Commandos now firmly committed to the Mediterranean, another four to South-East Asia, and No 10 (IA) Commando fragmented, this left only seven available in the United Kingdom. It was therefore decided to raise an additional RM Commando. There were no more Royal Marine battalions left in the United Kingdom, and it was not until 3 March 1944 that No 48 (RM) Commando came into existence under Lt Colonel J.L. Moulton RM at Deal in Kent, having had to await the return of the 7th RM Battalion from the Mediterranean. It was immediately rushed up to Achnacarry in order to make it operational in time for *Overlord*.

With regard to the continuation of *Hardtack* and *Manacle*, the weather prevented any operations being mounted during the January dark period. At the end of the month it was arranged that No 46 (RM) Commando should take over the role of No 4 Commando in *Manacle* in order to give it some operational experience. However, on 27 January, the Chief of Staff 21st Army Group, Major General Francis de Guingand, wrote to the Chief of Staff COSSAC* with a copy to Laycock requesting that no more cross-Channel raids should be mounted as they merely encouraged the enemy to further strengthen his defences.[23] This therefore brought about the cancellation of *Hardtack* and *Manacle*, and the Commandos now began to prepare themselves for the invasion itself. The only two exceptions were that raids could continue on the Dutch coast and Ushant, and that the embargo did not apply to COPP operations.

The COPPs were at the time performing their vital task of beach reconnaissance, which they had begun in earnest towards the end of December. Most of the work was done by No 1 COPP, which was led by Major L. Scott-Bowden DSO, MC RE, and one of the other star performers was Bruce Ogden-Smith, late of the SSRF. Commander Nigel Clogstoun-Wilmott DSO DSC RN, who had pioneered the idea on the beaches of Rhodes with Roger Courtney in early 1941, was also still closely involved. Their chief concern was the checking of beach

---

*This was how the latter was addressed, although at that time Supreme Headquarters Allied Expeditionary Force (SHAEF) was being set up at Bushy Park and it can be assumed that the letter was actually meant for Bedell Smith, Eisenhower's Chief of Staff.

gradients and bringing back soil samples. To do this they used X-Craft (midget submarines) and Landing Craft Navigation (LCN). Dressed in rubber suits, they swam ashore, and their method of measuring beach gradients was simple but ingenious. It consisted of a line with lead pellets mounted at 1ft intervals, which was pegged on the beach and then reeled out in the water, and a similar line which was used to measure depth. Measurements were recorded by the swimmer on a white slate with indelible pencil. It was tedious and very uncomfortable work, especially when being buffeted by breakers, but vital to the success of *Overlord* and the COPPists more than deserved the many decorations which they received. They were, however, transferred from Combined Operations to the Admiralty on 1 January 1944 in order to streamline the lines of communication. One Commando raid on the Dutch coast in early 1944 is recorded, which involved Captain Trepel and six French Commandos. This was mounted from Yarmouth on the night of 24/25 February, but, although they made a successful landing from their dory, leaving two men to man it, they ran into trouble, and it was not until June 1945 that their graves were found near where they had landed. Four had died of exposure and one had drowned.

As for the Commandos themselves, they gradually passed over from the command of the SS Group to that of 21st Army Group. On 5 February, HQ 1 SS Brigade, together with Nos 4, 6 and 45 (RM) Commandos, were transferred, to be followed a few days later by No 47 (RM) Commando of 4 SS Brigade, and by the end of March both brigades were firmly under 21st Army Group. By now the order of battle was as follows:

No 1 SS Brigade (Brigadier The Lord Lovat DSO MC)	Seaford, Sussex
No 3 Commando (Lt Colonel P. Young DSO MC, Beds & Herts)	Worthing
No 4 Commando (Lt Colonel R.W.F. Dawson, Loyals)	Bexhill
No 6 Commando (Lt Colonel D. Mills-Roberts DSO MC, Irish Guards)	Hove
No 45 (RM) Commando (Lt Colonel N.C. Ries RM)	Eastbourne
No 4 SS Brigade (Brigadier B. W. Leicester RM)	Canterbury, Kent
No 41 (RM) Commando (Lt Colonel T.M. Gray RM)	Ramsgate, but to move to Hastings in mid April

No 46 (RM) Commando (Lt Colonel C.R. Hardy RM)   Folkestone
No 47 (RM) Commando (Lt Colonel C.F. Phillips RM)   Herne Bay
No 48 (RM) Commando (Lt Colonel J.L. Moulton RM)   Gravesend

As for those elements still under command of the SS Group, No 10 (IA) Commando remained at Eastbourne. HQ Special Boat Unit had joined HQ SS Group at Pinner, its HQ at Coldhayes, Liss having been closed down at the beginning of February, being seen as nothing more than a 'gilded postbox',[24] and its constituent elements were now:

    Royal Marine Boom Patrol Unit   Southsea, Hants
    Combined Operations Pilotage Unit   South Hayling, Hants
    Special Boat Section   Lee-on-Solent, Hants

30 Assault Unit was at Littlehampton, the Holding Operational Commando was still at Wrexham, where it would remain throughout its life, the Depot remained at Achnacarry, but the Mountain Warfare & Training Centre had now moved to St Ives in Cornwall. One other Commando unit was the RM Engineer Commando. One of Bob Laycock's recommendations in his April 1943 paper for making the Commandos more self-sufficient was for them to have their own engineers. Consequently, in August 1943 the RM Engineer Commando Company was formed at Dorchester, and was then expanded into a complete Commando of three troops, one of which had been sent with 3 SS Brigade to India. The remainder moved to Wrexham in November 1943, and then to Steyning in Sussex in March 1944.

In outline, the allocation of Commandos to the assault forces on D-day was that 1 SS Brigade complete, with the two French Troops of No 10 (IA) Commando, would be under command of 3rd British Division for the landing on *Sword* beach. Also to be employed on *Sword*, but independently, was No 41 (RM) Commando, which was the reason for their move from Kent to Sussex in April 1944. Nos 46 and 48 (RM) Commandos would operate under the 3rd Canadian Division on *Juno* beach, while No 47 (RM) Commando would be with the 50th Northumbrian Division on *Gold*. As for their tasks, these are best described in the next chapter.

Notwithstanding 21st Army Group's imposed restriction on Commando operations during the months leading up to 6 June 1944, No 3 (Misc) Troop of No 10 (IA) Commando was to be involved in a further series, codenamed *Tarbrush*, in May. At the end of February they had been briefed and had trained for a series of raids, both sea and airborne, against German V weapon sites in the Pas de Calais area, as part of Operation *Crossbow*, which was the destruction of these installations. Nothing came of it, however, as it was considered that the RAF had caused them sufficient damage. Now, in early May, a small party of carefully selected individuals assembled under Captain Hilton-Jones at Dover to form Hiltforce. Their task was to gain further information on mines and other obstacles to be found on the beaches, but the area selected to do this was to be outside the invasion area, in order to reinforce the deception being practised on the Germans that the main assault would come in the Pas de Calais region. In order to assist security, these raids were to take place in the May dark period. The parties also needed to be able to inspect the various obstacles dryshod at half tide, to check whether the enemy was laying mines seaward of the beach obstacle belt. As for the types of mine which he was using, there was surprisingly little idea at this late stage in the invasion preparations, and it was thought that they could be of five types – magnetic, contact, electrically controlled, activated by the entry of sea water to set up an electric cell (voltaic) or acoustic.

The period chosen was 14-19 May, and no less than eight raids were mounted. Each party used an MTB, and then transferred to a dory with rubber dinghy. The actual reconnaissance would be carried out by a Royal Engineer officer and NCO, accompanied by a Commando signaller, while one officer and two other ranks would crew the dory, and a further man the dinghy. On the night of 15/16 May, *Tarbrush 3* (Bray Dunes), *5* (Les Hemmes), *8* (Quend Plage), and *10* (Onival) took place. *Tarbrush 3* and *5* were abortive because the weather prevented a landing, while *Tarbrush 10* suffered a similar fate when the MTB had to take evasive action after spotting a German naval patrol and there was not sufficient time left to carry out the reconnaissance. *Tarbrush 8* was successful, with the party spending 1½ hours ashore. They confirmed that there were no mines between the obstacle belt and low water line, and what mines there were were Tellermine 42s attached to stakes. They tried to remove one of these mines, but it was too firmly attached, and the Sapper officer slipped while doing this, and had to hang onto the mine itself. 'As nothing happened it did not appear very sensitive.'[25] The next night, *Tarbrush 3, 5* and *10* were repeated, with the last named again aborted because of the weather. Both *3* and *5* succeeded, bringing back much the same information as *Tarbrush 8*. In the former case, the party carried out their tasks undeterred by torch flashes while still 100 yds from the beach, and a man smoking a cigarette some 150 yds from their landing point. The *Tarbrush 5* party actually clashed with an enemy patrol, but the latter withdrew after shots had been exchanged. Finally, on the night of 17/18 May, *Tarbrush 10* was repeated once more. Having checked the obstacles in the area where they landed, Lieutenant Roy Woodbridge, the Sapper officer, accompanied by Lieutenant George Lane of No 3 Troop, moved further along the beach to see if they could locate any Element 'C' obstacles. As they did so, two German patrols on either side of them began firing. Lane and Woodbridge lay flat until the firing had finished and then crawled back towards the dinghy. In the meantime, the Sapper sergeant and the signaller had swum back to the dory, leaving the dinghy for the two officers. They picked up the dinghy and paddled out to sea, hoping to cross the Channel, but the tide was against them, and at dawn they saw a German patrol boat making its way towards them. They were captured, blind folded and taken to Abbeville, the nearest town, having been accused of being saboteurs and threatened with shooting. Eventually, after interrogation, they were driven to Rommel's Headquarters at La Roche-Guyon on the Seine, 50km west of Paris, where Lane found himself taking tea with the Field Marshal, at which they discussed the war in general. He subsequently survived Gestapo interrogation at the notorious Fresnes jail and ended up in a POW camp, where the information he gave on Rommel's HQ to the Senior British Officer there was smuggled back to London, and, a few days later on 17th July, Rommel was attacked by two RAF fighters, while returning to his HQ, and severely wounded.*

In spite of this setback, the information gained on *Tarbrush* was invaluable and did much to set the *Overlord* planners' minds at rest over what had been a nagging doubt, and No 3 Troop more than merited the awards of the MC made to Hilton-Jones and Lane, as well as a Mention in Despatches to another member.

---

*Lane returned to the scene of his meeting with Rommel exactly 40 years later, and a complete account was given in the Sunday Telegraph Magazine No 397, 3 June 1984. I have, however, been unable to substantiate whether the information given by Lane led directly to the attack on Rommel in his staff car.

CHAPTER EIGHT

From Normandy to the Elbe

The overall task of 1 SS Brigade on D-day was to land in the Ouist-reham area at the mouth of the River Orne, clear it and push inland to link up with 6th Airborne Division, who were tasked with seizing bridges over the Orne. Then, with the latter, they would be responsible for guarding the left flank of the beachhead on a line running along east of the river. 4 SS Brigade, with Nos 41 and 48 (RM) Commandos, were to destroy coastal defences in the area of Lion-sur-Mer (No 41) and St Aubin (No 48) and then seize the radar station at Douvres, which would then be searched by members of No 30 Commando. No 47 (RM) Commando, operating on its own, was to capture Port-en-Bessin, which lay between the British *Gold* and US *Omaha* beaches, while No 46 (RM) Commando was held in Army reserve with two possible tasks, both involving cliff assaults on coastal batteries to the east of the Orne. These tasks involved a certain amount of specialist training, with 1 SS Brigade and No 47 (RM) Commando concentrating on speed marching cross-country carrying 80-100 lbs per man, Nos 41 and 48 street fighting, and No 46 cliff climbing. Nos 1, 5, and 6 COPPs were to be responsible for beach marking, while, apart from the two French Troops with 1 SS Brigade, who were placed under No 4 Commando. No 10 (IA) Commando was also to be represented by elements of No 3 (Misc) Troop, which were distributed among the Commandos to act as special reconnaissance patrols for infil-trating the enemy lines, as well as tactical questioning of prisoners. Finally, in order to ensure that Commando interests were safe-guarded, Brigadier John Durnford-Slater headed a tactical HQ of the SS Group, which was attached to HQ Second British Army. The RN Commandos would also be strongly represented by *Fox, Jig, Love, Peter, Queen, Roger, Sugar* and *Tare. Charlie* would be in reserve, but was not called upon.

The Commandos embarked in LCI(S)s on 5 June. Many suffered from seasickness on their way across the channel to Normandy. The first to touch the shore on 6 June was No 4 Commando, who landed 500 men strong, having transferred to LCAs from the *Princess Astrid* and *Maid of Orleans,* on *Queen Red* beach, one mile west of Ouist-reham. The idea had been for 8 Infantry Brigade to land first and secure the beach, and then for No 4 to pass through. When No 4 landed at 0820 hours (H + 30 mins), however, it was to find the infantry pinned down under heavy fire from a strongpoint at the back of the beach. Mortar bombs were falling around the LCAs as they beached, and the Commandos suffered some forty casualties, including Lt Colonel Dawson wounded in the leg. It was clear that 8 Brigade were not going to be able to support them, and so Dawson decided to push on on his own, but was again wounded, this time in the head. He handed over to the second-in-command, Major Menday, and the Commandos managed to break out onto the coastal road running towards Ouistreham. Their next objective was a coastal battery, and they set off towards Ouistreham led by Nos 1 and 8 (French) Troops of No 10 (IA) Commando under Captain Philippe Kieffer, in the face of heavy harassing from snipers and machine guns positioned in various houses.

> Invaluable assistance was given by a gendarme, a member of the Resistance Movement, who helped the leading tps to by-pass enemy strong pts. The FRENCH Tps over-ran the casino area to the west of the Bty posn and the assault went in according to plan. Heavy cas were inflicted on the enemy, who put up stiff resistance from strong fortifications and cunningly camouflaged blockhouses. The concrete gun emplacements had withstood the terrific air and naval bombardment extremely well and severe fighting took place before the enemy posn became untenable and several surrendered. The Bty was taken, but cas on both sides were hy and after the engagement med orderlies from opposing sides worked side by side succouring the wounded.[1]

And then:

> No 4 Commando then withdrew to the area where the ruck-sacks had been left and prepared for a strenuous and back breaking 9 miles march under constant sniping and mortar fire to HAUGER across the CAEN Canal and the River Orne.[2]

Next to land, at 0840 hours and also on *Queen Red,* were Lord Lovat and his headquarters and No 6 Commando. They landed direct from LCI(S), but the beach was still under heavy gun and mortar fire, and three of the craft were hit, including one of the two HQ LCI (S)s. The beaches themselves, although under fire, 'seemed curiously deserted

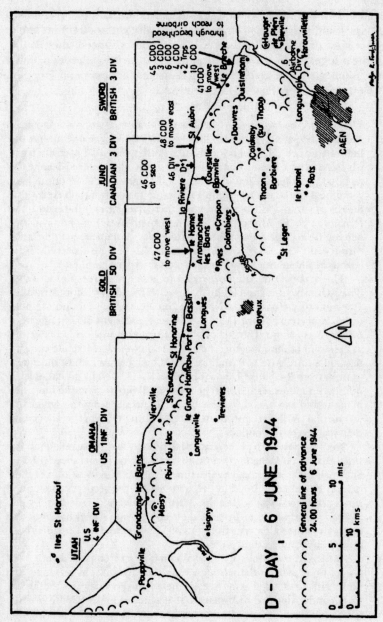

D - DAY, 6 JUNE 1944

as the men waded ashore and streamed up the sand. The gaunt and gutted buildings among a maze of tangled wire and shell craters made up a kind of martian landscape.'[3] They now advanced towards the Orne bridges, experiencing some difficulty in crossing the deep drainage ditches, which needed the help of scaling ladders. No 3 Troop of 6 Commando were leading the advance:

The country was by this time heavily wooded, and the troop stuck to fairly well defined paths, which were luckily going in the same direction as the line of advance. The enemy had stuck 'Minen' signs all over the place which must have been a bluff as no mines were encountered despite the fact that the troop walked over many of the signed areas. Continuing in a southerly direction the troop soon came to the two pillboxes which had been allotted to No 3 Troop to either attack or neutralise until the remainder of the Brigade had passed through. Although no firing was coming from these pill boxes at the time they could be seen quite easily through the trees – another strongpoint also being discovered in the corner of a field which was not shown on the photograph.

The Troop Commander decided to attack all three positions and despatched No 2 Section to the more westerly and went himself with No 1 Section to the other two. No 2 Section attacked and found the position had been vacated at a very short notice, and signs of bombing were evident everywhere. The section then returned to support No 1 Section in the event of their needing it. No 1 Section were formed into two parties and a third gave covering fire onto a hedge ahead whilst the attack went in from the flank. The first pill box was cleared by grenades after putting up minor resistance. The second pill box was attacked in a like manner and two prisoners were taken. Returning from this attack fire was turned on the section from a hedge in the rear. In the attack one man was severely wounded.

No 2 Section then proceeded off to destroy the six-barrelled mortar which had been firing fairly close all this time, in co-operation with two Sherman tanks which had by this time come up with some other infantry. On reaching the road in the area 084791 the section came under small arms fire from a distance. After penetrating a little further the mortar was nowhere to be seen and having gone somewhat over our boundary the section returned, and on the orders of the Brigadier continued the advance, to Bréville.

During the advance up several snipers were contacted, but they always fired and retired through the undergrowth. On reaching the Bénouville area small arms fire was heard in the village so the Troop Commander decided to by-pass the village and make for the bridges which had been reported captured by the Airborne. On nearing the bridge a group of men were seen through a hedge 200 yards away and these were first thought to be Germans; on looking at them through glasses, however, they were recognised as paratroops. The Troop Commander waved the Union Jack carried for this purpose and shouted. On seeing us the paratroops cheered frantically and moved towards us. The party consisted of a Paratroop Brigadier, Colonel Pine-Coffin* and their H.Q. The Brigadier said to our Troop Commander: 'We are very pleased to see you.' The Troop Commander characteristically answered, looking at his watch: 'I am afraid we are few minutes late, Sir.'

The Troop then continued across the bridges and so on to Bréville via Amfreville. Small parties of paratroops were met on route, but the ground ahead of us was undoubtedly unclaimed territory. Just this side of Bréville we met a civilian who informed us that Bréville was held by Germans. This was odd as we marched into the village without being fired on at all and took up a position around a fairly large house which we discovered to be the H.Q. of the Officer and R.S.M. in charge of the local troops. Leaving a section at this house the Troop Commander decided to attack another house which the enemy were reported to be living in and from which they were sniping at us.

The section tried to make its way round to the back of this house and take it from the rear in area 134744. It was at this point in the back garden of a house that the Troop Commander was killed, shot in the neck by a sniper. The section was then heavily mortared from the area 135745 and consequently withdrew to the position of the former house after having several casualties.

Little did the section realise that they were within 200 yards of a troop of four German 105mm Gun-Hows and a dual purpose 20mm gun, situated in the orchard 135746. These guns had not fired a single shot while the troop had been coming in.

Not being able to dig-in in the area allotted to the troop on account of enemy small arms fire the troop was ordered to dig-in in its present position. Not more than half an hour elapsed before heavy mortar fire descended on the Troop, also shots from the dual-purpose gun. Although the troop dug-in as much as possible in the time, heavy casualties were sustained in the first two hours and the position was regarded as impracticable to hold against a determined attack. The Troop was ordered back to the area of Commando HQ 130748 where it dug-in. The rest of the evening passed uneventfully.

At the end of the day the Troop had suffered 21 casualties. The body of Captain A.C.H. Pyman was recovered two days later and buried at Le Plein.[4]

---

*Brigader J.H.N. Poett commanding 5 Parachute and Lt Colonel R.G. Pine-Coffin commanding 7th Parachute Battalion.

The second half of the brigade, Nos 3 and 45 (RM) Commandos, landed at 0910 hours. Although there was now little opposition on the beaches, there was still some significant shelling, and No 3 suffered twenty missing when an LCI(S) received a direct hit. They soon caught the remainder up, but snipers continued to be a nuisance, and a number of casualties were inflicated by them, including Lt Colonel Ries of No 45, who was wounded in the leg, and Major Gray took over command. No 45's final objective for the day was the village of Franceville-Plage on the road to Cabourg, but they were held up by a strongpoint two miles short of this. In the meantime, No 3 Commando were sent to help out the 12th Parachute Battalion who were having a stiff fight in the village of Le Plein. No 3 Troop, mounted on bicycles, was given this task, and the village was cleared during the afternoon. The remainder of No 3 were ordered to provide protection for the 6th Airborne Divisional HQ at Le Bas de Ranville. It now became clear that the original plan of establishing a firm line east of the Orne could not be carried out that day. No 45 was therefore ordered to halt and to dig in at Merville, where they had just relieved the 9th Parachute Battalion at the battery there. No 6 Commando went firm between Le Plein and Bréville. Then, at 2000 hours, No 4 Commando finally rejoined and began to dig in at Hauger, between Sallanelles and Le Plein. With No 3 Commando detached, and No 45 isolated at Merville, the position of the brigade by last light on D-day was hardly secure, and the arrival of 6 Airlanding Brigade at 2100 hours was greeted with much relief. In spite of the fact that the final objectives had not been met, 1 SS Brigade had succeeded in its main task of linking up with the airborne troops and at least the bridges across the Orne were secure.

As to the fortunes of 4 SS Brigade, the Headquarters and No 48 (RM) Commando landed with the Canadian 3rd Division at St Aubin, also direct from LCI(S).

There was quite heavy fire on the beach and several of the LCI carrying the Commandos were holed on the beach obstacles. This led, in the state of the sea and owing to the weight carried, to a high proportion of casualties, many of whom were rescued after being 'partially' drowned. They were, however, lost as far as the initial operations were concerned.

German mortar fire and sniping caused losses, the beach defences appearing to come to life after being stunned by the bombardment and the LCI(S) not being the most suitable possible craft for a quick landing under fire in a rough sea.[5]

Nevertheless, they got ashore and No 48 (RM) Commando advanced as far as Langrune, two miles east of St Aubin. Here they came across a concrete strongpoint, which could only be reached through narrow streets dominated by fire. An attempt by one troop to capture it failed. Then a Centaur tank from the Royal Marine Armoured Support Group was brought up, but was knocked out on a mine, and the advance got no further that day. No 41 (RM) Commando, which had landed with the British 3rd Division, also experienced similar problems, and lost their second-in-command, Major Barclay, killed. In their attempts to move westwards in order to link up with No 48, they were halted by strong opposition in the area of Luc-sur-Mer.

No 47 (RM) Commando was to land with 231 Brigade in the area of Arromanches, on the western flank of *Gold* and then strike westwards to Port-en-Bessin. They transferred from HMS *Princess Josephine Charlotte* and SS *Victoria* to LCAs when 7½ miles offshore. Although the rough sea restricted the speed of the LCAs and resulted in some seasickness, they closed to the shore without too many problems. Once they recognised the various landmarks, they had to alter course to the east, and during this time they were under fire from a gun in the Arromanches area.

> On closing JIG GREEN beach, it was seen that the beach was still under fire. On the beach just east of LE HAMEL was a motionless tank with its gun depressed forlornly and apparently out of action. Two hundred yards further along the beach another tank was aflame and beyond an assortment of tanks, armoured bulldozers and stray vehicles. For 500 yds of beach east of LE HAMEL there wasn't a sign of life anywhere. No landing craft of any description had been stranded on this stretch of beach and it was most unlikely that any of the assault craft had been beached and got off again because there were not apparent gaps in the underwater obstacles. In the heavy sea running and from a plunging LCA, these looked very formidable indeed.
>
> There were spikes 6-8ft sticking out of the water and the next moment they would be completely submerged. Many of these spikes and poles had box type mines secured to their tops and, the view from a bucketing LCA was not a bright or pleasing one.[6]

In their final alteration of course, the LCAs were forced to run parallel to the coast under fire. Four out of the 14 landing craft were sunk. On one of these was Captain Wood:

Suddenly I found myself face downwards in the water not knowing what had hit me. I found that whatever it was had blown the bows off the LCA.

I had already removed my second Mae West, which was outside my equipment, but I still had the other one. I managed to slip my equipment without difficulty and swam around for a bit before I was helped on to the stern of the craft which was sticking out of the water.

There were altogether about nine of us perched on the stern. We signalled to one of the PJC's [*Princess Josephine Charlotte*] craft on her return journey and she came alongside. I supervised the transfer of the wounded. I went over to a badly wounded man and dragged him on the stern but when I turned round the boat was on its way back to the PJC. Needless to say I was pretty angry and shouted and gesticulated but they couldn't have heard me for they perservered with their course.

We made signs to various LCAs and LCTs without success and eventually I decided to swim for a rope leaving a corporal to look after the badly wounded man. I was quickly swept 200 yds along the beach. After about an hour I fetched up on the beach, having banged my head against several pointed bits of LCTs and LCIs and swallowed pints and pints of water.[7]

As for the remainder of the Commando:

When we assembled just off the beach, 4 officers and 68 other ranks were missing from our landing strength of 445 all ranks. The majority of men had had to swim for it and were soaked. Most of these had wisely slipped off their equipment and many were without arms and ammunition. Some of them had kicked off their boots and trousers.

The HW Tp had lost one MMG and had only one 3" mortar. This mortar had no sight.

The beach was a shambles. LCTs had beached and were stranded, some had breached to. There were landing craft of all types, in all positions, at all angles.

There appeared to be no beach organisation. There were no beach markings except for one or two exits which had been marked with white tapes. There was certainly no attempt made to call and guide in craft or put up leading marks to mark the channels through the underwater obstacles. Perhaps that was due to the fact that there were no channels. Wood and iron stakes tipped with mines, a varied assortment of iron obstacles, tetrahedra and the like, together with with the stranded craft bulldozers and drowned vehicles showed that any form of landing or arrival on to the beach was a hazardous business.

The CO, in the leading landing craft, continued Eastwards, parallel to the beach until he saw an LCT which appeared to have beached successfully.

At least it had its bows on the beach and its stern pointing out to sea. Thinking that this LCT had managed to find a gap, the CO turned in towards the beach following the course taken by this LCT, slipped up its port side, and jockeying between the side of the LCT, a drowned bulldozer, a submerged LCA and a drowned tank, the leading craft touched down and landed its troops almost dryshod.

Most of the following craft tried to follow suit but there wasn't enough room to manoeuvre in the rough sea and the men who could clambered from craft to drowned vehicles and thence wade ashore considered themselves very fortunate. Many of our landing craft were carried hundreds of yards further East before they discharged their contents, mostly into the sea. The scene on the beach beggars description. It was under intermittent mortar fire. Tanks burning, vehicles standing about either stranded, drowned or unable to move because there wasn't enough room to do so. No exit was marked. In fact there was no form of traffic control or direction on the beach whatever. The only markings I saw was a small Union Jack which marked, as far as I could see, a number of stretcher cases. I noticed one driver very pre-occupied digging a slit trench in the sand. I suppose he thought he was back in North Africa.

Although some of the 72 ranks who were missing have since rejoined the unit, none of them did so until after the capture of PORT-EN-BESSIN. The majority of the survivors were picked up by craft returning from the beach and were brought back to the UK.

Commando was first assembled by the 2 ic, Major DONNELL, at the junction of the coast road and the road leading inland to LES ROQUETTES about half hour after landing. The state of the unit was as follows:-

'A' Troop had not arrived; it was discovered later that at this time they were collecting themselves on the beach further East, where the coast road runs close behind the beach. 'B' Troop were complete. There was only one boatload of 'Q' Tp. 'X' Tp were present and fairly correct but there were only 6 men of 'Y' Tp. Cdo HQ had been divided among several craft loads and a number of them, particularly those who landed with 'Q' and 'Y' Tps, were missing, including some signallers with their equipment. HW Tp, which had shared four LCAs with 'Y' Tp, were also very depleted and much of their equipment was lost.

The CO was also missing. The plan was that, on landing, each boatload, irrespective of their unit or sub-unit organisation, would be led by the senior officer in the craft to the unit check pt at ASNELLES CHURCH, where we would sort ourselves out before proceeding further. I had arranged with Major WALTON, who was with me in the leading craft, that he would take charge of the leading boatload, which consisted mostly of 'X' Tp. I intended to make my own way to the check point with two orderlies. The first 50 yards I covered I spent struggling to free myself from my two mae wests and by the time I'd successfully accomplished this both the orderlies had disappeared. Major WALTON and a number of 'X' Tp were behind me as I made my way westward along the beach through the shambles already described. There was so much confusion that I wasn't really surprised when I next looked round to find that 'X' Tp had disappeared and that I was leading and commanding nobody.

However, it was no time to turn back so I continued up the beach and later through a gap on to the coast road just short of the LES ROQUETTES road junction. The coast road was under MG and either shell or mortar fire. I hadn't then learnt the almost unmistakable difference between the two. I found myself infiltrating through the Hampshires and it was rather uncomfortable. About four or five amphibious tanks passed through us in the direction of LE HAMEL but they withdrew shortly afterwards. The next thing to move along the road was a SP gun towing an ammunition sledge and I thought it was a good way of getting up the road towards LE HAMEL.

I was going too quickly to change my mind and I quickly found myself outstripping the almost halted Hampshires, covered with dust and choked with exhaust fumes but protected by the gun and screened by the high reeds on both sides of the road. I felt that there were many worse places.

However, when the SP gun reached the cross roads and on the outskirts of LE HAMEL it halted and then started to manoeuvre to turn back so I slipped off the sledge into a ditch on the left side of the road where, flattened out I was as frightened of the SP gun as I was of the enemy fire. A hundred yards down the road on the right a wooden bungalow was blazing. A large square, flat-roofed building further right almost on the sea front was plainly strongly held by the enemy. Over to my left, on the western outskirts of the town, I could hear several German MGs firing with their very marked high rate of fire.

After a long time I was joined in my ditch by a sapper officer who told me that his task was to recce the road from ASNELLES to RYES.

Spurred on by the fact that a sapper officer had got forward as far as I had, we turned left and, giving each other mutual support and confidence, we went up the road towards ASNELLES church. Rather cheap, nasty wooden seaside bungalows gave place to stone buildings. We saw a number of dead Germans lying about who looked as if they had very recently been killed.

We came across several Germans in an orchard on the right side of the road. Their carts all loaded and horses which had been harnessed ready for a move. There were at least 30 Germans in the orchard together, they were standing about, not attempting to take cover. The sapper and I rushed in to capture them but they almost completely ignored us and went on bandaging their wounded. We then noticed that none of them were carrying arms. We seemed rather unnecessary there so we continued towards the church. On our way in the narrow road we passed three or four SP guns and for a time our progress instead of the approved London District School of Street Fighting manner was more like crossing a street in a traffic jam, so narrow was the lane and so big the SP gun. There were more dead Germans and a live Frenchman who pointed up the road towards the church and said 'Boches', which is of course very plain English. On reaching the church we hid in the churchyard behind a nice solid wall and waited to see 47 (RM) Commando appear.

After some time, some British infantry appeared from a SE direction. I forget if they were the Hampshires or Dorsets, I think the Hampshires. I waited long enough to realise that 47 Cdo weren't coming that way after all, and, still accompanied by the sapper for whom I had acquired much respect, we went South as far as the road junction just less than a mile East of ST COME DE FRESNE. On arrival at the road junction we were met by a French gendarme who took off his steel helmet, put on a round peaked cap and gave me a very smart salute.

The first troops to appear were the Dorsets, coming from the direction of MEUVAINES, followed by a battery of SP guns belonging to 147 Fd Regt (Essex Yeomanry).

I later saw their 2 ic, from whom I learnt that Forfar [the MO] was either missing, hadn't landed, or had become a casualty and that a subaltern named IRVINE had been ordered to RV with us at LE ROSIERE in his place. About 1350 hours, the head of 47 (RM) Commando made their appearance, accompanied by a number of German mortar bombs.[8]

These delays prevented No 47 from reaching Port-en-Bessin and its capture had to wait until the next day.

Fighting in the Bocage
1 SS Brigade's main concern during 7 June was to strengthen their positions. In the early hours of the morning No 3 Commando rejoined and took up positions along the Ranville-Sallenelles road, to the south-west of Amfréville, while the cycle troop of No 6 was deployed to the same area. Its task was to cover the brigade's left flank and prevent enemy infiltration round the low ground near Sallenelles. The defences were based on the high feature at Le Plein. No 4 Commando continued to dig in around Hauger, although the hardness of the ground made this an exhausting task. Lt Colonel Dawson rejoined during the day, having had his wounds attended to, but two days later was ordered to the rear once more by the MO, and Major Menday reassumed command. No 45 were ordered by Lord Lovat to withdraw from their isolated position at Merville, and began to dig

in south of Sallenelles. General Gale, commanding 6th Airborne Division, then told Lovat that No 45 (RM) Commando's original D-day objective of Franceville-Plage must be taken, in order to secure the Allied left flank. The plan drawn up was for two troops of No 3 under Major J.B.V. Pooley MC to retake Merville, while No 45 went round the village to get into Franceville-Plage. The fighting on both objectives was very severe. The two No 3 troops did manage to recapture the Merville Battery, but only after suffering heavy casualties including Major Pooley killed. No 45 (RM) Commando succeeded in fighting its way into the northern end of Franceville-Plage, but with their 3" mortars knocked out, as well as the wireless link to Brigade HQ, they could not get any further and rejoined the two troops of No 3, who had withdrawn to the village of Merville. The only other action of note during the day was an attack launched by No 6 against Bréville in the late morning. They captured it and several prisoners, as well as four field guns, two 20mm guns and five machine guns, which were used to strengthen the Le Plein defences.

In the 4 SS Brigade area, the battle for Luc-sur-Mer continued throughout the morning. Tragically, No 41 (RM) Commando's HQ was attacked by three Heinkels with anti-personnel bombs, killing the FOO and wounding Lt Colonel Gray, the chaplain, the Rev Hughes RN, and nine others. Major J.A. Taplin, the adjutant, took over command. The Commando was then placed under command of the 5th Lincs who finally cleared the village and château, with No 41 in support. No 48 also renewed their efforts against Langrune. Three tanks were now used and employed their guns to knock a hole in the wall of the strongpoint. An assault party then went in and seized the houses on either side of the gap. One of these was blown up by a demolition party and the resultant rubble used to fill in the anti-tank ditch inside the wall. The tanks could now be brought into the strongpoint, and with their help the position was gradually subdued with the remaining defenders eventually surrendering.

No 47 (RM) Commando attacked Port-en-Bessin in the afternoon, using an artillery smoke screen and supported by the guns of HMS *Emerald*. Three strongpoints formed the framework of the defence, and two of these had been taken before the Germans counter-attacked and seized the hill which had been No 47's start line. Captain Cousins and fifty men managed, however, to seize the third strongpoint as dusk was falling, and the Germans surrendered, but Cousins himself was then killed by a grenade. No 46 (RM) Commando had not been required to carry out either of its D-day tasks as the naval bombardment had successfully neutralised the two batteries. They now came ashore 'in a fine state of rage at being cheated out of their raid on the batteries'.[9]

Brigadier Leicester gave them the task of capturing the strongpoint at Petit Enfer, two miles east of Langrune and supposedly even more formidable. Nevertheless, with assistance of a destroyer, artillery and two RM Armoured Support Group tanks, the Germans quickly surrendered in face of No 46's attack. The link up with No 41 was now made, and No 46 turned inland to capture la Délivrande and then advance on the radar station at Douvres. Enemy pockets of resistance on the coast were tidied up, but General Crocker, commanding I Corps, decided that since the garrison at Douvres was not interfering in his operations, it would be better to delay attacking it until he had gathered a sufficiently strong force together to deal with it without suffering needless casualties. No 41 was left to mask it, while the remainder of the brigade, with No 47 rejoining, were able to have a pause for breath.

1 SS Brigade were still under some pressure. No 45 (RM) Commando remained isolated in Merville, and efforts to send a relief force on the 8th were forestalled by continuous enemy pressure, especially on No 4 Commando. Both No 3 and No 6 were also forced to mount counter-attacks during the day in order to break up enemy attacks.

By the afternoon, casualties were mounting and ammunition, food and water running low. In view of this, Lord Lovat obtained General Gale's permission to cease his efforts to capture Franceville-Plage, and to concentrate on holding the high ground running from Hauger to Bréville. Accordingly, No 45 were given orders to break out southwards from Merville, which they did that evening, successfully gaining No 4's lines and, in view of the fact that they had been without rest or food for 36 hours, they were billeted in the church at Hauger for the night. By that evening the strength of the brigade was as follows:

Bde HQ	11 Officers 96 Other Ranks
3 Cdo	20 Officers 338 Other Ranks*
4 Cdo	15 Officers 239 Other Ranks
6 Cdo	22 Officers 329 Other Ranks
45 RM Cdo	17 Officers 286 Other Ranks

The enemy pressure continued during the 9th. No 45 (RM) Com-

---

* Peter Young later recalled that his strength was more like 15 officers.

mando occupied positions south and south-west of Amfréville, and Lord Lovat was now more confident than he had been. The next day, however, produced the climax to this long and exhausting battle. The enemy repeatedly made company strength attacks all along the brigade front, with the bulk of their efforts being against No 4 Commando. At one point two NCOs managed to crawl up to within ten yards of a deep ditch from which about 25 Germans were engaging the Commando positions. With Tommy guns and grenades, they succeeded in capturing or killing all. Another party of Germans, however, attempted to surrender to Captain D.C.W. Style MC. Sensing a trick, he went back for reinforcements, and on his return, a machine gun opened fire at pointblank range, seriously wounding him and killing three others. The remaining Germans were quickly despatched. Towards dusk, though, it became increasingly clear from the number of prisoners being brought in that the enemy had had enough, and the night was quiet. This enabled No 4 Commando to be withdrawn for a much needed rest, their place at Hauger being taken by the 12th Parachute Battalion. Next day was marked by a number of patrols, which went forward to investigate the villages which had been abandoned by the enemy, and the day was generally quiet. There was, too, welcome news from John Durnford-Slater, who visited and said that 4 SS Brigade were now moving to take over the 12th Parachute Battalion's positions in Hauger. The 4 SS Brigade, with Nos 47 and 48 (RM) Commandos, moved in on the night of 11/12th June, with No 48 taking over Hauger, while No 47 was placed in reserve at Ecarde. Up until then, they, along with No 41, had been masking the radar station at Douvres. This eventually fell to No 41 on the 15th, but the No 30 Commando detachment, Pikeforce, which had been standing by to investigate it on its capture, had been ordered not take part and had consequently moved across to join the remainder of the Commando, which was operating with the Americans, of which more later. No 46, meanwhile, had been placed under command of the 9 Canadian Brigade. On the night of the 10th they were given orders to move next day at first light to clear between Barbière and Rots the valley of the River Mue, which runs north-west of Caen into the sea. They were given a Canadian armoured squadron, RM Armoured Support Group tank, a section of Royal Canadian Engineers, a machine gun company and field artillery regiment to help them.

At 0615 hrs 11th June the Commando left ANGUERNY and married up with the supporting arms, here the C.O. gave his orders. The operation was to be carried out in four phases as follows:

Phase 1 – Clear woods from BARBIERE to outskirts of CAIRON
Phase 2 – Clear CAIRON
Phase 3 – Attack on ROSEL
Phase 4 – Attack on LE HAMEL and ROTS

The general plan for the first two phases was for the bulk of the Commando to move on the west bank of the river with two troops detailed to clear the woods on the east bank; the tanks were to move on the higher ground on the west side from which position they could shoot the Infantry into the woods. 'S' Troop, still without their heavy weapons, and 'B' Troop moved on the east bank. The first phase was completed without difficulty by 1100 hrs – 8 prisoners were taken in the woods without loss. On reaching the outskirts of CAIRON, the Commando came under fire from the 105mm Battery at ROSEL, but when the village was entered it was found to be already occupied by Canadian troops. Further progress was prevented by harassing fire from the ROSEL Battery, and it was not until 1320 hrs that the third phase commenced.

The attack was supported by two artillery concentrations and also by a Machine Gun Coy firing from the high ground above LASSON. The assaulting troops, 'X' and 'Z' Troops, formed up on the north west outskirts of LASSON closely supported by the tanks. They swept through LASSON and ROSEL without difficulty, being met by only a very small amount of enemy fire. Both villages were cleared by 1500 hrs; the ROSEL Battery, which by this time had ceased firing, was not located. The Unit then reformed on the west bank to prepare for the final phase. Information about the strength of the enemy in LE HAMEL and ROTS was scanty but a Company attack by a Canadian Unit earlier in the day had been beaten off.

The plan for the fourth phase was for 'A' and 'B' Troops to occupy the woods on the west bank just short of LE HAMEL and from there to protect the left flank. The artillery were to fire a battery concentration onto ROTS to enable 'A' and 'B' Troops to move into position, and then a regimental concentration on LE HAMEL prior to the assault on the latter village. This assault was to be made by 'Y' and 'S' Troops from the NW between the road and the river. The tanks were to move on the open ground on the right flank and shoot 'Y' and 'S' Troops into the village. During the assault on LE HAMEL, ROTS was to be contained by one field battery firing HE and Smoke. As soon as LE HAMEL was captured, 'A' and 'B' Troops were to pass through into ROTS. The fire plan included a concentration by the Troop of R.M.A.S. [Royal Marine Armoured Support] Gp firing intense immediately prior to the assault; as will be seen later, this proved very effective. The plan worked well. 'A' and 'B' Troops secured their position and helped to cover 'Y' and 'S'

Troop from considerable fire from the left flank. Major John LEE, who co-ordinated the attack of 'Y' and 'S' Troops described the subsequent action as follows:

' "Y" and "S" closed to within 150 yds of the Artillery concentration and then assaulted in line through the waist high corn. The tanks plastered the NE and NW sides of the village with their Besas and 6 pounders. There were five enemy machine guns in weapon slits about a hundred yards forward of the village on the axis of the assaulting troops. These held their fire until "Y" and "S" Troops were a hundred yards away and then let fly. Without any hesitation the assaulting troops went in firing their rifles, Brens and Tommy Guns from the hip. There were two hedgerow obstacles to cross, one of which was lightly wired, but the attack went on. While we were crossing the last obstacle, 30 yards from the enemy FDLs, the Boche flung their grenades and turned to run for the defended houses in the village. A number of them were shot down before they could reach the village.

"Y" Troop were on the right and moved on towards the group of defended buildings at the NE corner of the village. "S" Troop made for the road which runs through the centre of the village towards the main CAEN-BAYEUX road. For two hours, fierce street fighting took place, particularly LA HAUTE RUE south of the village. The enemy, subsequently identified as a Company of 26 Panzer Grenadier Regiment (12 S.S. Hitler Jugend Division), showed themselves to be troops of a very different quality from those manning the Coastal Defences. They were lightly equipped, well camouflaged and obviously very well trained. They darted about from house to house changing their positions all the time. Except on one occasion when confronted with a Sherman at close quarters, they showed no inclination to surrender. Their morale was obviously very high.

'A signal had been arranged that we should fire a white Very at low angle at any house which we wanted the tanks to engage; this worked very well, and we soon found that if we could get a tank close in, we could shift the enemy out of the most strongly defended houses. Several posts on the NW side of LA HAUTE RUE in the open fields away from the houses proved difficult to locate as they were so well concealed in the hedgerows and if there were any tanks in the neighbourhood the infantry would lie up opening fire on us from a distance after the tanks had moved away.

'It was found that the best method of advancing down the road was to have men moving in pairs well apart, dodging from door to door and supported by a well sited covering party. Lessons were learnt quickly; but the moment the assault commenced, one felt that we were on top, dominating the enemy, and without superior material support dictating to him the terms on which the battle was to be fought.

'Two 88mm guns were put out of action at LE HAMEL. Under cover of a further artillery concentration "A" and "B" Troops passed through into ROTS, preceded by one troop of tanks. "A" Troop were ordered to move towards the south end of the village, but immediately encountered a Panther tank lying up round a corner, which caused some casualties.

'In the meantime, "B" Troop had reached the north end of the village and were being engaged from the rear and from both flanks. While this was going on a tank-v-tank battle developed in the main street and two Shermans were knocked out, their 6 pounder guns being no match for the 88mm of the Panthers. "B" Troop then endeavoured to encircle the village by fighting their way through the open ground on the east side of the village; they met heavy opposition and suffered severe casualties. However, this encircling movement, combined with the arrival of "X" and "Z" Troops and a 17 pounder Sherman, caused the enemy to withdraw. During the subsequent tank action two Panthers were destroyed and enemy infantry suffered heavy casualties from the fire of Besas. There is no question that this village could not have been captured without the excellent and rapid support of the Sherman Squadron.'

The day's action represented an advance of some 7 miles and as progress on both flanks had only met with limited gains, the position of the Unit, if they remained in ROTS overnight, was likely to become precarious; appreciating this, the Brigade Commander ordered Colonel HARDY to withdraw back to CAIRON, but was informed that the newly won ground could be held overnight provided fresh assistance was forthcoming the following day. The expected counter attack during the night did not materialise and at 0400 hrs the following day, one Company of Regt DE CHAUDIERE arrived with carriers and a detachment of A/tk guns. Shortly after their arrival, however, orders were received from Div HQ for the whole force to withdraw before dawn.

Casualties in this action were 20 killed, 9 wounded and 31 missing: of the ranks posted as missing, the majority were members of 'B' Troop, many of whom had been wounded and were subsequently taken prisoner by the enemy. They were not released until May 1945 when their Camp was over-run by tanks of 11 Armoured Division on the outskirts of LUBECK shortly before the final capitulation. When ROTS and LE HAMEL were re-captured by the Canadians two days later, 122 German dead were found.

Colonel HARDY was subsequently awarded the D.S.O., Major LEE the M.C., and Sgt S. COOPER, L/Cpl R. McCARTHY, R.A.M.C., and Marine T. VARDY were each awarded the M.M. for the gallant part they played in this action.[10]

By now, 7th Armoured Division had been thrusting down towards Villiers Bocage and this seemed to be attracting the enemy's attention, thus reducing the threat of counter-attack against the Canadians. No 46 was therefore withdrawn to rejoin 4 SS Brigade, to be followed a few days later by No 41.

The next two months were to see the two SS Brigades, along with 6th Airborne Division, continuing to guard the Allied left flank. Both Commandos and Paratroops had hoped that, with the Normandy beachhead now secure, they might be relieved and sent home to prepare for future specialist operations. That this did not materialise was because of the serious manpower situation in 21st Army Group. The heavy toll of casualties was becoming increasingly difficult to make up from reinforcements, and, in early July, General Sir Ronald Adam, the Adjutant General, had visited Montgomery in Normandy and warned him that if infantry casualties continued at the same rate, it would be impossible to replace them and units would have to be cannibalised. It is thus understandable that Montgomery simply did not have the troops available to relieve the SS Brigades and 6th Airborne Division in their vital task, as much as he would like to have done so.

The main characteristic of this period was aggressive patrolling in order to dissuade the enemy from launching a major attack, but life took on a much more of a steady routine.

At 0445 hours the Commando stood-to for one hour – then weapons were cleaned, followed by breakfast. The forenoon was spent in improving positions, wiring, fetching headcover, and all the hundred and one jobs that required doing. The afternoon was devoted to sleep. In the evening any patrols going out that night were briefed – on air photographs which the patrol commander had studied and discussed in the afternoon with the patrol master (Major Freeman and later Major Sanders) and the Intelligence Officer (Lieutenant Smedley); in this country of woods and hedgerows these photographs were invaluable. Then during the hours of darkness double sentries were posted, patrols went out, and those with no other employment slept as best they could in spite of the mosquitoes. On some days half a troop would cross Pegasus Bridge and bathe on the beach at Luc, or would go back to B Echelon down by the river for a bathe. But B Echelon itself was no abode of peace; shellfire and, by night, enemy aircraft concentrated on this area and there were a few vehicles which did not bear some scar of battle. . .

Once for a week at the end of June, the whole Commando was taken out of the line for a rest, but what with the close proximity of our own guns and the apparent tendency of the enemy shells to follow the Commando around – three successive Headquarters received direct hits from shells – no one was sorry to return to the line . . . One consolation, for the officers at least – some men were heard to remark on people's peculiar tastes – was the glut of Camembert cheeses which added flavour to the monotony of Compo. On one occasion George Formby came forward to visit us with his wife and ukelele. He left amid such a storm of cheering that everyone retired below ground, but perhaps the enemy did not understand it as no reaction was noticed.[11]

Throughout the period there was a steady trickle of casualties, both from enemy artillery and mortar fire and the frequent patrol clashes. On 12 June, Lord Lovat was seriously wounded by an HE shell and had to be evacuated. His place was taken by Derek Mills-Roberts, even though he had been wounded as well. The Holding Operational Commando, however, ensured that a trickle of reinforcements was maintained.

Patrols penetrated up to 2000 yards in depth. Here is a typical report of a patrol carried out by No 45 (RM) Commando. The object was to destroy any enemy found in a particular area:

The start line was crossed on time at 0300 hrs, and the covering party preceded the raiding party through the wooded country NORTH of the road towards the objective. On reaching bend of road 143752 it was decided to by pass the difficult hedge, and the party utilised the road breaking out again into the small orchard NORTH of the road once this had been done. The covering party reached the road and took up posn while the raiding party crossed the road and entered a high cornfield which lay immediately in front of the objective 147751. This field contained high corn and progress was difficult. Lt Thomas, who was leading the raiding party, decided to utilise the hedge 146752-148752. Half way along this hedge the raiding party fanned out into open order to beat the ground in front of the objective. They encountered a well prepared and intricate wire fence made of wire netting and barbed wire immediately in front of the objective, and moved along this towards the road where a large house and a small house was situated. Grenades were thrown into these houses and the raiding party proceeded towards their main objective which was the destruction of enemy in the wooded area 148751. As soon as they proceeded beyond the houses, a maze of fox holes and dug outs presented themselves at 148751, it was here that the main slaughter took place. The raiding party came forward with Tommyguns and grenades and dealt speedily with every posn they could find. A suspected strong point was found at 147752, and 147749, a generous supply of grenades was fed through the apertures in each case. The objective had now been cleared out, but there was still time to go forward so Lt Thomas proceeded in an Easterly direction over a small lane which joins a road at 148752. He fired a green very light which was the pre-arranged signal that he was penetrating further forward to try to locate the suspected H.Q. The road at 148752 was crossed and the group of buildings at 149751 were cleared, but no enemy were found. Two of these buildings had been badly damaged presumably by the concentration, and the two larger and undamaged buildings were set on fire and destroyed by the raiding party. Between the road and the largest building a well camouflaged 15cwt vehicle was found, this was set alight and destroyed.

At this stage, the party had penetrated into an area which was presumably covered by other enemy localities on the SOUTH side of the road 148749. Voices could be heard and grenades were thrown over a thick and high hedge. At this time, Lt Thomas wisely decided that the alarm had been given and decided to withdraw the raiding party. They had to fight their way out, but it is considered that the concentration had been effective in keeping down the heads of many of the occupants of the forward weapon pits. These had now sprung into life and were endeavouring to take offensive action.

A sentry stepped forward to Lt Thomas and said 'Muller'. It is thought that he suspected Lt Thomas to be his friend. Lt Thomas disillusioned him with a burst of Tommy gun fire and a 77 grenade which set his stomach alight. The party continued to take vigorous offensive action on its way out, but the fire on both sides was heavy. Fortunately, the German small arms fire was inaccurate in the darkness and the many grenades that they slung at random from their weapon pits caused only 2 casualties, one of whom was Lt Thomas, the leader of the raiding party. The other casualty was caused by small arms fire.[12]

Not all, however, went on smoothly as this. On the night of 19/20 June Lieutenant R.R. Littlejohn of No 4 Commando and Sergeant W. Thompson of No 3 Troop, No 10 (IA) Commando set out to penetrate the enemy's line and carry out a reconnaissance in the area of Varaville in order to pinpoint enemy positions and supply routes:

Lt Littlejohn went out at 1430 hrs 19 June by way of LA GRANDE TERME DU BUISSON with the idea of crossing the enemy lines along the LONGUEMARE-GONNEVILLE Rd at a point about half way between GONNEVILLE and the X Rds at 144750. He crossed the open country between LA FERME and the rd by way of the orchard NORTH of the farm, and then through a field of standing corn NE to approx 144768 where enemy working party was heard at 141768 and another seen in area track juno 142749 thought to be preparing MG posns. The wood at 148767 was observed and found clear.

Then they crawled forward through long grass to stream at 144766 and on to a second stream across a field of alternate strips of standing corn and bare ground where they lay up to observe the enemy posns along the line of the rd. Enemy were heard all along track 145767 and 152764 and daylight outposts were suspected on fwd slope of large wood and field of bare ground at 147767 and 147765.

As soon as it was sufficiently dark an attempt was made to cross the GONNEVILLE-LONGUEMARE rd between 147757 and 150762.

They then crawled forward up to the rd which is bordered by trees and a thick hedge with bank, and keeping to the hedge crawled along it for a distance of about 500 yds, observing the enemy posns closely as far as a point where telegraph poles cross the rd 148757 where enemy were heard on the EAST side of the hedge. The enemy were not very alert as they reached the hedge unobserved and watched 2 posns from a distance of 5 yds. Lt Littlejohn and Sgt Thompson crawled back and explored the Northern end of the rd between 150765 and wood 145767, but discovered that here also the line was continuous and no penetration possible. Enemy were found to be thick on the ground with 2 posns every 20 yds and 2 men patrols visiting posts regularly.

They went back to the gully and lay up all day 20 June within 50 yds of the enemy posns. The enemy were in occupation of the whole line during daylight hours. Their posns were extremely well concealed and camouflaged. The whole of this area is pitted with shell holes which afford good cover.

No movement of M.T. was observed either by day or night.

No activity was seen along rd SW from 151763, but enemy heard working all along track 153764 NW to 144767 during the day.

Lt Littlejohn stated that the enemy seemed extremely jittery, firing and letting off flares and light signals at the slightest move. They are extremely alert and though probably low category tps, seem well disciplined. At about 1930 hrs 20 June, Lt Littlejohn decided to try and work his way between two of the posts and they crawled forward to the rd, reaching it about 2130 hrs. On raising his head to observe, Lt Littlejohn found himself looking straight down the muzzle of an enemy rifle. It had been decided that in the event of surprise being lost, grenades would be thrown and the party would separate and make a dash for it.

The enemy was apparently more surprised than Lt Littlejohn. At any rate his reactions were slower. Lt Littlejohn threw a grenade into the pit and dashed back, making for the cover of the gully, but was shot and badly wounded in the leg on the way. Sgt Thompson reached the shelter of a bomb crater on the open field.

Lt Littlejohn reached the gully however, and though wounded remained there observing, intending to make another attempt to penetrate further SOUTH, but was too badly injured to do so.

A search party about an hour later of about 10 men came out from enemy lines and fired at Lt Littlejohn from 2 yds range and missed him, Littlejohn unable to move shammed 'dead'.

The search party stripped him of his pistol and ammo but made no attempt to search him for maps or papers.

They checked that he was 'dead' by turning him over with a kick and prodded him in the face with a bayonet. Lt Littlejohn still made no move in spite of great pain, and eventually the Germans moved off leaving him for 'dead'.

Sgt Thomspon is presumed to be a prisoner as Lt Littlejohn heard the Germans who were searching him say 'der einer ist gefangen der ander ist tot'.[*]

Lt Littlejohn still had not the strength to move and about 40 minutes later a second looting party came out, who dragged him out of the gully into the open ground on the EAST of the stream where they removed his boots, compass, his watch and field glasses, but again did not take his papers or his map. Lt Littlejohn still made no move and pretended to be 'dead'.

By darkness, Lt Littlejohn mustered sufficient strength to move, and in spite of his wounded leg, crawled back over 2000 yds to No 47 Cdos lines, where he was picked up in an exhausted condition at 0530 hrs 21 June 44.[13]

No 3 (Misc) Troop, with their fluency in the German language, were in much demand. Unfortunately, on 14 June, Hilton-Jones was wounded and captured in an attempt to infiltrate two agents through the lines in the Gonneville-Varaville area. Later that night a man was found creeping towards No 4 Commando's forward positions. He failed to give the password when challenged and was shot and killed. He was later identified as one of the two agents. No 3 Troop was taken over by Lieutenant K.J. Griffith, another of its early members to be commissioned. A ruse tried by No 3 Commando was to stage a mock clash between two patrols, one equipped with capturing German weapons, in the hope that other Germans might come to its aid, in which case they would be ambushed. They refused to be tempted, however. No 6 Commando carried out a successful raid on the night of 4 July in conjunction with a propaganda broadcast directed at the German lines, using a loudspeaker system. By this time, however, the continuing domination of no man's land by the Commandos had made the enemy cautious, and it was noticeable that his positions were becoming very much more thoroughly wired and booby trapped.

---

[*] 'The one is captured and the other is dead.'

After the capture of Caen on 9 July, a fresh enemy formation appeared, which led to a higher incidence of sniping and enemy reconnaissance patrols, both by day and night.

On 18 July, Montgomery launched Operation *Goodwood*, a thrust by three armoured divisions southwards from the Ranville area and designed to seize the Bourgebus Ridge and, if possible, exploit southwards. Although it failed in this objective after three days' fighting, it did succeed in drawing the German armour onto the British front, thus making the American break-out easier. As far as the Commandos and 6th Airborne were concerned, their role of flank guard became even more important in order to prevent the Germans from counter-attacking the armoured divisions in the flank. This did not occur, and the period was marked mainly by artillery and mortar duels, which continued intermittently into August.

Then, on 1 August came Operation *Cobra*. The US break-out from St Lô began, when Patton's newly activated Third Army quickly overran Brittany, apart from the major ports, and then turned westwards. He beat off a German counter-attack at Mortain, and both 12th and 21st Army Groups now began to wheel anti-clockwise towards the Seine, with the Commandos and 6th Airborne Division being at the hub. It was not therefore until 19 August that the two SS Brigades began to come involved in the move east. On that day Mills-Roberts received orders from 6th Airborne Division to seize and hold a section of high ground by dawn the following day in order to support a further advance to Dozule. Led by No 4 Commando, with Nos 3, 45 and 6 following on behind, the brigade managed to infiltrate its way through the German lines and was on the feature before the Germans realised it. There were four counter-attacks throughout the day, but 1 SS Brigade held firm.

On the same day, 4 SS Brigade was ordered to seize Dozule. No 48 (RM) Commando was to move forward at dawn, bypassing the town and infiltrating through the woods to its south in order to seize Pt 120, a feature which dominated the town. They set off and soon came across traces of the withdrawing enemy. The close country and problems with radio communications made progress slow, but nevertheless they came up to Pt 120 in the late afternoon. Here they received a message from Brigade that Nos 41 and 47 (RM) Commandos were to attack Dozule from the south at 2000 hours, and Pt 120 must be secured by then. Lt Colonel Moulton, having organised a hot meal for his men, laid down H-Hour as 1900 hours, and the Commandos set off, encountering small pockets of resistance, which were dealt with. By last light, they were firm on their objective, but the enemy, making maximum use of the close country, was able to withdraw after suffering only light casualties. Lt Colonel Moulton now heard that the main attack had been postponed until first light on the 21st, but his men had a quiet night without being counter-attacked. While the main attack went in successfully, he sent out patrols westwards, but these failed to make any contact with the Germans and it became clear that they were pulling right back.

Both brigades now joined in the dash to the Seine, but 1 SS Brigade was soon halted in the area of Beuzeville, south-west of Honfleur, where it remained until returning to England on 7 September. 4 SS Brigade carried on from Beuzeville to St Maclou just short of the Seine, where they passed from under command of 6th Airborne Division to that of 1 Corps. Then, on 31 August, they crossed the Seine at Duclair before continuing the advance as far as Valmont, midway between Le Havre and Dieppe. They spent the remainder of the month containing the garrison of Dunkirk, apart from a brief spell of helping maintain law and order in the recently captured port of Le Havre.

No 30 Commando in Normandy

Both the RM and RN Wings of No 30 Commando were to take part in the Normandy Campaign, with the former now much enlarged. It was organised into a headquarters under Lt Colonel A.R. Woolley RM and three rifle troops, A, B, and X, each with a strength of two officers and 48 ORs. X Troop under Captain G. Pike RM, which was also parachute trained, had landed with the Canadians on D-day, but, as we have seen, it was foiled in its hope of investigating the radar station at Douvres. The remainder, known as Woolforce, did not land until D+4 and then on *Utah*. The reason for this was that it was expected that the Americans would have more scope for No 30's specialist role in their area of operations, and, indeed the Commando's first target was to be Cherbourg. Sadly, within three hours of landing they were attacked by a lone German aircraft with antipersonnel bombs, which left two dead and twenty wounded. They were now broken up into small parties to carry out another task before Cherbourg:

> . . . we spent the next few days in tracking down and reporting on 'V bomb' sites. From one seemingly innocuous farm with its concrete launching runways camouflaged with turf at La Haye-du-Puits the party

I was in moved on to Valognes where we found a massive concrete launching ramp still in the course of construction, a whole battery of concrete mixers lined up at its base.[14]

On 22 June, they all came together once more and joined the 9th US Infantry Division for the attack on Cherbourg.

A Troop began to move through the lines of G.I.s waiting patiently under the hedges of a country lane. The sight of Limeys, in their green berets, caused plenty of amusing comment and the buzz quickly spread that we were going forward to make the assault. Imagine the ribald comment as we returned later in the day, having been told that the attack could not be made until the morrow day. Just before dusk A Troop were given a sector of the front line to hold, a matter of lining a short stretch of hedgerow above a country lane, which was in turn about 500 yards from the main road into Cherbourg. As we took up position we heard German voices from the lane below and with a sharp 'Halt' and a couple of rounds three prisoners were quickly in the bag. A patrol was sent out at first light to reconnoitre the main road. It reported back having found nothing although we were being worried by a sniper. Another patrol was organised and set out towards a farmhouse on the edge of the main road. They had not been gone many minutes when we heard the sound of heavy firing from their direction. The patrol had brushed with a party of the enemy hiding in the farm and having sustained two casualties were forced to retreat. The courage of one member of the patrol in picking up his badly wounded comrade and running with him across a wide stretch of open ground to the safety of a hedge bordering the lane below us is worthy of mention. Not for this man the death by enemy action, he was later to die tragically by being gassed in his bath at Littlehampton, due to a faulty flue in the gas geyser.

Our troubles were not over, the sniper, taking advantage of the situation was able to hit two of our members, one the Troop SBA [Sick Berth Attendant], as they came over the bank to help. Both died of their wounds. We entered the outskirts of Cherbourg at Octaville that day bursting for a fight but it was not to be. The official report sent to the Admiralty stated: 'The Villa Maurice was secured without effort as all troops had retired to their underground positions.' We had encountered very little fighting aiid our pre-laid plans, exercised so assiduously at Littlehampton, of placing Beehive explosives over each of the ventilation shafts and rendering the tunnel occupants stupid by the blast were unnecessary. We did however obtain a little assistance from a couple of American tanks lined up on the hill opposite the firing armour piercing shells at the main entrance doors.

For two days we occupied the tunnel whilst our Boffins searched the HQ for enemy intelligence, incinerators were cleared, and all the burnt scraps carefully preserved, masses of paper and various pieces of equipment were prepared for shipment back to U.K. At the same time, the well stocked wine cellar was emptied of its contents and springs began to groan under the weight of cognac as the transport was loaded for our next move. Souvenirs abounded, in the form of Luger pistols, cameras, musical instruments. The tunnels had housed most of the enemy naval personnel in the port and they had marched out to a prison camp leaving most of their personal possessions behind.[15]

After the fall of Cherbourg, A and B Troops and Tac HQ moved to set up a camp at Cartaret opposite the Channel Islands, to be followed shortly by X Troop, who then returned to England. There they spent almost five weeks, waiting for the US break-out from Normandy, Operation *Cobra*, to take place. This commenced at the end of July, with Patton's drive through Brittany and both A and B Troops were involved. X Troop returned to France, only to return once more to England after some two weeks to take part in one of the many planned, but aborted airborne operations of this time. Consequently, they returned again to France four days later. They had the consolation, however, of being present at the liberation of Paris on 25 August. At the beginning of September, Tac HQ and A Troop had also established themselves in Paris. B Troop, on the other hand, were involved in the capture of Brest, and this kept them busy until almost the end of the month. During these operations they suffered three killed and one wounded. On 11 September, two sections of A Troop, one under Captain 'Red' Huntingdon-Whiteley, joined 51st Highland Division for the capture of Le Havre:

The attack on Le Havre was duly made and a report received that it had been successful and that the town had fallen. A small patrol, consisting of the Troop Commander and three marines, went into the town centre to recce the position as far as the Naval HQ was concerned. On reaching one of the main squares they came under attack from a party of Germans. The Troop Commander was killed by a grenade and after a short exchange of fire in which the marine bren gunner was killed the remaining two marines were taken prisoner. They were taken to the German HQ and had the doubtful honour of being present whilst the high command deliberated on surrender. After a while one marine was given a surrender note to deliver to the British HQ whilst the other was placed under guard in their main baggage store. It is doubtful whether a prisoner spent a happier time. The news of Red's death was a tremendous shock to his troop. He was one of the original members of the unit from its North African days and had earned the respect and admiration of all his men.[16]

With the fall of Brest and Le Havre, and the failure of the Arnhem operation, as well as the Americans coming to a halt in front of Metz, the Allied supply line, with Antwerp not yet open, had become too stretched to support a further major advance for the time being. All of No 30 Commando, with a mass of captured material, therefore returned to England towards the end of September, in order to re-equip and retrain, like 1 SS Brigade, for the final thrust into Germany.

Pause for Breath

1 SS Brigade landed at Southampton and Gosport on 8-9 September, and then moved by train to Petworth in Sussex, where HQ SS Group was now based. From here, Brigade HQ moved to Lewes, and the Commandos were located as follows: No 3 – Worthing, No 4 – Shanklin, Isle of Wight, No 6 – Hove, and No 45 (RM) – Bexhill. The first priority was leave, but there was also a requirement to find fresh volunteers. A trawl of the Infantry Training Centres in South-Eastern and Eastern Commands was made during September, and it is indicative that, of a total of 3,200 other ranks addressed, 300 volunteered and 135 were accepted for Commando training. In addition, out of 24 officers and 91 ORs who volunteered from the Field Army, 14 officers and 29 ORs were accepted.[17] Nevertheless, the casualties suffered by the Commandos serving in North-West Europe over the period 6 June – 30 September 1944 were no less than 39 officers and 371 ORs killed, 114 officers and 1324 ORs wounded and 7 officers and 162 ORs missing. This represented approximately 50% of the total war establishment, and illustrates just how tough the fighting in Normandy had been. Keeping the Commandos up to strength was a constant struggle.

One change to the organisation of the SS Group was that on 30 June 1944, 2 SBS was disbanded. Since the Allies were now firmly ashore in Normandy there seemed to be little left for them to do. SBS personnel now moved to SE Asia, along with the majority of the COPPs and RN Beachhead Commandos.

No 10 (IA) Commando, now under the command of Peter Laycock, who had succeeded Dudley Lister at the beginning of June, was at this time at very much greater strength at Eastbourne than it had been for a year. The reason for this was the natural wish of the national troops to take part in the liberation of their homelands now that the Allies had entered the Continent of Europe. As yet, only Nos 1 and 8 (French) Troops, who had been under command of No 4

Commando, had had this opportunity. To this end, the Belgian Troop had returned from Italy at the beginning of June and the Dutch Troop from India in July. The Norwegian Troop, too, with the realisation that the Allies were not intending to liberate their country at this stage, agitated to be relieved of their commitment in the Shetlands so that they could take a more active role, and they too came down to Eastbourne.

First to become involved were the Belgian Troop, but in an operation more akin to the traditional small raid. Operation *Rumford* was mounted on the night 25/26 August. Its object was a landing on the Isle of Yeu in the Bay of Biscay in order to secure and bring back a Frenchman, as information was needed on the harbour installations, whether there were any suitable landing beaches and if the Germans still had a garrison there. Lieutenant Dauppe and five ORs, along with two signallers from SS Group, embarked in the destroyer HMS *Albrighton* at Plymouth early on the 25th and had an uneventful passage. Shortly after 0100 hours on the 26th, the raiding party transferred to a dory. Lieutenant Dauppe:

> There is a strong swell but the Dory is going well. We can see the line of the island. I estimate our distance from the Island north end at 2½ miles. The moon is set. The sky is full of stars. Visibility good. At 0135 we are about 1 mile from the shore at what I estimate to be the height of 'Pointe de la Goumaise'. I continue on the same course although it seems to take us too much to the East. At 0150 after having increased speed to 4 knots I suddenly find myself at the entrance of 'Port Jaimille' harbour about 500 yards from the pier. I immediately turn round and steer a course north west along the coast. At 0205 I steer to the shore and land with rubber dinghy at 'Pointe de la Pulante' 407034. Landed: Lt W.V. Dauppe, Cpl. Deleener, L/Cpl. Legrand, Pte. Van den Bossche, Pte. Van den Daele.
>
> Deleener and Van den Daele have a T/G. The others a revolver. Lt. Dauppe carries a Walkie/Talkie. All have fighting knives.
>
> The dinghy is attached at some rocks and put ashore on rocks. The Dory drops anchor about 50 yards from the shore and stops engine. At about 70 yards inland is a large low building surrounded with some farmer's barbed wire. With many precautions we creep close and listen at the windows (which are shut) and door. It looks as if nobody is in it. At 0230 we leave this building in silence and proceed inland. 100 yards further inland we came across a country road (sand and stones, 3 yards wide) going from north-west to south-east to Port Joinville. On the N.W. side I notice something which looks like a building some 600 yards away. I decided to go left, S.E., in the direction of Port Joinville. We walked

about 400 yards with precautions and come to a cross-roads. Seeing no buildings at all in these surroundings I decide to go back to the building N.W. We do so and when we get closer realise that it is only a haystack. I then decide to go on again on the road to S.E. (Port Joinville) and to hurry things as time is pressing on – it is now 0300. At 0315 we arrive near these big buildings, 2 dark ones about 50 yards on the right of the road. They look like barns or farm buildings and one, close to the road, a white long house which looks inhabited. I order Cpl. Deleener and Van den Daele to go round the building in silence, with great precautions, to find out if there is any life or signs of enemy. After five minutes I got close with Legrand and Van den Bossche. Van den Daele shows me a bucket near the door which seems to indicate that there are people living here. I listened at the window and heard snoring. Deleener on one side and I on the other, we open the window shutters. The window blows open with a crack, a man gets up and comes to shut it. I spoke to him in French and he answered in the same language. I ask him if there were any Germans in his house and he says no. He opens the window. I persuaded him to leave his family (six children in the charge of a daughter of 13 years) and to come with us, promising him to bring him back in two or three days, and also that he would get a good reward. He gets some clothes and follows us, after kissing his children goodbye. He is 44 and his name is Leopold . . . and he is a widower. Fisherman is his job.

At 0330 we leave his house and proceed back to our landing spot. We get back to the Dory and leave the Island at 0345. Leopold . . . tells me that the Germans left the night before after evacuating all their guns, stores, ammunition, etc. in three days.

We steer course 330°, speed 2½ knots. The swell is stronger. We take some water in overboard. We are all very wet.

At 0440 we get in touch with the destroyer through Walkie/Talkie. At the same time we see the Destroyer. We come alongside in heavy swell at 0445. Very good steering of L/Cpl. Legrand. We come aboard and I report to Lieut.-Colonel P. Laycock at 0455 with Leopold . . . who tells the story.[18]

On the way back there was some excitement when a Beaufighter signalled that there were two German trawlers about. *Albrighton* was ordered by C-in-C Plymouth to intercept these, which she did. Shots were fired across their bows, and they ran up white flags. The Commandos made up one of the boarding parties, and in all 22 prisoners were taken, with the trawlers being sunk by gun fire. It transpired that the crew were mutineers, who had killed their officers, and were on their way to Spain.

It was now the turn of the Dutch. After he had been made aware that Operation *Market-Garden* was shortly to take place, Prince Bernhard of the Netherlands argued that it was only right and proper that there should be Dutch representation on it. Accordingly, at very short notice, the Dutch Troop were selected to take part, and they dropped with the airborne troops at Eindhoven, Nijmegen and Arnhem. There were used mainly as interpreters, which, in many ways, they found frustrating, feeling that their intimate knowledge of the local country and people would have been put to better use if they had been given specific intelligence roles. Many of them found themselves trapped after the failure of XXX Corps to link up with 1st Airborne Division at Arnhem in time, and had to hide up with friends for much of the winter. The liberation of Belgium and large parts of the Netherlands did, however, result in several fresh volunteers for the Belgian and Dutch Commandos. The Belgians were able to raise two additional troops (Nos 9 and 10), while the Dutch were able to make good the losses suffered by No 2 Troop in *Market-Garden*. All these volunteers attended Achnacarry before being posted to No 10 (IA) Commando.

At the end of September, it was decided that No 4 Commando should be sent back to the Continent in order to exchange with No 46 (RM) Commando, which had now a strength of only 200 men. By this time 4 SS Brigade had moved to the Ostend area, where they began to prepare for another major amphibious assault operation.

Walcheren

Crucial to the success of the Allied advance into Germany was the need to shorten the ever stretching supply lines, which, with the Germans still holding onto the Channel ports, were still, in early October, dependent on the Normandy ports. Of even greater use than the Channel ports, because of its very much larger capacity, was Antwerp. Although this, and the port installations had been seized by Dempsey's Second British Army in early September, Montgomery's attention was now drawn to seizing the vital bridge over the Rhine at Arnhem in a belief that this would enable a lightning advance into Germany and the ending of the war in the West in 1944. Unfortunately, he failed to grasp the significance of the fact that the port of Antwerp lay 25 miles up the Scheldt. On 14 September, Montgomery did order Crerar's First Canadian Army to open up Antwerp, but it was still required to also capture Boulogne and Calais. In the meantime, the mouth of the Scheldt was occupied by the Fifteenth German Army, and Hitler had ordered the island of

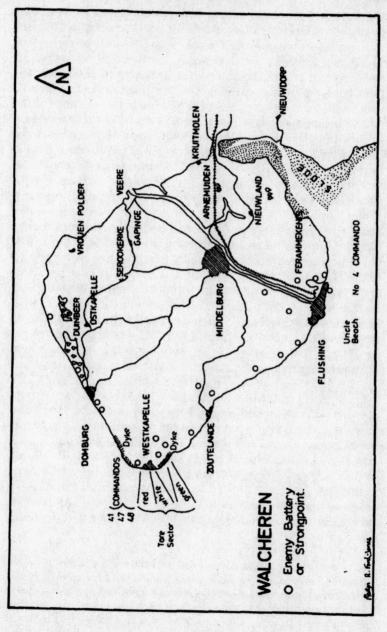

WALCHEREN

o Enemy Battery
   or Strongpoint.

Walcheren, which dominated it, to be turned into a fortress. Boulogne fell on 22 September and Calais on 1 October, but Crerar's attempts to secure the south bank of the Scheldt opposite Walcheren was foiled by the Germans in the Breskens pocket, which rested on the Leopold Canal. Then, at the beginning of October, the Canadians, advancing north from Antwerp, attempted to approach Walcheren from the east, but were held up at the entrance of the narrow isthmus which connects South Beveland to the mainland.

To Admiral Sir Bertram Ramsay, Eisenhower's naval commander, the importance of opening up Antwerp was still paramount and, by the beginning of October, he was convinced that this could only be done by an amphibious assault on Walcheren. It took time for his ideas to be accepted by 21st Army Group, although he had a strong supporter in General Simonds, who had taken command of First Canadian Army when Crerar had been evacuated sick back to England. Indeed, he had already earmarked 4 SS Brigade for this. On 9 October, Montgomery issued a new directive giving priority to the clearing of the Scheldt, and some ten days later the Canadians began to attack along the isthmus as well as breaking into the Breskens pocket. By the end of the month the Germans in the Breskens pocket had been cornered in Zeebrugge, surrendering on 2 November, and both South and North Beveland had been virtually cleared. The moment for the assault of Walcheren, Operation *Infatuate*, had arrived.

The outline plan was for the three RM Commandos of 4 SS Brigade, along with No 4 (Belgian) and No 5 (Norwegian) Troops of No 10 (IA) Commando, who were to be commanded by Peter Laycock, to land at Westkapelle on the western side of the island. No 4 Commando, with Nos 1 and 8 (French) Troops under command, would cross from Breskens and attack Flushing, supported by 155 Infantry Brigade. During October the brigade trained in the Ostend area. This had been chosen because the German defences there were similar to those on Walcheren. RAF Bomber Command had attacked the dykes during October, and the result was that:

> The sea pouring in had transformed the centre of the island into a vast lagoon, rimmed by the massive dykes. But the Germans, tunnelling and boring, with their usual industry and ingenuity, and employing masses of reinforced concrete, had turned this dyke into an almost continuous fortification, bristling with guns of every calibre, of which the largest were 220mm. Along this rim the Marines had to fight their way, with no

room to manoeuvre – just a grim slog through the deep, loose sand dunes against an enemy well protected by his solid concrete.[19]

The idea was that the Royal Marine Commandos would seize the shoulders of the gap created by the dyke by RAF Bomber Command at Westkapelle, and then fan out north and south to roll up the remainder of the defences, the southern thrust linking up with No 4 Commando. Because of the flooded ground behind the dyke, much reliance was to be placed on the use of Weasel and Buffalo tracked amphibious vehicles (LVTs), and much of the preparatory training concentrated on familiarisation on these. Support would be given by the RAF, batteries based in the Breskens area, specialist armour from 79th Armoured Division, naval gunfire support, which included landing craft and multiple rocket launch systems, and Landing Craft Gun (Medium) (LCG(M)) armed with two 17 pdr anti-tank guns in armoured turrets. After some debate over when the sea conditions would be suitable, the operation was planned for launching on 1 November. No 4 Commando were to land at 0545 hours and the remainder at 1000 hours.

A heavy mist on the Dutch and Belgian airfields limited the RAF support for the actual landings, although the skies over Walcheren were clear. For No 4 Commando, once more commanded by Lt Colonel Dawson, now fully recovered from his wounds and wearing the DSO for his performance on D-day and thereafter, the main problem was finding a suitable place to get ashore. Accordingly, Dawson planned for a small reconnaissance party, known as Keepforce, to lead the way in in two LCPs. Once they had located a suitable spot, Nos 1 and 2 Troops, along with RN Commandos, and under the command of Major Boucher-Myers, would establish a beachhead. Once this was firm, the main body would land and carry on with the attack on the town of Flushing itself.

> The night of Oct 31/Nov 1 was spent in most cramped and uncomfortable quarters among the ruined houses of BRESKENS, Reveille was at 0200 hours and the Commando was formed up ready to move down to the harbour along what was left of BRESKENS main street at 0315 hours. It was cold, and very wet, with a steady drizzle which limited visibility very considerably, and heavy low cloud. We knew by now that the bombing programme had had to be called off and that the increased artillery fire plan was to take its place. As we filed down to the harbour a Mosquito was circling overhead, and swooping over FLUSHING to strafe at regular intervals.

Loading was completed by 0415 hrs, and at about 0440 hrs the leading craft slipped and passed the harbour mouth. At almost the same moment the artillery barrage commenced, and the mainland was from now on silhouetted against the flickering muzzle flashes of three hundred guns. We gazed anxiously over to FLUSHING, straining our eyes for the answering flashes of the German artillery, but all that we could see were the sudden bright pin points of light all along the waterfront which were our own shells exploding and one glow somewhere in the town where the Mosquitoes had started a fire. Sometimes our shells struck the steel antilanding stakes and then there was a shower of red sparks reminiscent of a fireworks display. But the German guns remained silent.

For an hour the landing craft cruised placidly around between BRESKENS and FLUSHING, watching this one-sided artillery battle. This hour was not without its alarms and excursions, for we were constantly on the watch for mines and for one man torpedoes, a number of which were known to be kept at FLUSHING. Gradually the fire in the town was gaining hold, and suddenly the unmistakeable silhouette of the windmill – the ORANJE MOLEN – was thrown into relief against the glare. We could have no clearer indication of our landing point.[20]

Keepforce and Boucher-Myers' two troops got ashore successfully and secured the beachhead with minimal casualties, and soon began to take prisoners. The main body came in at 0630 hours, but by this time the Germans were thoroughly alerted and opened heavy fire with machine guns and 20mm cannon. Nevertheless, they managed to land with only two or three casualties, although the LCA containing the heavier equipment, including the two 3in mortars, hit a stake and sank some 20 yards from the shore. The mortars were, however, very successfully salvaged.

It was now a question of fighting through from one strongpoint to another. Much of the problem lay in the fact that each troop had to leave parties in its rear in order to guard against infiltration, but they were helped when the leading battalion of 155 Brigade began to land at 0830 hours, although they lost two LCAs from the fire of one of the heavy coastal batteries. It was important to get the stores unloaded quickly, and for this prisoners were pressed into service. 'Without their invaluable contribution the usual chaos on the beaches would have been inevitable, and they undoubtedly did more for us in the battle of FLUSHING than they did for the Third Reich.'[21] It must be pointed out, though, that the defenders were largely low quality troops, either elderly or of low medical category, many of them suffering from stomach complaints. It was as well, since the defences were 'formidable in the extreme; they were very well stocked with ammunition and food; they were filled with all the painstaking and admirably executed range of cards and panoramic sketches which we were accustomed to find in them'.[22] By 1600 hours, the Commando had reached most of its objectives, but with the day now drawing to a close, it was decided to consolidate where they were rather than attempt to reduce the remainder that day.

Brigadier Leicester's plan for the attack on Westkapelle called for three troops of No 41 (RM) Commando (Lt Colonel E.C.E. Palmer RM) to land on the north shoulder of the gap blown in the dyke, and clear between here and the village Westkapelle itself. The remainder of the Commando, along with the two No 10 (IA) Commando troops would then come ashore in Weasels and Buffaloes launched from LCTs, clear Westkapelle and then move north. No 48 (RM) Commando (Lt Colonel J.L. Moulton DSO) would use the same method of landing, but their prime target was the south of the gap, from where they would advance on Zoutelande, some two miles to the south. Finally, No 47 (RM) Commando (Lt Colonel C.F. Phillips DSO) would land behind No 48 and drive on to meet up with No 4 Commando near Flushing.

The force set sail from Ostend at 0315 hours, and by 0930 hours were off the objective. The ships now began to bombard the defences with 15in and smaller calibre guns. This produced no reaction from the enemy, and neither did the LCGs and rocket craft, nor a squadron of rocket-firing Typhoons, which had managed to take off from their airfield. Then, as the assault craft began to make for the shore, the coast defences opened up.

. . . a little way off on starboard side, a rocket LCT went up in smoke from a direct hit, and other craft could be seen in difficulties, and as we neared the beaches several appeared to be on fire and out of control.

We had several near misses, and as we get very close in, being a little way off the allotted beach, we ran foul of tetrahedra stakes and became a sitting bird, coming under fire from the guns North of West Kapelle and the heavy mortars which were even more effective. The ramp could only be partly lowered because of the obstruction, and the landing vehicles could not be got off. We received a hit too, and the Adjutant was the first casualty, losing the third and fourth fingers of his right hand. The commotion was tremendous, and a concerted movement out of the question, so section leaders had to use their own discretion. The stakes were all round, and mines were attached to them, and the Scheldt very cold this November morning.[23]

Peter Smithson landed with No 41 (RM) Commando:

> Scampering down the ramps and glad to fill my lungs with fresh air after
> the many hours of diesel oil on board the landing craft, I ran with other
> members of No 41 across the sands. Cross fire was heavy, also shelling,
> and working on the theory that a shell never lands in the same spot twice,
> jumped down into a large crater with others and after a few moments
> ran across the beach and teamed up with other members of No 41. *War-
> spite* with other large RN ships had bombarded the enemy gun emplace-
> ments, but the thick reinforced concrete bunkers still stood engulfed
> in sand with just the narrow slit and large barrel standing out from the
> dunes, but now in no position to sink shipping intending to enter the
> Antwerp port.[24]

No 41 succeeded in overcoming a pillbox immediately to their
front and then pushed on to Westkapelle itself, where they came
up against a battery of four 150mm guns. This was reduced with the
help of some of the tanks which had got ashore. They now began to
move northwards along the dyke.

No 48, also after initial quick progress, came up against a battery
of 150mm guns. They tried a quick assault, but lost the leading troop
commander killed and several men wounded. Another attempt was
met with intense mortar fire, resulting in several more casualties.
'I must ask you to imagine what this fighting was like, struggling
through soft deep sand that clogged rifles and machine guns and
filled your mouth, eyes and hair.'[25] Supporting fire from field batteries in the Breskens area and Typhoon attacks was now arranged.
Using smoke as a cover, another troop went in, and finally reached
the centre of the battery. By now dusk was falling, and the rest of the
position was mopped up by patrols under cover of darkness.

The next day saw No 4 Commando continuing, along with 5
KOSB, the battle for Flushing. Typical of the many actions that day
was that involving the French Commandos of No 5 Troop* for the
operation against a strongpoint which had been nicknamed *Dover*.

> No. 5 Troop began their attack on Dover at about 0700 hrs. The line
> of approach was down GOOSJE BUSKEN STRAAT, but progress was
> necessarily very slow as the enemy in DOVER were still very much on

---

*Both French troops were under command of No 4 Commando as they had been
in Normandy. For ease of control they were called Nos 5 and 6 Troops, with Nos 1-4
Troops being made up by No 4 Commando themselves.

the alert. One section entered a cinema in the street, and gained the roof, from where they opened fire against the strongpoint with their PIAT. Gradually both sections worked their way forward 'mouseholing' their way through the walls of the back gardens. No 1 Section crossed over to the far side under heavy fire, and the Troop was preparing for the final assault when they were ordered to withdraw and let the Typhoons make another attack on the position. In the afternoon they resumed their advance, clearing a number of houses and reaching the corner immediately over looking their objective. In the course of the house clearing they discovered a member of No. 6 Troop who had been cut off during the previous day's fighting and had been compelled to spend the night in the same house as a number of Germans. The Germans had re-entered this house after our troops had left it, and, finding British equipment lying in it, had taken the entire family who lived there outside and shot them in cold blood.

As a result of this advance through the GOOSJE BUSKEN STRAAT during which a number of casualties had been inflicted upon the enemy, the Germans were now confined to the DOVER strongpoint itself and to the house on the corner of the BOULEVARD BANKERT. From this building they made a bolt for it at about 1630 hrs, but were met by the concentrated fire of the whole of No 5 Troop, and suffered several casualties. No 1 was by now at the Anti-Tank wall which blocks the end of GOOSJE BUSKEN STRAAT, and firing PIAT bombs at very short range into the embrasures of the strongpoint. As there was still no sign of surrender from the occupants, it was decided to blow an entrance with a made-up charge, and Cpl. LAFONT volunteered to carry out this hazardous task. Just as he was about to dash forward, a white flag appeared from the embrasure, and the battle for DOVER had been won.[26]

This occupied the Commando until the evening when they were given fresh orders resulting from the progress of the remainder of the brigade.

No 48 (RM) Commando had pushed on at first light and taken Zoutelande, meeting only light opposition. No 47 now took over the advance but soon came up against a strong position fortified with an anti-tank ditch and huge Dragon's teeth. The weather had closed in, and hence no air support was available, and so they attacked supported by artillery alone, coming under heavy mortar fire and suffering several casualties. The other half of the Commando had moved along the dyke and were faced by another 150mm battery, but could not get into it because of running up against pockets of resistance in front of it. Not until nightfall were these cleared. The three troops involved now halted in front of the battery, but had to repulse a German counter-attack, luckily just after they had received much needed replenishment of ammunition, food and water. Resupply to the brigade across the beaches did, however, present problems:

> Throughout D-day and D plus 1 big guns could still be brought to bear on the gap. In addition, the only possible place for a craft to beach, the massive masonry that formed the foundation of the dyke, bristled with stakes and mines that had to be cleared. The first two supply craft which closed the beach on D-Day came under heavy fire and one of them was hit. They were ordered to withdraw. Not until high tide on the night of D plus I could they be called in and beached successfully under difficult conditions. Then began a race against time to unload so that the craft could get away with the next tide with the wounded and also with some of the fast-mounting number of Prisoners, whose presence in the restricted area of the dyke was an embarrassment. The Pioneers tackled the unloading heroically but the weather decided to take a hand. The wind blew up to a gale force and one of the landing craft was torn away from its moorings and flung up the beach. The other was driven against a groyne and was immovable. The gale, lashing up 8ft waves, made it impossible to get craft in or out . . .[27]

The Commandos had to endure the next two days on captured German rations, and the situation was only relieved on the fifth day when the RAF dropped supplies by parachute near Zoutelande.

As for No 41 and No 10, they reached Domburg on the morning of D+l, where they encountered strong resistance. That evening, Brigadier Leicester decided to send No 41 less one troop to assist No 47 in the south, leaving the two troops of No 10 and the one of No 41 to finish mopping up Domburg. No 4 Commando was ordered to hand over its tasks to 155 Brigade and embark by LVT to assault two batteries, W3 and W4, situated north-west of Flushing, landing in a gap in the dyke to do so. This was, however, fraught with difficulties. Little was known about the gap or possible landing places in it, it was long after dark when the orders were received, which made the relief by 155 Brigade a complicated business, and the Commandos had now been fighting for some forty hours without respite and were hardly fresh. In view of this, Lt Colonel Dawson contacted Brigadier Leicester, and the plan was postponed for 24 hours. The relief operation duly took place, and this at least gave No 4 the opportunity for a pause for breath next day. In the event, No 47 (RM) Commando overcame the opposition south of Zoutelande on that day, and then linked up with No 4. While this was taking place, No 10 cleared Domburg, with the Norwegians showing particular dash in the face of heavy opposition, which cost them a number of casualties, including their troop commander, Captain Risnes, wounded.

Nos 4, 47 (RM) and 48 (RM) Commandos now concentrated at Zoutelande, and there was a pause for two days while the resupply situation was sorted out. The remaining enemy resistance was now concentrated in the area north-west of Domburg, and Nos 4 and 48 were sent up here by foot, although they used LVTs to cross the gap at Westkapelle, in order to reinforce No 10 and No 41. While No 41 was to assault the last remaining battery, W19, No 4 Commando would clear the Overduin woods, where most of the remaining Germans were thought to be, and then push on to Vrouwenpolder opposite North Beveland. No 48 (RM) Commando would remain in reserve, but be prepared to move through No 4 if the opposition could not be dealt with by the latter. This operation was launched on 8 November, and, as far as No 4 Commando was concerned:

> The Commando column formed up in DOMBURG at 0345 hours, with 3 Troop in the lead. A Belgian guide from 10 (IA) Commando was charged with leading the column to the forward defence lines occupied by our own Troops. After a few preliminary excursions, including one seemingly pointless circumambulation of a not especially delectable villa, the Commando got under way and had reached the chosen jumping-off point at 0530 hours. At this time the artillery barrage on the area of the wood came down with gratifying promptitude and was accompanied by a mortar barrage from the brigaded mortars of 4,41 (RM) and 48 (RM) Commandos. One solitary German gun fired a few rounds in reply, well off anything that might have been a target. When the mortars had ceased firing, No 3 Troop moved off down the line of the light railway, and were closely followed by No 5 Troop, who were to advance through the wood to the South of the light railway line, and by No 6 Troop, who were to advance North of the line.
>
> Very soon prisoners began to come back to Commando Headquarters which was moving up the railway line very close behind the leading troops. The prisoners were all taken North of the railway, and admitted that they had been put into positions all over the dunes, generally in small groups and with no special prepared defences. It was by now beginning to get light, and the Commando column was in some danger of being caught in very open country between the commanding heights of the dunes on the left, and the Wood on the right.
>
> At about 0630 hours a machine gun high on the dunes, and to the rear of the Commando column, opened fire, firing tracer in short bursts very

high. The rear section of No 1 Troop was detached into the dunes to deal with this post. At about the same time No 5 Troop in the wood came upon a number of buildings which were occupied in some strength by the enemy, and sent a request for assistance in clearing the area. No 2 Troop were diverted from the railway line into the wood to help, and these two Troops together carried out a near pincer movement on the buildings and collected about 50 prisoners. No 3 Troop was by then established on the forward edge of the wood, where they had been joined by No 1 Section of No 1 Troop and No 6 Troop was almost up to the waterworks, having cleared up a small number of minor positions on the way. Commando Headquarters was on the edge of the wood in some empty German bunkers. There was a considerable amount of scattered small arms fire from the dunes and from the western strip of the wood, and prisoners were being brought in in small bunches at fairly regular intervals. One German gun was firing our heads in the general direction of DOMBURG.

At 0815 hours, while a batch of German prisoners were being searched in the Headquarters area, four Germans were seen walking through the undergrowth nearby. They were at once called to order by the RSM who thought they were part of a fresh batch of prisoners. These men, however, were fully armed, and on being interrogated stated that they had been sent forward by their officer to establish contact with an English officer in order to make a formal surrender of all remaining German troops in the area. An Intelligence Officer and a runner accompanied the Germans back to their company headquarters, a dug-out situated surprisingly close to the Commando Headquarters area, where the German officer phoned through to his Regimental Commander at VROUWENPOLDER, and told him that he was in contact with the attacking force. The Regimental Commander, Oberst-Leutnant VEIGELE sent down a car with one of his headquarters officers, and the Commanding Officer of No 4 Commando and the Intelligence Officer returned to VROUWENPOLDER in it to negotiate the surrender. The order to cease fire and consolidate in the present positions had been given by both sides, and we had in addition stopped the artillery bombardment and air attacks which were due on the VROUWENPOLDER area at 0900 hours.

With the Canadian 2nd Infantry Division now down the Beveland causeway and Middelburg in their hands, the German opposition on Walcheren ceased, although, while the surrender negotiations were taking place with No 4, No 41, being unaware of them, continued their advance. This resulted in fire being opened from German strongpoints and accusations that a flagrant breach of the truce had been made. It was eventually sorted out on the German telephone system.

The advance had been hard. The weather had broken up from the third day, with a tempestuous wind blowing. The ground was strewn with mines and progress had been slow, and deadly . . . 40,000 Germans had been put out of action by this operation.

After a short time, we left the island and, on our arrival at Ostend, we presented the classic sight of soldiers returning from the front. Our clothes stiffened by dried mud which was glued to them, we bent under the load of our rucksacks filled with many memories. . .

Our eyelids were reddened through lack of sleep and more than one chin sported a hairy beard. In spite of our tiredness, we had the feeling of having accomplished something.[29]

This had not been without cost, however. The brigade suffered 103 killed, 325 wounded and 68 missing during the eight days' fighting. Yet, they had the comfort of knowing that, after a massive minesweeping operation, the first cargoes began to be unloaded at Antwerp by the end of November.

The Overrunning of Germany

On 6 December 1944, the Special Service Group was renamed the Commando Group, and the SS Brigades became Commando brigades. 4 Commando Brigade, after a period of refitting and resting at Ostend, returned to the Walcheren area, being made responsible for it, as well as North and South Beveland. With the launching of the German counter-attack in the Ardennes on 16 December 1944, No 47 (RM) Commando was sent to the River Maas, and came under command of the British 1 Corps, and was later followed by three troops from No 48 (RM) Commando. This situation, with one Commando detached to the Maas, would remain in being until the end of hostilities.

1 Commando Brigade had expected to be sent to the Far East early in January 1945, but on 7 January came orders that they were to return within seven days to North-West Europe. Although by this time the German counter-offensive in the Ardennes had been beaten back, there was still a certain amount of nervousness that the Germans might still try to disrupt the port of Antwerp and other arteries. Also, looking ahead to the advance into and through Germany, there were a number of river lines, of which the foremost was the Rhine, which would have to be crossed, and it was thought that the Commandos would be particularly useful for this. There had been one or two changes in the hierarchy of the brigade. While Derek Mills-Roberts still commanded it, two of the Commanding Officers were

new. Both Campbell Hardy, who had won the DSO in Normandy, and Peter Young had by now departed for South-East Asia, the first to command and the second to be his deputy in 3 Commando Brigade. Lt Colonel Arthur Komrower commanded No 3 and Lt Colonel T.M. Gray MC RM had taken over No 46 (RM) Commando. On arrival at Ostend, No 46 was detached from the rest of the Brigade and sent to Antwerp in order to help guard against surprise airborne attacks. The remainder were, like No 47, sent to hold the line of the River Maas.

At this stage, First Canadian Army was preparing for Operation *Veritable*, designed to clear the enemy between the Maas and the Rhine, while the US Ninth Army, also under command of Montgomery's 21st Army Group, launched *Grenade* across the River Roer, and would then join hands with *Veritable*. The first action involving 1 Commando Brigade was in preparation for *Grenade*, and took place on the night of 23/24 January. This was Operation *Blackcock*, which was designed to clear the enemy from the Roermond Triangle. For it the Brigade was placed under command of 7th Armoured Division, and was given the task of crossing the Juliana Canal and driving on through Massbracht and Brachterbeck in order to capture the town of Linne. The crossing, which was done over the ice, was successfully accomplished by No 6 Commando on the night of 22/23 January. No 45 (RM) Commando then passed through and captured Brachterbeck without casualties. Advancing on to Montefortebeck, they found themselves pinned down under heavy fire. A Troop, who were leading, suffered particularly, with thirteen wounded and two killed, and were in a very exposed position.

Totally disregarding the dangers, Lance Corporal H.E. Harden RAMC, one of the Commando's sick berth attendants, went forward and attended to the wounds of one officer and two marines. As he dragged one of them back into cover, he was hit in the side. In spite of being ordered not to risk his life any further, Corporal Harden twice returned with stretcher bearers to evacuate these wounded men. On the third occasion he was hit in the head and killed. His supreme self-sacrifice was in the highest traditions of both the Commandos and the RAMC and he was awarded a posthumous Victoria Cross.

Enemy counter-attacks were beaten off, and then No 3 Commando passed through to capture the town of Linne. German resistance was, however, fanatical and they were unable to break into the town until tanks of the 8th Hussars were brought up to support them. The brigade took up positions just to the north of Linne facing part of the formidable defences of the Siegfried Line, and No 6 Commando began a week of close cooperation with the tanks of the 8th Hussars in a series of sweeps designed to gain detailed information on the enemy defences.

> These sweeps were made by two or three troops of tanks carrying one troop of J [No 6] Commando on their backs. The force was usually commanded by the Commando Troop Leader, the Infantry dismounting in close country to protect the tanks and to search houses and woods, and the tanks supporting the infantry forward. This series of patrols began on 26 Jan and continued till 1 Feb, when a general thaw began to limit armoured movement. An immense amount of detailed information was obtained, and casualties were inflicted on the enemy.[30]

In the meantime, No. 45 (RM) Commando were, on the night of 27/28 January, detailed by 7th Armoured Division to find out more about the enemy in the Merem area. This necessitated crossing the Maas, checking on two small islands, Belle and Anchor, in the middle, and then crossing over to the far bank. As the initial crossing was made, there was some sniping, but once the Commandos landed, the enemy on Belle picked them up against an background of the snow, even though they were wearing white suits. A fierce battle broke out, with casualties being inflicted on both sides. Enemy artillery and machine gun fire broke out from the far bank, and it was clear that the second phase of the operation could not take place with all surprise now lost. Attempts were made to extricate the party, but:

> Owing to the very strong current all attempts to establish a line across the river failed. Even with 8 men paddling and with the use of a stern oar, boats were swept down stream as far as 400 yds before crossings were achieved. This meant that no boat could return without a full load to paddle it. However, two boat loads of the raiding party were landed on the island to assist in holding the bridgehead and bringing back the wounded. A SA [Small Arms] battle still continued and walking wounded came into the bridgehead. Other wounded men were brought in by the raiding party. Great difficulty was experienced in getting back these wounded, owing to the fact that they took up a great deal of boat space and there was not enough room to provide a crew strong enough to paddle. The boats were eventually brought across with the help of men swimming alongside.
>
> The battle noises continued, but gradually died down and eventually ceased.
>
> An officer led patrol was then sent across to search again for wounded

men and to attempt to clarify the situation. This patrol found 5 dead
Germans, including the Arty Observation Officer and 1 PW was taken.
He stated that his information about our wounded was very vague and
second hand. He knew of 3 seriously wounded Germans nearby guarded
by 5 men in position within 100 yds of us. He explained the positions to
the patrol, but was not prepared to call on them to surrender. The officer in charge of the patrol did not consider himself justified in running
into an ambush for 3 wounded Germans.

Wounded were evacuated to RAP [Regimental Aid Post], and all
boats possible were retrieved. Meanwhile, the covering party kept a
sharp lookout across the river. When a shout was heard another boat
crossed to find a sergeant who had managed to escape after capture. He
knew the whereabouts of 1 other wounded man, so the patrol was sent
to bring him in. This was done, although it brought on another SA battle
and 3" mortars had to be used to extricate the party. As the exact whereabouts of the remaining missing or wounded ranks was very indefinite,
and in view of the fact that two casualties occurred from enemy SA during this final effort, it was decided reluctantly that more crossings could
not be made.[31]

On 1 February, No 46 (RM) Commando rejoined the brigade and
took up positions alongside No 45, and they too, became involved
in the problem of how to shift the enemy off Belle. The increasing
floods were threatening to engulf it and the Psychological Warfare
Department (PWD) was also brought in to help. Eventually, the
enemy began to relinquish his hold and a number crossed over and
gave themselves up to No 46.

Towards the end of February, the brigade shifted position to the
area Venraij-Meerlo-Oostrum, ten miles north of Venlo, but still on
the Maas. Further to the north, the Canadians launched *Veritable*
on 9 February and slogged their way through the Reichswald and
Hochwald forests to close up to the Rhine. Then came *Grenade*, and
the stage was set for the biggest river crossing of the war, Operation
Plunder.

Although the US First Army had fortuitously seized the Remagen
Bridge, south of Bonn, intact as early as 7 March, the attention of
the Allies was concentrated more on the Ruhr, and 21st Army Group
were to cross just north of it. Accordingly, the British Second Army
now began to prepare for what would be an opposed crossing in
the area between Rees and Wesel. The fortnight's breathing space
also gave the Germans time to strengthen their defences in the area.
XXX Corps were to assault on the left, with XII Corps on the right,

and the task given to 1 Commando Brigade, who were under XII Corps for the operation, was to secure the right flank of the bridge-head by seizing the town of Wesel after a heavy attack by RAF Bomber Command.

The Commandos now set about intensive water training:

> Goatley boats, rubber dinghies, Dories and later Buffaloes and Weasels were collected and on one sunny afternoon an Inter-Troop regatta was staged at Well. Although falling slightly below the standard of pre-war Henley, this was undoubtedly the most successful afternoon's boating since the Unit was ferried across the Seine the previous September.[32]

Mills-Roberts' plan was for No 46 (RM) Commando to lead the assault by crossing with Brigade HQ and securing a temporary bridgehead two miles downstream of Wesel in an area of low marshy ground known as Grav Insel. The rest of the brigade would then cross and made their way cross-country to the town, with No 46 following on at the end, since it was essential that the bridgehead be cleared by first light as it was dominated by high ground inland.

At 1730 hours on 23 March 1945, 77 Lancasters of RAF Bomber Command's No 3 Group dropped 435 tons of bombs on Wesel. Thirty minutes later, the preliminary artillery bombardment by six regiments began, switching to actual landing site an hour before H-hour. At 2100 hours, No 46 embarked in their Buffaloes about one mile from the river and began their approach. The leading troops landed shortly after 2200 hours and began clearing the trench systems overlooking it. The artillery bombardment had done its job well, and the defenders were very dazed. The remaining troops came in and, within thirty minutes, the bridgehead was secured. No 6 Commando passed through, although they had suffered a number of casualties as they crossed the river. RAF Bomber Command now attacked the town for a second time, 200 bombers dropping over 1100 tons of HE. 'It seemed as if more than mortal powers had been unleashed', as Lt Colonel Bartholomew, who had now taken over from Arthur Komrower in command of No 3, noted in his diary.[33] No 3 and No 45 had by now come across, and established themselves in a tight line on the northern outskirts of the town. During this, Lt Colonel W.N. Gray DSO, now commanding No 45, was wounded, but remained in command for the next two days.

No 46 followed, and all now prepared to beat off counter-attacks. One did develop, but was easily broken up. Then, in mid-morning,

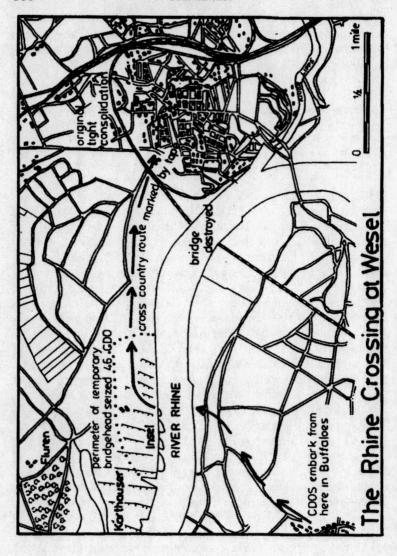

Fluren

Karthauser

perimeter of temporary
bridgehead seized 45 CDO

Insel

RIVER RHINE

original
tight
consolidation

cross country route marked by

bridge
destroyed

CDOS embark from
here in Buffaloes

The Rhine Crossing at Wesel

0   ½   1 mile

came reinforcements in the shape of the US XVIII Airborne Corps, who began dropping on the high ground east of Wesel. The Commandos now began clearing the town, and on the following day met up with the 1st Cheshires, who had been landed on the river side of Wesel. That night a bridge across the river was put in, and 1 Commando Brigade's task was done. At a cost of 95 casualties, they had captured 850 prisoners and killed a large number of the enemy, as well as playing the leading role in the capture of Wesel.

1 Commando Brigade was now placed in reserve of VIII Corps, but with the break-out into Germany now well underway, they were soon on the move once more. On 3 April, 11th Armoured Division bypassed the town of Osnabrück and the brigade, once again under command of 6th Airborne Division, were rushed by lorry with orders to capture the town at dawn the following day. They were in position by 0300 hours and, with No 3 Commando leading the way, encountered only light opposition and were in the centre of the town by 0800 hours. 450 prisoners were taken and fifty Germans killed or wounded. Included among the dead was the local Gestapo chief, who was tracked down and shot by Major Vicomte de Jonghe, the Brigade Security Officer. Once again, there was little pause for breath, and on the 6th the brigade found itself under command of 11th Armoured Division, and faced with the task of crossing the next river line, the Weser.

A company of the 1st Rifle Brigade had established a small bridgehead at Stolzenau the previous evening, and No 45 (RM) Commando were rushed up to this, with orders to capture the town of Leese a mile to the east. Passing through the Rifle Brigade at 1345 hours on the 6th, the Commando quickly met strong opposition from the fanatical members of the 12th SS Training Battalion. That night they were ordered back into the Rifle Brigade bridgehead, and the rest of the Commando Brigade moved up. No 3 Commando joined No 45 in the bridgehead. Mills-Roberts wanted to do an infiltration across the river by night, but this required boats to be brought up. There was now a delay, and the operation was not mounted until the night of the 7th/8th.

The Brigade plan was to leave all the heavy weapons troops of the Brigade to hold the bridgehead and for the remainder to break out and, after a long cross-country march around the right flank to attack Leese from the rear. 6 Commando led the way, laying out a white tape as they had done on the Rhine; 46 (RM) followed; with 45 (RM) and 3 Commando in the rear. The going proved to be very difficult; several streams, thick hedges, a steep railway embankment, ditches and marshland were traversed during the night. The enemy appeared to be unaware that anything unusual was going on. 6 Commando were confronted with a 20mm AA post just outside the town and dealt with it more than adequately. The town was occupied without any great opposition by 0700 hours. Eight prisoners were captured by the Unit [No 46] and on interrogation revealed that their battalion had withdrawn northwards at 0430 hrs. The booty they left behind included the weekly NAAFI ration for the whole battalion.[34]

The following twenty-four hours were spent in winkling out small' pockets of resistance and extending the bridgehead.

The next obstacle was the River Aller, a tributary of the Weser, and, still under command of 11th Armoured Division, 1 Commando Brigade was to force a passage across it at Essel. There was a road bridge leading to the town, but Mills-Roberts concluded that an attack across this would merely lead the Germans to blow it up. He therefore selected another bridge, a railway one, at Schwarmstedt a mile downstream. This time No 3 Commando led the way, and at midnight on the 10th/11th approached the bridge. The Germans spotted them and set off demolition charges, which destroyed the first span on the home bank, but that was all. No 6 Troop under Lieutenant A. Wardle, took their boots off in order to make no sound and began to charge across. A machine gun opened up on them, causing five wounded, but the remainder got across, overpowered a position at the far end and then removed the remaining charges. The other three Commandos now came across.

Next morning the Germans, who belonged to the 2nd Marine Division, launched some fierce counter-attacks, and at one point Mills-Roberts himself had to shoot a sniper. No 6 Commando were now detailed to capture the road bridge, which they did with much dash – hunting horns sounding and bayonets fixed. They, too, were now subjected to counter-attacks, and No 46 (RM) Commando were ordered to reinforce them. A KSLI battalion was sent to reinforce the original bridgehead during the night, but then it became clear that the enemy had managed to infiltrate back into the woods between the two bridges. A combined force of the two Royal Marine Commandos under Lt Colonel T.M. Gray DSO MC RM was therefore ordered to retrace their steps and clear this opposition. This proved to be easier said than done:

Enemy opened fire with MG small arms and Panzerfaust. Very strong defensive firepower was met. Forward troops after pushing the enemy from their forward positions consolidated. Immediately the enemy counter attacked and with Arty support counter attack was beaten off. 0930 hrs two Troops holding right flank were counter attacked. Attack beaten off with aid of Arty support. Right flank Troop pinned down area 297588 with very accurate MG fire. Another strong counter attack with simultaneous flanking attack at 298588 which cut the flanking Troop completely off and caused heavy cas. 1025 hrs the two flanking Troops ordered to withdraw to area 295583.[35]

Although the Commandos were foiled in their attempt to clear the woods', it transpired from interrogation of prisoners that a marine battalion had moved in during the night, and that they had caught it on the point of counter-attacking the brigade. Next day, Friday the 13th, the enemy's resistance began to weaken, and the bridgehead could now be expanded. No 46 (RM) Commando were ordered to capture the village of Hademstorf, which dominated the bridge the Sappers had now laid in place of the damaged road bridge. They carried out a two prong attack. While the left hand prong had considered trouble from concealed machine guns, the right hand fared better and was soon in the village. With this captured, the fighting came to an end, and 1 Commando Brigade moved on.

By 19 April, the brigade had reached Luneburg, where they left 11th Armoured Division and came under 15th Scottish Division for what was to be their last operation of the war. This was to be the crossing of the River Elbe. The brigade was given orders to capture the town of Lauenburg and the bridges across the Elbe-Trave Canal. The river at this point was as wide as the Rhine and a further problem was that the far bank rose steeply to a height of some 150 feet. The original idea was for a repeat of *Plunder*, with RAF Bomber Command softening up the objective and 5th Parachute Brigade dropping beyond. Bad weather precluded both from taking place, and the brigade had to carry out the assault with just artillery support. D-day was fixed for the 28th, and at 2200 hours the previous evening the artillery softening up began. At 0200 hours the Buffaloes carrying No 6 Commando entered the water, to be followed by No 46. On reaching the far bank, No 6 came under a hail of grenades from the top but, undeterred, they scaled it and cleared the enemy from the area. No 46 then began to advance towards Lauenburg, meeting a little opposition apart from the fire of one mortar. They

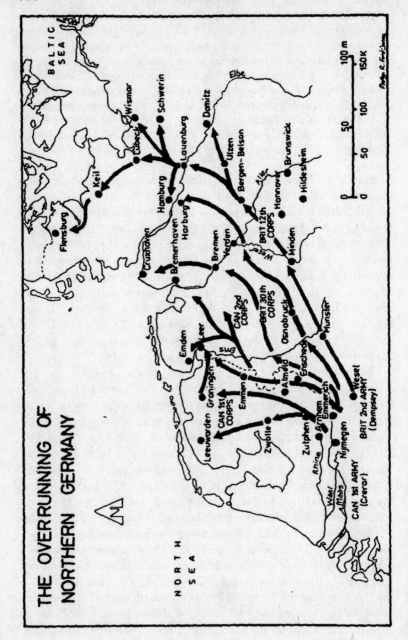

THE OVERRUNNING OF NORTHERN GERMANY

reached their objective, a sandpit on the northern edge of the town and began to dig in.

> As night turned into day, some confusion and amusement was caused when it was found that British and German troops were digging side by side. No fight was left in the Boche, who were promptly disarmed and then made to adjust their positions to suit our own requirements.[36]

The rest of the brigade now passed through the town was cleared, No 6 Commando then moved on and captured the main road bridge across the Canal intact. On the 30th, 11th Armoured Division and 6th Airborne Division passed on eastwards through the bridgehead and 1 Commando Brigade's final task was completed.

The brigade now moved up to Neustadt, where they were joined by the three Belgian Troops of No 10 (IA) Commando.* It was here on 4 May that Derek Mills-Roberts took the surrender of Field Marshal Erhard Milch, former Inspector-General of the Luftwaffe and its pre-war architect. It was a fitting end to the brigade's trail of success which it had blazed across Germany during the past six weeks.

Throughout all this time, 4 Commando Brigade had remained relatively static. With Montgomery's attention firmly on the Rhine, the Germans in Holland were, during the winter months, left very much to themselves, with First Canadian Army being responsible for ensuring that they did not interfere with the thrust towards and beyond the Rhine. 4 Commando Brigade, now under command of the Canadians, carried out a number of raids. Initially, these concentrated on the islands north of the two Bevelands. Typical of them was one that took place on the mouth of the Maas on the night of 23/24 January. It was carried out by a patrol of No 41 (RM) Commando under Captain T.M.P. Stevens MC RM, and illustrates well the conditions under which the brigade had to operate.

Time	Map Ref	Action
0245	989496	Firm Base SOUTH bank established.
0245	975497	The patrol left DRIMMELN harbour in 2 Mk 3 Assault Boats, proceeding up stream 1200 yds maintaining an average distance of 25 yds from the SOUTH bank.

---

*Members of No 3 Troop had been operating with both 1 and 4 Commando Brigades throughout the campaign and the reconstituted No 2 (Dutch) Troop joined 4 Commando Brigade at the end of April.

Time	Map Ref	Action
Unknown	985496	The river was crossed, progress being much impeded by the ice and the current. The whole crossing and journey up stream took 1½ hrs of which a good ½ hr was occupied in clearing a passage through the ice on the NORTH side of the river.
0415	987501	The patrol disembarked and proceeded along the path to its junction with the dyke. A considerable amount of unavoidable noise was caused owing to the freezing of the marshy ground up to the dyke.
0430	987503	Firm Base NORTH bank took up a posn covering the WESTERN approaches to the dyke and the patrol proceeded along the dyke. The dyke is constructed of hardened earth flanked on either side by frozen, impenetrable willow and reed swamp. No tracks of any description were found on the surface of the dyke.
0500	991503	The first house was reached which was found to be derelict and unoccupied. The patrol proceed along the dyke to the next house.
0530	996504	At a point 50 yds before the house on the dyke a double apron fence was encountered stretching the whole width of the dyke.
0535	996504	2 members of the patrol cut a gap in the wire. Trip wires were also encountered in the fence which were cut. The patrol commenced to move through the gap.
0540	996504	4 men had passed through the gap when simultaneously a Verey pistol was fired and 2 LMGs opened up. The patrol was caught in the open on the dyke and went to ground. The first burst wounded the Patrol Comd, I OR and the Dutch Guide. The fusillade was followed by several hand grenades (some of which were thought to be British 36s). The Patrol Comd. gave the order to withdraw into the reeds on the SOUTH side of the dyke. While withdrawing aimed MG fire continued supplemented by 5cm mortar HE. Progress through the dyke was found impossible.
0550	993504	The patrol withdrew to reed hut. The enemy made NO attempt to follow up the withdrawal. It was here discovered that I OR (previously reported wounded) was missing. A rear guard of 2 men was left to wait for the missing man at MR 993504.

Time	Map Ref	Action
0605	987513	The patrol arrived back at firm base. The rear guard returned at 0615 without the missing soldier. The whole patrol then waited a further 15 minutes.
0630	987513	The patrol re-embarked and proceeded by direct route back to harbour. Ice encountered was worse than on the outgoing journey but the current helped the boats along.
0705	975497	The patrol arrived back in harbour.

In all, during the period 1 December 1944 until the end of the war at the beginning of May, the brigade carried out twenty fighting patrols, fourteen reconnaissances and six longer patrols of 2-3 days duration. One of the last-named was, in fact, the final operation by 4 Commando Brigade, and involved No 48 (RM) Commando, now commanded by Lt Colonel Martin Price, since Jim Moulton had assumed command of the brigade. It took place between the Maas and Waal rivers, and began on the night of 19/20 April. By this time, First Canadian Army was pushing up into northern Holland towards Groningen, leaving the remaining Germans in the area Rotterdam north to Den Helder isolated, and the brigade had been masking them.

Major P.H.B. Wall RM, who was No 48's Patrol Master, and responsible for the detailed planning of all patrol activity, had gone to spend the night with a standing patrol on the Maas. While there, two Dutch civilians came through to the observation post and reported that the Germans were evacuating Biesbosch on the southern bank of the Waal. They were escorted to the local Dutch Underground co-ordinator, who wanted his Resistance group to attack the Germans, but needed Commando back-up and weapons in order to do this. Price was in favour of this, especially since there now appeared to be few Germans left to the south of the Waal. However, he needed more information before formulating a proper plan, and sent a patrol under Major Wall to check whether any Germans still remained on the island of Steenen Muur, in the Waal. Nothing was heard from them after a message at 0600 hours on the 21st that the enemy were close by. He waited another twelve hours and then sent two troops across the Maas, who landed without meeting any opposition, but encountered many mines, through which it took time to clear passages. Both went firm at last light. In the early hours of the following morning, an officer of No 4 Commando, who had been in charge of the dories in which Wall and his patrol had crossed to the island, turned up and said that he had waited in vain at the rendezvous previously arranged with Wall, although he had been given much information on the enemy's dispositions by a member of the underground.

Brigadier Moulton now visited and decided that the Commando should land on Steenen Muur, establish a firm base there, rescue Wall and his men, and check whether indeed the enemy had evacuated Biesbosch. This operation was mounted later that day. In the meantime, a patrol had moved to the outskirts of Biesbosch. 'This party was armed with TMCs [Thompson Machine Carbines] only, and were mortified to find that an enemy patrol of one offr and 4 were out of killing range whilst moving down the rd 016566 without taking any mil precaution until 50 yds before the br into STEEN MUUR. Here they crawled in full observation, retiring at speed having probably observed our arrival on the island.'[38] The main body were met by the bulk of Wall's patrol under his 2ic. They looked 'very tired, very wet, and very hungry and very very pleased.'[39] Wall, his batman and attached Dutch interpreter were found, lying in a bed of straw in a barn trying to get warm after a fruitless attempt to swim across to the home bank.

Before dark, Brigadier Moulton came up to see for himself and appreciating how exposed the island was to shellfire, ordered the Commando to withdraw. As he himself later wrote: 'The end was very near and those of us in responsible positions had to remember that a man could still be killed just as dead as on 6 June, but with infinitely less justification.'[40]

4 Commando Brigade had not had the excitement of the fast moving advance that their sister brigade had experienced, but the part they played, even if much less dramatic, had been equally as important in contributing to final victory. It must be remembered, too, that they did not have the opportunity to recover their strength back in England and had remained in the European theatre throughout. Also, after Walcheren, they were made up of 50% of unblooded replacements, who had to be acclimatised to battle conditions.

No 30 Assault Unit, as No 30 Commando was now formally called, also played a significant part in the final assault on Germany. During the autumn of 1944 the Admiralty had drawn up a wide range of targets, and 30 Assault Unit had a room in the basement in order to prepare for these, with Colonel R.H. Quill MVO RM appointed as formation commander and responsible for co-ordination with the Admiralty. As for the targets themselves, these mainly concerned torpedoes and submarines; indeed, anything relating to the Battle of the Atlantic. It was also important to establish what technical information the Germans had passed across to the Japanese.

At the beginning of February 1945, Lt Colonel B.W. de Courcy-Ireland DSC RM, then second-in-command of No 45 (RM) Commando, was ordered back to England to take over the RM wing of 30 Assault Unit from Colonel Woolley. He was briefed by General Sir Robert Sturges at Commando Group Headquarters, and the first he saw of his command was on 21 February as 'a long line of vehicles drawn up on the A3 Guildford by-pass'.[41] The RM wing was still organised in three troops, A, B and X, but the last-named were carrying out airborne and glider training in East Anglia at the time as part of a plan for them to drop into the Kiel area. Two days later the unit was across at Genappe in Belgium, and the next month was taken up with detailed planning and liaison with the various formations involved in the spring offensive.

The general concept of operations was for the RM Wing to provide escorts for the Technical Intelligence Officers of the RN Wing, and the various teams were given special passes to enable them to operate in the area of any Allied formation at will. This naturally took a certain amount of careful liaison, which is what both Quill and de Courcy-Ireland turned most of their attention to. As for vehicles, de Courcy-Ireland:

> After the slender establishment of vehicles in wartime Commando. I was pleased to see the wide variety and numbers of vehicles in 30 AU. Five armoured cars (Staghounds) for close support, armoured scout cars for carrying the scientists to their targets, Jeeps, 15cwts and 3 tonner trucks. The Unit being mobile with its own resources.[42]

The Staghounds were, however, quickly swopped for seven more scout cars since it soon became apparent that spare parts for them were virtually unobtainable. As for the detailing of troops to tasks, A Troop was to cover the Ruhr and Harz Mountains, and would eventually penetrate as far as Leipzig, B Troop was to make for the northern ports up to Hamburg, while X would be responsible for the Kiel area.

The first operation was carried out by a team led by Lt Commander Patrick Dalzel-Job RNVR:

My Recce Group crossed the German frontier on 3rd March, searched some targets in the Eifel hills, and entered the almost completely ruined city of Köln four days later. To our astonishment, the civilian inhabitants were friendly and their information was reliable. We had no difficulty in penetrating our main target, the Schmidding works, 24 hours ahead of other troops; and we made a very big haul of documents and technical equipment. We also found a new type of German mine, and apprehended the Works Manager and Chief Engineer before they were able to disappear. More important than all this, we were able to establish beyond any doubt that movement ahead of Allied troops was scarcely more difficult in Germany than it had been in France. My only change in tactics was to lash a heavy, belt-fed German machine gun to the bonnet of my leading jeep, to make ourselves look more aggressive and to give us rather more fire-power in the Recce Group.[43]

Once Operation *Plunder* had been mounted, the teams began to spread out into Germany. Commander (later Rear Admiral) I.G. Aylen RN found himself operating in the sector of Patton's US Third Army:

In Patton's area a tin hat was a 'must' day or night, it seemed, since this dashing and flamboyant leader, reputed to always be carrying a brace of jewelled pistols, had so ordained (I had a problem here – the RM Commandos scorned tin hats, always wearing the green beret, to which I was not of course entitled. My alternative was a naval brass hat, blue topped as the white plastic top had not yet been adopted, and a right Charlie I felt with naval shoulder straps and khaki battle dress, with the Army, let alone the American army, could never quite understand!)[44]

HQ 30 Assault Unit quickly moved to Venlo and here they were joined by X Troop still under Captain Pike, who had been denied their airborne landing at Kiel because of a shortage of gliders after *Plunder*. The ports of Emden and Wilhelmshaven fell, with the unit's teams invariably succeeding in reaching their targets ahead of other troops. Nowhere was this more marked that at Bremen. Patrick Dalzel-Job:

As we came slowly nearer to Bremen, the importance of the Deschimag shipyard became clearer to me. From what we were told by our prisoners and by civilians, there might be as many as twenty German submarines in the yards, mostly the new and much-feared 'Type 21' U-boats in various stages of construction; and we heard rumours that there was a very secret research workshop. Getting into the shipyard would not be easy, however, because it lay on the right bank of the Weser, beyond Bremen on our line of approach.[45]

The British XXX Corps, in whose area Dalzel-Job's team was in, wanted to bring him under T Force, similar to S Force in the Mediterranean, but he managed to resist this, and entered Bremen on 25 April.

Early on Thursday, 26th, we moved gingerly past burning tanks and debris of battle and slipped to the side of the 52nd Division's line of advance to enter the Haus des Reiches area of Government buildings. We grabbed a dozen naval officers from basements, but found no material of interest, so I went forward again with my Recce Group into the Altstadt (the Old City area).

Moving circumspectly from corner to corner, we came to the empty City Square, and faced the high brick front of the City Hall. There was no firing and no sign of troops, but a German policeman in a steel helmet popped out of an air-raid shelter, and was lucky not to be shot for his temerity. Please, the City of Bremen wished to surrender; please would I come into the Rathaus, where the Burgomaster was waiting for me? Several citizens had now appeared from cellars and air-raid shelters, and the atmosphere seemed very friendly. I left the scout cars on guard in the square, and went in to the City Hall with Miles Cooke and Johnny Rose; inside, I found the Burgomaster, dressed very formally in black and standing all alone in the echoing empty hall.

The Burgomaster desired me to accept the formal surrender of the City of Bremen; the police and all other services would be placed at the disposal of the British Army, and everything would be done to get electricity, telephones, water and such things functioning efficiently again.

I asked whether he could give an assurance that there would be no attempt at any form of sabotage? Most certainly he would give that assurance, and the police would be instructed – especially instructed – to take the strongest action against any persons who failed in any way to cooperate with the British authorities. Anything which we ordered would be done immediately.

This seemed satisfactory, so I went back with my scout cars to rejoin the Support Carrier Group at the Haus des Reiches, and sent a message to 52nd Division Headquarters to tell them about the surrender of the City. Bremen was now almost clear of enemy, except in the dock area, which was the only part of real interest or importance for me. When they had finished clearing Bremen, 52nd Division intended to shell the docks during the night, as a precursor to clearing the shipyard with infantry. This would be disastrous from my point of view, because almost everything of intelligence value would probably be destroyed; I was therefore determined to get into Deschimag shipyard, whatever the risk, in time to show Divisional Headquarters that shelling was unnecessary.[46]

Leaving the rest of his team outside the Rathaus, Dalzel-Job took his own scout car on to the docks. Unfortunately he ran out of petrol just in front of the dock gates. Since he had also lost wireless contact, he had to seize a bicycle off a startled German workman in order to go and bring up the rest of his group.

Several times, I nearly fell off the bicycle when the front wheel hit a brick from one of the bombed houses; but I kept on pedalling, until I came unsteadily round the last corner. The waiting vehicles of 30 A.U. did not need to be told to get moving, and I was hauled on board the leading scout car as it passed.

I took the bicycle with me; its owner was surprised to see it again. My scout car was still intact, standing forlorn in front of the iron gates, with the Royal Marine gunner alert in his turret.

We opened the gates of the shipyard, and went inside, followed almost immediately by the Carrier Group. The Royal Marines tumbled out of their vehicles to sweep through the maze of slips and buildings in the fading light; there were 16 submarines of the newest German type of the slips, as well as two destroyers, and several others lay sunk or partly sunk alongside the quays.

We had forestalled nearly all the plans for demolition, and we were just in time to intercept all the Directors of the Company except one, as well as most of the technicians, while they were still trying to decide whether or not to abscond while the going was good. There were masses of the latest technical papers and equipment, and our search of the vast and labyrinthine workshops and offices went on all night; in the process, we collected a considerable number of prisoners, but met no organised resistance and had no casualties.

Just before daylight next morning, infantry and tanks of the Cameronians appeared, and we guided them round the shipyard. During the day, no less than two other powerful bodies of British troops arrived with orders to clear the shipyard, followed somewhat later by the Press – a series of incursions which became something of a nuisance while we were photographing all the highly technical equipment and interrogating hordes of prisoners and technicians. When a Staff Officer arrived from 52nd Division and asked me to sign a receipt for the 16 submarines, it was the last straw. I told the Royal Marines to put up a sign saying that the shipyard belonged to 30 A.U. Unfortunately (perhaps) we had one Royal Marine who had been a sign-painter in civil life; he raided the shipyard store and spent a happy afternoon in painstaking brushwork. The splendid arrogance of the finished product on the iron gate made 30

A.U. very unpopular with some people at Divisional Headquarters, but it enabled us to get on with our work in peace for the rest of the time we were there.[47]

His team then went on to Bremerhaven, while that of Commander Aylen entered Hamburg where they came across examples of the Walter U-boat with its revolutionary drive and captured Dr Walter himself. Another, under Dunstan Curtis, along with an SAS troop, also entered Kiel.

Unlike the Army Troop (see next chapter), the RM and RN wings were able to build on the experience gained in the Mediterranean and France, and the final campaign saw them operating as they had always wanted to. The result was a vast haul of highly valuable technical intelligence, which they would not have obtained if they had not been allowed the free rein which was essential to their operations.

CHAPTER NINE

Italy and the Adriatic
1944–5

By the end of 1943, the British Eighth Army had decided that it had no immediate need for the Commandos on the eastern side of Italy, while the more difficult country in the west might well require Commando assistance in order to continue the advance. Consequently, 2 SS Brigade, less No 2 Commando, moved there at the beginning of January 1944 and set up a base in the Castellamare area, ready to undertake operations with the US Fifth Army. They would not have long to wait.

On 12 January, No 40 (RM) Commando, still under the command of Lt Colonel J.C. Manners DSO RM, was placed under the British X Corps. They were to return to the scene of No 9 Commando's activities in the area of the mouth of the River Garigliano at the end of December. This time, however, instead of being a feint, 56th Division had been given the task of crossing the river, which they planned to do on a two brigade front. No 40 would be equally split between the two brigades with the task of exploiting the initial crossing into the hills north of the river. B and Q Troops under Captain E.W. Ecrupont RM would form Force I under command of 169 Brigade, who were to cross some 1200 yards from the river mouth, while A, P and X Troops, commanded by Captain L.G.B. Marshall MC RM, composed Force II under 167 Brigade, whose crossing place was to be some 5,000 yards further east.

The crossings took place on the night 17/18 January and were successfully achieved. Force 1 reached the far bank, and followed a minetape for 700 yards, but then it petered out in an orchard. Having not found the infantry battalion which he was supposed to contact, Ecrupont attempted to skirt round the orchard, but ran into a minefield, losing three men. They got through these eventually, but then came under accurate fire from a machine gun, which was knocked out. Dawn was now upon them, and so they dug in where they were and stayed there throughout the day. In the early hours of the following morning they resumed their advance, knocking out another machine gun post, and established themselves on their final objective, which was found to be unoccupied by the enemy. They remained here for the next two days, capturing a number of prisoners through patrolling and suffering one or two casualties from enemy harassing fire, before being relieved and sent into reserve.

Force II experienced considerably heavier harassing fire during their advance from the river, but nevertheless got into the foothills of Monte Salvatito, which was their objective. Part of P Troop was then sent to clear the eastern end of this feature. This they did and spent the next three days here guarding an artillery FOO, who was able to call down fire on several useful targets. The remainder spent the day mopping up Monte Savatito and had a number of brushes with the enemy. That night, the brigade intended to push on further, and Force II was given the task of infiltrating the German lines and seizing a dominant feature called Monte Rotondo. This achieved, they were to disrupt traffic on the road running north-west from Castel Forte, which was one of the main objectives of the attack.

The force consisted of X. Troop, A. Troop and 1 platoon of P. Troop, and the plan was to split up and move off at half an hour intervals and join up again at ROTONDO, where it was to contain the feature, cut the road, destroy and harass the enemy in the vicinity until relieved by the infantry. The going was very hard and finding one's way was very difficult. Apart from hearing German voices in the distance, no contact was made with the enemy. On reaching the low ground at Pt. 820003 a German sentry was seen guarding what appeared to be a barracks. It was by-passed. At this time owing to the darkness, the force had become split up and the men badly needed a rest, so it was decided to lie up for a short period in the area 826003. Here 2 Italians were brought in who gave us very useful information as to the strength and disposition of the Germans. The strength of the force was 2 officers, 1 TSM and 10 O.R.s. Daylight arrived and it was obvious that the attack by the infantry had not materialised, and as it was impossible for such a small force to hold ROTONDO we turned ourselves into Guerillas and proceeded to act as such. Several telephone lines were cut and M/C [Motor Cycle] combinations were knocked out, the occupants killed. One armoured car appeared which was fired upon, but it continued on in the direction of CASTELFORTE and was lost to view. German voices were heard to the right of our position and on investigation it was found to be a gun emplacement. A sharp engagement followed and a great deal of 'Pepper Potting',* the site was captured, containing 2 field guns which had already been prepared for demolition. These were destroyed. A quick

* Fire and movement by small groups.

reconnaissance was made and an assortment of motor cycles, staff cars, and 2 armoured cars were discovered at the side of the road. The position was attacked and owing to the closeness of the country, the enemy's fire was not accurate and only one casualty was sustained, the armoured car put up a stiff resistance but was eventually knocked out by a 77 grenade, one German being killed and one wounded. A Red Cross armoured car got away during the attack but was manned by machine guns which opened fire at our troops, although we were unable to reply.

A road block was being constructed when the first thing that came along was a Mk IV tank, this was engaged with 77 grenades which set the tank alight and although not knocking it out, the tank made away in the opposite direction.

By this time 3 more Mk IV Tanks had arrived and they opened up on the rest of the party at point blank range, the patrol receiving 2 casualties. A German Officer alighted from one of the tanks and in perfect English said, 'Come here, I have orders for you,' to which the reply was a burst of L.M.G. fire.

By this time the German were far more numerous and with their tanks had a greater fire power, and the force under Capt. Marshall made its way into a gulley. It was ascertained that ammunition was getting very short, the force commander decided to return. After concealing themselves during daylight hours, our own lines were reached by about dawn having passed through one of our own artillery concentrations. Thus ended a very useful patrol which did a considerable amount of damage.[1]*

Force II now changed position and reinforced a battalion of the Oxfordshire and Buckinghamshire Light Infantry, carrying out some patrolling, as well as dealing with an enemy counter-attack. They were then withdrawn into brigade reserve, before moving back into the line again on the night of the 21st. More patrolling took place, before going into corps reserve and meeting up once more with Force I and the rest of the Commando. There then followed further spells in the line before they were finally relieved on 21 February and returned to their billets in Vico Equense. Their operations on the Garigliano had cost them 12 killed, three missing and 63 wounded, and, apart from Captain Marshall's patrol, their role had been very much that of an ordinary infantry battalion.

Anzio
Throughout this time, Alexander's thoughts had centred on Rome. The failure of his original plan to force the enemy to give ground in

---

* It was to earn Marshall a Bar to his MC.

front of the US Fifth Army by applying pressure with the British Eighth Army, and the realisation that the nature of the terrain was making frontal attacks unproductive, caused him to alight on a new and ambitious plan. The Fifth Army was to be heavily reinforced from the Eighth, and would break the German Gustav Line with an assault on Monte Cassino, in conjunction with an amphibious landing at Anzio (*Shingle*), south of Rome. The crossings of the Garigliano represented, along with similar operations on the Rapido, the first phase of this plan. But the latter failed, and enabled Kesselring to rush reserves to Cassino when General Mark Clark began his attacks here.

As far as 2 SS Brigade were concerned, they knew little about *Shingle* until a very late hour. In the meantime, No 40 (RM) Commando was operating with X Corps, and the Polish and Belgian Troops had also been sent here to act as additional infantry. Indeed, at the time the Fifth Army seemed to view the brigade as little more than a source of infantry reinforcements. The first Brigadier Tom Churchill heard on Anzio was:

> . . . a suggestion that we should create a diversion on the night of the landing by coming ashore North of the Tiber and proceeding directly to ROME. General Clark, Commanding Fifth Army, sent for the Commander No 2 S.S. Brigade and asked him if he was prepared to undertake this task. He agreed and proceeded to study the project in conjunction with his staff at Fifth Army. When details came to be worked out it was found that the best place for a landing was at a point on the coast some 15 miles North of the Tiber where the road ROME-CIVITA VECCHIA passes close to the coast. The intention was to force a passage Eastwards down the ROME road, to create as much as havoc as possible in ROME and to withdraw North Westwards into foothills where they would have to fend for themselves until the main armies advanced to the ROME area.
>
> It is unnecessary here to go into the many details of the planning and it will suffice to say that after due consideration the Commander 2 S.S. Brigade reported to the Commander Fifth Army in the following terms:-
>
> a) The shipping and transport available was only sufficient to move 210 men in 30 Jeeps from the landing place to the city of ROME on the night of the landing;
>
> b) That as such a force would have a strictly limited effect on a city as big as ROME it would be desirable to land one or two Commandos to provide some base upon which the flying column could retire and also to make a second descent on ROME on foot on a subsequent night to increase the effect of alarm initiated by the flying column.

c) Owing to the impossibility of stating when these forces could expect to join up with the main army and after taking full acount of the possibilities of dropping supplies from the air it was the considered opinion of the S.S. Brigade that 80 per cent of any force so landed would in all probability be killed, wounded or taken prisoner.

d) That the Brigade was perfectly prepared to undertake the task provided Commander Fifth Army considered that the results which could be achieved justified the probable loss of specialised troops and equipment on the scale suggested at paragraph (c) above.

After due consideration Commander Fifth Army decided to abandon the project and instead the Brigade was to be prepared to embark with the 'SHINGLE' expedition with the following tasks:-

either   (a)   To be used in the bridgehead if the landings were strongly opposed or

          (b)   to undertake flying missions from the bridgehead if opportunities offered.

Much anxious work was done by the Brigade staff in endeavouring to ensure that the essential transport and stores were allotted shipping space in the already completed loading and shipping tables for Operation 'SHINGLE' but at no time was any guarantee given that *anything*, other than the personnel of the Brigade, would be embarked. Planners in London will readily understand the misgivings of the Brigade's staff on this account.[2]

Shingle was to take place on 22 January, and would involve the 3rd US and 1st British Divisions, along with three battalions of US Rangers. On the evening of the 15th, Tom Churchill was present at a coordinating conference. The original plan called for airborne troops from the US 504th Parachute Regiment to seize high ground inland, which dominated the US landing, but it now transpired that this might not now take place. The Commander 3rd US Division now turned to Churchill and asked him whether he could seize the vital feature north of Anzio. Churchill agreed that he could, but warned that, in view of the limited supplies which the Commandos could take with them on the initial landings, they would have to be relieved within 48 hours. They could then return to Naples and collect their vehicle for any follow-up operations for which they might be required. This was agreed, and preparations for the change in plan were hurriedly got underway. This was not helped by the sudden death of the Brigade Major, Major Henderson, on the 16th. His place was taken by Captain A.L. Blake RM.

A skeleton Brigade HQ, along with Nos 9 and 43. (RM) Comman-

dos embarked in HMS *Derbyshire* on the morning of 20 January.
Next day they sailed with the rest of the armada, and arrived off the
beaches shortly after midnight on the night 21/22 January. They
got ashore on the 1st Division beach without problems, although
they suffered a few casualties from an aircraft attack shortly after
daylight. Then, led by No 9 Commando, they began the hike to
their objective. Each man was carrying some 70 lbs and they were
dragging heavily laden handcarts as well. The going was muddy, and
hence progress was slow. Odd enemy parties were encountered on
the way, but, nevertheless, both Commandos were in position for
the main assault by 1330 hours. They attacked from the north-east
and west, and within an hour they were firm on the objective. Next
morning they made contact with the US Rangers and were placed in
reserve before being embarked in an LST, which brought them back
to Naples on the morning of the 25th. Thus, in spite of the concern
prior to the operation, it had proved remarkably easy, but little did
the Commandos know how fierce the fighting at Anzio was about to
become.

Monte Ornito

2 SS Brigade was warned that, on its return to Naples, it must be prepared for further operations at short notice. The summons was not
long in coming. Brigadier Churchill was ordered to report to HQ X
Corps on the 29th, and was told that he was to move with Nos 9 and
43 (RM) Commandos to join No 40 (RM) Commando with 56th
Division and make up a counter-attack force. They were to move to
an assembly area, while Tom Churchill reported to Divisional HQ.
Unfortunately, the transport provided by X Corps to move the Commandos did not arrive until that night, and they did not reach their
destination until almost dawn on the 31st. In the meantime, General Richard McCreery, the Commander X Corps, had amended his
plan, and decided to use Nos 9 and 43 (RM) Commandos to extend
his foothold in the hills west of the Garigliano, by seizing the three
peaks which made up the dominant Monte Ornito. For this they
were to come under the command of 46th Division.

> The ground consisted of rough hills devoid of any cover and strewn
> with rocks and boulders. The hills rose precipitously from deep uneven
> valleys and movement was impeded by loose stones and screeze [scree].
> M.TUGA is 2000 ft high, and to climb it it was necessary to start from
> the river bed which was to be the Commandos' assembly area, which is

only 300 ft above sea level. The objective, M. ORNITO, is 2400 ft high and M. FAITO beyond is nearly 3000 ft. Digging was extremely difficult and only in places could the surface foot of soil be removed to form a shallow trench. Round any such trench it was necessary to build protective walls of rocks and boulders to provide cover for the troops from mortar, shell and small arms fire. Mules could only be brought halfway up M.TUGA, and from there supplies had to be carried by Porters to the troops on top of the hill. Even to live in this area involved considerable fatigue in carrying water, ammunition, food and supplies to the troops.[3]

Tom Churchill took his two Commanding Officers, Lt Colonels Tod and Simonds, to view the ground, and then they went back to meet their men at a forward assembly area. Once again, there were problems over the transport, and this, as well as the fact that they had to cover the last part on foot, meant that they did not arrive until almost dawn on 1 February. Since they had now had two nights with virtually no sleep, Brigadier Churchill requested and obtained agreement from 46th Division for the attack to be postponed for 24 hours. Unfortunately, no further reconnaissance could take place because the landscape was blotted out by a thick mist. Sadly, too, enemy shellfire caused No 9 Commando sixteen casualties including five killed.

The original plan called for the two Commandos to launch their attack north-westwards from Monte Tuga, but during the 2nd, 138 Brigade informed Tom Churchill that the enemy held a post, which would dominate the route of the advance, in some strength. Consequently, the plan was changed that afternoon and the Commandos were now to work their way round the right flank of Monte Tuga, then move north-west until they were north of Monte Ornito. Once they had taken the latter, No 43 (RM) Commando would move south to capture Pt 711, while No 9, who would follow No 43 on the initial approach, made their way round to the north-east of Monte Ornito in order to seize Monte Faito. The Belgian Troop, who had now rejoined, would be in reserve, and 6th Battalion Yorks and Lancs would provide some flank protection as well as clearing the valley floors. There was time only for the two Commanding Officers to have another quick look at the ground before the operation was launched. No 43 (RM) Commando: .

At 1830 hrs after being shelled by an 88mm gun, the advance commenced on a very narrow and rocky track leading from Mount TUGA through the foothills of Mount ORNITO and Pt 711, which towered above us. In bright moonlight we encountered intense MG and mortar fire from enemy outposts, but the leading tps D, B and A ignored these and after many hours' arduous climbing and against MG and intense mortar fire secured Mount ORNITO and Pt 711. C Tp were left behind to mop up the foothills which they accomplished, not without casualties, by first light. Capt John BLAKE RM received the MC for the magnificent example leading the three leading troops, and the dash with which the two objectives were seized, despite the extreme weariness of all ranks, was due to his example and leadership. Over 30 PW including officers were taken, but owing to the enormous size of the objectives it was impossible to winkle more out. Two big problems had been the extreme difficulty of maintaining wireless contact, particularly with Bde, and the fact that we had to advance and climb over three miles under fire, and many men were cut off from their Troops. However soon after first light the majority had rejoined their Troops who had been very thin on the ground.[4]

Meanwhile, No 9 Commando had moved round Monte Tuga and pushed on north-west from Monte Ornito. They now came under heavy fire from a feature in front of Monte Faito. Three troops took this in the face of heavy mortar and shell fire, which caused some casualties, and this fire continued during the consolidation and reorganisation which followed. Advancing once more, they met further opposition. More casualties were suffered, including Ronnie Tod, who received a bad wound in the arm, Major E.W. Clark, the second-in-command, killed and six other officers wounded. The intensity of the fire made Ronnie Tod decide that to continue the advance would be suicidal, and the Commando withdrew to Monte Ornito. Come daylight and Tod managed to get through to Churchill on the wireless and explain the situation to him, and he arranged for resupply to be sent up. Interrogation of prisoners revealed that the enemy had withdrawn to Monte Faito, and that it was likely that he would put in a counter-attack. Churchill now went up to see for himself and ordered Ronnie Tod, in view of his wound, to stand down. Captain M.R.H. Allen took over command in his place. Churchill saw that it was not possible to attack Monte Faito until further reinforcements had been sent up, and ordered a programme of active patrolling until this could be done. Much of the day was marked by extensive artillery duels, and the gradual build up of enemy fire indicated that a counter-attack was likely. This took place at 1600 hours and fell on

No 43 (RM) Commando. Although the enemy got within grenade range in some places and inflicted casualties, No 43 succeeded in beating it off, and then came the welcome news that 2 SS Brigade would be relieved that night. First, however, the Belgian Troop had to seize a small feature lying between Monte Ornito and Monte Faito, which they luckily found unoccupied. The relief itself went smoothly, and on 5 February X Corps ordered the brigade back to its rest areas in the Bay of Naples.

General Dick McCreery, in a letter to Tom Churchill, congratulated the Commandos on the work they had done. 'The country was extremely difficult, and the courage, enterprise and endurance shown by many parties, after officer casualties had made control difficult, were in the best traditions of the Commandos.'[8] Casualties had been heavy, especially for No 9 Commando, and the ultimate objective of Monte Faito had not been captured. During the next few months, however, the Commandos could take consolation in the fact that, such was the German determination to deny the Monte Ornito feature to the Allies, it would be captured and recaptured no less than six times during the coming months before finally falling to French Goums.

Return to Anzio

On their return to the Bay of Naples, Nos 9 and 43 (RM) Commandos were rejoined by No 40, who had been finally released by 56th Division, now bound for Anzio. A day later, however, on 23 February, the brigade was ordered to send one Commando to the Adriatic to reinforce No 2 Commando, now on the island of Vis, and No 43 was selected for this, to be followed shortly afterwards by Brigade HQ. To the north the Germans were reacting strongly to the Allied beachhead at Anzio. It was the threat to his lines of communication running north from Rome which concerned Kesselring, and from the end of January he had been constantly counter-attacking. Two US Divisions and 56th Division had been sent as reinforcements, but these were still not enough, and on 29 February, Nos 9 and 40 (RM) Commandos were also ordered there. They arrived on 2 March, and were placed under 56th Division. No 9 Commando, with Ronnie Tod once more in command, went to 167 Brigade and No 40 to 169 Brigade. Both began with a period of offensive patrolling, which No 40 would continue throughout their stay without being involved in a major action.

No 9, on the other hand, received, on 10 March, a warning order for an operation. By now they were under command of 5th Division, which had just arrived at Anzio. The original idea was for a two division spoiling attack to disrupt further German counter-attacks, but this was boiled down to merely a local attack by No 9 designed to clear three wadis, which the Germans had been in the habit of using as forming up points for their counter-attacks. The area of this operation was some eleven miles north of Anzio and two miles west of the main road running north from it. The wadis themselves formed a 'U' with a small hillock in the centre, and there was high ground below the base of the 'U'. The Commando was given just over a week to prepare for it. Ronnie Tod's plan was for a night attack on the wadi forming the left hand arm of the 'U' (*Haydon*), and then, in Phase 2, clear *Charles* at the base and secure the junction of this with the other arm *(Laycock).** Finally, *Laycock* would be cleared and a defensive position established. To carry this out, Tod split the Commando into three two-troop squadrons, A, B, and C.

At 0200 hours on 19 March, B and C Squadrons crossed the start line and seized *Haydon* with little problem. Some machine gun fire was now encountered, but was quickly silenced. The start line also came under artillery fire as A Squadron and Tod's HQ were crossing it, but they joined the first wave in *Haydon*. Preparations were now made to clear *Charles*, but when the attack began at 0530 hours it was met with heavy fire, and Tod ordered all back to *Haydon*. An enemy counter-attack and heavy sniper fire made this a difficult operation, but nevertheless it was done. The enemy now began to pour heavy fire onto *Haydon*, and so intense was it that it proved impossible for porters to bring up supplies, which were now urgently needed. As for the wounded, it was very difficult to extricate them, but eventually a Red Cross flag was hoisted, which the Germans respected, and some were got back behind cover. With the coming of darkness the enemy put in a number of counter-attacks, which were beaten off, but it was clear that to hold onto *Haydon* was going to be an expensive and risky undertaking in view of the fierce enemy reaction. Indeed, orders to withdraw to the start line had come from 15 Brigade before the counter-attacks broke out, and once they had been stopped this now took place. All the riflemen were detailed to help carry out the wounded, using improvised stretchers made from rifles, greatcoats and ground sheets, and they were covered back by the machine gunners, with

---

*These names, together with *Bob* (Laycock), *Tom* (Churchill) and *Angie* (Bob Laycock's wife), were often used in 2 SS Brigade operations at this time.

friendly artillery fire being laid down to prevent the enemy following up too closely. Once back in their own lines, No 9 Commando, who had lost 19 killed, 50 wounded and four missing, were withdrawn into Anzio, where they met up with No 40.

Both Commandos left Anzio on 25 March and returned to Naples, but were to remain here for only a few days before joining the rest of the brigade in the Adriatic. Here they had become involved in something as close as any to the traditional Commando concept.

The Island of Vis

Although Trevor Glanville's attempts in October 1943 to set up joint operations by No 30 Commando and Tito's partisans in Yugoslavia had come to naught, the efforts of Fitzroy Maclean and others in the Balkans had improved relations between the British and the Communist-inspired resistance groups. Tito, especially, had demonstrated greater determination and organisation to drive out the Axis invader than his Royalist counterpart, Mihailovic, whom SOE had originally backed, and liason officers had been sent to help him. With the Italian surrender, Tito had quickly stepped into the vacuum and seized large areas of the mainland coast, as well as the Dalmatian Islands, which had been formerly garrisoned by the Italians. The Germans reacted quickly, however, and by the end of 1943 had regained control of the coast and forced Tito back into the mountainous hinterland. He was now desperately in need of help, but, at the time, with the Americans and British fully committed in Italy, there was little that could be done besides disrupting German shipping in the Adriatic with MTBs and MGBs and providing some air support.

This was not enough to reassure Tito, suspicious as he was of Anglo-American intentions. Accordingly, it was decided to set up an advanced headquarters of Force 133, which was based in Cairo and responsible for coordinating operations in the Balkans, at Bari, and on 2 January 1944, No 2 Commando was placed under its command. It would shortly be designated Force 266. It was obvious that the Germans intended to wrest the Dalmatian Islands from the Partisans, but the Allies needed to at least retain a foothold on them, if they were to keep communications with Tito open. It was therefore decided to set up a Force 133 base on Vis, the nearest island of any size to the Italian mainland, and this would be built around No 2 Commando. At the time, they were still training their replacements at Molfetta, and would not be fully operational until mid-February, but with the Germans seemingly poised to seize the islands of Brae and Solta, troops had to be deployed to Vis well before this date.

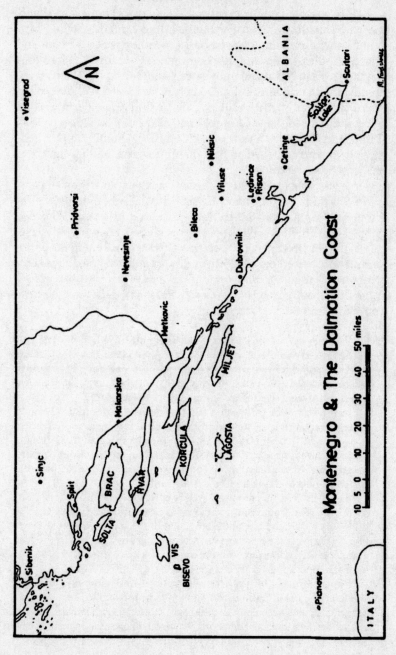

Montenegro & The Dalmatian Coast

Before any such deployment could take place, however, contact had to be made with the Partisans and agreement reached with them. Thus, after being delayed by bad weather, Jack Churchill and Brigadier Miles, commanding Force 133, set out for Vis. Here they met the Partisan Naval and military commanders in the Dalmatians, Commander Cerni and Colonel Millic, who agreed to 1,000 Allied troops being sent to the island, and that a joint Anglo-Partisan command should be set up. Churchill and Miles then went on to look at Brae and Hvar with a view to raids on them should the Germans seize them, and returned to Bari on 15 January. On that same day Brac and Solta were invaded.

Time was now short, and on the very next day an advanced party of No 2, under the Adjutant, Captain R.W. Keep, landed on Vis. Three days later, Hvar fell to the Germans, and on the 20th two troops and the Heavy Weapons Troop landed, together with elements of a US OSS Special Operation Group. More elements of the Commando arrived on the 25th, and by 12 February No 2 was complete on Vis, together with one officer and seven men from No 7 (Yugoslav) Troop of No 10 (IA) Commando. As for the voyage across from Bari, Stan Buckmaster:

Our journey across the Adriactic was uneventful. We left in a LSI and were escorted part of the way by a Motor Torpedo Boat and a Motor Gun Boat, both of which had a useful complement of weaponry. They turned away as dusk settled over us, and our vessel ploughed on through a fairly even swell at what seemed to be slightly increased speed.

I stayed on deck for most of the voyage until, at about 0130 hours, there was an abrupt slackening of speed and, although as yet the moon had not risen, I could make out through the gloom a land mass straight ahead and what appeared to be a small island on the port side. We were passing the island of Bisevo and shortly we would arrive at the harbour and small port of Komiza at the western end of Vis.

As we entered the sheltered waters of this natural harbour, several shots were fired from small arms towards us, but over the vessel. On the bridge an Aldis lamp began flashing, one or two more shots were fired, then the firing ceased as the recognition signal was accepted by the Partisan lookouts. RN seamen busied themselves as we drew alongside the mole that now appeared to our starboard.

Ropes were hurled over the side and secured, gangways lowered, and a small party of Commando soldiers came forward to assist with the baggage. Orders were given to disembark. So, laden with kitbags, valises, ammo and weapons, we edged our way down on to the solid concrete of the mole. Stepping across to the shelter of the wall that ran continuously along our right side I read for the first time the slogan SMRT FASCISMU SLOBODA NARODNA.* We had arrived. . .[6]

At the time, the Partisans were some 1,000 strong and organised into three brigades, which were tied down to coastal defence. No 2 Commando therefore took over responsibility for the central plain and was also to act as a counter-attack force in the event of a German invasion on this, the last of the Dalmatian Islands in Partisan hands. Jack Churchill was made Garrison Commander of Allied troops, which were shortly swelled by a light Ack-Ack battery, RAF elements and a machine gun detachment from the Raiding Support Regiment.† Later, at the end of February, No 43 (RM) Commando also arrived. This put much strain on Jack Churchill's small HQ, especially as he was anxious to begin offensive action as soon as possible. Before he could do this, however, it was essential to gain accurate intelligence on the enemy. The Partisans had much of this, but it was uncoordinated, and initially the Commandos had to rely on scraps fed to them by Commander Cerni.

There was also the problem of maintaining good relations. While the Partisan welcome had been very warm in the belief that the arrival of the Commandos marked the end of recognition of Mihailovic and his Cetniks, and that the tide would now dramatically turn, when the latter did not happen an element of suspicion arose. They felt, too, that the British were taking too much advantage of their hospitality and considered themselves better and more experienced soldiers. The execution of two women Partisans convicted of pregnancy in the sight of three British soldiers was considered barbaric by the British, even though it was a laid down rule among the Partisans that men and women should not indulge in sexual relations. Then, towards the end of February, the Partisans began week long celebrations in honour of the anniversary of the Red Army, while the British garrison went on full alert since invasion was now considered immi-

---

* 'Death to Fascism, Freedom to the People'
† This had been formed in November 1943 by Raiding Forces Middle East and was designed to provide heavy weapons back-up to the other elements in the formation. All members were parachute trained, and they had their own unique capbadge of a mailed fist descending from a pair of high crested wings. They were organised into five batteries equipped with mountain guns, 3in mortars, MMGs, anti-tank (usually captured Italian) and anti-aircraft guns. For a personal account of their activities see Reid, Francis *I Was in Noah's Ark* (Chambers, London 1957).

nent, but neither party really understood what the other was doing. The fact, too, that by the beginning of March the Anglo-American garrison had risen above the stipulated 1,000 men also did not help. Nevertheless, relations between the British and Partisan leaders did remain cordial until at least June 1944, and at the lower levels, in spite of mutual misunderstandings, they continued workable.

Much of Cerni's intelligence on what was happening on the other islands came from the schooners which he ran to them with the help of an OSS team based at Monopoli, 30 miles south of Bari, in order to supply the Partisans still there. He agreed with Jack Churchill on 20 January to use these on a raid on Hvar before the Germans could consolidate their position. Unfortunately, the weather as it so often did, took a hand, and it was not until the 27th that they were able to sail. Churchill took four schooners with three troops of No 2 Commando and thirty members of the US Operations Group. Two of the schooners developed steering problems and had to turn back, but the other two landed, contacted the local Partisans, and the force set out for the town of Hvar. They attacked a German outpost in a house on the outskirts, killing two Germans and capturing four, and then withdrew to the schooners which had been left in Milna Bay, and re-embarked. The intelligence gained from the prisoners was valuable. The German 118th Jaeger Division was holding the islands very lightly, but seemed to be keeping a regiment in reserve for the invasion of Vis, and details of the two divisions holding the coastal region of the mainland were also obtained.

In view of the threat to Vis, Churchill decided that attack was the best form of defence; the best way to prevent a German invasion of Vis was to force the enemy onto the defensive. A series of reconnaissance operations were now mounted against Hvar, and these noted that by night the Germans vacated their outposts and withdrew into the security of the town of Hvar itself. In order to persuade them to occupy the outposts by night, which would make them better targets, the Partisans lit fires in these positions and this was partially successful. On 2 February, Captain Bare, OC No 2 Troop, who had led many of the reconnaissances, landed on Hvar once more, and identified a German platoon position in the village of Grablje, which he decided to attack. His troop came across to join him the following night and four Germans were killed and four captured. Unfortunately Bare himself was badly wounded in the stomach and died before he could be put on the schooner. One other man, Private

Tuck, had a bad chest wound and was considered to be too ill to be moved and had to be left, apparently dying, and two other men were missing. Attempts to mount a rescue operation were thwarted by the weather, but another British officer on the island, Major Corbett, made contact with the two missing men and also with Tuck, who had dragged himself back to the landing place at Dubovica, a distance of three miles, living on his emergency chocolate ration and melted snow. On 6 February, the party returned to Vis where happily Tuck recovered and returned to duty.

Throughout this time the Royal Navy had been busy in its cease-less battle with German shipping supplying their island garrisons. The Senior Naval Officer on Vis, Lt Commander (later Rear Admiral) Morgan Giles OBE CM RN, agreed with Churchill that small parties of his Commandos should go out on the MTBs on these expeditions, and this provided added excitement. The Commandos were used as boarding parties, and a number of prisoners were made in this way. Often they returned empty-handed and, once, after a schooner had been boarded, it was decided that it was too late on in the night to tow her back to Vis and she was sunk. Unfortunately, she had a cargo of canteen supplies, which would have been very welcome to the garrison on Vis, whose resupply from the mainland was often haphazard.

Churchill had by now turned his attention to the island of Solta, and two reconnaissance parties were sent there in early February. As on Hvar, the enemy quickly altered his dispositions by night, concentrating his forces in the town of Grohote, and Churchill decided to attack this target. An interesting operation was also mounted against Brac in the middle of the month, when Lieutenant B.J. Barton MC and a party of ten were sent to harass the Germans there. He made contact with the local Partisans, but had a narrow escape when one of them was captured and mentioned that his patrol was on the island. Luckily, local Partisan intelligence was one step ahead of the Germans. The latter now began to maltreat the local population and Barton offered to assassinate the German Commandant, which was readily agreed to. The Partisans gave him details of where the Commandant lived, in a house in the village of Nerezisce, and, disguised as a shepherd, with his sten gun hidden in pieces in a bundle of faggots carried by a donkey, Barton managed to slip into the village. Helped by Partisans, he got into the house and killed the Commandant. Next day, 23 February, he was ordered back to Vis.

By this time, analysis of German shipping movements indicated that an invasion of the island was imminent, and Churchill decided to cease offensive operations for the time being in order to concentrate on the defences of Vis. He was still woefully short of troops, but efforts by Brigadier Miles brought about the dispatch of No 43 (RM) Commando to the island, and they arrived on 28 February, as did the rest of the Raiding Support Regiment. HQ 2 SS Brigade and the Belgian Troop followed a few days later. The Yugoslav Troop detachment, however, returned to North Africa since the Royalist allegiance of its members did not rest easily with the Partisans, and the troop was disbanded in April. The Royal Navy was reinforced by some destroyers and Allied aircraft bombed concentrations of German shipping. The invasion threat receded by the first week in March, when Brigadier Tom Churchill took over from his brother, but reinforcement of the Vis garrison continued, which enabled the Commandos to devote more time to the offensive operations.

At the end of February, a small American party returned to Hvar and Lieutenant Barton to Brac. The former had a sharp exciting brush with the enemy which ended in both sides withdrawing, while Barton took out an eight man German outpost. For this and his previous expeditions to the island, he was later awarded the DSO. In the meantime, once Brigade HQ had relieved Jack Churchill of his responsibilities for commanding the garrison, preparations for the raid on Solta were resumed. The plan which was eventually evolved was for the force to land one night, surround the town, and then, next morning, after attacks by RAF aircraft, the main assault would go in. Taking part would be No 2 Commando, elements from No 43, the US Special Operations Group and some members of the Light Ack Ack battery armed with 47mm guns. The force set sail on the night 17/18 March, and Stan Buckmaster describes what happened:

We boarded the landing craft at dusk, and sailed from Komiza about an hour later. The sea was calm, and the journey uneventful. We passed the time checking weapons, priming grenades and chatting to off duty sailors below deck. Most of the Navy chaps seemed to have a horror of grenades, a weapon with which they were not familiar. Some seemed to be fascinated by the fact that one has to be in very close proximity to the enemy before being able to use them.

Most of the riflemen had been detailed to carry six 3 inch mortar bombs apiece, a weight of slightly more than 60 lbs, add to this their own ammunition and ration pack, weapons, personal gear and water bottle, etc, and each man would be carrying about 100 lbs in weight. No transport of any description would be landed, and guns, mortars, heavy machine guns, were also to be carried on shoulders and backs.

Shortly after 0130 hours we were approaching Solta. The outline of the island could now be clearly seen, and soon we were nosing into a small cove. The shallow draught of landing ships enabled them to run their bows to within a few feet of the beach. We were lined up along the rails on either side of the vessel in order to disembark, and seamen were standing by to lower the gangways that face forward on port and starboard sides of the bows.

A slight judder, followed by the grinding of shingle under the ship, and we were beached. The starboard gangway went down almost silently, but not so the port side which refused to budge. A burly seaman stepped forward with a sledge hammer and after a few hefty blows the offending locking pin was removed, the gangway going down with a tremendous rattling of chains over pulleys.

We hurried down to the beach to try to get back into our correct position of advance from the start line, whilst a second L.S.I. alongside our vessel had almost completed the disembarkation of its troops. Beyond the narrow stretch of the shingle a rocky escarpment rose steeply upwards for about a hundred feet, and across its face a boulder strewn path ran towards the top at an angle of 45 degrees or so. The leading troop was already swarming up this path, whilst two 3 inch mortars had been set up for immediate action, and also to cover the eventual withdrawal. The accidental discharge of a rifle at this point, by a soldier who had slipped off the path, infuriated nearby officers and brought forth the order to 'check safety catches'.

Those of us carrying the mortar bombs found the going very strenuous and by the time we reached the top of the path, were somewhat exhausted. Any reaction from the enemy at this stage would have found us all at our most vulnerable. However, there was no opposition so far and we carried on along a gravel path, that had dry-stone walls running along either side. There were many halts, while the leading scouts went forward to reconnoitre the way ahead. We took the opportunity to rest our bomb packs during these halts, on the top of the dry-stone walls, probably centuries old, just fell away with a cascade of stones and the dried earth between them. The noise generated by these minor avalanches, over and above the crunch of boots on the gravel, set off an incessant howling and barking of dogs, from the somewhat isolated homesteads that lay mainly to the right of the track. Now to our left a cemetery, with its ugly ornate crumbling tombstones, and tall wrought iron hollow crossed that stood stark against a lightening sky. Another mile and we could see Grohote; it lay in a basin formed by the low hills around the town. A slight mist had formed and added to the chill of the morning, but visibility was not affected.

At this point an officer of the mortar detachment directed us to make a stockpile of our bombs. Relieved of the burden, we then moved forward to join in ringing the town as far as our members would permit. A sudden and unmistakable burst of fire from a Schmeisser, heralded that start of the battle. The morning patrol of German troops had bumped into our leading scouts, thus ending any hope of surprise. 3 inch mortars fired a few rounds but then had to stop, as a force of bombers from the RAF operating from Italy were due to arrive at 0600.

Germans attempting to man the gun platforms had to abandon them, for no sooner had they started to climb up to the guns, our gunners with the 'squeeze gun'* opened fire and smashed two of the supporting struts with the first two shots.

Using a Loud Hailer Lt Col Jack Churchill called upon the garrison to give up and surrender, he also informed them that they were about to be bombed unless they did so. As this demand was being made through an interpreter, thirty-six Kitty Hawks arrived over the town. They flew in low at the start, over the roof tops, then swept upwards to form a 'Cab rank'. Then, taking directions from a ground control officer who was with the colonel, peeled off into a steep dive a dozen at a time. As the dive commenced they opened fire with their 20mm cannon and machine guns, which were firing tracer, and at the point where they flattened out, released their bombs. From below it appeared as though they were descending on golden rails, the unbroken lines of tracer giving this effect. The assault troop fixed bayonets, and as the last wave of aircraft dived down over the target, they dashed into the main street and commenced clearing the houses of the enemy. This part of the plan was a master stroke, as these planes were firing blank ammunition, allowing the Commandos to move in under a curtain of noise rather than fire, whilst the Germans had their 'heads down'.

During the air attack those of us immediately below the flight path of the aircraft were showered with the spent cannon shell and machine gun cartridge castings as they fell away from the planes. We had been informed that this was likely, and were warned to wear our steel helmets to avoid injury.

Among the early captives during the street fighting was the German garrison Commandant. He was brought to where Colonel Churchill had made his surrender demand, and in turn called upon his men to stop fighting. He was able to assure them that the attacking force was British, and that they would be treated correctly as P.O.W. under the terms of the Geneva convention. Partisans were apt to give their prisoners short shrift, largely as a result of the manner in which they themselves had been treated by the enemy.

---

*A 2 pdr anti-tank gun with an attachment, which squeezed the projectile as it traversed up the barrel, thus imparting greater velocity and accuracy. Known also as the Littlejohn conversion, it was used on the Daimler armoured car.

Gradually the firing died away, as various sections of the defenders were rounded up, disarmed and made prisoner. Many civilians had made a mass exodus from the town whilst the fighting was actually going on. We had no idea as to the extent of casualties among them, although there most have been some, as many houses had been destroyed or damaged during the bombing. Among the prisoners were several Ustachi, and local collaborators. A thorough search of the town ensured that all the garrison were in the net. Eventually all was ready to return to the beach, and the prisoners were lined up, some being detailed to assist with carrying the heavy equipment. Col. Jack Churchill took his place at the head of the column and we marched away from Grohote to the tune 'Road to the Isles' played by the Colonel on his bagpipes. We had lost two men killed and had several wounded, but we had well over a hundred prisoners, and they had lost at least eight dead and many wounded.[7]

This was an exceptionally successful operation and it was gratifying that civilian casualties were limited to four killed and two badly wounded. It also made a significant contribution to forcing the Germans onto the defensive and shelving ideas for invading Vis.

The next target was Hvar, and this was given to No 43 (RM) Commando. In the middle of March they sent two patrols to the island to study the German routine, and on 22 March established that the enemy was intending to evacuate Jelsa that night. Cerni and Millic suggested to Tom Churchill that a joint force should attack the town as the Germans were about to withdraw, and this was agreed. Some 280 members of No 43, together with two battalions of Partisans (some 400 men), set sail that afternoon.

Despite heavy loads and extremely steep and rough country the Commando had surrounded the town of JELSA soon after midnight, covering in some cases many miles. However it was not until Cdo HQ and A Troop, the reserve Troop bumped and split into two enemy columns, that it was realised that the garrison had flown and were withdrawing in the same direction from which we had come, in order to get to the east end of the island. A terrific fire fight ensued, and A Tp and Cdo HQ were assaulted from all sides. All attacks were driven off despite the fact that it was 180 against 45 Commandos. We captured some PW and their complete Mule Train. Major (then Capt) J.C.D. HUDSPITH RM won a very fine MC in this action. Our casualties were only a few wounded.

The enemy column broke off and tried to make for the East but bumped the 1 Dalamatian Pzn Bde who had now landed. A terrific hand-to-hand battle took place with heavy casualties on both sides. The enemy again assaulted A Tp and Cdo HQ but were dispersed with heavy casualties. By now it was daylight the Cdo had re-grouped and set off to chase the enemy for about eight miles to the east end of the island. Some of the enemy got away but many were captured, and a memorable shoot by a 3" Mortar which had been man carried with its bombs for miles, caught an unsuspecting enemy group resting, and accounted for fifteen of them. The Commando retired that night, re-embarked and returned to Vis. In all 80 enemy were captured and 50 confirmed killed. This action was memorable in that it was the first action fought by British tps and Tito's Partisans and commanded by a British commander Lt Col R.W.B. SIMONDS RM. We had our first insight of the excitability of the Partisans, who were at times in the depths of depression about the outcome of the battle, only overcome by the Force Comd and also when we were fired on by the Partisans wounded one of our men. A letter from the Partisans Bde Comd was received by the Commando addressed to 'Our Comrades in the Fight against the German Barbars' commemorating this first action together.[8]

Once again, this had been highly successful, with no less than 160 enemy put out of action at a cost of 21 Commando/Partisan casualties. This reduced the enemy garrison to some ninety men only, who now clung on to the eastern tip of the island.

There now followed a pause in major operations. The Germans took steps to reinforce the islands, and carried out largescale sweeps on them. Vis itself became the target of a number of air attacks, which caused casualties. Churchill turned his attention to the southern group of the Dalmatian Islands, and a number of reconnaissance and sabotage parties were sent to them. He also mounted a propaganda campaign, arranging for leaflets to be dropped from aircraft. At this time the Belgian Troop left Vis to return to the UK to take part in *Overlord*, and the Polish Troop, which had originally wanted to take part in *Overlord*, joined II Polish Corps in Italy. It was now called the 1st Independent Commando Company, and later the 2nd Motorised Commando Battalion, and particularly distinguished itself in the battles for Monte Cassino. In the meantime, life on Vis went on, and Sir Alfred Blake, then Brigade Major of 2 SS Brigade, describes something of the bizarre life the Commandos led:

It was a very unreal existence. Conditions were cramped to say the least, especially with more and more Yugoslavs coming in – they used to come by boat from the mainland under the cover of darkness. Apart from the local anchovies and wine, all the food came from Italy including carrier pigeons supplied to take messages back and thereby supplement our rather shaky communications, but could you blame us for a tasty but rare change of menu? We were also the haven for scores of US Liberators, and the Partisans built a very rough emergency airstrip so that those damaged during their raids on Southern Europe could crash land or bail out. The strip itself was very short, with a vineyard at one end, and once down-the Liberators had to be stripped of everything in order to have any chance of a successful take-off. I remember particularly when General Sturges came to visit us by air and his aircraft overshot and landed in the vineyard. I was there to greet him with a Guard of Honour, and, in order to be opposite the door when he came out, we too had to crash our way into the vineyard. As he alighted he looked somewhat shaken, but the bizarre sight of the Guard of Honour and myself attempting to pay him the due military courtesies in the middle of the vines was too much.

Strangest of all was our 'rest and recreation' centre. This was on the nearby island of Hvar, which, of course, was occupied by the Germans. To get away from the constant hurly-burly of Vis, we would telephone the Postmaster of Hvar town, using the civil line between the two islands, of which the Germans were totally unaware, and check that the coast was clear. We would then take a Yugoslav schooner across by night and land at the jetty in the harbour, put up with the local Partisans, and then spend the next day swimming and sightseeing, returning to Vis and the war the next night.[9]

This is, too, perhaps the moment to make mention of one of the more unique Commando characters who was present on the island. Admiral Sir Walter Cowan, had joined the Royal Navy in 1884, and had won the DSO serving in gunboats during the Omdurman campaign of 1898. After a distinguished career during the First World War, which included being present at the Battle of Jutland, he had retired at the age of sixty in 1931. On the formation of the Commandos, he managed to persuade his close friend Lord Keyes for him to be attached to them, and served with No 8 Commando as their Naval Liaison Officer in North Africa. When they were disbanded, he attached himself to the 18th Indian Cavalry, with whom No 8 had served in Tobruk, and after the war became their Colonel. He was captured by the Italians at Bir Hacheim in May 1942 while in typical fashion trying to fight a tank crew with just his revolver, and was sent to Italy. In 1943 he was repatriated, being considered by the Italians as too old to take any further part in the war, and immediately rejoined his beloved Commandos, serving as Tom Churchill's Liaison officer. He was small and slight in stature, lived an aescetic life, but was utterly fearless, and became very much 2 SS Brigade's 'mascot'. His bravery and complete disregard for danger were an example to all, and this was recognised in the award of a bar to his DSO, 46 years after he had won the original decoration.

In the meantime, the Royal Navy had been reinforced on Vis by Lt Commander Fuller RCN and a flotilla of MGBs. He and Giles developed a method of ambushing enemy shipping:

Acting on Lieut Commander GILES' orders, he [Fuller] would head his flotilla to a pre-arranged ambush. Usually, he hid his craft in the shadow of one of the islands, close inshore, with a Commando boarding party of an officer and six men amidships, lying flat on the deck, ready for his orders to board any enemy craft he came alongside. He would wait thus, in the darkness, and in absolute silence, with one engine ticking over softly, its noise drowned by the lap-lap of the water on the nearby ashore and his craft.

Enemy shipping sailed in convoy about six at a time in line ahead, and about 100 yards from the shore. Usually such a convoy would be led by an E-boat or I-lighter, and have a second E-boat in the rear. These E-boats were usually armed with up to 4-20mm Oerlikon guns, while the schooners, or caiques, which made up the convoy, were armed with one or two machine guns. The convoy would make about 5 knots and would chug along, watching anxiously to seaward, ready for any attack from that direction by our dreaded MGBs.

Suddenly, from inland of the enemy convoy, would come the noise of engines springing into life, and the deafening roar of gunfire. The decks of the enemy craft would be swept with fire, and, at the same time, three or four MGBs would flash across the bows of the convoy, turn sharply in a shower of spray, and come down the line of the convoy from the front and on the seaward side. The panicking enemy gun crews would swing their guns shoreward at the first sound of life, then find the enemy on their other side. By the time the schooners' guns were round again to face the foe, the leading MGB would be abreast of the rearmost E-boat and covering it with deadly fire. The centre MGB would swing in to board a schooner, and the rearmost MGB would concentrate its fire onto the leading E-boat. Luck invariably favoured the attackers, and with their first well aimed burst of fire, one of the schooners and one of the E-boats was usually sunk. By the time they were round on the seaward side of the convoy, the second E-boat was often sinking. As soon as one of the E-boats was destroyed, a second MGB would be freed to join the first in boarding one of the enemy schooners, while the third MGB would finish off the second E-boat and then stand off to watch fair play.

The Commando boarding party for such attacks usually consisted of one officer and six men. At a word from the bridge, they would leap up from the MGB deck and jump on the enemy craft alongside, shouting and brandishing their weapons. They seldom had to fight, for the frightened German crews were only too eager to surrender. Sometimes the boarded enemy craft would be found in a sinking condition. A quick search to round up prisoners and seize the ship's papers would be carried out, then back on to the MGBs would climb the boarding party, often to board the next schooner in the convoy a few minutes later. Only the superb seamanship of the MGB crews in keeping their craft alongside the sinking schooners prevented any of the boarding parties from ever going down with a sinking schooner.[10]

Such was the success of this type of operation, that during the month of April 1944 alone, seven schooners were captured and a further 28 enemy craft sunk.

During this time, the Partisans, assisted by the Royal Navy, carried out a number of successful raids on their own, and in May further reinforcements arrived on Vis, including No 40 (RM) Commando, now once again up to strength. No 9 Commando, which had found replacements in the same way as No 2, took little longer to become operational and remained at Molfetta for the time being. May, like April, was marked by reconnaissance of the islands, but plans to raid the northern islands of Uljan and Pasman, in view of the distance involved, had to be cancelled. Instead, it was decided to go for the slightly closer target of Mljet. Operation Farrier was launched by Nos 2 and 43 (RM) Commando on 22 May, after a.48 hour postponement because of the weather, but proved abortive. Little sign of the enemy was found, and the force was re-embarked. No 43 had a particularly frustrating time, scaling mountains and hacking through undergrowth. 'Scarcely a man had a pair of denims left, so much had the bush ripped them about, and in many cases there were no soles left on the felt soled boots worn by the Commando, because of the sharp rocks, on the mountains, had cut them to pieces.'[11] Nine men were also missing, although a rescue party sent back a few days later did find three of them who had temporarily joined the Partisans. The others had been either killed or captured.

At the end of May, Tom Churchill returned on a short visit to England in order to brief the Special Service Group on the activities of his brigade, and left brother Jack in command. At the same time, on 26 May, news came through that the Germans had launched a major offensive against Tito and his forces in Bosnia. All but trapped, the Partisans fought fanatically and managed to break through the German ring, but the situation was still desperate and Tito sent an urgent request to both Allied Forces Headquarters (AFHQ) and Commander Cerni on Vis for a large scale diversion to be mounted in Dalmatia in order to take some of the pressure off him. On the 29th, the Chief Staff Officer of Force 266* arrived on Vis and, after discussions with Jack Churchill and the Partisan leaders, it was decided to mount an attack against Brac under the codename of *Flounced.* It was hoped that not only would this prevent the Germans reinforcing Bosnia from Dalmatia, but also force them to reinforce the islands from the mainland. As for the immediate objective, this was the destruction of the German garrison, believed to be of regimental size (some 1200 men with artillery), on Brac. The main enemy position was in the centre of the island, south-east of Nerezisce, and consisted of a number of mutually supporting strongpoints, each on a hill top. An OP on the highest hill on the island covered the whole of the south coast of the island, and there was another series of strongpoints on the eastern tip of the island. Finally, a force of 280 men defended the port of Supetar on the north coast.

The plan, the joint product of the British and Partisans, was for two forces to be landed by schooner on the night D-2/D-1. One, consisting of a company of 2nd Highland Light Infantry, part of the British garrison on Vis, and some twenty Partisans, would be responsible for eliminating the dominant OP on the following night. Once this had been achieved, the main landing would take place. The second group, 400 Partisans, would contain and then attack the enemy force in Supetar, thus preventing any reinforcement of the main position from the north. Then, on the night D-1/D Day, three landings would take place on the south-west corner of the island. These would be carried out by No 43 (RM) Commando, with Heavy Weapons Troop of No 40 under command, 1300 Partisans of the 13 Brigade, a rifle troop of No 40 to act as porters and a troop from the Raiding Support Regiment with two captured Italian 47/32 antitank guns. Under the joint command of HQ 2 SS Brigade, with Jack Churchill in charge, and HQ 26 Partisan Division, they were to destroy the main enemy position in the centre of the island. Simultaneously, 1400 Partisans would take care of the enemy on the eastern end of the island. Some artillery was to be landed with both these forces and air support would be available. D-Day was fixed for 2 June.

The two advanced parties landed unobserved on the night 31

---

*This had been formed in view of the increased military commitment in the Adriatic, as an off shoot of Force 133.

May/1 June and moved into position. The attack on the OP ran into trouble when the enemy became alerted while the HLI were breaching a minefield in front of it. Heavy fire broke out and the attackers were beaten back, leaving two officers wounded in the middle of the minefield. A second assault succeeded in rescuing them, but got no further, and a third attack seemed pointless, especially since the main force was now landing and was not under artillery fire. They therefore contented themselves with harassing the OP garrison in order to neutralise it. The Partisans in the north had slightly more success, quickly capturing an enemy position south-west of Supetar and completing a tight ring around the port. Efforts to break into it, however, proved fruitless.

At first light, the RAF put in attacks on the main position and Supetar with rocket firing Hurricanes. Following this, No 43 (RM) Commando set out to attack the northernmost of the strongpoints of the main position, Pt 542. Like the HLI, they were foiled by a minefield, as were the Partisans, who were approaching it from another direction. One problem found was that the limited artillery support was not sufficient to support two simultaneous attacks, and so it was agreed that the Partisans should attack Pts 648 and 622 immediately to the south in the morning, while No 43 and one of the Partisan battalions had another attempt on Pt 542 in the afternoon. In the meantime, the HLI company was reinforced by a Partisan company, who made another attack, gallant but unsuccessful, on the OP. The RAF were then called in, and the position finally taken. It is significant that the garrison was found to be only twenty men, but the strength of the concrete defences and skilled siting of the minefield had caused them to seem many times this number.

Air attacks also preceded the Partisan attacks on Pts 648 and 622, but, although they overran two outposts, wire and mines again proved their undoing. The same happened to No 43's attack on Pt 542, and further Partisan attacks that night were also unsuccessful. By now, reinforcements had been called for from Vis, and they landed in the shape of three more troops of No 40 under Lt Colonel Manners, 300 Partisans and two 25 pdr guns, in the early hours of the 3rd. The only bright spot in the proceedings was the fact that the Partisans in the east had enjoyed some considerable success, capturing or killing a large number of the enemy, and by midday on the 3rd they had the remainder bottled up in the town of Sumartin.

In the meantime, Jack Churchill went on a long reconnaissance, and that afternoon a fresh plan was formulated for dealing with the main position. Nos 40 and 43 (RM) Commandos would attack Pt 622 at dusk, while the Partisans harassed Pts 542 and 648. The Commandos would then similarly support the Partisans onto the two last-named objectives. Problems in communication now arose. No 43 deciphered their radio orders to read that they alone were to make the attack with Partisan support on the flanks. Meanwhile, one of Churchill's staff officers, Captain Wakefield, with a guide from No 40, was sent to brief Lt Colonel Manners.

No 43 (RM) Commando began their attack under supporting artillery fire as planned at 2030 hours. They got through the minefield using Bangalore torpedoes and reached the top of the hill shortly before 2200 hours. They had, however suffered several casualties from fire from both flanks, in spite of the plan that the Partisans should suppress this. Almost immediately, they were heavily counter-attacked and lost touch with B Troop on the right. With no wireless communication to Brigade HQ, steadily mounting casualties and concern that further counter-attacks from the flanks would cut off his retreat, Lt Colonel Simmonds decided to withdraw. B Troop, however, had never even reached the objective, being held up by a suspected minefield, and No 43's withdrawal took them far to the left of No 40. In the meantime, unaware of all this, Jack Churchill had run across 'Pops' Manners at 2030 hours and discovered the Captain Wakefield had not met up with him.

I told Col Manners to collect his Commando, as there was an attack by 43 at 9.0 p.m. and his people were the reserve for this attack. We met again as arranged and I guided the Cmdo to the starting line. On the way we met Captain Wakefield and his guide who had hopelessly lost the way. They were both very tired from wandering about the island all the afternoon.

Close to the starting line we halted and sat on the ground. The hill could be seen clearly in the moonlight – several small fires were burning on it, where the gorse or scrub had been set alight by the artillery bombardment. I explained the situation and plan, but added that as we were so late (1½ hours) we might have no fight. 43 Cmdo, by this time, were probably already going up the hill, and in any case might not need us – we were the reserve elm.

Some machine-gun fire went over our heads at this time, but hit no-one. It was the usual German intimidation fire, and was shot off at random. After I had given everyone the general picture and plan, Col Manners gave the officers certain detailed orders. We then advanced towards the hill, descending into the crossing a wide shallow valley. We tried to make a wireless contact with Col Simonds but failed.

At the foot of hill 633 our leading troop ran into 43 Cmdo [B Troop]. On hearing this Col Manners and I went forward and heard from an officer of 43 that they had been held up by mortar fire and mines.

The 81mm mortar fire did not seem to me severe enough to prevent a further advance, and on enquiring about the minefields I learnt that (a) no-one had been blown up and (b) No-one had found a mine. Furthermore it looked to me as though the advance was really being delayed by a simple fence (two strands of barbed wire) of the type that often surrounds minefields to prevent one's own troops from straying on to them.

There were a number of shouts of 'mine' from men of 40 Cmdo, so I sent Capt Pirie R.E. No 2 S.S. Brigade to investigate.

In the meantime, I told the officer of 43, that 40 Cmdo would attack straight up the hill, that his troop was to do the same on our right, and that my orders to Col Simmonds, with whom he said he was in touch, were to press on up the hill immediately, with his Commando, and to ignore the minefields. These I thought were of the trip-wire variety – probably not very deep, and, I hoped would not cause series losses. We were now about 2 hrs late. 43 were on the right of 40 at the bottom of the hill. Captain Pirie returned to say that no mines had been found and that the alarm was due to the suspect minefield fence.

I organised 40 in subsection single file – 4 single files to each troop – two troops abreast, A and Y in front and Q in the rear – thus:-

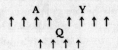

Bayonets were fixed and rifle magazines loaded with 10 rounds. I led a file of Y Troop. We crossed the wire, and I blew my pipes up the hill. There was a certain amount of mortar-fire, but I did not see or hear any obvious mine explosions. About half-way up the hill Y Troop formed line. We passed out of the mortar fire area and came under small arms fire. Two posts were assaulted, one an L.M.G. position. About 5 Germans were allowed to surrender. Y Troop, 40 Cmdo were magnificent, all in line, and shouting and firing from the hip as if on an assault course at Achnacarry. The top of the hill was soon cleared, some Germans taking to their heels in the darkness. The success signal, two green very lights was shot off as arranged. No success signals had been seen from the neighbouring hills – those being attacked by the Partisans.

We took up defensive positions, but it was evident that there were not many men on the hill-top. Col Manners moved over to the left of the summit, while I went to the right, to supervise the consolidation and try to discover the whereabouts of 43. We tried, but failed, to contact them on the wireless. Col Manners and I met again a few minutes later, neither having found 43.

Shortly afterwards, I moved off again to speak to Q Troop Commander and give him his defence area on the hill-top. When about 40 yards away he called out that he'd been hit and an artery cut. I ran across, to find that his left arm had been badly smashed. I stopped the bleeding with a tourniquet made from my handkerchief, and dragged him over to where Roger Wakefield was already lying, badly wounded.

Enemy fire was now fairly heavy, from 47mm mortars, rifles, grenades and machine-guns. I sent 2 Marines to bring up Q Troop, 40 R.M.C. and to try and find 43 R.M.C. I also told Corporal Verri to go back a little way down the hill to a more sheltered position, and make further efforts to contact 43, and Brigade HQ on his wireless set. He was to ask Major Blake to have artillery fire put down on the further slopes of the hill, which we would observe.

This reduced my post to 6 including Col Manners, Captain Wakefield, and a wounded Marine.

Enemy fire was now heavy, and a counter-attack seemed imminent. I was distressed to find that everyone was armed with revolvers, except myself, who had an American carbine. Colonel Manners was firing his revolver, as were some of the men. A mortar-bomb fell among us and killed Capt Wakefield and 2 Marines and wounded another. Soon Col Manners was hit again, this time through the right shoulder. While I was trying to remove his equipment and small pack, a Marine – I think Mne Wood of the Intelligence section – suddenly joined me, and asked, 'Can I help you Sir?' While helping me to remove the Colonel's equipment, he was shot through the head. About 20-30 enemy advanced towards us, but were stopped by rapid fire, and took cover perhaps 75 yds away. Some men on our flanks began to withdraw, but we shouted to them to stay. A small post to our left rear was holding well and firing, and called back. I believe Lt Beadle of Y Troop was commanding it.

I rolled over onto my back, and played 'Will ye no' come back again', on the pipes, to indicate that we still held the hill-top, and hoping to attract 43. Soon afterwards we heard shouts, and D Troop 43 under Capt Blake put in a timely appearance nearby. Our position was growing precarious.

The revolver ammunition was finished, but I still had one magazine (15 rounds) for the carbine. The enemy now appeared to have got round our right flank. The small arms fire was very severe, and the dead and wounded in my post were continually being hit. Col Manners was the only one still conscious.

Finally there was a flurry of grenades and a fragment cut a furrow in my helmet, slightly cutting my scalp, and stunning me. This must have preceded the assault, as on coming to, I found German soldiers prodding us, apparently to discover who was alive.

Shortly afterwards 4 Marines, including 2 wounded were brought along and the 5 of us were taken to the BnH.Q. dugout. We were not allowed to carry any of our wounded, but the Germans said they would be collected after their own troops had been brought in. We were put in a pit 10ft deep, with a petrol engine driving a small dynamo, at the bottom, and our numbers increased to 13.

Before dawn the Germans were out of their trenches re-camouflaging everything with gorse and scrub. The wounded and dead were collected, and we were led down the back of the hill, and into a very small stone hut. Later in the morning the unwounded prisoners were taken out to collect further casualties. At midday our last prisoner Cpl Verri joined us – he had been captured at dawn. He had not retreated with the remainder of the British force, but stayed with his wireless set, under shelter of a rock, trying to make wireless contact.[12]

Sadly, 'Pops' Manners died of his wounds a couple of days later. The remainder of No 40 and B Troop of No 43 withdrew under Major Maude to the start line, and there met up with No 43. Because of the atmospheric conditions, news of the failure of the attack did not reach Brigade HQ until 0300 hours. Alf Blake, the Brigade Major, automatically assumed temporary command and sent a message to Simonds asking him to come and take over, as the senior British officer left. He then set about establishing the number of casualties suffered by both Commandos. Ten officers and 41 other ranks were killed or missing and six and 70 wounded. The HLI company had 16 casualties and the Partisans some 260.

Given this information on his arrival at Brigade HQ, Simonds conferred with the Partisan commander, and Lieutenant Webb RNR, the naval representative, and they decided that, in view of the fierce German resistance, it was unlikely that they would be able to destroy the German garrison without unacceptable further numbers of casualties. In any event, it was very likely that the enemy would bring in reinforcements. Withdrawal of the force would therefore take place that day. In fact, this had already been organised the previous night when Captain Keep, Adjutant of No 2 Commando, had been sent across by Brigadier Miles, who was following events on Vis, to confer with Jack Churchill on the situation. Keep, having reported back to Miles, had then returned with two troops from his own Commando and thirty additional porters from No 40 in order to help in the withdrawal. This went smoothly, assisted by the Hurricanes of No 242 Group RAF, who provided cover throughout and the efficiency of the Royal Navy. Keep, with two other officers and 12 men of

No 2, remained behind on Brac to try and establish the fate of those missing. After much excitement and several brushes with the enemy, as well as an attempt by a party from No 40 (RM) Commando to help in a possible rescue, they all eventually returned empty-handed to Vis on 11 June.

On the surface, *Flounced* appeared to have been little short of a disaster, but, although not immediately apparent, it did succeed in making the Germans draw troops off Tito and send them to the coast.

At this time there was a reorganisation of the Allied Forces in the Adriatic. By now an airfield had been built on Vis, which meant that more effective air support to the Partisans in the Balkans. On the other hand, the size of the Vis garrison was becoming a distraction to Force 266. It was therefore decided that the Air Forces would take the lead in the Adriatic and a new command, the Balkan Air Force, was formed. The land element became a subsidiary command to it, and was called Land Forces Adriatic, with Brigadier G.M.O. Davey CBE DSO being appointed to command it. His first step was to summon Ronnie Tod across to Vis to take temporary command of the garrison until Tom Churchill's return on 21 June. Before this, there had been an important event when, on 13 June, Tito arrived on Vis, having been collected from the mainland by a British destroyer. For a few days his whereabouts on the island were kept secret, but then, on Tom Churchill's return, he gave a lunch party for the British and Partisan commanders. What was vital, however, was that now Tito had appeared to have sought the protection of the British, the defence of Vis became paramount once more. As far as offensive operations were concerned, *Flounced* had demonstrated that the Germans would prefer to die than fall prisoner, and another intensive propaganda campaign was mounted on the islands, which began to bear fruit. In terms of raids, the emphasis was once more on reconnaissance, although the Raiding Support Regiment and the Americans did carry out some operations involving landing 75mm guns on the islands and bombarding enemy positions. For the Commandos, however, the pause was necessary since all three were badly in need of a rest.

Back on the mainland, No 9 Commando, now once more fully operational, had not been idle. On the night of 25/26 May, 75 men under Major M.R.H. Allen MC, the second-in-command, took part in an operation to rescue Allied prisoners of war. They were to sail from Termoli in an LCI to a point some thirty miles south of Ancona and seventy miles north of the Allied lines. Here they were to rendezvous with agents of A Force, who were responsible for handling escaped prisoners of war, and act as a protection party, after being guided in by a US Navy 'Beach Jumper Party' (the equivalent of the RN Commandos). After an initial navigation error, this was successfully achieved and 120 ex-prisoners were evacuated. The success of *Darlington 11* prompted A Force to consider a more adventurous operation. Popski's Private Army was to land with their jeeps in the same area and create havoc on the German lines of communication, and then withdraw. No 9 Commando were called on once more to provide the protection party for the landing, this time under Captain M. Long MC.

The party set sail in an LCT from Manfredonia on the evening of 14 June. Contact was made with the A Force agents ashore, who reported much traffic using the coast road. It was therefore decided that it would be too risky to try to use the jeeps and the party was therefore to be re-embarked. Unfortunately the LCT could not unbeach, being hard aground, and all had to swim to the escorting ML. The LCT was abandoned and destroyed with delayed action limpet mines, and the party then returned to Manfredonia in an overladen ML.

On 1 July Lt Colonel R.W. Sankey DSC RM assumed command of No 40 (RM) Commando, which was still very much under strength after *Flounced*. No 2 Commando had also become somewhat stale after its lone sojourn on Vis, and so it was decided that both should return to the mainland. They initially went back to Molfetta, and then to Monopoli, where Land Forces Adriatic had a camp. While No 2 Commando, now under Lt Col F.W. Fynn MC of Fynn Force fame,* began preparation for operations in Albania, No 40, on 15th August, were sent to Malta for two months retraining and re-equipment. Another who left at the same time was Admiral Sir Walter Cowan. Distressed by the loss of jack Churchill and 'Pops' Manners, he decided to return to England, but not before his parting was marked with a salute of guns and Commando and Partisan Guards of Honour.† This left 2 SS Brigade HQ and No 43, along with the other units from all three services and the Americans, on Vis. During

---

* He had been 2ic of the Commando at the time of Jack Churchill's capture.
† This was not quite Sir Walter's last contact with the Commandos. In March 1945 he visited HQ 30 Assault Unit and insisted on being shown the Rhine so that he could relieve himself in its waters to demonstrate his contempt for the Nazi regime.

this month, No 43 mounted a very successful little operation on Hvar. On 1 July, Major Hudspith MC went across with a small party to study the movements of a well known German patrol which operated in the area of the village of Docomolje. As a result of his information, Lt Colonel Simonds took three of the troops across on the 11th with the intention of ambushing it.

> After landing ambush positions were taken up round the village. The next morning at the expected time of the patrol a thick mist had descended rendering visibility nil. The enemy patrol of about thirty managed to slip through between the Troop and the first information of their presence was when the Medical Officer, Captain R.W. BAZE-LEY RAMC was captured with his RAP. However, it was not long before the Commando realised this and descended on the village with great vigour. The enemy prepared to defend themselves in the houses but were quickly evicted. The MO states that he would rather be attacked by The Germans than suffer another attack by the 'Banshee and Bayo-net' methods of the Commando; he also claimed that he recaptured his own RAP after escaping and running the gauntlet of several Schmeiss-ers. Capt CLARKE RM and Capt M.R. NUNNS RM were both wounded when charging Spandaus in houses. Capt Nunns managing to get a direct hit with a grenade on a spandau in the window of a house. Sgt FRENCH, whose prowess before and since with the Tommy Gun from the hip is legend, won a very fine MM. He chased a great lumbering German for hundreds of yards before bringing him down. The patrol was accounted for in quick time, and after burying the enemy dead, we brought eighteen prisoners back to Vis, the Navy bringing the force back, crammed in MTBs.[13]

In the middle of the month a long term reconnaissance patrol was also sent to Korcula. Sadly, at the end of the month, Lt Colonel Simonds was posted back to England. His place was taken by Lt Col-onel McAlpine, who, after being evacuated sick from Tunisia when in command of No 6, had been sent to the USA, from where he had agitated strongy to get back to the Commandos.

On 12 August, HQ 2 SS Brigade was ordered to return to the mainland in order to begin planning for a new operation with Land Forces Adriatic, leaving just No 43 to represent the Commandos on Vis. They were, however, kept busy with a number of reconnais-sances and drawing up plans for operations, the majority of which never came off. Then, on 11th September came news that the Ger-mans were withdrawing from Brac, and it was decided to land and catch the last two remaining garrisons on the island. The Partisans landed at Supetar once more, but failed to prevent the Germans there from slipping away by sea to Split.

No 43, meanwhile, secured the mountains in the north-west of the island, and then the fighting moved to the south-west corner, where the garrison there resisted stubbornly for a week before surrendering. At least, it vindicated the memory of those who had fallen or been made prisoner during *Flounced*. On their return to Vis on 15 September, they were ordered to mount a similar attack on Solta, this time on their own. The defences on this island were as formidable as those on Brac, and again much trouble was experienced with mines. Nevertheless, persistence and determination won through, and after five days of fighting, the enemy garrison attempted, on the night 22/23 September to escape to Split by lighter and E-boat. Lt Commander Giles's craft were waiting for them, and only one third got through, the rest being destroyed. Next day, the final mopping up was completed and Solta came securely under British control. The last operation mounted from Vis, *Blue Pencil*, was an attempt by Lieutenant Preston's troop to negotiate the surrender of the German garrison on Uljan. After a week's efforts these broke down, and they returned to Vis on 8 October. At the same time, Lt Colonel McAlpine had another bout of the malaria which had laid him low in Tunisia, and had to be evacuated, command passing temporarily to Major Munro. In the middle of October, the Commando was ordered back to the mainland.

The period on Vis was for Sir Alfred Blake 'the most fascinating experience of my war'[14] and for Stan Buckmaster something 'that I suspect few of us would have missed'[15]. This echoes the views of all Commandos who served there, to whom I have talked. Coming especially after the frustrations of being used as little more than ordinary infantry on the mainland, the opportunities to carry out traditional style Commando raiding operations, and the added interest of operating with the Partisans, as well as being on a relatively 'free rein', came as a refreshing contrast. Undoubtedly, the joint operations with the Partisans first stopped the Germans from overrunning all the Dalmatian Islands, reduced pressure of the mainland Partisans at a crucial time and forced the enemy first to relax and then begin to abandon his hold on Dalmatia. The role that 2 SS Brigade played was remembered by the Yugoslavs for many years, and the many ex-Commandos who served on Vis and revisited in the years since the war were always made warmly welcome.

Albania

The operation for which No 2 Commando began planning on their return from Vis at the beginning of July 1943 was directed at Albania. The Partisans here were desperately in need of additional arms. The idea, therefore, was to open up the coastline in the Mirara area, south of the Linguetta Peninsula, and use this as a beachhead through which supplies could be passed. In order to do this, the German garrison at Spilje had to be destroyed, and this was the primary task facing No 2 Commando. The secondary aim, which could be achieved through the first, was to force the Germans to commit troops in an effort to recapture the area, and hopefully the Partisans would resist this. The garrison itself consisted of some 150 men, with the nearest enemy troops some six miles way. The troops selected for the operations were No 2 Commando complete (now 250 all ranks), a company of the HLI from Vis, about 180 men of the Raiding Support Regiment with four Italian 47mm anti-tank guns, six heavy machine guns and some 3in mortars, and 1 Mobile Protection Troop. No 9 Commando were to provide forty porters, No 40 a medical detachment and the LRDG would have twenty men for reconnaissance duties. Naval and air fire support would also be available.

Because the lay-out of the German defences meant that an unopposed landing could not be made close to the objective, a spot some four miles to the south was chosen. The attack was to be made at dawn, having made an approach march in darkness immediately after landing. Five hours were allowed for subduing the garrison, which meant that the withdrawal had to be done in daylight, making air cover essential at this stage. The LRDG and Force 266 Liaison Officers with the Partisans carried out the necessary preliminary reconnaissances, and the force embarked in LCIs at Monopoli at breakfast time on 28 July.

The landing went according to plan and LRDG and Force 266 representatives were met on the beach. Then began the approach march, which was marked by the barking of many dogs. It afterwards transpired that the Germans had received warning from Albanian Quislings two days before, and the dogs merely confirmed their suspicions. Nevertheless, the Commandos reached their battle positions without incident. Communications problems now arose because wireless sets were screened by trees, and this upset the fire programme. The heavy mortar teams were also fired on by a machine gun as they moved into position forcing them to drop their mortars and go to ground. In spite of these problems, the attack was launched, but the enemy proved resolute. Machine gun nests brought about a mounting toll of casualties, and the enemy positions could only be cleared slowly.

Finally, at 1030 hours, after a unsuccessful attempt to clean up a strongpoint near the garrison headquarters, Lt Colonel Fynn realised that he was running out of time and that he would not be able to complete that task in what little time was left. He therefore ordered a withdrawal. This was no easy task, with the exhaustion of the men and the number of wounded, and smoke and artillery had to be used to prevent the enemy following up. Yet, it was achieved without further loss and the force re-embarked and sailed back to Monopoli.

Operation *Healing II* seemed to have been only partially success-ful, and casualties had been high – 20 killed or missing, of whom three members of No 2 joined the Partisans temporarily until they could be evacuated to Italy, and sixty wounded. Yet Colonel Fynn could take comfort in a letter received from Brigadier Davey:

> I congratulate you on the excellent work done by you and the troops under your command in the HIMARA operation. Thanks to your care-ful planning and their very gallant fighting against a determined enemy and some objectionable Albanian quislings (some of whom were killed) the operation was a complete success. The object was the destruction of a German garrison. We know that it consisted of good German troops. You accounted for most of these, and the only remaining Germans were yesterday rounded up by the partisans, who now control the coastal belt in that area. Your casualties were not light, but against them you must measure the set-back the enemy has suffered morally and materi-ally in Albania. Then you will realise the extent of your achievement. Your No 2 Commando has maintained and enhanced its already great reputation, and I should be grateful if you would convey my thanks to every member of it for his collective and individual part in a successful battle, the results of which are out all proportion to the size of the Force engaged.[16]

The only operation mounted during August 1944 was *Gradient 1*, which was carried out by No 9 Commando. This was designed to interfere with enemy shipping in the northern Adriatic, by destroy-ing the swing bridge linking the islands of Lussino Piccolo and Lus-sino Grande. This would mean that shipping plying between Istria and Yugoslavia would have to take a longer route, and if the ships went south, they would be in range of Allied naval forces at Ancona. The operation was mounted from this port, with 109 members of No

9 sailing in three MTBs and an MGB. While one party was to seize and demolish the bridge, a second equipped with bicycles was to attack and destroy a nearby garrison. The operation took place on the night of 9/10 August. The bridge was captured without a fight, with two Italian guards being taken prisoner, but there was no sign of the garrison, and so the bicycle party destroyed the telephone exchange and equipment and brought back documents and some civilians for questioning to the bridge, which was destroyed. On the return trip to Ancona, they picked up an American pilot who had been adrift for a week in the Adriatic.

A number of plans were considered and drawn up by Land Forces Adriatic and 2 SS Brigade, but most were cancelled. There was an idea to seize the island of Molat in the Northern Adriatic and turn it into another Vis. *Workbasket* was a plan to destroy the German garrison on Korcula, and Tom Churchill even carried out a personal reconnaissance of the island before this was scrapped. Then, No 2 Commando were to attack the Ljogara Pass in Albania, but this was postponed indefinitely after another reconnaissance had been mounted. No 9 Commando, however, were given the task of destroying a radar station on the island of Kithera at the southern tip of Greece. A reconnaissance party parachuted in on the night of 10/11 September, and discovered that the Germans had left the day before. This gave the opportunity to establish a naval base there for operations against German shipping in the Aegean, and No 9 Commando were landed on the island on 17 September to begin what would be a period of five and a half months in Greece, of which more later. The main problem, however, with operations on the Balkan coast at this time was that the Germans had reinforced their positions, because of previous Commando operations, and most of the likely beaches were now defended by concrete strongpoints, which, given the paucity of forces available, made most projected operations very risky. Nevertheless, the opportunity to put thought into action did come again towards the end of September.

After the Spilje operation, the Albanian Partisans had succeeded in holding onto their beachhead. They now wanted to expand it by capturing Borsch, which would also provide them with a useful small port. There was a snag to this, in that the Germans maintained a strong garrison at Sarande, which was able to react quickly to any movement on Borsch. It was therefore agreed that No 2 Commando should land north of this town, carry out demolitions on the Sarande-Delvine road and generally keep the garrison contained, while the

Partisans carried out their operation. The idea was that the Commandos should be withdrawn after 36 hours, by which time it was thought that the Partisans' position would be secure and that they would be able to take out Sarande themselves and thereby isolate the German garrison on the island of Corfu.

Accompanied by Tom Churchill and elements of the Raiding Support Regiment with their heavy weapons, No 2 Commando landed on the night of 21/22 September. A small reconnaissance party had gone across two days earlier and having very nearly been surprised by a German foraging party, which in turn was ambushed by the Partisans, they had established that the German garrison in Sarande was about 500 strong, with that at Delvine to the north-east having as many as 1,200 men. They also seemed to be well equipped with heavy weapons. Furthermore, the Germans had now withdrawn from Borsch. It was therefore a question of what to do now. Sarande was the obvious objective and, in view of the enemy force, the Partisans would still require Commando help in order to capture this. Churchill and Fynn therefore decided that No 2 should first seize the high ground overlooking Commando Valley, which adjoined the landing beach, and then patrol the area beyond the block the Sarande-Borsch and Sarande-Delvine roads with demolitions. In the meantime, Churchill would return to Italy in order to bring across further reinforcements.

No 2 quickly discovered the main problem, the physical nature of the country:

Maps and air photographs had already revealed the high mountains rising steeply from the shore to over 2,000 feet, intersected with sharply defined valleys filled with thick woods and tangled bushes. But neither the maps nor the photographs had shown the difficulties of moving about in this country. Not only were the woods extremely thick, but there were very few paths through them, and no reasonably easy means of keeping direction. The mountains were not only high and rocky, but their surface was so uneven that anybody working there was in constant danger of breaking an ankle. In parts, the surface consisted of innumerable pointed rock projections about nine inches high and six inches apart, so that one either had to walk from rock point to rock point, in which case the points hurt one's feet even through army boots, or else step between the rock points, in which case one's feet invariably got stuck between two pieces of rock. In either case, walking was painful and dangerous, but yet men had to carry equipment, food and ammunition over these rocky surfaces, for no mule could traverse such ground. So first it was thought that the dry beds of the streams and rivulets in the valleys would assist movement, but in most cases this was found to be untrue, for huge boulders blocked one's path, and matted undergrowth forced one to crawl or abandon the river bed.[17]

It would therefore take a little while before the Commandos could get themselves in a position to begin offensive operations. In the meantime, Brigadier Churchill briefed Brigadier George Davey and arranged for No 40 (RM) Commando, with another Raiding Support Regiment troop, to join No 2. Brigadier Davey also realised that, since the Germans were now beginning to evacuate Greece, the capture of Sarande was even more significant in that it would mean that the garrison on the island of Corfu would be entirely cut off. No 40 (RM) Commando landed on the night of 24/25 September, and a number of reconnaissances were made, although often frustrated by the going and enemy artillery, and liaison was set up with the Partisans. Matters improved slightly when a battery of 25 pounders of 111 Field Regiment RA was landed on the 28th, but the Germans brought up heavier guns, and continued to dominate the area by fire. Even worse, there was a period of heavy and persistent rain. Lack of dry clothing and exposure meant that, by 2 October, only a third of the force could be considered fit to fight. Trench foot and other ailments had caused 130 to be evacuated back to Italy, while another 200 were lying sick in the beachhead. Finally, the Royal Navy came up with a solution, which was to make LCIs available so that the troops could rest, have a hot shower, wash and dry their clothes and have a properly cooked hot meal, in itself a welcome contrast to the 24 hour ration packs in which they had been subsisting. The weather began to improve as well, and by 6 October preparations could resume for the attack on Sarande.

The overall plan was for the main attack to come through the mountains from the north, while diversions were made from the south and east, as well as against Delvine. In order to overcome the enemy's superiority in artillery, destroyers and LCGs were brought in, and further reinforcements in the shape of No 1 Parachute Company of the RAF Levies. Pioneers and medical personnel had also by now arrived. The Pioneers, in particular were a godsend in that they could now relieve the Commandos of the onerous task of humping supplies up to the forward positions. The enemy, meanwhile, apart from desultory artillery fire, and one or two reconnaissance patrols, remained inactive, being more concerned over the evacuation of the Corfu garrison, which was passing back through Sarande and

Delvine on its way north into Yugoslavia and Greece. In terms of troops to tasks, the main attack would be carried out by Nos 2 and 40, with 200 Partisans operating on the left of No 2 on the Sarande-Delvine road. The RAF Levies were to land south of Sarande, in order to carry out a diversionary attack, while 300 Partisans attacked Delvine from the north. A small party was to also seize and hold a bridge on the Sarande-Delvine road.

On 8 October the troops deployed to their positions, and that night the diversionary operations were mounted.

> Dawn the following morning and our guns and mortars got down a barrage while the Commando [No 40] moved in. 43 Cdo [sic-No 2 Cdo] could be heard firing in the mountains on our left flank, and withering machine gun fire pinned down our attack in open ground at the approaches to the town. Captain 'Jock' Angus crawled back, under fire, and reported that concentrated Spandau fire was coming from a large building covered with red crosses. After brief thought, Lt Col R.W. Sankey called for shell and mortar fire to be brought down on the building; the effect was immediate; the Spandaus ceased to chatter: At the same time a German gun battery, on the inland flank of the town, ceased fire. 43 Cdo [No 2] had moved in closing the jaws of the pincers. We, No 40 RM, Cdo were soon firmly established in the town and, by mid-afternoon it was over, with hundreds of prisoners captured and the town formally surrendered.[18]

A considerable amount of equipment was captured, including twenty artillery guns, a ferry and various other craft, some still loaded with stores from Corfu. The Germans, however, as it was quickly discovered, had booby-trapped many of the houses, and it was only thanks to the alertness of Lieutenant D.G. McNab of the Royal New Zealand Engineers that nobody was caught in the delayed action explosions, which virtually destroyed the centre of the town in the next few days. To round off what had been a highly successful operation, especially when the initial difficulties were taken into account, the Germans evacuated Delvine on the 12th, which was immediately occupied by the Partisans, while on the same day, the remainder of the garrison on Corfu surrendered, and the island was occupied by 40 (RM) Commando.

The aftermath of *Mercerised* was not so happy. Land Forces Adriatic now decided that 2 SS Brigade should follow up the Germans during their retreat northwards through Albania. Given the nature of the terrain, the fact that the Germans would obviously blow all the bridges in the wake of their retreat, and the brigade possessed no mechanical transport in Albania, this seemed to Churchill to be wholly impracticable proposition. His remonstrations were, alas, to no avail, and in the end he offered his resignation as Brigade Commander, which was accepted. Tom Churchill had commanded 2 SS Brigade for over a year. During this time, as we have seen, it had been highly successful, and much of this was due to Churchill himself, both in his leadership and his imaginative planning. He had never been afraid to lead from the front, and had been an inspiration to all. It was indeed a sad way to have to leave the brigade, but his integrity could not have been illustrated in a better way.

The force in Albania, excluding No 40 (RM) Commando, who remained on Corfu, was now ordered to return to Italy. On its return, Ronnie Tod was summoned across from Greece to take over command of the brigade.

Greek Interlude

No 9 Commando had been landed on the island of Kithera on 17 September. They made up the bulk of what was called *Foxforce*, which included elements of the LRDG, SBS and Raiding Support Regiment, and later some Sappers and 350 men of the Greek Sacred Heart Regiment. Ronnie Tod was in overall command, and his initial task was to guard the naval base at Avlemon, on the eastern end of the island. This was soon moved to Kapsali, on the south-west corner, because communications, accommodation and the prevailing wind were more favourable. Within a few days, however, he received a new directive.

With the Germans now beginning to withdraw from Greece, Headquarters Middle East began to set up a scheme, Operation *Manna*, to send Allied troops to the Greek mainland, especially to Athens, once the Germans had left. In support of this, Tod was now ordered by Land Forces Adriatic to do what he could to hasten German withdrawal from the Peloponnese and follow the retreating Germans up the Aegean. Furthermore, he was to secure the approaches to the port of Piraeus so that relief convoys could use it. A number of exploratory patrols, mainly LRDG and SBS, were sent to the islands, to establish what the exact situation was, and by 24 September, these had found that, apart from Corinth, the enemy had withdrawn from the Peloponnese, leaving Greek security battalions to maintain law and order in the towns. It was now that Foxforce found itself embroiled in what would eventually become the Greek Civil War.

By this time, there were three main resistance groups in Greece, two, EAM and ELAS, its military wing, were controlled by the Greek Communist Party, while the third EDES, although anti-monarchial, was noncommunist. The first indications of the unrest lying below the surface were seen on Kithera, where HQ *Foxforce* was constantly besieged by individuals who were full of malicious tales about one another. *Foxforce* was entirely unprepared and ill equipped to be involved in what was clearly an internal political arena. Ronnie Tod, however, quickly realised the impending threat of civil war between the communists and non-communists and did all in his power to prevent this from happening. On the mainland, ELAS, the main guerrilla group, quickly attempted to seize the towns as the Germans left, and were quite prepared to butcher the security battalions left in them. The Allied Military Mission realised that this would precipitate the civil war, now asked *Foxforce* to help. Accordingly, Tod and seventy men went to the mainland and, assisted by the Swedish Red Cross, managed to prevent bloodshed, arranging for the security battalions to be imprisoned on the island of Spetsai for their own safety.

The Germans, even though they had evacuated the Peloponnese, still retained a tight hold on most of the islands in the Aegean, as well as Crete. They did, however, evacuate Poros, and it was decided to move the naval base from Kithera to here, since it would enable the Royal Navy to operate more effectively in the Aegean, as well as being a better launching pad for *Manna*. Before leaving Kithera, in order to avert civil conflict, Tod arranged for the Partisan leaders, church and civil population to sign a document agreeing to uphold the Greek Government, keep the peace and not to deport any individual or faction.

The move to Poros took the Germans by surprise and triggered their withdrawal from both Pireaus and Athens. Even so, during the early days on the island, the threat of a German counter-attack was ever present. There was, too, the constant problem of the civilian population, especially as Poros was now flooded with refugees from the mainland. This was mainly as a result of the Caserta Agreement, which had been drawn up at the end of September by General Wilson in order to help avert civil war. Both EAM and EDES undertook to support the government of Papandreou, which in turn would come under the British. In return, the two resistance groups were allowed to retain areas of influence, and Poros bordered the area controlled by ELAS. The new arrivals in the island were those who felt threatened by ELAS, but there was little that *Foxforce* could do to immediately help them.

After various changes of plan, caused in the main by further evacuations of the islands by the Germans, *Manna* was finally mounted on 14 October. *Foxforce*'s objective was Piraeus and, after negotiating enemy minefields in the Gulf of Athens, they landed to a tumultuous welcome from the local people, the Germans having evacuated the port the day before. One troop was left to guard the airfield at Kalamaki, while the rest found themselves taking part in a parade in Athens to celebrate its liberation, and Tod was made a Freeman of the City. Along with 2 Parachute Brigade, *Foxforce* now found itself guarding vital installations in the capital. Then, within a few days, the SBS and LRDG left Tod's command, which was known as *Commandoforce*. He himself now returned to Italy to take over 2 SS Brigade, and Major M.R.H. Allen MC assumed command of No 9 Commando. At the end of October, the Commando moved to Salonika, where it undertook normal garrison duties, and on 1 December Lt Colonel J.M. Dunning-White arrived from the UK to take command. December, however, proved to be a tense month, with civil war now raging in Athens, but luckily, in spite of indications to the contrary, it did not spill over into Salonika, and, by the beginning of February 1945, the situation was quiet enough for the Commando to return to Italy.

No 40 (RM) Commando had experienced similar problems on Corfu. Initially, they were welcomed with open arms by the population, who saw their presence as a means of averting civil war. Under the Caserta Agreement, Corfu was EDES territory, but to show too much favour to this faction would merely incite EAM supporters to violence. Hence Sankey found himself walking a tightrope. He saw his priority in re-establishing the confidence of the local population in the Greek Government, and to this end divided the island in four, positioning elements of the Commando in each sector with the task of constantly showing the flag. There was also much to be done in identifying the minefields, booby traps and obstacles left by the Germans. Yet, Sankey could never feel confident that violence would not break out unless he took steps to disarm the Partisans. Since EDES was nominally in control, he allowed them to maintain one of their regiments, but wanted the remainder, together with the ELAS units, to hand in their arms. A series of meetings with the various factions during October resulted in deadlock, and in the end, on the 25th, Sankey had to act unilaterally. Disarmament was achieved without bloodshed, and from then on the threat of violence was considerably diminished, although political strife continued, especially when civil war broke out in Athens.

No 40's main task, however, was trying to get the island back onto a sound peacetime footing after the ravages of war. This meant combatting the problem of inflation and stamping out the inevitable Black Market, clearing up the physical damage and getting the public utilities working once more. In all this, the Commandos were helped by the local officials, but it was an unusual and daunting task, and very different from what they had been used to. On 10 November, the situation was favourable enough for the majority of the Commando to return to Italy, leaving just two troops under Major P.R. Matters RM on the island. The Allied Military Mission gradually took over the Commando's responsibilities, and Matters and his men joined up with the main body in Italy on 31 December.

It was to be but a few days before they returned once more to Corfu. By this time the build up of ELAS forces on the mainland, and a large number of Albanian troops at Sarande made the authorities on Corfu very nervous of attack. No 40 was therefore sent back on 10 January in order to help EDES troops guard against invasion. Internal unrest continued, and there were isolated incidents of violence, which the Commandos managed to contain by prompt action. By January 1945, it was generally realised that one step which had to be taken if peace was to come to Greece was to disband the politically motivated security forces and form a new force, the National Guard. Towards the end of February 1945, this was sufficiently organised to replace the EDES troops on the island, and the latter were disbanded. This task completed, No 40 (RM) Commando rejoined the rest of 2 Commando Brigade in Italy.

Both No 9 and No 40 (RM) Commandos had coped well with the difficult and unusual task which they had been given to them and it says much for the quality of the individual Commandos that they were able to prevent civil war in their respective areas of responsibility. Their experiences in peacetime reconstruction were to be a foretaste of what was to follow later in 1945, both in Europe and the Far East.

Montenegro

While No 2 and 40 (RM) Commandos had been busy in Albania, and No 9 in Greece, No 43 (RM) Commando had also been independently committed in the Balkans. They had returned from Vis to the mainland in mid-October 1944, but the German withdrawal from the Balkans meant that they had little opportunity to rest and recuperate after their eight months on Vis, and they immediately became involved in projected operations to harry the retreating Germans. Four operations were proposed and cancelled in as many days, but then on 21 October, the opportunity came.

The German XXI Mountain Corps was pulling back through the mountain fastnesses of Montenegro in Southern Yugoslavia. With the Yugoslav Partisans harrying them from in front and the Albanian Partisans from behind, the insertion of Allied troops could bring about a complete destruction of the corps. Land Forces Adriatic therefore hurriedly assembled a force composed of No 43, 111 Field Regiment RA, Raiding Support Regiment elements and an RAF Regiment Squadron, and these were sent across to Dubrovnik. One of the first things that the Commandos noticed was that the relatively carefree relationship which they had enjoyed with the Yugoslav Partisans on Vis was no longer. They had now come even more under the influence of Moscow, and the British were regarded with deep suspicion, it being made very clear that the liberation of the country would be carried out by the communists alone. Indeed, it was only with extreme reluctance that they agreed to what was called Floyd-force being sent in the first place, and then only because of their extreme lack of artillery.

At this time the Germans were attempting to move up the coast road from Risan and Ledinice towards Trebinje, and the Commandos' first task was to send a troop, C Troop, to escort a battery of 25 pdr guns to harass the coast road. Major General Loudon was the troop commander:

> Having left Dubrovnik C Troop and 211 Battery moved 30 miles inland to the small town of Viluse, then South to an area from which the guns could support the Partisans in the Ledinice area. At this time the German defences had the upper hand and the Partisan Dalmatian Brigade, brave as they were, could do little directly against them. It was of course impossible for the Germans to move away from their strong defended positions without being molested.
>
> The German main body was to the South and the troops we encountered were mainly concerned in keeping a supply route to the North open. In our immediate area the Germans at this time had a Battalion in Risan, supplied from Kotor, with a one or two company detachment in Ledinice. Ledinice again maintained outposts on the high ground to its North and West. These latter outposts occupied some of the enemy old

Turkish forts to be found in this part, massive stone buildings with walls anything up to a couple of yards thick. Against the lightly armed Partisans these forts were ideal, but now, with the arrival of field guns, the situation began to change.

In a series of small operations these forts were reduced and the German defence pushed back to its main position in Ledinice. The reduction of two of these forts remains clear in my mind. In one case the job was simply accomplished by setting up a 25 pounder just out of small arms range and reducing the building by pointblank fire. The gun was aimed by opening the breech and looking down the barrel! The other case was not so simple. Here, owing to the mountainous ground, a suitable 25 pounder position was not available. In this case C Tp, remembering what little it had learnt about explosives, prepared a massive pole charge for a partisan assault party to use. This consisted of a large box about 4 x 2½ feet square and 6 inches deep which was filled with some German guncotton the Partisans managed to produce. This box, with sturdy poles fixed at either end, was to be propped against the fort wall and detonated. It took two men to lift and was a very clumsy load. However, three very gallant Partisans were found and rehearsed in their job which they managed to perform with a measure of success – sufficiently so to allow an assault to be made which drove the Germans out of their stronghold.

Once cooped up in the village of Ledinice and the Town of Risan, life was made unbearable for the Germans. The outposts gone, the Partisans could get close to the German perimeter and snipe to their hearts content. This was supplemented by 25 pounder and MMG fire, the latter from 43 Cdo Heavy Weapons Troop which had joined the party, on any movement by day.[19]

The rest of the Commando remained in Dubrovnik for the time being in order to defend it against enemy attack, although a second troop was sent to the Risan-Viluse road to act as a backstop in the event of C Troop having to make a hurried withdrawal. Plans were made for an attack on Risan, but this was cancelled when the Partisans stated that the Germans were planning an attack on Dubrovnik from the north, and the Commandos were now deployed in Trebinje.

By mid-November, however, it became clear that the Germans had abandoned their attempts to move up the coast road and had switched their efforts to the Danilovgrad-Niksic road further inland. South of Niksic was a vital bridge, which, if blown, could foil the enemy movement up the road should they succeed in breaking through the Partisan positions at Danilovgrad. No 43, less B and C Troops, and half of D Troop, which was now acting as escort to four

75mm Raiding Support Regiment guns supporting the Partisans in Danilovgrad, was moved to hold this bridge. On 22 November, B Troop rejoined. With Ledinice now in partisan hands and Risan about to be evacuated by the Germans, D Troop was now concentrated south of the bridge with the 75mm guns. At this point Lt Colonel I.H. Riches RM arrived to take over command from Major Munro. It was not a particularly satisfactory position:

> The dispersal of the unit presented many difficulties, and the fact that troops of the Commando were under command of other units did not help matters. Worse problems than these had to be faced. Severe winter conditions now began to set in. The snow was soon several feet deep, and strong winds pierced the thin bivouacs and inadequate clothing of the troops, making life miserable and almost unbearable on the bare rocky hill-sides. The whole force was living more that a thousand metres above sea level, and no special equipment was available to protect them from the cold. Yet they remained cheerful and resolute, and the small sickness rate of the unit demonstrated amply their physical toughness and mental stamina. The discomfort of the troops was not to be compensated by any pleasant relaxation. Relations with the partisans gradually worsened during the period, and deprived the troops even of the feeling that they were at least appreciated and welcome on those bare hill-sides. They only had their training and discipline, their belief in their own officers, and in the strategy which made it necessary for them to go to MONTENEGRO, to keep them from the desire to leave the partisans to their own fate.[20]

While the Germans remained firm in front of Danilovgrad, they now gradually switched their efforts even further eastwards, and began to break out towards Berane. Efforts were now made to forestall this, and at the beginning of December a plan was drawn up for one Commando troop and four 75mm guns to be flown into the Berane area in order to hold up the enemy. Bad weather forced the cancellation of this, but then this same force was sent to help the Partisans drive the enemy out of their positions south of Danilovgrad, while the remainder were made responsible once more for the protection of the 25 pdrs of 111 Field Regiment RA. Spuz fell on 16 December, but the problems of crossing the River Morasha and Partisan unwillingness for Floydforce to share any more of the laurels of victory meant that a week later No 43 (RM) Commando were withdrawn to billets in Niksic, where at least they were able to celebrate Christmas in peace. It now became clear that the Partisans considered the British superfluous and the force was withdrawn to Italy on 20 January 1945. It had been a frustrating business, but at least a third of the XXI Mountain Corps never got out of Montenegro, and the remainder who did escape were in a very woebegone condition.

Lake Comacchio

It had now been almost a year since the Commandos had operated with the Field Army on the Italian mainland. During it, the US Fifth and British Eighth Armies had broken through the Gothic Line, captured Rome and then gradually slogged their way northwards through successive defensive lines. The previous autumn had seen the Arno Line overrun, but the Allies had been forced to a halt fifty miles south of the River Po, and Alexander decided that they should now pause before mounting the final offensive in the spring of 1945. General McCreery, now commanding the Eighth Army, wanted to use 2 Commando Brigade in this final offensive, and Brigadier Ronnie Tod asked him if the Commandos could spend time in the front line in order to get used once more to operating with the Field Army. This was agreed, and during the second half of February and throughout March they came under V Corps in the Ravenna area. HQ 2 Commando Brigade became a normal brigade headquarters, with initially Nos 2 and 43 (RM) Commandos under command, along with the 12th Lancers, a field regiment RA, anti-tank troop and a squadron of tanks from the North Irish Horse. On 14 March, Nos 9 and 40 (RM) Commandos rejoined the brigade, which now found itself with also the Partisan 28 Garibaldi Brigade under command. There were the old problems of lack of heavy weapons and transport, but HQ V Corps was able to solve these. More important was that the Commandos were occupying the ground overlooking the scene of what was to be their area of operations when the spring offensive started. This was Lake Comacchio.

The task given to Ronnie Tod in early March was to seize the spit of land running between Lake Comacchio and the sea and then tie down the enemy forces in the area, while the main assault through the Argenta Gap took place. If possible, 2 Commando Brigade was then to exploit northwards to Comacchio Town, but only if the enemy had been sufficiently routed in the initial attack. Ronnie Tod was left to make his own plan and could call on the assets of V Corps, now commanded by General Keightley, who had known the brigade well from his days with 78th Division. The only guidance was that the Commandos should cross the lake and take the enemy in his right

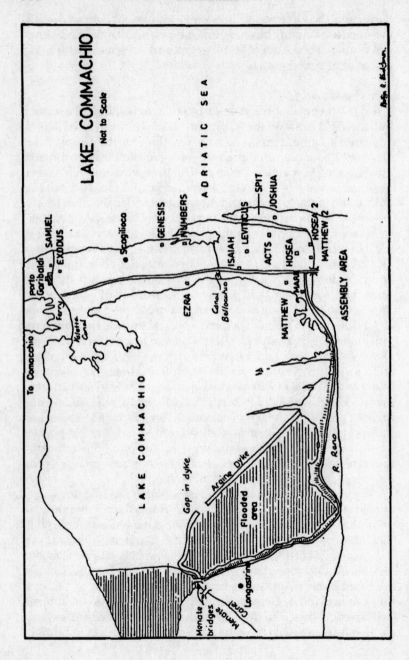

flank, while simultaneously thrusting from the south across the River Reno. The Spit itself was reckoned to be held by some 1200 men, mainly of the somewhat unreliable 162nd Turkoman Division, but stiffened by Germans. Nevertheless, the area was riddled with trenches and fortifications, and the enemy seemed to be prepared for an attack from every quarter, apart from across the lake itself, although there were a number of trenches facing in this direction. General Keightley's suggestion of attacking across the lake was therefore sound, but Tod felt that the success of this could be enhanced by making a subsidiary attack up the narrow tongue of land separating the Reno from the sea in order to make the enemy feel that he was being squeezed. To disconcert him further, he also decided to put in a small feint, rather than a major thrust, across the Reno.

Within a few days Tod had briefed his Commanding Officers. No 2 Commando (Lt Colonel F. W. Fynn MC) were to cross the lake north of the Bellocchio Canal and seize two bridges over the latter, nicknamed *Amos* and *Peter*. They were then to hold the line of the canal in order to prevent enemy reinforcements from the north and prevent him from withdrawing from the south. No 9 Commando (Lt Colonel J.M. Dunning-White) would also cross the lake and clear the enemy from the south-western half of the Spit, while No 43 (RM) Commando (Lt Colonel I.H. Riches RM) attacked up the Tongue, crossed the Reno and cleared the south-eastern half. This left No 40 (RM) Commando (Lt Colonel R.W. Sankey DSO DSC RM), who were to hold the south bank of the Reno at the base of the Spit, put in a feint attack, and also send one troop, along with two troops of tanks of the North Irish Horse, across the Reno in the west by ferry and then begin clearing the northern bank. Once the southern part of the Spit had been cleared, No 2 Commando would advance north-wards on the left and No 43 (RM) Commando on the right and seize the southern bank of the Canale di Valetta. No 9 Commando would then pass through them and capture Porto Garibaldi.

One major problem had to be overcome and that was the nature of the lake itself. It was shallow, very muddy and there was an artificial dyke running along the line of much of the eastern shore. A detailed reconnaissance was therefore carried out by COPP 2 under Lieutenant Richard Fyson RN, using canoes. Because of the particular shallowness of the southern shore, the storm-boats which were to be used would have to be carried 500 yards through the mud before they could be floated empty and then pushed a further 1000 yards before the eighteen men, which they could take, could get aboard. A few hundred yards' paddle would then bring them to sufficient depth so that the outboard engines could be fitted. Navigation, because the flatness of the land meant there was no discernible horizon, was also very difficult, as the COPPists found. Indeed, so concerned was Ronnie Tod that he tried to get hold of a parachute battalion to carry out No 2 Commando's task, but none was available. LVTs were produced and the V Corps Sappers were also on hand to help get the boats across the Reno and onto the lake. Every effort, too, was made to ensure that each Commando had sufficient artillery fire support, which would be immediately available on call.

By 1 April, all was ready and the Commandos moved into position, although not without some artillery harassing by the enemy, which caused Brigade HQ five casualties. At last light began the complicated business of getting the 'armada' formed up on the lake and ensuring that they found the gaps in the dyke identified by COPP 2. First to set out were navigation parties from M Squadron SBS, which was commanded by Major Anders Lassen MC, who had made his name with *Maid Honor* Force and the SSRF and had then gone on to even greater things with Jellicoe's SBS in the Eastern Mediterranean. These parties laid out navigation lights across the lake and also where the craft were to form up. Accompanying them were two gap control parties, each of one artillery observer and a gap control officer with wireless, one for No 2 Commando's gap, and the other at the southern end of the dyke by which No 9 Commando would land. This meant that they could both monitor progress and call down artillery fire if need be. Meanwhile, to drown the noise, RAF bombers circled overhead, tanks rumbled up and down the lateral road just behind the front line, and No 40 (RM) Commando played Wagner over a loudspeaker across the Reno at the base of the Spit. On top of this was the normal artillery harassing fire. Although two hours behind schedule, Nos 2 and 9 Commandos successfully married up with their LVTs and assault craft, but now a snag arose.

There had been a spell of dry weather over the past six weeks, and this had lowered the water level in the lake by some six inches, No 2 Commando embarked on LVTs, but then reported that they were bogged down just a few yards from the shore. Accordingly, the Commandos were ordered to transfer to the spare storm-boats and Goatleys, but inevitably this brought about much confusion, with the two Commandos

. . . inextricably mixed, some in storm-boats, some in assault boats, all trying to find their leaders and their own sub-units. The scene was a nightmare mixture of 'Venice by Moonlight' and the end of the Henley Regatta transferred to a setting of mud, slime and a few inches of stinking water.[21]

Both Fynn and Dunning-White wanted to postpone the operation, but Ronnie Tod, recognising that a repeat attempt would produce the same problems, refused to countenance this. The crossing therefore continued with the storm-boats towing strings of Goatleys, but such was the confusion in No 2 Commando that in the end the initial landing was made just by the HQ, Heavy Weapons Troop and one section from the line troops. In the event, the landing would not now be made until first light, and this meant hurried amendments to the artillery fire plan, including the institution of a 6,000 yard smokescreen to cover the landings if need be. In the meantime, No 40 (RM) Commando prepared to make their feint attack at the same time, and No 43 began to form up for their attack on the Tongue.

Just before first light, No 9 Commando reported that they were coming under fire, and the supporting artillery began to lay down covering fire. Both Royal Marine Commando attacks were now ordered for 0500 hours. No 40's feint, which included putting assault boats and dummies into the river, worked well and drew much enemy fire, and the leading troops of No 43 began to advance on their first objective, a company position on the Tongue, under enemy artillery and machine gun fire. As for No 2, Desmond Rochford recalls:

It was not until 0530 hours that we got ashore and by then it was growing light. This was to our advantage as the Germans had been expecting us earlier and, when we did show up, had relaxed, thinking it all a false alarm. Furthermore, being Easter Monday, they had decided to celebrate, and the officers and NCOs had begun drinking, leaving their Turkoman soldiers to it. We caught them in their dugouts and I remember one found wearing a long white nightshirt. Our initial objectives were two bridges. As we came to the first, a German officer dashed out and it was clear that he was going to blow the bridge. Hopkins, our sniper, could not get into a firing position in time, and up it went, although he got the officer with his second shot. By this stage a lot of us were having problems with our weapons, which were clogged with mud. Rifle oil was in heavy demand. I saw a bottle with flannelette stuffed in the top. I pointed it out some of my friends, but it turned out to be vintage brandy and we all had a much welcome swig.

No 2 Commando were approaching the enemy from behind and when we came up towards the second bridge, which was codenamed *Peter*, we formed up in column of threes. This confused the enemy, who thought we were paratroops coming up to reinforce them. Thus we were able to capture the bridge intact. We took up positions around it and gathered in prisoners. One German captain evaded capture and opened fire with a Spandau on a group of prisoners guarded by some of our chaps. All fell dead or wounded apart from one of the guards. The German captain was then killed. I took up position with my Bren gun team behind a mound, from out of which appeared a young German – it was a strongpoint facing the other way. By now we were under heavy mortar and Spandau fire and found what shelter we could. I was in a foxhole and was joined by a bearded German sergeant whom I persuaded to become my prisoner. Those manning the first aid post were similarly surprised. They had been dealing with the casualties of both sides under incessant sniper fire. It then stopped and two German snipers surrendered to them, complaining that our chaps had taken not the slightest notice of their fire![22]

No 2 Commando had firmly established themselves along the line of the Bellocchio Canal by 1100 hours. Meanwhile, No 9 had successfully landed by 0630 hours, but experienced much difficulty in clearing the maze of dug-outs and strongpoints, many excellently camouflaged. Nevertheless, they succeeded, apart from one particular position, codenamed *Leviticus*, which resisted all attempts to capture it, including having the support of artillery, mortars and the 'cab rank' fighter-bombers. No 43 (RM) Commando got three troops across the Reno and set about attacking a position codenamed *Acts*, a company strength strongpoint, which included an 88mm gun and an Italian 47/32 anti-tank gun.

This coy posn was sighted amongst scrubby sand dunes elevated above, and with a perfect fd of fire over the flat hinterland of the river. An extremely hy arty conc was put down on the target incl a very effective and prolonged smoke screen and under this B and D Tps aslted the posn at 1042 hrs with E Tp in res. So perfect was the timing between the arty conc and the mov of the two Tps that the enemy was unable to offer any serious resistance. From this posn over 80 PW were taken.[23]

'A' Troop of No 40 (RM) Commando had also been advancing with the tanks of the North Irish Horse along the northern bank of the Reno.

At the first ditch it was found necessary to use fascines to get over the dyke as the width of the supporting sub-soil had been under estimated. The tks kept getting bogged and more fascines were brought up. At 1130 hrs the first tk had crossed the dyke. The tp moved up in sections clearing foxholes on the way. The leading tp fired 2 or 3 shells into a house and about 5 mins later the enemy opened up causing 3 cas in the tk gp. The remainder took cover behind the tks and 2" mortars gave smoke and HE on the left as cover for Lt Marsh's sec. The wounded were brought in under cover of this screen and of LMG fire of Mne William-son who stayed out in the open with absolutely no cover at all for a full 18 mins whilst he was being sniped at and fired upon by enemy MGs. At approx 1515 hours enemy were observed waving a white flag and PWs came through their minefields towards us, being fired on by their own tps. Cpl Ward's sec was brought up to the second tk, and the first one carried on through the minefield ahead. Lt Marsh was contacted and found to be wounded and he ordered Lt Seales to carry on to MARK with 'A' Tp under his command. The first tk got bogged after leaving C . . . the second going back some 500X to a house and then coming back again by the lower river bank. The other tk was knocked out by a Tell-ermine. No enemy posns were contacted, and it was heard that 43 Cdo were in MATTHEW and contact was made.[24]

No 9 Commando mounted another attack on *Leviticus* that after-noon, this time using a smoke screen. Unfortunately it cleared too quickly and Nos 1 and 2 Troops had to advance the last 150 yards with no cover and under heavy Spandau and mortar fire. This, they did led by a piper playing *The Road to the Isles* and the position finally fell, yielding almost a hundred prisoners.

With the Spit up to the canal now in the hands of the Comman-dos, there was now a pause for reorganisation. No 43 (RM) Com-mando took over *Peter* from No 2, and No 9 was placed in reserve. Since the day was now drawing to a close and all were exhausted after the events of the previous night and a day's fierce fighting, Ronnie Tod decided not to continue the advance until the follow-ing day. That night was relatively peaceful, and Nos 2 and 43 (RM) Commandos were ordered to resume the advance at 1100 hours, supported by tanks. Problems in getting these forward caused delays and it was not until 1400 hours that they got going. After moving some 1,000 yards, No 2 Commando was pinned down by heavy artil-lery and mortar fire, while No 43 cleared the small village of Sca-glioca, and moved on towards the Valetta Canal. The ground here was very open, and the leading troop, C, was pinned down by heavy fire from the north bank of the canal. Several individuals managed to reach the bank, and Corporal Tom Hunter, with complete disregard for his own safety, took on five or six Spandaus with his Bren gun from a very exposed position. This took the pressure off the remainder of the troop, but the contest was too unequal and Hunter fell, later to be awarded a posthumous Victoria Cross. In view of the enemy's strength on the canal, only a set-piece attack could dislodge him, but the Commandos were now ordered to hold their positions until relieved by 24 Guards Brigade. This took place at last light on the 4th.

As to what the Commandos had achieved, this is aptly summed up in a message sent by General Sir Richard McCreery to Ronnie Tod on 4 April:

> My best congratulations to you and all ranks of your force on your most successful operation which has captured or destroyed the whole enemy garrison south of **PORTO GARIBALDI**. Your operation demanded very careful and detailed planning and skill in execution. All ranks have shown a splendid enterprise, endurance and determination to surmount difficulties. Your success has helped the whole army plan. Well done indeed![25]

When Charles Keightley had originally briefed Ronnie Tod in early March on Operation *Roast*, he also tasked the Commandos with another operation, *Fry*, which was to be carried out at much the same time. It called for the seizing of four islands in the middle of Lake Comacchio, and then using these as bases from which to raid enemy positions on the north shore of the lake. *Fry* was to be launched within three days of the mounting of *Roast* and was also designed to tie down enemy troops, and thus help the main attack through the Argenta Gap. With the enemy strength on the four islands estimated at not more than sixty men, and the fact that the bulk of the brigade was still actively involved in *Roast*, Brigadier Tod gave the task to Anders Lassen's M Squadron SBS and the Partisans of the 28 Garibaldi Brigade, who along with sappers and a medium regiment RA, formed *Fry Force* under Lt Colonel R.P. Menday MC, commander of the 2 Commando Brigade Training Wing. The attack took place on the night 4/5 April, but all four islands were found to be unoccupied, although small parties of Germans were captured as they came out to check on the situation on the islands. Colonel Menday now returned to the mainland, leaving Lassen in charge. From interrogation of the prisoners, it transpired that enemy reinforcements were to be landed on the islands during the night of 5/6 April. Three boats were spotted and the occupants of one captured, although the others got away.

Lassen now began his raiding operations. On the following night two patrols set out, but were hindered by an artificial dyke, in which they blew holes. The night after, three more patrols were sent, but were beaten back by strong winds. Then, on the night 8/9 April, four patrols set off. Two of these were under command of Anders Lassen himself, and they landed between Porto Garibaldi and Comacchio Town on the narrow causeway carrying the road which connected the two, and made their way towards Comacchio Town. Some two miles short of it they came under Spandau fire, which they silenced with grenades and small arms fire, capturing two men and killing two. Five hundred yards further on, they came to a blockhouse, which was engaged, and six enemy came out with their hands up. As Lassen went forward to secure them, fire was opened up by a Spandau on the other side of the causeway, which caused casualties, including Lassen himself wounded. There was now a sharp firefight, which produced further casualties. Lassen therefore decided to withdraw, but heavy fire frustrated all attempts to recover the wounded. He therefore ordered those fit enough to pull back and gave covering fire until he himself was killed. A boat was left for any others who might make their way back, and four did so, including two wounded, reaching the boat just before dawn. They lay up on a nearby island that day and returned to their base that night. The operation had cost three killed, including Lassen, one missing and three wounded, but two prisoners had been captured and up to eight enemy had been killed. The death of Lassen after all that he had been through during the past four years was nothing short of a tragedy and there was much sadness among those who had known him. A few weeks later, his gallantry in this last fight was marked by the award of a Victoria Cross to add to the three Military Crosses which he had already won.

The other two patrols that night were not successful in meeting the enemy, being thwarted by the deep water canal west of Comacchio Town, but a reconnaissance party did manage to gather useful information from civilians in the area of the salt pans at the north-east corner of the lake. On the following two nights, patrols were landed on the dyke covering the north shore and engaged houses and other targets, forcing the enemy into nervous retaliation, and the patrols then withdrew. On the 11th, *Fryforce* was relieved by the Partisans. A subsidiary operation, *Cinderella*, concerned a troop of No 9 Commando, was planned, but not mounted. This was to be a simulated landing on the north coast, north of Porto Garibaldi, but heavy defences and the fact that a similar operation had already been planned resulted in its cancellation.

After the end of *Roast*, 2 Commando Brigade found itself placed under command of 56th Division for a series of operations aimed at outflanking the enemy positions in front of the Argenta Gap by a series of right hooks through the flooded area south of Lake Comacchio. The first of these had already been carried out by 167 Brigade, and the second, *Impact*, was to involve 169 Brigade with 40 (RM) Commando under command. While the main attack across the Senio and Santerno rivers had been launched on the 9th, *Impact* was to be carried out on the night 10/11th. No 40 (RM) Commando's task was to advance along the dyke running north-west from Urmana, seize the pumping station at its northern end and then capture a bridge, called 'Commando Bridge' which ran over the Menate Canal just north of Menate. 2/5 Queens would assault the latter early next morning and link up with the Commandos guarding the right flank. Crucial to the success of the plan was the ability of the Commandos to clear any mines and cross a thirty foot gap in the dyke and the mouth of the Menate Canal before first light, as they would be very vulnerable if caught on the dyke in daylight.

After a 90 minute delay caused by the lorries carrying the stormboats and assault boats becoming bogged, No 40 eventually started out along the dyke at 2330 hours. At first all went well, and the gap in the dyke was reached after two hours' hard marching. Y Troop were leading the way with the Sapper mine clearance party:

> . . . a position was taken to cover the Bren Sec under Lt Atkinson. The gap was too muddy and Capt Thomson asked for the assault boats to come up. These came up on the right and the Tp started to cross the gap and formed up on the right of the bank.
>
> A few minutes later a mine exploded. This seemed to throw the boat sec into some confusion and Lt Parker went forward to see what had happened. Capt Thomson had been brought back to the gap and was lying on the bank, wounded. He said that he could not go on and that Lt Parker would have to take over the Tp. Lt Parker went forward across the gap and found that the entire Bren sec including Lt Atkinson were lying wounded about 50 yds across on the bank. They were told to wait there and the Sappers started prodding a path towards them and the

Sick Bay Attendant and stretchers were sent for. The Tp was reorganised and the front Bren gunners replaced.[26]

It took some two hours to get this problem sorted out, and then Tac HQ and three troops pushed on, leaving the remainder to be ferried across the gap and bring on the storm-boats and stores. Y Troop reached the Menate Canal at 0430 hours and spread out along the east bank, while P Troop passed through and crossed the Canal with the aid of their toggle ropes, and made their way towards the Commando Bridge. By now the first glimmers of light were appearing. Worse, the enemy had now woken up as to what was happening and began to engage the dyke with artillery, mortars and machine guns, causing a number of casualties. This prevented X Troop from crossing the canal in order to seize the pumping station, and only friendly artillery support prevented the situation from becoming any worse. P Troop managed to get within 200 yards of the bridge and were able to cover it with fire to prevent the enemy blowing it, but lacking any support, the enemy were able to inflict an increasing number of casualties on the troop, especially when fire was opened by a self-propelled gun positioned in the pumping station. Air strikes were called down, and these subdued the enemy in the pumping station, enabling it to be captured. This was the key to the enemy defences, and Commando Bridge now fell. Not until 0400 hours on the 12th was physical contact made with 2/5 Queens, and next day the Commando was withdrawn into reserve. It had not been an easy operation, and indicative of this is that No 40 suffered 88 casualties out of a total strength of 350.

The next outflanking operation helped 24 Guards Brigade, which was relieved in the line south of the Valetta Canal by No 43 (RM) Commando, and No 9 Commando. The objective for *Impact Royal* was another canal, the Fossa Marina, which ran from Lake Comacchio to the Reno at Argenta, and No 9's task was to seize a bridge over it some 5,000 yards north-east of Argenta. The original plan called for a landing north of the bridge, but a high bank was found, after a reconnaissance, to be impassable to LVTs, and so the Commandos were now to land, with a battalion of the Buffs, to the south-east and then advance up the road to Strada Della Pioppa, which crossed over their objective. They landed on 13th April, not far forward of 169 Brigade's positions in the Renate area, and a linkup was quickly made with them. The Buffs, in spite of suffering casualties in their landing, also quickly went firm. There was then a pause while the beachhead was consolidated. The Buffs and Scots

Guards then advanced towards Fossa Marina, but were held up by the enemy short of it. No 9 Commando were therefore ordered to pass through and seize the original objective, together with another crossing over the canal, which was a hydro-electric plant. They attacked on the night of 14/15th, got up to the canal, but heavy fire prevented them from seizing the two crossing places. A second attempt the following night was also foiled when it was discovered that the enemy had blown a thirty foot gap in the bridge and that the canal itself, which they had hoped to cross in assault boats, was but a few inches deep and the mud at the bottom proved to be impassable on foot. Those who tried quickly sank up to the waist and, in some cases, the neck. During the next day a very careful watch was kept on the enemy positions and it was possible to draw up a very accurate lay-out of his dispositions. No 9 Commando were relieved, but had the satisfaction of knowing that the information they had gained was of much help to 24 Guards Brigade when they finally overcame the enemy's defences the following night.

While Nos 9 and 40 (RM) Commandos continued under command of 56th Division, the remainder of the brigade was placed under the direct command of V Corps on 14 April, No 43 having been relieved north of the Spit by the 28 Garibaldi Brigade. They were now to take a more direct part in the forcing of the Argenta Gap and were put into the line just south of Bastia, with 78th Division on their right and 8th Indian Division on their left. While the Indians advanced across the Sillaro river and drive on north-west of Bologna, the Commandos were to establish a force in the bend of the River Reno north-west of Argenta, thus outflanking the Gap, and then help 78th Division break through it. The area over which they had to advance was mainly below sea level and was flooded. Crossing it were a number of canals running east-west, each with banks rising above the water.

The first task was to seize the Quaderna Canal, which was done by No 43 (RM) Commando on the night of the 16th/17th. The axis of the advance to the bend in the river was now to be the two canals which ran parallel to the river to the west of Argenta itself. No 2 Commando now took over, and advancing in the early hours of the 17th got as far as the bridges crossing the river and canals just by Argenta. There they were held up by machine gun fire. In the meantime, 78th Division had begun their advance, but were meeting heavy opposition south-west of Argenta. Ronnie Tod ordered No 2 Commando to put in a set-piece attack on the bridges, which went in, with artillery support, at 0945 hours on the same morning.

> The nature of the country precluded any use of ground or manoeuvre in the attack, which was put in as a series of straight forward charges up each flood-bank with covering fire from the remaining flood-banks, so that the whole attack became a series of section charges, the result of each depending on the use of superiority of small arms and artillery fire by the attackers. The enemy put up a stubborn resistance, but as each charge was successfully driven home, he was forced to withdraw from one position to another, and by 1030 hours the area of the bridges had been completely cleared, and eight prisoners taken.[27]

Attempts to exploit northwards were once again foiled by heavy fire, and the enemy then put in four quick counter-attacks, all of which were broken up by artillery and small arms fire. Two troops of No 40 (RM) Commando were brought in to relieve No 43 on the Quaderna Canal, and the latter were ordered to pass through No 2 Commando and continue the advance to the river bend. They launched their attack at 0330 hours.

> The Commando came under murderous fire the moment it passed the Start Line, in fact 2 Commando had at the time been counterattacked again. The positions the enemy held on the banks of the RENO had been very well constructed with a main second line of defence, six months previously. The attacking troops were caught out by almost point blank fire by enemy SP guns, panzerfausts used in an anti-personnel role, and by murderous spandau fire. On the left both Troop Commanders of E and D Troops were wounded. Capt R.N. Parkinson-Cumine MC RM received a spandau burst across his chest puncturing one lung. He was extremely lucky in that one bullet broke the shoulders holding the safety pin of a 36 grenade. The grenade handle by chance did not fly off. Lieut R.J. EVE RA received a burst of spandau in his leg. Lieut W.G. JENKINS RM, with outstanding courage and leadership, although wounded in the neck, charged down on an enemy spandau position, and leading E Troop with great dash, cleared an enemy platoon from the village.* 25 prisoners were taken. E and D Troops moved in, and were continually shelled and fired on by spandaus from the flanks.
>
> On the right A and B Troops were being heavily engaged, but kept on advancing. Capt NUNNS (although wounded in the leg, his third received in action) reached his objective a thousand yards from the start line, but only one sub section with him, as the rest of his Troop with A

---

*Jenkins was awarded the DSO for this.

Troop were heavily counter attacked from the east by over a hundred of the enemy.

With very accurate support fire from 2 Commando, they accounted for an estimate of fifty of the enemy (enemy casualties were evacuated later under a white flag). Lieut McConville was wounded early on in this attack.

Owing to the exposed nature of the ground, and the fact that the Irish Bde had apparently not yet reached the R. Reno on our right, the Commando had ordered to withdraw back to the start line. Capt M.R. NUNNS RM and his party, now cut off, did not get back until midday. They too were counter attacked, but turned the tables on the enemy and charged them, taking 1 Officer and 4 ORs prisoners, and inflicting casualties on the attackers. Our casualties were four Officers wounded, six ORs killed and nineteen wounded, a heavy price to pay considering that the four assaulting troops were little over thirty strong in each case.[28]

The 78th Division had by now outflanked Argenta to the east and were advancing westwards some 1500 yards north of the town. A number of patrols were sent out by the Commandos that day to check on the enemy, but during the afternoon, a message was sent to Brigade HQ stating that 6th Armoured Division was now to be passed through the Argenta Gap at first light next day (19th). The Commandos were to clear both banks of the Reno up to at least the bend that night, while 78th Division continued to mop up the enemy north of Argenta. No 43 (RM) Commando were given the task, and succeeded in getting to the bend in the river with little difficulty. Orders were now received to exploit this success by continuing to advance westwards a further 1000 yards between the river and the canal immediately to its south. Once No 2 had taken over No 43's positions in the bend, No 43 (RM) Commando carried out this operation, again meeting little opposition. Then, No 2 Commando were ordered to exploit even further westwards until such time as 6th Armoured Division linked up with 10th Indian Division. Contact with the enemy had now been lost, and so jeeps and motor-cycles were brought up, and in these No 2 Commando advanced another 5,000 yards before encountering any opposition. On the 20th, two troops of No 43 (RM) Commando came up and continued the move westwards, reaching Molinella on the 21st. This was the limit of the advance, for on that day the link-up between 6th Armoured and 10th Indian Divisions was achieved, and the battle rolled on northwards.

This was the end of the fighting for 2 Commando Brigade. They returned to Ravenna and Porto Corsino for a much needed rest. They were still there when, on 2 May, the German forces in North Italy and Austria finally surrendered.

During almost two years' hard campaigning in the Mediterranean, the Commandos had seldom been out of action. They had participated in all the major amphibious operations, had taken their place in the front lines as normal infantry, bolstered up the partisans of Yugoslavia and Albania and done their bit to limit the spread of civil war in Greece. Finally, the part they played in the forcing of the Argenta Gap was crucial to the success of this operation. And it was this, perhaps more than anything else, which finally convinced the enemy that the game was up. The cost, however, had been severe. Excluding the casualties suffered by Nos 3 and 41 (RM) Commandos in the late summer of 1943 before they returned to the United Kingdom, the brigade had incurred almost 1500 casualties, including over 300 killed.

Before leaving the Italian theatre, mention must be made of No 34 Troop of 30 Commando. After the frustrations on Corsica towards the end of 1943, the troop, which retained the cover name of Special Engineering Unit throughout, returned to the Italian mainland. It took part in the advance on Rome, being placed, along with other intelligence agencies, under No 1 Intelligence Collection Unit (ICU), the new name for S Force. It appears to have had little opportunity to put its specialist skills into action, and the same applied to the operations leading to the capture of Florence towards the end of August 1944. For these, the troop was given specific targets in the city to search, but was not allowed to go in ahead of the main body. As it so happened, they discovered that these establishments, including the local Abwehr school, had been evacuated by the Germans some weeks before, and they came away empty-handed. Also, during the advance into Florence, Major Ward, the Troop Commander, was wounded* and his place was taken by Major Strachan, whose conclusion on the way the troop had been used was:

To ensure any degrees of success, Intelligence targets of importance such as were allotted to this Unit must be tackled well in advance of the Allied Armies – in this case 5-6 weeks before the Army was due to reach Florence. Had this been possible, in short, had the opportunity of operating

---

* He recovered in time to command B Troop of the RM Wing of 30 Assault Unit in the closing stages of the war in Germany.

as it is intended to operate, is 'behind enemy lines' when necessary, the above targets might have yielded some information of value – at worst, they could not have yielded less.[29]

He also tried to get the establishment of four officers and twenty other ranks raised, as that of No 33 Troop had been for *Overlord*, but in vain. The winter of 1944-5 was spent in training, but the troop did eventually get the opportunity it had been waiting for for so long during the final offensive. Operating with SOE and the Partisans, they were involved in the advance on Genoa and took a leading part in the capture of the city on 27 April 1945.

CHAPTER TEN

South-East Asia

In August 1943, Lord Louis Mountbatten had arrived in India and set up a new Allied command in order to wage war against the Japanese in Burma, South-East Asia Command (SEAC). After the disasters of 1942, the British had attempted to regain the initiative with an abortive offensive in the Arakan in early 1943. The Allies now agreed that the main priority was the re-occupation of Northern Burma in order to help bolster the Chinese, but plans were also made to renew the offensive in the Arakan, and, as part of this a number of amphibious operations were considered. A Combined Training Centre had already been set up on Lake Kharakvasla in the hills near Poona in 1942, and, as a part of the preparations for these amphibious operations, COPP 7 under Lieutenant (later Admiral) G. Hall DSC RN arrived in India in August 1943 to begin reconnaissance of possible landing beaches. At the same time, 3 SS Brigade under Brigadier W.I. Nonweiler was also earmarked for the theatre, and he with his Brigade Major and DAA & QMG arrived in India in early December.

Nonweiler was not, however, pleased with what he found. For a start, he was warned by Mountbatten that there was little prospect of the brigade as a whole being used in a major operation for the next twelve months, although efforts would be made to employ parts in minor operations. The reason for this was lack of landing craft, since priority for these now lay with *Overlord*, and there was also, as we have seen, still a requirement for them in the Mediterranean In terms of minor Commando operations, Mountbatten said that he was thinking along the lines of an amphibious assault, followed by a twelve week jungle penetration similar to that of Wingate's Chindits. Nonweiler was somewhat cynical about this, although he did not totally dismiss it, noting that an Army brigade operating in the Arakan had recently had to be pulled out after suffering 80% malarial casualties.[1] As for administration, it was proposed to put the brigade in a tented camp near Poona, but it was clear that few on the staff had much idea of the brigade's organisation or realised that it possessed very little administrative tail of its own.

The Commandos themselves set sail from Gourock on 15 November 1943, but the *Ranchi* carrying No 1 Commando, with Ken Trevor in command, and No 42 (RM) Commando (Lt Colonel R.E. de M. Leathes RM), was attacked by German bombers in the Mediterranean and had to put into Alexandria for repairs. It did mean, however, that both were able to celebrate Christmas ashore. The other vessel, the *Reina del Pacifico*, was unscathed and Nos 5 (Lt Colonel D.M. Shaw MC) and 44 (RM) Commando (Lt Colonel F.C. Horton RM) arrived at Bombay on 19 December, and moved by train to the camp at Kedgaon near Poona. A month later, the other two Commandos finally arrived at Bombay and were also sent to Kedgaon. Also to join the brigade was No 2 (Dutch) Troop of No 10 (IA) Commando, who left the United Kingdom on 11 December. It was the ultimate intention that they should take part in the liberation of the Dutch East Indies. Kedgaon itself, as Brigadier Nonweiler had found, was not at first sight a pleasing prospect:

> A cold, windswept, bleak and bare hill, mottled with large black rocks crept into view. An occasional tent and bamboo building remained standing in the wilderness. Just as 'Quisling' and 'Coventrate'* have their special meaning, so 'Kedgaon' should mean acres and acres of sweet nothing.
>
> Nothing was quickly organised and a blanket and mosquito net were hastily issued. A mad rush for beds was halted by the news that they were all bug infested, somehow and somewhere we spent our first miserable night in India.[2]

Nos 5 and 44 (RM) Commandos were not to remain here long.

In late December 1943, XV Indian Corps launched the second Arakan offensive, and on 9 January, 5th Indian Division had captured Maungdaw. Three weeks later, the Japanese launched their own offensive, Operation *Ha Go*, which took 5th Indian Division in the flank. Nos 5 and 44 (RM) Commandos were brought round aboard HMS *Keren* from Bombay, leaving there on 22 February as *Ha Go* ground itself to a halt. Along with a skeleton Brigade HQ, they arrived at Cox's Bazaar on 5 March, and began to prepare for Operation *Screwdriver*. With *Ha Go* having been beaten off, XV Corps were now preparing to clear the Maungdaw-Buthidaung road, and the

---

*A term for the blitzing of cities by air attack introduced after the bombing of Coventry on the night 14/15 November 1940.

idea was that the Commandos should land in the enemy's rear in the Alethangyaw area in support of this. This was mounted on 11 March and to assist them in their landing they had RN Beach Commando *Hotel.* John Hill:

> The Naval Commando were given half an hour to prepare for the main body and dig the defences. The beach and the country inland, as far as could be seen, were deserted and only the rushing surf disturbed the tranquillity. In a little while we were ready.
>
> The assault boats were called in by the letter G flashed by a shaded torch, in morse, and, with only two exceptions, they landed spot on, and the Marines drifted silently over the sandhills and out of sight. Two maverick craft were stuck on a sandbar, broadside on to the sweeping rollers, in spite of the beach party's attempts to float them, and there they stayed. The Marines struggled ashore with difficulty and in no state to march and fight, but this they did, nevertheless. Hardly had we settled down to a state of alert when the sounds of battle were heard in the direction of Aleythangyau. The kettledrum staccatos of the automatic weapons were interspersed with the crump of mortar shells and the explosions reflected briefly from the cloudy, night sky. This went on for an hour or two and seemed, gradually to recede. The Beach Party stayed on guard all night but nothing exciting came our way although our main anxiety and irritation centred on those wretched landing craft, standing out like landmarks when the moon shone through the clouds. The crews were told that if they were found wandering around the shore they would be shot.[3]

Buthidaung and the Japanese stronghold of Razabil were both captured, and No 5 Commando then returned to Maungdaw to be followed later by No 44. On 23 March, two troops were called out at short notice to help an artillery battery to extricate itself from an exposed position. On their way back, they were ambushed in a narrow defile, but, although suffering heavy casualties, they managed to extricate themselves, and their success in doing this was later recognised by the awards of two MCs, an MM and two Mentions in Despatches. As for the initial impressions of their new enemy, the Commando view was that:

> Any units who come here in future will, of course, have had battle experience but *this* is a completely different type of war and you are fighting against a genuine fanatic who fires and expects no quarter. Even in our short experience we have had played against us all the tricks you read about in pamphlets – snipers tied to treetops – moving a wounded man

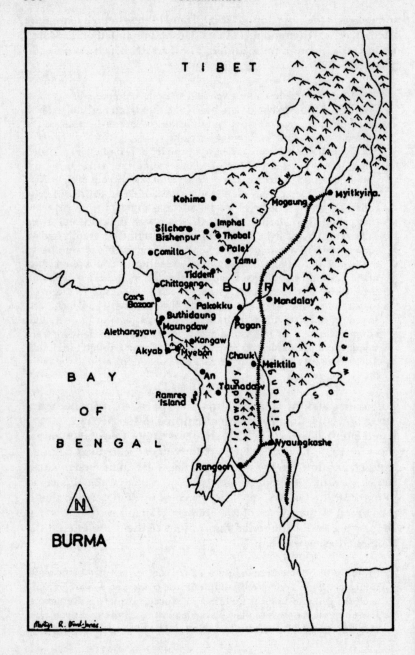

Martyn R. Ford-Jones.

into a field and tempting you to come and get him – shouting in English – making a noise in one direction you coming in the other. Tps must be prepared for all this or they will be caught on the wrong foot. It sounds obvious but both our units were caught. The Jap is a very good defensive soldier – he must not be given time to dig.[4]

Another Japanese ploy detected was their ability to break in on wireless nets. No 44 (RM) Commando noted:

Within 1½ hours of landing it was clear that the enemy was listening in on the Unit net, several messages being received that had obviously not originated within the Unit. Early on D+1 'Sunray' [Officer Commanding] was called to the set and asked to 'pass a short message'. The CO stated in no uncertain way that he had more important things to attend to and received a reply to the effect 'Thank you, I know your voice'.[5]

Screwdriver was therefore invaluable in giving the brigade some hard practical experience on which to build.

The Japanese Fifteenth Army now launched its offensive in Northern Burma, which culminated in the desperate battles of Imphal and Kohima. After a period of patrolling south of Maungdaw, Nos 5 and 44 were rushed up to Silchar arriving there on 11 April. This was a vital communications junction, and 3-4 day patrols into the Assam hills were mounted. They remained here until August, enduring the monsoon, with its continuous rains and mud, and then returned by rail to Bangalore via Calcutta, where everyone was able to take 14 days' leave. During September, they were deployed to Trincomalee in Ceylon, where Nos 1 and 42 (RM) Commandos rejoined the brigade. They had spent the spring doing jungle training at Belgaum and then had endured an uncomfortable summer in the heat and humidity of Cocanada on the east coast of India. During this time, the Dutch Troop, seeing little prospect of operations being mounted against the Dutch East Indies for a long time and keen to take part in the liberation of Holland, were allowed to return to the United Kingdom.

The stay in Ceylon was not for long. The brigade staff flew to Urma at the end of September to begin planning for further operations in the Arakan with XV Indian Corps. The four Commandos themselves then set off in two parties going via Calcutta and Chittagong before arriving at Teknaf. Brigadier Nonweiler now returned to England for leave and conferences and Peter Young, who had recently arrived, took over temporary command of the brigade until Campbell Hardy's arrival at the beginning of December.

Small Operations Group

COPP 8 had followed COPP 7 to India in November 1943. Also, at Mountbatten's insistence, elements of the SBS were sent out in February 1944, and were known as A and B Squadrons. Another amphibious reconnaissance unit formed in 1944 was Royal Marine Detachment 385, which arrived in India in the early summer of 1944. Coordinating the training of these units was 'Blondie' Hasler, and in June 1944 it was decided to bring them all formally under on umbrella, the Small Operations Group (SOG), which was to based on Karaitivi Island of the Jaffna Peninsula in Ceylon. Its role was:

> To provide small parties of uniformed troops trained and equipped to operate against enemy coastal, river or lake areas, using as their final means of approach various types of small craft (all of capacity less than 12 men), inflatable boats, paddle boards or swimmers.[6]

While the COPPs continued to specialise in their role of beach reconnaissance, and more were to join SOG as the requirement for them in the European theatres receded, the SBS concentrated on operations ashore, and were also parachute trained. RM Detachment 385, on the other hand, were trained more in boatwork. Later in 1944, another unit, the Sea Reconnaissance Unit (SRU) also joined SOG. Their particular speciality was 'long distance swimming, landing and withdrawing through heavy surf, the use of paddle-boards and underwater swimming with oxygen breathing apparatus'[7]. They were also trained parachutists, and on arrival on Karaitivi were introduced to small boats and navigation.

The SOG operations were to be of two distinct types. The first were independently mounted operations, in which the SOG Commander was responsible for all planning and execution, merely calling on the use of facilities of formation HQs. These were normally administrative, since the SOG was entirely operational and possessed no logistic assets of its own. The second type were called 'Force Commanders' Operations'. Here the teams were detached to the formation HQ concerned for use in conjunction with a major operation, and the SOG Commander was merely responsible for team selection, liaison and advice. These were by far the most numerous and by the end of the war in the Far East, no less than 154 had been carried out, as opposed to only nineteen independent operations. While the COPPs were always attached to Force W, the naval amphibious force, the other SOG units were under command of either Fourteenth Army or XV Corps, and, frequently the latter placed them under the operational control of 3 Commando Brigade, as it became titled at the beginning of December 1944, during the early phases of the final offensive in Burma.

The SBS had been reorganised into three groups – A, B and C – each of four officers and sixteen other ranks. After 3 Commando Brigade had returned to the Arakan in November 1944, A Group was placed under its command and carried out a number of operations on the coast and offshore islands. A typical operation was *Barbarism*, which was carried out by Captain G. Barnes MM and No 2 Sub-Section:

On the night of 15/16 Dec. 1944, at 2210 hrs, 3 canoes slipped from M.L. 438 which was under the command of Commander MacDonald, from a position about 2½ miles off the North of KALAYAUNG village, and proceeded in line astern on a course of 47 degrees. Progress was rather hard as the tide was ebbing strongly in a South-West direction. Capt. Barnes drew ahead as the beach was in sight, landed first, the other 2 canoes coming in on getting the 'all clear' sign; all canoes were beached safely without any surf, at 2345 hrs, and the M.L. contacted by Walkie-Talkie to report landing. The Group took up a defensive position on the beach and Capt. Barnes went ahead to recce inland to the scrub, and returned. Leaving Cpl. Longhurst as guard on the canoes, the remainder advanced in file towards the village across a narrow belt of sand-dunes, a narrow strip of paddy, and into the trees where a basha was found about 400 yds from High Water mark.

At 2358 hrs, Lt. Ryan and Cpl. Kiernan were posted as sentries to stop anyone approaching or leaving the basha. Capt. Barnes, Sgt. Barney, and Sgt. Tough entered the door of the basha, awakened the native and his family. On questioning the native, it was found that he was rather dull, with little knowledge of the enemy, but he said the fishermen of the village knew much more than he did and supplied the Japs at Taungup with fish. Capt. Barnes persuaded him to guide them to the fisherman's basha which he did readily. The Group crossed small paddy fields for about 300 yds inland, and the fisherman proved to be a very old man, but he had quite a lot of knowledge about the enemy, and he called a younger man about 20 years of age who knew still more than himself, so it was decided to bring him back. The simple native and the old man were both given a small amount of money and warned not to say anything of the visit to which they readily agreed. The young man came down to the beach willingly and got into the canoe of his own accord.

The time was now 0110 hrs, and all 3 canoes put to sea on a course of 230 degrees, without getting contact on the Walkie-Talkie to the M.L. After about 20 minutes on the course, Capt. Barnes flashed torch to sea, as arranged by M.L. which was to light mast head-lamp. A light was seen South-West of original position of M.L. and it was believed that the craft had moved out to sea on ebb tide to avoid grounding. Course was then changed and the mast-light approached. After 25 minutes paddling, the light turned shorewards, and Capt. Barnes decided that it was a native boat, as an ML could not get into that depth of water; through the night-glasses, it was visible as a large sailing boat either fishing or a Jap patrol. A new course was worked out to rectify mistake, and after paddling for 15 minutes, Capt. Barnes tried Walkie-Talkie and got contact with M.L. As it was impossible to see signal light, Capt. Barnes asked for Verey light which was instantly seen directly ahead. From this time on, both canoes and M.L. exchanged signals on lamp, and all canoes were aboard at 0345 hrs.

The anchor was weighed and, going slow ahead, at 0355 hrs. M.L.s engaged with their guns the vessel with mast head-light, which went out immediately as did the lights ashore. Owing to the distance between M.L.s and unknown craft, it was impossible to say whether the shoot was successful or not. At 0405 hrs, a course was set for the base, and all except the duty-watch turned in.

The native who had been brought aboard seemed quite happy and content and enjoyed a good meal with the Indian seamen.[8]

During this time 3 Commando Brigade were under command of 25th Indian Division, and Nos 1 and 42 (RM) Commandos took over a section of the line south of Maungdaw. While No 42 had a relatively peaceful time, No 1 was split into two. Half under Major J.H.S. Turnbull MC was in the hills and carried out a number of exhausting patrols, but saw little of the enemy. The other, under Major Davies, had several brushes with the Japanese on the plains, and inflicted a number of casualties on them. 3 Troop also captured a live prisoner, the first on the 25th Division's front for nine months. This was all achieved at a cost of one officer killed in an ambush, but there were awards in the shape of one MC and three MMs. Each Commando also carried out an amphibious raid, No 42 (RM) Commando on Elizabeth Island and No 1 on Ramree.

Akyab, Myebon and Kangaw

XV Indian Corps was, by the end of December, poised to take to the offensive once more, ready to support the attacks by IV and XXXIII Corps from Kohima and Imphal, which had already begun. In order to drive the Japanese 28th Army out of the Arakan, General Christison, the Corps Commander, proposed to use 3 Commando Brigade in a series of outflanking assaults from the sea. A target on which he had long set his eyes was the island of Akyab, and by the end of December, with the Japanese showing signs of withdrawing, it seemed that it was only lightly defended. He therefore decided to attack, with the Commandos landing on beaches on the north of the island. A brigade of 25th Indian Division, under whose command the Commandos still were, would then take over the returning landing craft and be ferried across from the mainland. D-Day was fixed for 3 January, which gave only four days in which to plan the operation. Air reconnaissance drew no fire from the island, and on 1 January a light aircraft of 656 Air OP (Observation Post) Squadron actually landed on the island, to be greeted by enthusiastic villagers, who told the pilot that the last Japanese had left the night before. Christison, nevertheless, decided to go ahead with the operation, considering that it would be good practice. On D-Day, he himself:

> . . . like King Xerxes at the battle of Salamis, took his seat on a high viewpoint overlooking the narrow waters. With him were the GOC and a group of senior Naval, Military and Air Force Officers. Out at sea to the west they saw a host of landing craft of all types approaching in neat formation. Far out to their flank lay the escorting cruisers and destroyers. As the landing craft approached the beach, the naval vessels swung South and took up the positions from which they would have made their bombardment had the landing been contested. But all was quiet as the first craft touched down.[9]

The island was quickly occupied and turned into a supply base for subsequent operations. The Commandos also sent out a number of reconnaissance patrols in LCAs to neighbouring islands, and on one of these No 5 Commando had a satisfactory brush with the enemy, killing four at no loss to themselves.

General Christison's intention now was to destroy the 28th Army before it could get back across the mountains to the Irrawaddy valley. His next target was the Myebon Peninsula, situated thirty miles south-east of Akyab, which commanded the two main waterways used by the Japanese, the Kyatsin River and the Daingbon chaung (river). The plan was for 3 Commando Brigade to land on the south-eastern face of the Peninsula. In the early morning of 10 January,

Brigadier Campbell Hardy carried out a personal reconnaissance of the beach in an ML. He was fired on by a gun in the area of the beach, but noticed a line of coconut stakes some 300 yards from the shore and just above the low water mark. To deal with this, a COPP team was sent out on the night 11/12 January to create a gap in the stakes with delayed action charges designed to detonate just before H-Hour. The following morning the assault was made, with No 42 (RM) Commando making the first landings. The COPPists had succeeded in creating a 25 yard gap through which the landing craft passed, meeting only desultory fire from the shore, and only one was hit. An air smoke screen also helped to cover the landing.

Two problems now arose. First, the Royal Marine Commandos discovered that they had to wade ashore in soft mud, and as successive waves followed, the receding tide aggravated this even more, and prevented tanks of the 19th Indian Lancers from being landed. By the afternoon, it was therefore decided to switch to another beach, which was open from early next morning after it had been prepared by the Indian Engineers. The second problem was anti-personnel mines, the first time that these had been encountered on the beaches of Burma, and one killed the Beachmaster as he stepped ashore.

Nevertheless, No 42 quickly seized their objectives and secured the beachhead, and No 5 Commando passed through. They met little opposition until they came to a hill, codenamed *Rose*, where they came under machine gun fire and suffered a number of casualties.

1 Cdo followed up 5 Cdo and, on ldg, were ordered to clear TIGER feature and also to send a party to DOG ISLAND where there was a suspected enemy gun posn. A suspicion which eventually proved unfounded. As it was now almost low tide it was decided to direct 44 Cdo to DOG BEACH where ldg was easier. However, due to a misunderstanding, this did not occur. As a result the unit had to struggle ashore for a distance of 300 yds through waist deep mud. This took them 3 hrs and neither men nor weapons were in a fighting state by the time they reached the beach. It was then decided to try and land the tks on BAKER Beach but this attempt was met by hy shell and only one tk succeeded in getting ashore. The LCTs were then directed to EASY beach. The tks were able to get ashore but could not get round the pt on CHARLIE RED [the original landing beach] until a rd had been cleared through the boulders by the Engr Tp.* By this time it was apparent that

---

* 3 Troop of the RM Engineer Commando had been part of the Brigade since October 1943. They carried out all normal engineer tasks and were also used as beach parties for amphibious landings. The second troop had operated with 1 Commando Brigade and a third was raised, but never saw active service.

no further adv could be made until Rose feature had been captured and that this would involve a full scale attack. It was too late to lay it on that day, therefore disposns . . . were taken up for the night and plans made for an attack by 5 Cdo supported by tks to take place the next morning. The attack was to be preceded by an air strike and naval bombardment.[10]

At 0830 hours the next day, after the air strike and naval bombardment had gone in, No 5 Commando mounted their attack, supported by A Squadron of the 19th Lancers. The latter employed what was known as a Forward Tank Officer (FTO), who advanced on foot with the Commandos in order to direct the fire of the tanks onto strongpoints which were in danger of holding up the attack. The feature was cleared, although no prisoners were taken, the Japanese preferring to fight until they were killed. No 42 (RM) Commando then came through to attack Myebon village, whch they took with little difficulty, again supported by A Squadron 19th Lancers, but came up against heavy opposition from another feature, *Cabbage*. In spite of casualties, including Lt Colonel H.D. Fellowes, who had taken over command from Lt Colonel de Leathes the previous summer, wounded, they captured this too. No 1 Commando also seized a feature, *Onion*, and just before nightfall No 44 (RM) Commando were brought up from the beachhead and placed in direct support of No 42. This next day was marked by extensive patrolling, which established that the enemy held a series of further hills in some strength, and a brigade attack was planned for the 15th. This was successful, although the planned preparatory air strike did not materialise. The MO of No 42 (RM) Commando, Captain J.W.F. Richardson RAMC, gave his impressions of it:

We advanced via a tortuous hill track in rear of 1 Commando. Halting just behind the top of the hill facing our objective we listened to the clatter of machine gun fire as No 1 went into the attack. With the assistance of tanks they were soon on top of their objective. A message was sent back for eight of our stretcher bearers to go to them immediately and four more were called forward a few minutes later. Throughout our concealed journey we did not meet any snipers ourselves, but a press photographer who was moving about in the jungle was very nearly taken for one. Our Commando formed up under cover of the hillside opposite our objective. We had a hundred yards of open paddy to charge across before we got to it. The first wave streaked across the paddy which was already burning furiously as a result of the smoke from our mortars which had been fired into it to give us concealment. Although heavily bunkered the Japs were in no mood to stand and fight. They were seen retreating at the double over the hilltop. Someone said they were going faster than our bullets. We boxed* there that night and rum was issued with the evening meal (this consisted of a fraction of a tin of self heating soup!).[11]

The next two days were spent patrolling and mopping up, until, on the 18th, 74 Brigade passed through and cleared the remaining Japanese from the peninsula. From captured documents and the interrogation of the only two prisoners captured, it was established that there had been some 250 Japanese on the peninsula in 3 Commando Brigade's area, and only forty of these had got away. In comparison, especially bearing in mind the enemy's initial fanaticism, the Commando casualties were surprisingly light – five killed and thirty wounded. The brigade now withdrew to the beachhead for a welcome two days' rest.

With the Myebon Peninsula now cleared, the enemy was denied the use of the waterways in order to evacuate the Arakan, and the only escape route left to him was the Myobaung-Tamandu road. General Christison decided, therefore, that this should be cut, and selected Kangaw, where there was a bend in the road as it left the plain and swung east into the hills. To advance by land would take too long, since three water obstacles would have to be crossed, and a water-borne advance direct from the Myebon river would likely as not alert the enemy. He therefore decided on an indirect water-borne approach, advancing south-east from Myebon into the lower Daingbon chaung and then north for a distance of 18 miles. This was clearly a task for 3 Commando Brigade and on the nights 19/20 and 20/21 January, COPP teams were sent up to find suitable beaches. Campbell Hardy's general plan was for No 1 Commando to land first and seize the dominant Hill 170, which lay between the chaung and the village of Kangaw. No 42 would then establish the bridgehead, which would be bounded by *Thames* and *Mersey*, two tributaries of the Daingbon chaung, and No 5 would pass through to help No 1. No 44 would land and be held in reserve. In support there was a battery of 25 pdrs, which were placed on Z craft (lighters), and from the day after the initial landing the 8th Hyderabads and a troop of the 19th Lancers would be under command. One major problem was that information about the enemy in the area was scanty.

---

*A piece of jargon from the Burma campaign which meant establishing an all round defensive position.

The Commandos joined up with their landing craft on the following night, and set off on what Peter Young called 'a most hazardous procession of boats up the chaung'.[12] Luckily, only in the last stage was there any indication of the enemy, when the flotilla was subjected to some shellfire.

As for the landing, Peter Young again:

> There was no road. The landing was through mangrove; the paddy for about 3/4 mile, leading up to [Hill] 170 was swamped by the spring tides. Even the bunds didn't make proper footpaths being broken in many places. No tanks could be got ashore – or guns – the first few days, but we had air support, mediums for the Myebon area and a lighter battery and a sloop. MLs and LCs guarded the chaung L of C.[13]

Nevertheless, No 1 Commando were quickly ashore, landing at 1300 hours on that day, the 22nd, under the cover of an aircraft laid smokescreen. They cleared the area of the bridgehead and then pushed onto Hill 170. This they succeeded in securing, apart from a small pocket on the northern tip. With No 42 now ashore, No 5 Commando were moved to help No 1, and No 44 were stood by to put in an attack on another feature just east of Hill 170, *Milford*. This they did at 1930 hours and captured it without meeting any opposition. During the night, the enemy launched a counter-attack on No 1 Commando from the northern tip of Hill 170, but this was beaten back, although not without hand-to-hand fighting. At first light next morning they cleared the remaining enemy from Hill 170, and No 44 were then ordered forward to *Pinner*, a small feature south-west of Kangaw. By now, the 8th Hyderabads had been landed, and they took over No 42 (RM) Commando's role in the bridgehead, and No 42 now held *Milford*. During the day there was intermittent shelling of the bridgehead, but it had been possible to get the troop of tanks ashore, and these joined No 1 Commando on the north end of Hill 170. No 44 sent a reconnaissance patrol to *Nuns* and reported a small enemy post just to the north of it. That night the enemy mounted a strong counter-attack on *Pinner* with artillery support.

> Those of us who were not on watch were soon dozing in our trenches, but at approximately nine o'clock in the evening we were rudely awakened by shells landing on the centre of the hill some fifty yards away. It was not long before long bursts of MG tore through the trees above our heads. The shelling increased in intensity and mortars then joined in as the cresendo reached its climax. Before this we had had little respect for

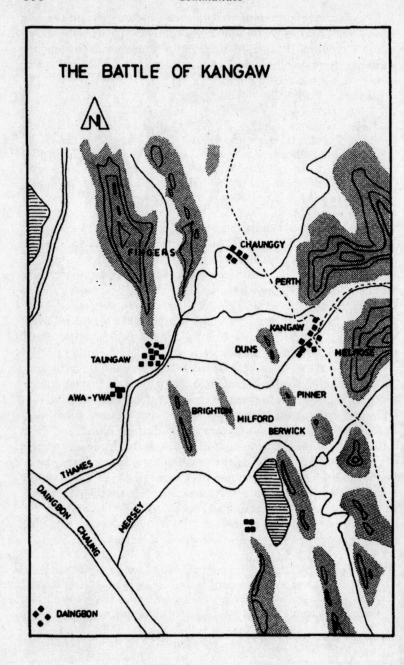

THE BATTLE OF KANGAW

the Jap artillery, but the officer in command of these guns had obviously read his amendments for the shells were bursting right on the target.

Our comrades to our left were surrounded by dust, and periodically the area was illuminated by exploding shells and the smell of cordite hung in the air. The guns were not very far away as the flashes and shell-bursts were almost simultaneous. Soon the Japs appeared clambering up a little reentrant at the top of which we had three sections – two from my troop, and one from the troop on our left. The MMG continued its uninterrupted task as we could not spare an LMG to engage it. The first wave of Japs were not very persistent and were soon tumbling down the hill again having come face to face with the steady and accurate fire from our two LMGs. It was evident that we had inflicted casualties as the excited Nip was squealing in the paddy below and near the summit of the hill sickly groans punctuated the eerie stillness. My right hand platoon on the end of the hill had remained silent.

We waited motionless. The shelling had subsided and below in the undergrowth confused Japs were calling to each other in an effort to reorganise, and having done so they came again – this time with more determination and considerably less silence. Once more the MMG began its monotonous stutter and some of the Japs succeeded in crawling to some 5 yards from the top of the hill under its accurate cover. There, however, their journey ended for once again our LMGs took their hungry toll and grenades lobbed down the hill made life very unpleasant for those who were following in the wake of their braver comrades. We sustained two casualties from the MMG and these had to be dragged from their trenches to a safer area. The Japs continued to come and discharger cups were now being used from the foot of the hill in an effort to assist the assaulting troops to penetrate our defences. These grenades could be clearly seen silhouetted against the moon dropping through the trees into the trenches of the left hand section of the reentrant. Moving across to this area it did not take long for one to appreciate that things were pretty serious and that reinforcements were required. The grenades had inflicted severe casualties on the section and an equal number of men were dragging away the wounded and dying to safety. The remainder of the section were only armed with pistols and grenades and were running out. The wireless was not working so an orderly was sent to HQ, but returned with the information that nobody could be spared from other sectors as the enemy shelling had considerably depleted our numbers.

During this period a medical orderly was busy crawling from trench to trench administering to the wounded. As he crawled into one trench a grenade landed beside him. Instantly he picked it up and threw it to one side, but it burst in its flight, wounding him in the face and shoulder.

It was decided to reinforce this section with a section which had been given the task of guarding a track to our rear – leaving two men behind on the track as sentries to warn us of the approach of the enemy up the track. The Bren gun was first to arrive in the new position, but it remainded silent as the number one was immediately killed and the number two wounded in the head. Fortunately a marine following flung himself down by the gun and brought it into action. He was soon followed by Tommy-gunners and riflemen so the evacuation of the casualties was able to proceed. The marine firing the Bren was subsequently wounded, but remained as number two of the gun refusing to be evacuated. The right hand platoon was still silent – The Japs appeared at a loss to know what to do and one shouted, 'Play the game Johnny Commando – come down here and fight'. The proverbial comic immediately replied, 'Send your pals away and I'll come right down and sort you out, you little yellow b—d'. In the meantime, the Japs had moved a mortar into the paddy below and the orders given to the crew could be clearly heard followed by explosions in the trees above our heads.

Again the bewildered babble of fanatical Japs was heard and it appeared that an O [Orders] Group was in progress at the bottom of the hill. Our last grenade went down and from the subsequent confusion it had obviously not been wasted.

They tried to break through in force again but the fire from our Brens and the steady shooting of the riflemen who sat and waited until they could actually see a target before firing frustrated this attempt as successfully as the previous two.

It was now necessary to fill Bren mags from bandoliers and several were collected from the riflemen. It was fortunate that at this stage the Jap decided to think again and for the next half an hour only odd parties of one or two endeavoured to approach our positions on the hilltop – but down below they could still be heard rummaging about in the undergrowth calling for one another dazed from the punishment they had received and which had been so savagely dealt out.

It was just after two o'clock in the morning and the moon was still shining brightly. As one visited the various sections with the initial intention of cheering up the men one soon realised how futile was the idea. Superfluous words were not required as every man was so obviously determined and confident of the outcome of the struggle. One of the sentries on the track, a cockney, smiled and said 'Don't worry, Sir, they will not get up here'. That remark indicated the spirit all round. We were later able to send a Bren gun to the track; the gun had been sent over from another sector where there was nobody left to fire it. The odd parties coming up the hill grew more frequent, and suddenly the platoon on the right came to life providing the solution to the interrupted Jap 0 group some time previously. Their efforts against this platoon were equally unsuccessful and after a second final attempt they gave up and joined with those they had left behind below. A few minutes later an ambitious Jap tried to get up the track and to our rear. One shot rang out. It was sufficient. Our smiling cockney friend had kept his word.

The moon had now gone down as it was now after three o'clock. From below a voice shouted, 'All right, we will be back in the morning'. 'Tata for now', replied the comic. We heard the mortar being dismantled but waited nodding with fatigue.

Sure enough they came back about two hours later, but little effort was made to gain the hill. It was obvious that the Nip had really returned to collect his less fortunate comrades who were unable to make their own way back. We hindered them in their task and as dawn came we could see the stragglers disappearing in the half light. So it was all over. Our own casualties had been heavy and the night long – but the hill had been held.[14]

No 44 suffered some sixty casualties during this battle, including 26 killed, and on the morning of the 24th they were relieved by the Hyderabads and withdrew to Hill 170.

The brigade was now ordered to stand firm and not attempt to exploit further. Then, on the 25th, Hill 170 came under heavy shellfire, with no less than 182 shells landing in one half hour spell. This was to continue over the next four days. On the 26th, 51 Brigade landed and took over *Melford* and *Pinner* and No 42 was withdrawn to the beachhead area. On 28 January, 51 Brigade launched an attack on Kangaw, and the two features which dominated it to the east, *Perth* and *Melrose*, which also marked the entrance of the Myoang-Tamandu road into the hills. That on *Perth* failed to make any impression, but by nightfall most of *Melrose* was in the hands of the Indians. This attack was resumed next day, while No 5 Commando laid an ambush and patrolled Kangaw, but no signs of the enemy using the road were seen. On the 30th, orders were given that the Commandos should be relieved, and were to begin thinning out the next day. While No 5 Commando remained under command of 51 Brigade on *Pinner*, No 44 returned to Daingbon and was placed under command of 51 Brigade. This left No 1 and No 42 on Hill 170.

On the morning of 31 January, just before first light, the defenders of Hill 170 were preparing to stand to. The northern end of the feature was held by No 4 Troop of No 1 Commando, and also here was the 19th Lancers' tank leaguer. From the diary of Captain Merriam, second-in-command of the Lancers' A Squadron:

We were rudely awakened by some very fast and accurate shell-fire at about 0545 which continued until about 0620 when a babble of voices in the nearby bushes west of our position followed by the noise of machine-guns indicated that we were being attacked. The first twenty minutes were more confused as it was definitely a case of the queen getting into the back line in as much as the Japs got into our perimeter![15]

Two out of the three tanks managed to get out, but the third was blown up by Japanese engineers, killing the complete crew. Meanwhile, No 4 Troop under Lieutenant Semple were hotly engaged, with the platoon* under Lieutenant G.A. Knowland, Royal Norfolks, taking the brunt. By 0830 hours, with ammunition running low, Knowland's men were finally forced to give up some of their positions. Twenty-four men had held up 300 Japanese for over two hours, and he himself had constantly been in the forefront of the battle.

> . . . he took over a 2" Mortar, whose crew had been spent to replace casualties in forward trenches. Once again, in spite of heavy fire and the closeness of the enemy, he stood up in the open to face them, firing the Mortar from his hip, and killing 6 of them with his first bomb. When all bombs were expended he went back through heavy grenade, mortar and machine-gun fire to get more, which he fired in the same way from the open in front of his platoon positions. When these bombs were finished he went back to his own trench and still standing up fired his rifle at them. Being hard pressed and with enemy closing on him from only 10 yds away, he had no time to recharge his magazine. Snatching up the Tommy gun of a casualty he sprayed the enemy and was mortally wounded in stemming this assault, though not before he had killed and wounded some ten of them.[16]

His inspiration to his men was such that the survivors managed to cling on to their remaining positions for the rest of the day. There are few incidents where the Victoria Cross had been better earned.†

Colonel Trevor now came up to see for himself, and arranged for a platoon from W Troop of No 42 (RM) Commando to help No 4 Troop. Part of this put in a counter-attack, which was beaten back, and then a platoon of No 3 Troop arrived, and were ordered by Lieutenant Semple to clear the east side slope of the position. J.J. Edmans was one of the section commanders:

---

*Unlike in the other Commandos, troops in 3 Commando Brigade were organised into platoons rather than sections, probably to avoid confusion in XV Indian Corps, who considered the latter term as an element of a platoon.

†Naik (Corporal) Jag Mai of the 8th Hyderabads also won the VC during the fighting around Kangaw.

We moved forward in single file, bullets ripping through the trees. The fighting on our left got fierce. We were moving down the side of the hill when Pte Dearden went down. On looking at him we could see that he was dead. We carried on, crouching low. Then Sgt Roberts went down, but was able to crawl back without help.

At least we reached the bottom of the hill and stopped to appreciate our situation. A few yards away from the bottom of the hill, in the paddy field, was an old bamboo hut. From this hut you could see round the other side of the hill. Pte Hobbs dashed to the hut and then let off a couple of bursts from his Tommy Gun. He came back to say that he had got four Japs who had been waiting round the other side of the hill. He then dashed back to the hut again, but unfortunately a sniper must have spotted him as he came running back holding his jaw, which was pouring with blood, having been smashed by a bullet. We took up position at the bottom of the hill, facing upwards. Ptes McFall and Sweeney, our Bren team, were on the flank. They let off a couple of bursts as they had seen movement. Then a grenade fell between them, but failed to go off. Another grenade came down and this caught them in the body and face. Our position was now hopeless down at the bottom, and so we decided to move to higher ground. Having moved up the hill we heard someone moaning. We looked back towards the hut and saw Gnr Beaney lying in the open. A couple of the lads went back to pick him up, but as soon as they got to the paddy field all hell was let loose in front of them. We tossed down some smoke grenades, but with no effect. A wall of fire was being put down which would have been suicide to pass through. We made several attempt to try and get him out, but it was to no avail. What made things worse was that all the time this was going on, he kept calling out 'They're gone now' and shouting our names.

We passed the word back to HQ about Beaney and what we had done to try and get him out, but the order came back that were not to try any more, and so we carried on to the higher ground, hoping that we would be able to pick him up later. We also heard that Sgt Lander, who had been with us since Independent Company days, had been killed by a sniper. We got to the top of the hill and took up positions. Then they came, swarms of them charging up the hill, shouting and yelling. We let them come on and waited. When they were near enough so that we could not miss, we gave them the lot. After some time, and very, very depleted, they gave up, leaving their dead and wounded.[17]

While this battle was going on, the Brigade Commander himself came up onto the hill, and decided to use X Troop of No 42 to recover the lost ground. This attack went in at 1230 hours supported by one tank of the 19th Lancers. The leading platoon suffered heavy casualties from machine gun fire, and the second platoon could not get any further forward, and eventually joined the remainder of 4 Troop in their positions. A platoon of No 6 Troop then made an attempt, but had 50% casualties, and the rest of the troop also joined 4 Troop. By now it was mid afternoon and the Brigade Commander ordered no more counter-attacks until nightfall. Lt Colonel C.J.B. Pollitt MC, formerly of No 1 and now commanding No 5 Commando, came forward with one of his troops, which was made available to Ken Trevor, as was, on Campbell Hardy's orders, a second troop. Returning to his own headquarters, Pollitt was wounded in the knee and his place was taken by Major Robin Stuart, the Second-in-Command.

By this time, 1700 hours, the enemy's attacks had ceased, and only a few snipers were in evidence. Ken Trevor therefore set about trying to tidy up the situation, with the troops of three Commandos now intermingled on the north end of Hill 170. The two troops of No 42 pulled back, and 2 Troop of No 5 Commando relieved the forward elements of No 1 Commando. The enemy made no further attacks during the night, and early on the following morning No 5 Commando cleared and reconsolidated the position. It was only then that the Commandos began to realise what had happened. No less than 340 Japanese dead were found. As for the battle itself, Peter Young:

> Jap dead were inter-locked with our own in a proportion of at least 3 to 1. The back slopes of the hill were thick with the victims of our 25 pdrs and 3" mortars which respectively fired at positions 100 and 40 yds ahead of our own troops! It was a real epic. I never saw dead so thick. The bosche could not have stood five hours of it! We got 4 PW – all wounded. At least 10 officers swords were picked up and 2 MMG besides a number of Brens (not necessarily taken from US [sic] for the Japs love to use them). They used many 36 grenades. I found one Jap with his finger in the pin of one . . . Several 1 Cdo soldiers were found well forward alone, dead, in the middle of the Japs, having pushed on in these counter-attacks after their first sections were finished. One RM officer killed 4 Japs and got 4 wounds . . . All this in about 2 acres of ground, where manoeuvre off the hill was pretty impossible, except at long range, being open paddy . . . I'm convinced that no British troops ever fought better than ours on that day . . .[18]

One officer of No 5 Commando concluded: 'Kangaw was no picnic, and I've never been so bloody scared in all my life. It wasn't so much the fighting as the shelling that got us down. They had about 20 guns firing at us all the time.'[19] Another wrote:

The bravery shown must go down in the annals of Military History. 12 men, one after another, were hit behind one vital Bren gun, each accounting for a number of Japs . . . Today I'm a proud man to think that I was beside such gallant fellows.[20]

The cost, however, had been high. When the Commandos were relieved later on 1 February, five officers and forty other ranks lay buried on the hill, while a further six and 84 had been wounded.

Back in Myebon, where No 44 rejoined, it became clear what they had achieved. If the Japanese had seized Hill 170, they would have:

. . . cut off our troops on the road from the beaches, their source of supply. Had this action been successful it would have been impossible for 51 st Indian Infantry Brigade to maintain their strangle-hold on the road at this particular time, and the whole of the Kangaw operation would have been doomed to failure.[21]

Indeed, as General Christison himself wrote in a Special Order of the Day to 3 Commando Brigade: 'The battle of KANGAW has been the decisive battle of the whole ARAKAN campaign and that it was won was very largely due to your magnificent defence of Hill 170.'[22] Awards flowed in, including a third DSO for Campbell Hardy and a DSO for Ken Trevor, besides Knowland's VC, and the brigade was flooded with publicity:

We were cheered by all (including Indians) when we went out. The Divisional General* has said and written officially, that he has never seen a braver crowd – that we are the finest fighting troops in all Burma etc etc.

It's very embarrassing going round wearing the green beret really – Mountbatten is beside himself with joy – we've been given the privilege of choosing our own monsoon quarters in India or Ceylon. The Division has presented us with a complete set of clothing per man and this is only two days after the battle. We're being bothered by newspaper men now and I'm up to my neck writing an account of it all.[23]

In the event, the brigade moved first to Akyab, and then back to Madras, where all were given leave. Short spells outside Poona and at Ahmednagar followed, and then they finally came to rest at Kharakvasla, where they began preparations for the invasion of Malaya, Operation *Zipper*.

---

*Major General G.H. Wood OBE MC Commanding 25th Indian Division.

No 30 Commando Activities in South-East Asia

In the summer of 1943 Mountbatten asked for two officers from No 30 to be sent out to South-East Asia in order to examine the possibility of employing intelligence assault units in various operations which were being envisaged at that time. Eventually, in February 1944, the Director of Naval Intelligence sent Quentin Riley out. On his arrival, he discovered that an inter-service assault intelligence unit was in the process of being set up under Lt Colonel Cass, the original commander of the Army Troop in No 30, and that this would be part of the Small Operations Group. As Brigadier Nonweiler had already found, however, there were no suitable operations being mounted in the immediate future, and Riley and Cass contented themselves with a lengthy tour of the front in Burma and visits to all higher commanders and intelligence agencies with whom they might have to coordinate in the future. Riley then returned to the United Kingdom.

Nothing further happened until March 1945, when Colonel Quill suggested that a detachment of 30 Assault Unit be transferred from North-West Europe in order to obtain samples of Japanese weapons and investigate the organisation and operational planning techniques of the Japanese Naval Staff. While this received the approval of Admiral Godfrey, the DNI, SEAC were initially not in favour, stating that other arrangements had already been made. Nevertheless, a few days later, SEAC obviously remembered Cass's unit, and stated that it was to include a naval section of three or four officers and five or six other ranks, which they asked to be sent from Europe, to arrive at Kandy in Ceylon no later than the end of July.

Trevor Glanville was selected to lead the detachment, and he took with him Lt Commander Rouson OBE GM RNVR and Lieutenant Pratchett GM RNVR, as underwater specialists, and five Royal Marines. The reason for this sudden change of mind was *Zipper*, and Glanville was informed by the Director of Intelligence at HQ SEAC of the outline of the plan, which involved an initial landing at Penang, followed by a drive down to and across the Straits of Johore to Singapore. As for the Intelligence Assault Unit's role, they were to land on D+3 and follow the advance of the 5th Indian Armoured Division down to Singapore. To Glanville this bore all the hallmarks of the early misuse of No 30 Commando in the Mediterranean in that they would be arriving too late to find anything of value. Instead, he proposed that his team should land with 3 Commando Brigade at Cape Rachado, where there was a Japanese radar station. At this late stage it was going to be difficult to find room in the assault craft and, in any event, as it was pointed out, the Intelligence Assault Unit was largely made up of members of the Secret Services, Civil Affairs and the Psychological Warfare Board, who had not been trained for a combat role. Eventually it was agreed that Glanville should accompany 3 Commando Brigade and that arrangements would also be made for him and four of his men to join up with the Indian Airborne Division for their drop into Singapore.

By this time, momentous events had taken place in the Pacific with the dropping of the atomic bombs on Hiroshima on 6 August and on Nagasaki three days later. The Soviet Union had finally declared war on Japan on the 8th, and on the 14th the Emperor Hirohito announced that Japan was accepting the Allied surrender terms. For 3 Commando Brigade this meant that plans had to be hurriedly recast for what was now to be just the occupation of Penang, but, on setting sail, the Commandos were then told that their destination was to be Hong Kong, and it was perhaps symbolic that one of the two ships which took them there was one of the first of the Commando ships, *Glengyle*.

Glanville was told that he was also to take part in the occupation of Penang and Singapore, which went under the codename of *Tideracer*, but, on arrival at Calcutta, he was informed that he was now to go to Indo-China. He protested that, from a naval intelligence point of view, Singapore was much more important. After some discussion, it was agreed that he should continue to Indo-China, leaving Rouson to handle Singapore and Pratchett Penang. They managed to recover a number of examples of Japanese torpedoes, but Flag Officer Malaya blocked Rouson's request to extend his activities to Saigon, Hong Kong and Tokyo, and this was only reversed when Glanville visited Singapore in November. He himself now found that he was with the bulk of Cass's unit, which also had an Army and RAF sections, in Indo-China. Initially, Glanville found himself very restricted by an edict which stated that he was not to do anything until the problem of the liquidation of the Japanese Secret Police, the Kempei Tei, had been resolved. Nevertheless, he did obtain a signed order from the Japanese Commander-in-Chief, Count Terrauchi, that all under his command were to give Glanville any assistance that he might require, and eventually he obtained much useful material.[24]

Thus, unlike in Italy and Germany, the campaign in South-East Asia ended as a 'whisper' rather than a 'bang' for the Commandos, and for 30 Assault Unit it proved to be particularly frustrating that their operational techniques, which had become finally honed in North-West Europe, should not have been understood by SEAC.

CHAPTER ELEVEN

Appraisal and Aftermath

While there is no doubt that from *Torch* onwards, the Commandos made a significant contribution to victory, both in Europe and the Far East, the achievements of both UK-based Commandos prior to D-Day and those who served in the Middle East in the early days are more a matter of debate. Their origins lay in the need to instil an offensive spirit in an army bewildered by the events of May 1940. Yet that army, now faced with invasion of the homeland and short of equipment, could do no more than remain on the defensive for the time being. It was, too, imperative that any offensive operations be mounted from a secure base. The idea of earmarking a regular formation of the Field Army was considered, but quickly dropped in view of the paucity of troops to guard the coastline. Also, equipment was far too short to consider anything more than minor 'smash and grab' operations in the early days. It was thus logical that a special force should be formed and trained accordingly, and that it should be made up of volunteers. Yet, those who volunteer for hazardous operations are invariably those who can be ill spared from their units, and it was understandable that there should have been some resentment in Home Forces, especially after the abortive raids in the summer of 1940, and then a long period of time when it seemed that the Commandos were not doing anything to 'earn their keep'.

It was always the intention that the Commandos should be but the steel tip to a much larger amphibious assault shaft. Once the threat of invasion had receded, efforts were made to begin training Home Forces formations in amphibious offensive operations. As we have seen, this quickly came to naught with the decisions to send Force Z to the Mediterranean and, later, *Tonic* to West Africa, which tied up the amphibious capability at the time, and left little for UK-based operations. The projected operation against Rhodes fitted well into the account of Churchill's desire to give physical support to the Greeks, but the arrival of the Afrika Korps in Libya and Rommel's counter-offensive put paid to it, and Wavell, desperately short of men on all fronts, was forced to use Layforce on other tasks. They now found themselves suffering from much the same problems which had dogged the original Middle East Commandos.

The Commandos raised in the Middle East in the summer of 1940 operated in a very different environment to those at home. While in Britain the Army was not actually engaged with the enemy, the Middle East Forces found themselves quickly involved in a series of campaigns, against the Italians in Libya, East Africa and later Abyssinia. Equipment for the Commandos was therefore in even shorter supply than it was back in England, and there was less appreciation of their strengths and limitations. Too often, therefore, the Middle East Commandos, and Layforce as well, found themselves being regarded more as a source of manpower rather than for their specialist skills. This was especially so in East Africa and Abyssinia, and particularly during the Crete disaster. When they were correctly used, they fell victims to poor intelligence and slipshod planning from above.

After the disbandment of Layforce and No 51 ME Commando in the autumn of 1941, the reconstituted Middle East Commando found itself pulled in too many directions. Above were GHQ Middle East and the Royal Navy and SOE, while within there were David Stirling's concept of reducing Axis air power by destroying aircraft on the ground, the activities of the SBS and the more shadowy intelligence roles developed by SOE and G(R) Branch. With other 'private armies' such as the Long Range Desert Group and Popski's Private Army also in the field, there was understandable confusion, and Stirling's steps to resolve this by bringing all the Commandos *per se* under the umbrella of the SAS in August 1942 were logical. From now on, there was a clearcut definition of tasks with the LRDG continuing its role of reconnaissance, the SBS being responsible for raiding behind enemy lines and Popski's assisting both with his indigenous force. Nevertheless, the anathema towards private armies in the Middle East persisted, and indicative of this was the refusal of Cairo to accept a Phantom* unit, the only theatre of war in which this happened.

Both Brooke and Paget also had understandable resentment towards the Commandos at home. It was as if they alone were being allowed the privilege of developing the offensive spirit which the Field Force as a whole so desperately needed if it was going to go

---

*Phantom, or the GHQ Liaison Regiment, was originally formed in 1939 with the object of pinpointing forward troop positions for the RAF. It was later developed into a means of passing back immediate battle information to the commander. For a full account see Warner, Philip *Phantom* (Kimber, London, 1982).

from the defensive to the attack, which had to happen for the war to be won. Yet, the resources simply did not exist for each formation in Home Force to carry out offensive operations during 1941 and the early part of 1942. As we have seen, the one formation which did attempt this, V Corps, was able to only mount one operation during the year's life of its School of Raiding.

During this time, the Commandos mounted major raids on the Norwegian coastline and small operations across the Channel. The Norwegian raids were very successful and laid the foundation of the strategy designed to firstly prevent the Germans reinforcing the Eastern Front from here, as well as, later on part of the deception plan for *Overlord*. The cross-Channel raids were of more questionable value. Few of them were entirely successful *per se*, but, on the other hand, the indirect benefits were large. Firstly, they forced the Germans to tie down troops on the coast, which again prevented reinforcement of the Eastern Front at a very critical periods for the Russians. Secondly, the lessons learnt in both execution and planning were invaluable in perfecting the technique of raiding and, more important, amphibious landings. Lastly, they helped maintain the morale of not just the Commandos themselves, but the country at large. It generated the same feeling as the fledgling strategic bombing offensive that the country was hitting back at the enemy. Yet the publicity given to these raids was a two-edged weapon as it also tended to increase the resentment in Home Forces towards the Commandos.

Madagascar marked the first occasion when the Commandos were used in what was to become their fundamental role, the spearheading of major amphibious assaults on opposed shores. Dieppe, although a disaster, did confirm how important they were in this role, and the Royal Navy would have suffered many more casualties in ships without the efforts of No 3 and No 4 Commandos against the coastal batteries. From now on, the inclusion of Commandos would be a vital ingredient of success in any landing.

The small raiding operations in the post Dieppe era turned now to specialist small raiding forces – SSRF, Nos 10, 12 and 14 Commandos, SBS. Here again, they ensured that the enemy slept uneasily, but it was realised by the end of 1943 that, with *Overlord* only months away, they would also encourage the enemy to strengthen his coastal defences in France still further. There was, too, the clash of interests which had been experienced in the Middle East, with Combined Operations, SOE, SIS and the Admiralty finding themselves in competition with one another, and it was this which brought about the demise of No 62 Commando. On the other hand, the intelligence gained was especially important for the planning of *Overlord*, and here the part played by the COPPs and the *Tarbrush* operations of No 3 (Misc) Troop of No 10 (IA) Commando in May 1944 deserve particular mention.

Indeed, Combined Operations spawned many offshoots of the Commandos, and all had a particular role to play. A prerequisite of any successful amphibious landing was detailed information on the beaches, and the art of beach reconnaissance, as pioneered by Courtney and Clogstoun-Willmott at Rhodes in early 1941, contributed much to the success of subsequent landings from *Torch* onwards. Likewise, it was quickly realised that, although the initial landing might be successful, unless the beach itself was properly organised, chaos would quickly ensue, and hence the formation of the Royal Naval Beachhead Commandos. The water skills of the SBS and Royal Marine Boom Patrol Detachment also contributed, and indicative of their value was the high demand for the services of the Small Operations Group in South-East Asia. Not to be forgotten, as well, was the part played by No 30 Commando. Without the use of their particular expertise much valuable technical intelligence would have been lost, and indeed much more would have been gained if commanders in some theatres had woken up earlier to No 30's intended role.

As for the individual Commando himself, the publicity given to him during the war tended to make him out to be some form of cut-throat, highly individualistic and with little regard for the niceties and discipline of ordinary military life. This was an unfortunate misrepresentation, and only helped to fuel resentment in some quarters against the Commando concept. All the early ex-Commandos to whom I have talked, both UK-based and Middle East, joined, not so much to get away from the monotony of life in a normal unit, but because they wanted to take a more active part in the war in order to see it won sooner rather than later. While in very early days, emphasis was on the Commando operating as an individual, it was quickly realised that unless the necessary self- and corporate discipline was instilled, he would be of little value. The same went for basic military skills, and it was competence in these which gave the Commando his inherent flexibility. Thus, apart from his specialist roles, he could fight just as well as an ordinary infantryman, as Crete, Tunisia, Normandy and Hill 170 showed. What marked him as different from the ordinary soldier was that he had to be physically fitter, capable of operating both as part of a large body and on his own, and have a greater versatility of skills. As good a definition as any of what was demanded of him is in a post-war Royal Marine pamphlet on Commando training. It defines the tactical characteristics of Commandos as:

> The Commando must firstly be a highly skilled infantryman. Secondly, he must be expert in his own branch of infantry work. He must:-
> (a) Be able to move fast across any country and be independent of roads.
> (b) Be very happy to fight at night.
> (c) Be ready to work in small parties or on his own.
> (d) Be able to land on coasts impracticable to normal infantry and follow up climbing leaders in cliff assaults.

The pamphlet recognised, however, that more important than anything else was the incalculation of the right psychological attitude. This is called 'the Commando spirit', which was made up of:

> (a) Determination.
> (b) Enthusiasm and cheerfulness, especially under bad conditions.
> (c) Individual initiative and self reliance.
> (d) Comradeship.[1]

This enabled the Commando to operate conventionally in the front line and behind the enemy's lines with equal impunity.

The Army Commando always lived under the threat that he would be returned to his parent unit should he fail to meet the high standards demanded, and he initially resented the later Royal Marine Commandos in that they were straightforward conversions of existing battalions, who did not go through the same filter that he had. The Royal Marine, on the other hand, considered that his army counterpart had usurped a role which was rightfully his. General Sturges quickly recognised the rift between the two, and rightly realised that the original concept of having separate RM and Army Commando Brigades was a mistake. Once the two found themselves alongside one another in action, they quickly appreciated that they were both the same. While the Royal Marine Commando came to respect the skills and experience built up by his Army counterpart, the Army Commando recognised the adaptability of the Royal Marine, who had been brought up to be equally at home on board ship as on the land. Indeed, it had only been pre-war parsimony that had prevented the Royal Marines from taking on the role in the first place. As it was, amphibious strike forces, without which ultimate victory could not be gained, had to be built up from scratch, and it was the Commandos Who pioneered the concept and handed the torch on to the Field Army.

Aftermath

With the end of the war in Europe, 1 and 4 Commando Brigades found themselves tussling with the problems of the occupation of Germany. Their experiences in the early days are well summed up in this No 10 (IA) Commando account:

> Problems were many and varied, and owing to lack of directives had to be dealt with on the spot and at the local Commander's discretion. First essential was to show the local inhabitants that we were the conquering army and the second to establish some sort of check and control on the swarms of miscellaneous wanderers.
>
> This was done by the imposition of a 24 hrs curfew, the organisation of road pickets and stragglers' camps, the collection of arms, the appointment of a Burgomeister and the presentation to him of a list of tasks which he was to set about without delay.
>
> The following day a Mil.Gov [Military Government] Office was established, and water and electricity supply were regulated, instructions on the treatment and disposal of POWs were received from higher authority, and a quick round-up of the local Nazis was made, aided by a flood of denunciations.
>
> It is impossible to describe all the tasks which demanded accomplishment, but amongst the problems which kept us continually occupied were the following: displaced persons, numbering many thousands; these took very unkindly to discipline and found looting a more profitable pastime than obedience. Prisoners: these included ex-army stragglers, civilian refugees without papers, Nazi officials that had been rounded up, and German civilians who had committed some breach of the regulations. The total number of all these detainees became so vast that the problem of feeding, accommodating and exercising them was a serious one. Questioning and interpreting: in spite of the excellent work done by the few members of No 3 Troop 10 Commando whom we had attacked to us, we were seriously handicapped by a shortage of interpreters. Guards: our commitment in this respect taxed our manpower resources to the utmost.
>
> Such were the main problems, but there were many besides, which called for all our ingenuity.[2]

After a few weeks a more permanent scheme was worked out, and much of the load was taken off the shoulders of the fighting troops with the setting up of a proper government of occupation, and this gave some opportunity to unwind after the long years of war. 2 Commando Brigade, in view of the time which they had spent in the Mediterranean theatre, managed to escape this role. They returned to England in June 1945 and were quartered around Hampshire.

No 3 Commando Brigade arrived in Hong Kong on 12 September 1945, and one of their first duties was to help the Royal Navy accept the formal surrender of the Japanese forces in the colony, which took place on the 16th. In many ways, the task which they faced was even more difficult than that in Germany. There was no government infrastructure, apart from those government servants who had survived almost four years of captivity, and the Commandos found themselves acting as the local police force. Their two main problems were dealing with looters and rioting among the mercurial Chinese population, but their tasks also extended to such local government problems as keeping the streets clean. For this they were dispersed throughout the colony and the New Territories. They also had to guard the Japanese internment camps. Sadly, shortly after their arrival, Campbell Hardy left for England and his place was taken by Brigadier H.D. Fellowes DSO, now fully recovered from the wound which he received at Myebon. He had earlier taken over as Deputy Commander from Peter Young.

During this time much thought had been taking place in London on the future of the Commandos in Britain's post-war armed forces. In mid-1944 a committee had been set up under the chairmanship of Air Marshal Sir Norman Bottomley, the Deputy Chief of the Air Staff, to consider the future inter-Service responsibility for amphibious warfare, with special reference to the Royal Marines, and its findings were approved by Churchill in August 1944. In essence, it was recommended that the Royal Marines resume responsibility for amphibious striking forces, as had been originally recommended by the Madden Committee in 1924. The Chiefs of Staff at their meeting of 27 September 1945 reconsidered the matter, and it was agreed that the Army Commandos, who, in any event, had remained merely seconded from their parent regiments and corps, should be disbanded forthwith, and that the Royal Marines be responsible for manning one Commando Brigade of three Commandos for peacetime service.[3] In conjunction with this the Commando Group would also be dismantled.

Bob Laycock, who had fought in vain to keep the Army Commandos in being, chose to break the news by addressing the Army Commandos of 1 Commando Brigade, who had returned to Sussex from

Germany in July 1945. This was on the day of the formal announce-
ment, 25 October.

> Officers and gentlemen of the Commandos, since your formation in
> 1940 I have spoken to you on many occasions. In the early days as a Com-
> mander of one of your units, later, as your Brigade Commander, and later
> still I have spoken to you as Chief of Combined Operations; but whenever
> I have spoken to you before it has always been in connection with opera-
> tions either in exhaltation before a battle or praise after one . . .
>
> Today there is no battle in store for you, nor have you lately fought
> one, yet nevertheless I am today more moved in speaking to you than
> ever before, for my emotions are not now those which I felt when I spoke
> to you in the past – the inspiration of battle and the exhilaration of com-
> ing danger – but they are deeper and more poignant emotions and they
> are these.
>
> First, the emotions of unbounded gratitude which I feel for every
> one of you who has helped make the Green Beret of the Commandos a
> symbol of bravery and honour whenever it has been worn. Secondly I am
> very conscious of the great privilege which I myself feel in having been
> associated with you and lastly, and most poignant of all, the emotions of
> sadness of farewell. . . .
>
> . . . out of all the frightfulness of war there emerges something of
> excellence and something to be admired; for who can say that there
> is a more splendid example of endeavour than that which the Com-
> mandos have set during the dark misery which the world has just been
> through – the high resolve to volunteer and not count the cost in the
> service of your King and Country, the love of adventure, and the skill
> and loyalty, and bravery unsurpassed which sometimes ended so tragi-
> cally in supreme sacrifice of many of your comrades – this is the spirit of
> the Commandos which Great Britain is so justly proud.
>
> I therefore admit to you, however grateful I am that the war is over,
> and it is a feeling of very deep regret than it has fallen to my lot to tell
> you – the Commandos, who have fought with such distinction in Norway
> and the islands of the North, in France, in Belgium, in Holland and in
> Germany, in Africa and in Egypt, in Crete and in Syria, in Sicily and in
> Italy, on the shores and in the islands of the Adriatic, and on the beaches
> and in the Jungles of the Arakan and of Burma – it is, I repeat, with deep
> regret that I must tell you today that you are to be disbanded.[4]

He also stated that the Green Beret would die with the Army Commandos. A short time later this was rescinded through the efforts of
Mountbatten and the Royal Marine Commandos continue to wear
it to this day.

It was understandably a sad blow, especially since most of the
Army Commandos considered that their Commando unit was their

regiment, particularly those who had been in it from the beginning. Nevertheless, as they had always been proud of their discipline, so they set out to carry out this last order.

Disbandment began in mid-November with Nos 2, 3, 6, and 9 Commandos, those personnel who had not already been demobilised, being sent back to their parent regiments. This was completed by 17 December, and the Headquarters 1 and 2 Commando Brigades suffered a similar fate. In November 1945, 4 Commando Brigade, less No 4 Commando, returned to England. No 4 had been operating on a strength of 180 men only since the end of June, having sent the majority off to Nos 3 and 6 Commandos and the Holding Operational Commando in preparation for 1 Commando Brigade's planned move to the Far East, which never took place because of the Japanese surrender. It was thus wound down in Germany. As for No 10 (IA) Commando, the Norwegian Troop had been returned to the Norwegian Government in April 1945, the French Troops in July and the Belgian and Dutch Troops in September. The British Troop was disbanded in Germany, and the Headquarters returned to Eastbourne in mid-September and was finally disbanded on 1 November 1945.

This left Nos 1 and 5 Commandos in Hong Kong, but this disbandment was tied up in the formation of the new Royal Marine Commando Brigade. Because there was no immediate prospect of 3 Commando Brigade being relieved of its duties, it was decided that it would be simplest for the new formation to be formed around this. It was to have an establishment of three rather than four Commandos, and hence one RM Commando would have to be sent to join it from England. No 45 (RM) Commando under Lt Colonel T.M. Gray DSO MC RM was selected and set sail for Hong Kong in HMS *Rajah* on 31 January 1946. On their arrival, Nos 1 and 5 Commandos, which had been allowed to run down through demobilisation, were merged to form No 1/5 Commando, and No 45 gradually took over the duties of the amalgamated Army Commando. No 1/5 was finally disbanded in January 1947. As for the other Royal Marine Commandos in the United Kingdom, the disbandment of Nos 40 and 43 was completed on 31 January 1946, and Nos 41,46,47 and 48 by 28 February. HQ Commando Group and ancillary units including the Commando Basic Training Centre at Achnacarry wire disbanded on 31 March 1946. The Holding Operational Commando was allowed a temporary stay of execution because it was handling demolition.

General Sir Thomas Hunton, the Commandant General Royal Marines, laid down that the new 3 Commando Brigade should reflect something of the wartime Royal Marine Commandos as a whole. Thus, No 42 (RM) Commando represented the Royal Marine Commandos of the old 3 Commando Brigade which had fought in the Arakan, and No 45 those who had served in North-West Europe. This left Italy and the Adriatic, and so No 44 became No 40 (RM) Commando in order to represent 2 Commando Brigade.

3 Commando Brigade has proved itself many times since 1945 as a worthy successor to the wartime Commandos. It did its share of 'jungle bashing' duties during the long years of the Malayan Emergency. Royal Marine Commandos fought alongside the US Marine Corps in Korea, were involved in counter-terrorist operations in Cyprus and spearheaded the amphibious landings in Suez in 1956. They served in Aden and the Radfan in the Sixties, played the leading role in putting down the revolt in Brunei at the end of 1962 and patrolling the jungles of Borneo. It was they who bloodlessly put down the army mutinies in East Africa in 1964. Since then, they helped shoulder the burden of Northern Ireland, and the Brigade as a whole, with battalions of the Parachute Regiment under command, thus reversing the relationship of NW Europe 1944-5, bore the brunt of the fighting in the Falklands in 1982. The wartime connection with Norway was also not forgotten, since the brigade's primary role within NATO was on the Northern Flank. Since the end of the Cold War, the Royal Marine Commandos have been heavily engaged in the Balkans, Sierra Leone, Iraq and Afghanistan. Thus, they remain a living embodiment of those first who wore the green beret.

The wartime Commandos still live on, however. As early as 1943 the Army Commando's Benevolent Fund was set up and the Commando Association formed at Achnacarry by Charles Vaughan. With the closing down of the Commando Basic Training Centre in early 1946, the Association moved down to COHQ in Richmond Terrace and shortly after this Henry Brown, who had served with Scissors Force in Norway and then with No 1 Commando throughout the rest of the war, took over the Secretaryship, which he held for almost fifty years. It is open to membership to those who served with the Commandos during 1940-45, and such is the strength of comradeship engendered during the war years that at the annual reunion at the Porchester Hall, London, in 1984, no fewer than 650 members were present – something which few other Old Comrades' Associations can match.

In September 1957, Her Majesty The Queen approved the award of no less than 38 battle honours to the Commando Association. They ranged from Norway through to St Nazaire and Dieppe, Normandy, Walcheren and North-West Europe, Syria, North Africa, the Middle East, Italy, the Adriatic, Greece and Burma. The only omission was that the achievements of the original Middle East Commandos in Eritrea and Abyssinia were not recognised. With their break up in 1941, those who served with them were either prisoners of war, or had gone on to other things and had quickly formed other affiliations, and their story was sadly quickly forgotten. The honours themselves are emblazoned on the Association's Battle Honours Flag, which was laid up in St George's Chapel, Westminster Abbey, in 1971. Within the Abbey, there are two other memorials to the Commandos, the Commando Memorial itself and also the Roll of Honour Book, which contains the names of no less than 1,706 Army and Royal Marine Commandos who lost their lives during the Second World War. At Spean Bridge, near Achnacarry, there is a further reminder in the Scottish Commando Memorial, and Normandy and Walcheren are the sites of further memorials.

As for the surviving members of the Association, the years may have rolled on, the step may not be as light as it was, but see two or more together, and it is clear that the wartime Commando Spirit is still as strong as ever.

Source Notes

PRO represents the National Archives (formerly Public Record Office) at Kew, London. Of the categories of papers preserved there and used in this book, ADM = Admiralty, CAB = Cabinet, DEFE = Defence (Defence Committee), FO = Foreign Office, PREM = Premier (Prime Minister's own files), WO = War Office. RM Museum is the Royal Marines Museum at Eastney, Portsmouth, and IWM, the Imperial War Museum, London.

CHAPTER ONE

[1] PRO WO 260/3

[2] PRO WO 260/32

[3] Account dated 1 June 1940 in PRO DEFE 2/1

[4] Dated 30 April 1940 PRO WO 106/1944

[5] HQ Norwegian Expeditionary Force Instructions dated 2 May 1940 PRO WO 165/55

[6] PRO WO 168/107

[7] *No 4 Independent Company* by Lt Col JR Paterson, Dept of Docs, IWM (83/4/1) and Liverpool Scottish Regimental Museum, Liverpool, on which this account is based.

[8] PRO CAB 120/414

[9] Ibid.

[10] Account dated 30 October 1942 PRO DEFE 2/4

[11] Memo dated 13 June 1940 PRO WO 193/384

[12] PRO CAB 106/3

[13] *Geoffrey: Major John Geoffrey Appleyard DSO MC and Bar MA* by JEA (Blandford Press, 1947) p 51.

[14] Account communicated to the author.

[15] Transcript of Interview with General Sir Alan Bourne KCB DSO MVO, Adjutant General Royal Marines (formerly DCO) 4 August 1942, RM Museum Archive 2/14/1.

[16] Report on Operation COLLAR by OC No 11 Independent Company dated 26 June 1940, PRO WO 106/1740

[17] Bourne op cit.

[18] PRO PREM 3/330/9

[19] Bourne op cit.

[20] PRO PREM 3/330/9

[21] Churchill to Eden, 23 July 1940, Ibid.

[22] PRO CAB 120/414

[23] PRO WO 260/11.

[24] *Geoffrey* op cit pp 53-4.

[25] PRO PREM 3/103/1.

[26] Ibid.

[27] COS (40) 256th Meeting.

[28] Minute General Haining to Keyes dated 12 Ocotober 1940, PRO WO 216/54.

[29] *Seven Assignments* p 219.

[30] PRO WO 218/12.

CHAPTER TWO

[1] *The Origin and Work of the Commandos* PRO DEFE 2/699.

[2] PRO WO 218/19.

[3] Phillott op cit.

[4] Ibid.

[5] Diary, Dept of Docts, IWM, Microfilm

No PP/MCR/149.
[6] March-Phillipps, Henrietta, *The Quest for Gus* broadcast on BBC Radio 4, 16 May 1972
[7] Description based on Langley, Mike *Anders Lassen VC MC of the SAS* (New English Library, 1988)
[8] PRO ADM 199/395.
[9] PRO FO 371/26922.
[10] PRO CAB 100/8.
[11] PRO ADM 199/653.
[12] Henrietta March-Phillipps op cit.
[13] Ibid.
[14] Account by Major Leslie Prout from *Geoffrey* op cit p 76.
[15] For information on the later history of both ships I am indebted to Leslie Wright for his research with both Charles Howe and Canadian Pacific.
[16] Raid report PRO DEFE 2/136.
[17] Ibid.
[18] COS(41)487.
[19] Quoted Bryant, Arthur *The Turn of the Tide* 1939-1943 pp 255-6 (Collins, London, 1957).
[20] PRO CAB 106/7.
[21] Joseph, Michael *The Sword in the Scabbard* pp 165-6 (Joseph, London, 1942).
[22] PRO WO 106/4125.
[23] Letter dated 30 September 1941 PRO DEFE 2/1.
[24] PRO DEFE 2/2.
[25] letter dated 21 October 1941, Ibid.
[26] PRO DEFE 2/703.

CHAPTER THREE

[1] Account communicated to the author.
[2] Middle East Commandos Historical Research Group (MECHRG) Papers.
[3] Cator Diary 14 June 1940.
[4] Ibid 16/17 June 1940.
[5] Ibid 17 July 1940.
[6] Rose op cit.
[7] Cator Diary 14 November 1940.
[8] MECHRG Papers.
[9] Ibid.
[10] Ibid.
[11] Cator Diary 20 November 1940.
[12] Middle East Commando Narrative, MECHRG Papers.
[13] Lt Col John Millman, then 2ic of No 52 ME Commando, MECHRG Papers.
[14] MECHRG Papers.
[15] Cator Diary 2 March 1941.
[16] MECHRG Papers.
[17] Cator Diary 8 March 1941.
[18] Account written shortly after Amba Alagi, MECHRG Papers.
[19] Letter to Cator, 22 May 1941, Cator Diary.
[20] MECHRG Papers.
[21] Report by Major SM Rose, 2ic, No 50 ME Commando, dated 3 March 1941, MECHRG Papers.
[22] Ibid.
[23] MECHRG Papers.

CHAPTER FOUR

[1] PRO WO218/166.
[2] PRO WO201/731.
[3] PRO WO218/166.
[4] PRO DEFE 2/71 1B.
[5] Graham, Lt Col FCC *Cretan Crazy Week*, account dated 4 April 1948, MECHRG Papers also, Dept of Docs IWM 76/180/1D
[6] MECHRG Papers.
[7] Papers of Capt FRJ Nicholls RA, Dept of Docs, IWM, 78/1/1.
[8] MECHRG Papers.
[9] Ibid.
[10] Graham op cit.
[11] MECHRG Papers.
[12] PRO WO 218/166.
[13] PRO WO 218/171.
[14] PRO DEFE 2/71 IB.
[15] Ibid.
[16] Ibid.
[17] Churchill to Ismay 23 July 1941, PRO PREM 3/330/9.
[18] Churchill to Ismay 16 August 1941, PRO CAB 120/414.
[19] PRO WO 201/720.
[20] Ibid.
[21] Clarke to Daniell 10 July 1941, PRO WO 193/405.

CHAPTER FIVE

[1] Account communicated to the Author.
[2] V Corps Instruction dated 31 December 1941, PRO WO 166/6099.
[3] PRO ADM 199/1199.
[4] Barber op cit.
[5] PRO PREM 4/14/10.
[6] The Reverend Joe Nicholl Manuscript, IWM Dept of Docs 78/43/1.
[7] Ibid.
[8] Account dated 8 December 1943 PRO ADM 199/1199.
[9] Ibid.
[10] PRO ADM 199/1199.
[11] Account communicated to the Author.
[12] Letter dated 15 August 1942, The Polish Institute and Sikorski Museum, A.XII 1/4.
[13] Account by CR Featherstone dated May 1946, PRO DEFE 2/977.
[14] *No 3 Troop: No 10 Commando: A Brief History* by B Hilton-Jones dated 25 April 1946, PRO DEFE 2/977.
[15] Fuhrer Order OKW/WFSE 551213/42, Enemy Documents Section, National Archives, Washington, D.C.
[16] Barber op cit.
[17] RM Museum Archive 7/19/12.
[18] PRO WO 106/4196.
[19] Largely drawn from Dear, Ian, *Ten Commando 1942–1945*, pp. 21–22 (Leo Cooper, London, 1987).
[20] *London Gazette* 2 October 1942.
[21] PRO WO 106/4117.
[22] *The Mounting of Raids* by Rear Admiral J. Hughes-Hallett CB DSO, The Journal of the Royal United Services Institute, November 1950.
[23] Beamish, Derek, Burnett, Harold and Hiller, John *Poole and World War II* pp 127-8 (Poole Historical Trust, 1980).
[24] Post-Raid Report by March-Phillipps PRO DEFE 2/109.
[25] Henrietta March-Phillipps op cit.
[26] Appleyard's Post-Raid Report dated 16 September 1942, PRO DEFE 2/109.
[27] Conversation with Author 7 November 1984.
[28] Kemp, Peter *No Colours or Crest* p 58 (Cassell, London, 1958).
[29] PRO DEFE 2/109.
[30] Post-Raid Report by Appleyard.
[31] Translation held in RM Museum Archive.
[32] Mountbatten instruction dated 22 October 1942, PRO DEFE 2/622.
[33] Kemp op cit p 59.
[34] Ibid pp 65-6.
[35] Diary entry 8 November 1942.
[36] Major WG Cass paper entitled *30 Commando – Military Section* dated 6 April 1943, PRO WO 218/71.
[37] Lt Cdr TJ Glanville DSC RNVR *History of 30 Assault Unit* p 23 PRO ADM 223/214.
[38] Account communicated to the Author.
[39] Account communicated to the Author.
[40] PRO DEFE 2/4.
[41] PRO PREM 3/103/3.
[42] Hasler's Post-Raid Report Dated 8 April 1943, RM Museum Archive 7/19/13.
[43] Ibid.

CHAPTER SIX

[1] Jordan, Phillip *Jordan's Tunis Diary* p 90 (Collins, London, 1943)
[2] From Greenslade, Leslie J *The Road to Bizerta*. Copy lent to the Author by JJ Edmans.
[3] Letter dated 15 April 1943 PRO WO 218/49.
[4] Cator Diary 30 May 1943.
[5] Mitchell Manuscript pp 22-3 RM Museum Archive 2/14/6.
[6] Letter Laycock to Sturges dated 8-15 August 1943 PRO DEFE 2/55.
[7] Ibid.
[8] PRO DEFE 2/58.
[9] Letter to Sturges dated 19July 1943 PRO ADM 202/103.
[10] Letter Laycock to Sturges 8-15 August 1943 op cit.
[11] Cator Diary 19-22 July 1943.
[12] *The History of the Commandos in the Medi-*

terranean, September 1943 – May 1945 p31.
[13] Ibid pp 52-3.
[14] Account communicated to the Author.
[15] Account communicated to the Author.
[16] *A History of the Period of Active Service of 43 Royal Marine Commando in the Central Mediterranean Force until the end of the War in Italy.* Copy lent to the Author by the Hon Sec of 43rd Royal Marines Commando Reunion.
[17] Glanville op cit. Ch V Para 4.
[18] Ibid Ch V Paras 13-14.
[19] Letter Martin-Smith to Ward 15 November 1943 PRO WO 218/71.
[20] Glanville op cit Ch V Paras 43-45.
[21] Ibid Ch VII Paras 12-18.
[22] Report by Cpl Levy, Pte McDiarmid and Gnr McLellan dated 26 November 1943 PRO WO 218/71.
[23] No 2 SS Brigade Report PRO DEFE 2/1073.
[24] *Interim Report on the Activities of the Polish and Belgian Troops of No 10 Commando for Period 13 Dec '43 to 21 Dec '43* PRO DEFE 2/1016.
[25] Ibid.
[26] Segers, Carlo G *Donnez-Nous un Champ de Bataille* (Brussels, undated) pp 110-114.

CHAPTER SEVEN

[1] Curtis Report dated 17 March 1943 PRO DEFE 2/9.
[2] Conversation with Peter Kemp 19 October 1984.
[3] PRO DEFE 2/8.
[4] Information from former SSRF members.
[5] Minutes of a Meeting held at COHQ 24 February 1943 PRO DEFE 2/8.
[6] Post Raid Report dated 28 February 1943 PRO DEFE2/122.
[7] Report by Lt D Rommetveldt dated 20 May 1943 PRO WO 218/56.
[8] PRO DEFE 2/1051.
[9] Letter Lt Gen RM Weekes (DCIGS) to Mountbatten 24 June 1943 Ibid.
[10] PRO WO 106/4158.
[11] PRO ADM 202/74.
[12] *The Royal Marines* p 101 (Sphere Paperback edition 1973).
[13] See PRO PREM 3/103/2 and PREM 4/14/3.
[14] Dept of Docs IWM 76/143/1.
[15] Saunders, Hilary St George *The Green-Beret* pp 213-4.
[16] Post-Raid Report, PRO DEFE 2/211.
[17] Ibid.
[18] COS (43) 525(0).
[19] PRO DEFE 2/1231.
[20] Post Raid Report dated 30 November 1943, PRO ADM 202/74.
[21] Hilton-Jones PRO DEFE 2/977 op cit.
[22] PRO WO 106/4158.
[23] PRO DEFE 2/1093.
[24] PRO DEFE 2/927.
[25] *Op Tarbrush* Report PRO PREM 3/330/8.

CHAPTER EIGHT

[1] SS Group Monthly Letter No 8, June 1944 PRODEFE 2/1073.
[2] No 4 Commando War Diary PRO DEFE 2/40.
[3] SSGroupMonthlyLetterNo8opcit.
[4] *3 Troop VI Commando: Report on D-Day* dated 2 July 1944 by Lts D Colquhoun Scots Guards and MJ Leaphard Reconnaissance Corps, PRO DEFE 2/43.
[5] *Royal Marine Commandos in Normandy* PRO ADM 202/99.
[6] Anonymous account RM Museum Archieve2/14/12.
[7] Ibid.
[8] Ibid.
[9] *Royal Marines in Normandy* op cit.
[10] PRODEFE2/977.
[11] *No 48 Royal Marine Commando 1944-6* PRO ADM 202/111.
[12] PRO ADM 202/75.
[13] Patrol Report. Copy lent to the Author by Ken Phillott.

[14] Account by Capt FC Townsend RM Museum Archive 2/16/4.

[15] Ibid.

[16] Anonymous account RM Museum Archive 2/16/4.

[17] Figures derived from PRO ADM 202/75.

[18] PRO WO 218/70.

[19] Major WR Sendall RM *The Royal Marine Landing at Westkapelle* PRO ADM 202/99.

[20] PRO DEFE 2/40.

[21] Ibid.

[22] Ibid.

[23] CR Featherstone *No 10 (IA) Commando's Role in the Walcheren Operation,* account dated 10 May 1946, PRO DEFE 2/977.

[24] Smithson op cit.

[25] Sendall op cit.

[26] PRO DEFE 2/40.

[27] Sendall op cit.

[28] PRO DEFE 2/40.

[29] Segers op cit p 174.

[30] Commando Group Immediate Report PRO DEFE 2/1091.

[31] 1 Cdo Bde Report PRO ADM 202/83.

[32] Capt PKW Johnson RM *The Story of No 46 Commando Royal Marines* pp 24-5 (Gale and Polden, Aldershot, 1946)

[33] Quoted Saunders op cit p 329.

[34] Johnson op cit.

[35] 45(RM) Commando Summary of Events for April 1-30, 1945 PRO ADM 202/83.

[36] Johnson op cit p 36.

[37] PRO ADM 202/101.

[38] Report on *Op Bograt* by CO 48 (RM) Commando, Ibid.

[39] Ibid.

[40] *Haste in Battle* p 186 (Cassell, 1963)

[41] *Notes Concerning 30 Assault Unit in NW Europe Feb-Aug 1945* RM Museum Archives 2/16/4.

[42] Ibid.

[43] Dalzel-Job, Patrick, unpublished ms *Special Service* pp 202-3. Loaned by the Author, but a further copy is to be found in the Liddell Hart Centre for Military Archives, King's College, London.

[44] *Recollection of Assault Unit No 30 Part 1* Naval Review Vol LXV No 4, 1977.

[45] Dalzel-Job op cit p 210.

[46] Ibid pp 212-3.

[47] Ibid pp 215-6.

CHAPTER NINE

[1] Report by Lt Col JC Manners DSO RM, RM Museum Archives 7/19/26.

[2] Report on *Shingle* dated 29 January 1944 PRO ADM 202/75.

[3] *Commandos in the Mediterranean* op cit p 110.

[4] No 43 (RM) Commando History op cit p 4.

[5] Letter dated 10 February 1944 quoted in *Commandos in the Mediterranean* op cit Appendix N. 4.

[6] Buckmaster op cit.

[7] Ibid.

[8] No 43 (RM) Commando History op cit pp 5-6.

[9] Account communicated to the Author.

[10] *Commandos in the Mediterranean* op cit pp 189-191.

[11] No 43 (RM) Commandos History op cit p 7.

[12] Undated handwritten account in PRO DEFE 2/693.

[13] No 43 (RM) Commando History op cit p 11.

[14] Blake op cit.

[15] Buckmaster op cit.

[16] Quoted *Commandos in the Mediterranean* op cit p 284.

[17] Ibid pp 304-5.

[18] Account by Lt GS Marshall RMR, RM Museum Archives 7/19/29.

[19] Account communicated to the Author.

[20] *Commandos in the Mediterranean* op cit pp 343-4.

[21] Official Report on Operation *Roast* by Major I De'Ath DSO RM, Brigade Major, 2 Commando Brigade, quoted Ibid pp 397-8.

[22] Account communicated to the Author.

[23] Report on *Roast* by CO No 43 RM Cdo dated 6 April 1945 PRO DEFE 2/49.

[24] No 40 (RM) Commando Report on Operation *Roast* PRO DEFE 2/48.
[25] Quoted *Commandos in the Mediterranean* op cit p 408.
[26] Battle Report of 'Y' Troop by Lt D Parker RM dated 15 April 1945 PRO DEFE 2/48.
[27] *Commandos in the Mediterranean* op cit p 441.
[28] No 43 (RM) Commandos History op cit pp 19-20.
[29] Report dated 7 September 1944 PRO WO 218/71.

CHAPTER TEN

[1] 3 SS Bde Interim Progress Report dated 13 December 1943, PRO DEFE 2/1051.
[2] No 44 (RM) Commando Notes *The Third Jungle Book* (The Journal of the 3 Cdo Bde) No 9, March 1946.
[3] Hill op cit.
[4] 3 SS Bde letter quoted in *44 (RM) Cdo in the Arakan* PRO ADM 202/95.
[5] Ibid.
[6] Lt Col HG Hasler DSO OBE RM *History of the Small Operations Group (SOG) in SE Asia* PRO DEFE 2/780.
[7] Ibid.
[8] Post Operation Report by Capt G Barnes MM dated 17 December 1944, PRO ADM 202/90.
[9] *The Arakan Campaign of the Twenty-Fifth Indian Division* p 45. Copy lent to the Author by the late General Sir Campbell Hardy.
[10] *Interim Report Ops – 3 Cdo Bde: Nov 1944–Jan 1945* PRO ADM 202/91.
[11] *Account of Some of the Operations of 44 (RM) Commando* RM Museum Archive 7/19/8.
[12] Extracts from letters from Young to Durnford-Slater PRO ADM 202/94.
[13] Ibid.
[14] Anonymous account RM Museum Archive 7/19/8.
[15] Quoted Pocock, Brigadier JG *The History of 19th King George V's Own Lancers 1921-1947* p 81 (Gale & Polden, Aldershot, 1962).
[16] *The Third Jungle Book* No 8, September 1945.
[17] Account communicated to the Author.
[18] Young to Durnford-Slater op cit.
[19] Extract from personal letter from Lt Salt No 5 Cdo PRO ADM 202/94.
[20] Report and Extract from personal letter from Captain RJ Dashwood 15/19H No 5 Cdo, Ibid.
[21] XV Indian Corps *History of the Arakan Campaign* 1944-1945 p 50. Copy lent to the Author by the late General Sir Campbell Hardy.
[22] XV Corps Special Order of the Day dated 17 February 1945.
[23] Dashwood op cit.
[24] This account largely based on Glanville op cit Ch XV.

CHAPTER ELEVEN

[1] *Commando Training Notes* 1953.
[2] PRO DEFE 2/977.
[3] PRO DEFE 2/1325.
[4] Reproduced in *The Third Jungle Book* No 9, March 1946.

Select Bibliography

History of the Combined Operations Organisation 1940–1945 (Amphibious Warfare Headquarters, London, 1956)

History of the Commandos in the Mediterranean Sept 1943 to May 1945 (HQ Commando Group, 1946)

JEA *Geoffrey: Major John Geoffrey Appleyard DSO MC & Bar MA* (Blandford Press, London, 1947)

Buckley, Christopher *Norway: The Commandos: Dieppe* (HMSO, London 1951)

Clarke, Dudley *Seven Assignments* (Cape, London, 1948)

Courtney, GB *SBS in World War Two* (Hale, London, 1983)

Durnford-Slater, John *Commando* (Kimber, London, 1953)

Fergusson, Bernard *The Watery Maze: The Story of Combined Operations* (Collins, London, 1961)

Foot, MRD *SOE in France* (HMSO, London, 1966)

Foot, MRD *SOE: The Special Operations Executive 1940–46* (BBC, London, 1984)

Hampshire, A Cecil *The Secret Navies* (Kimber, London, 1978)

Hampshire, A Cecil *The Beachhead Commandos* (Kimber, London, 1983)

Johnson, Capt PKW *The Story of 46 Commando Royal Marines* (Gale and Polden, Aldershot, 1946)

Kemp, Peter *No Colours or Crest* (Cassell, London, 1958)

Ladd, James *Commandos and Rangers of World War II* (Macdonald and Jane's, London, 1978)

Ladd, James *SBS: The Invisible Raiders* (Arms and Armour Press, London, 1983)

Lassen, Suzanne *Anders Lassen VC* (Muller, London, 1965)

Lovat, The Lord *March Past* (Weidenfeld & Nicolson, London, 1978)

McDougall, Murdoch C, *Swiftly They Struck: The Story of No 4 Commando* (Odhams, London, 1952)

Mills-Roberts, Derek *Clash by Night* (Kimber, London, 1956)

Moulton, JL *Haste into Battle: 48 Marine Commando at War* (Cassell, London, 1963)

Saunders, Hilary St George *The Green Beret: The Story of the Commandos 1940–1945* (Michael Joseph, London, 1949)

Strawson, John *A History of the SAS Regiment* (Seeker & Warburg, London, 1984)

Sweet-Escott, Bickham *Baker Street Irregular* (Methuen, London, 1965)

Young, Peter *Commando* (Macdonald, London, 1970)

Young, Peter *Storm from the Sea* (Kimber, London, 1956)

INDEX

Ranks given are those eventually achieved
(where known)

Index